Mathematics and Computers in Archaeology

J. E. Doran and F. R. Hodson

J. E. DORAN AND F. R. HODSON

*

Mathematics

and

Computers

in

Archaeology

*

HARVARD UNIVERSITY PRESS
CAMBRIDGE, MASSACHUSETTS

© 1975 J. E. Doran & F. R. Hodson
All rights reserved
Library of Congress
Catalog Card Number 75-7605
ISBN 0–674–55455–8

Second printing 1976

Printed in the United States of America

Contents

Contents   vii

Preface

This book is intended for archaeologists or budding archaeologists who may have no specialised mathematical knowledge, but who wish to assess the relevance of mathematics to their subject and the quality of mathematical work carried out by their colleagues. If the reader is inclined to follow a mathematical approach before or after consulting this text, we hope that it will help him to proceed without too much risk. He will certainly need to discuss his ideas with mathematicians, and this book should facilitate the dialogue.

Although mathematical and computer applications in archaeology have often been naive, not to say inept, yet they have drawn on a wide range of mathematical and statistical concepts that are not collectively described or assessed in any standard texts. Consequently the working archaeologist finds it difficult to track down accounts of methods that some of his colleagues have sought out and applied. A good deal of help is available from handbooks in other subjects that share some of the problems of archaeological research: geology, geography, the 'behavioural sciences' and sociology in general, and history. Many such works will be cited in later chapters. However, they cannot tackle the really basic archaeological problems concerning the nature of archaeological data and the relevance of techniques developed in other disciplines. For more specific guidance, the archaeologist has had to turn to the proceedings of specialist conferences, where the really fundamental problems tend to be masked by more detailed interests, or to short, scattered review articles. There does seem to be a pressing need for a more general and yet a specifically archaeological text on mathematical and computer applications, and so we have written this book.

The nature and content of the following chapters reflect their dual authorship. We have accepted that our views differ on a number of points and that our modes of expression are largely irreconcilable. In this situation it has seemed appropriate to state for each chapter the author whose primary responsibility it is, while stressing that criticisms of the co-author have always modified, sometimes drastically, its final content and form. Where inelegant contrasts of style and approach remain we ask indulgence.

Chapter 1 (F.R.H.) is a very brief introduction to archaeology as we see it, and to its relationship with mathematics.

Chapters 2–4 (J.E.D.) introduce basic concepts of mathematics, statistics and computer science respectively. These chapters are directed to the non-mathematical reader, but there can be no pretence that all archaeologists will find them immediately straightforward (perhaps chapter 3 especially). This will be due in part to the necessarily compressed presentation, but mainly to the nature of the subject matter itself: no mathematical text can be fully appreciated at a first reading. However, with re-reading and thought the content of these chapters and, perhaps more important, their general tenor should be clear.

Chapters 5–9 (F.R.H.) attempt to relate standard archaeological procedures and concepts to mathematics. In general, this section concentrates on numerical approaches that at present seem well suited to traditional archaeological practices, and that are generally referred to as *data analysis* (in contrast to conventional statistical analysis). The computer plays an essential role in this approach and in fact has largely inspired its development. These chapters deal with the quantitative description of archaeological evidence and its subsequent presentation and ordering or classification. This is an area where archaeologists have been very active over the last decade, and an attempt is made to review key examples of this work as a major part of the exposition.

Chapter 10 (J.E.D.) examines as a separate topic the various automatic seriation techniques which have been developed by archaeologists and mathematicians specifically for application to archaeological problems, especially to problems of chronology. While these techniques are of limited value and are often less useful than more general purpose data analytic procedures, they have attracted much attention in the past and lead naturally to a consideration, in chapter 11, of mathematical models and their use.

Chapters 11–13 (J.E.D.) are more speculative. They present and evaluate some further mathematical concepts and techniques which we and other authors have suggested might play an important part in the future role of mathematics in archaeology. Thus chapter 11 considers mathematical models and computer simulations, chapter 12 considers computer-oriented data-banks, and chapter 13 discusses such topics as General Systems Theory and 'scientific methodology'. Since little practical archaeological work has as yet made use of the concepts and techniques discussed in these chapters, there is ample room for disagreement about their value. Readers, therefore, must be prepared to think and judge for themselves!

Finally, it may be useful to say something about the terminology we have used. Archaeologists, mathematicians, and computer scientists all employ technical terms and we make no apology for using these, suitably defined, where their avoidance would involve ambiguity or tedious repetition. A few basic words like 'population' and 'random' are used by both archaeologists and mathematicians but with quite different meanings. In such cases we have taken special care to avoid confusion. The archaeologist, especially the British archaeologist, should be prepared for a few apparent vagaries of spelling: for example, computer scientists write computer 'program', not computer 'programme' and we have adhered to this convention.

Acknowledgements

Both authors would like to express their gratitude first to the Science Research Council Atlas Computer Laboratory, Chilton, Berkshire and to its Director Jack Howlett. This book is largely the outcome of Senior Research Fellowships held jointly at the Atlas Laboratory and at St Catherine's College, Oxford (from 1970–73, J.E.D.) and Churchill College, Cambridge (1966–68, F.R.H.).

J.E.D. also thanks the Centre d'Analyse Documentaire pour l'Archéologie, Centre National de la Recherche Scientifique, Marseilles for hospitality during the Spring of 1972. He is very grateful to Marion Doran and Carl-Axel Moberg for their critical reading of his section of the text, and to Trude Trewin for her admirably efficient and patient typing.

F.R.H. would like to thank, in addition, the London University Institute of Archaeology where he has received great encouragement in this work, and the Leverhulme Foundation that supported it with a grant for a research assistant between 1970 and 1972. He also acknowledges the Computer facilities and help that have been extending ungrudgingly to him by the staff of the University College London Computer Centre. Of the very many personal friends who have helped over the past years, F.R.H. is happy to acknowledge a special debt to David Kendall, Peter Sneath and John Gower. He also acknowledges with thanks specific help with his text from May Ashmore, Rosaly Evnine, Patricia Hodson, Carl-Axel Moberg and Mark Newcomer.

PART ONE
Basic Archaeological and Mathematical Tools

Introduction

1.1. THE ARCHAEOLOGIST AND HIS TASK

Archaeology involves a great variety of different disciplines from Prehistoric Archaeology, where material remains are the only direct source of information, to Classical or Industrial Archaeology, where the material remains simply fill out and give life to an existing, though often scanty historical account. Then, some of the most interesting and difficult branches of archaeology lie between these two extremes, where historical or direct ethnographic evidence competes with material evidence as the primary source.

However, in all these areas of specialisation, the contribution of the archaeologist as archaeologist rather than as biologist, historian or anthropologist, is to study with all the means at his disposal *material* evidence for man's activity and achievements in the past. This dictates that the archaeologist's real specialisation is the study of artifacts and their context, accepting in this instance as artifacts not only handaxes and pots but domesticated animals, cleared forests and whole settlements and settlement patterns. Because this evidence is more clearly separated from competing evidence in prehistoric archaeology, and because of the experience and inclination of the authors, most of this book will be dealing with prehistory. However, other disciplines are not excluded, and in general it is probably not unreasonable to suppose that quantitative methods proved in a prehistoric context will be suitable for other archaeological contexts as well.

1.2. THE STATUS OF MATHEMATICS IN MAINSTREAM ARCHAEOLOGY

What is, or should be the relationship between mathematics and this study of material remains? Is mathematics really relevant? If so, is the mathematician an outside specialist called in to perform a routine, if difficult, analysis comparable with a radiocarbon assay or a spectrographic analysis of metal; or is mathematics more pervasive: a part of the basic equipment not only of scientists performing such specialist analyses but of anyone, including the archaeologist, who wishes to study material evidence objectively? If this is accepted, can the archaeologist justifiably separate off a mathematical from a non-mathematical part of his study and hand over the former to an outside specialist? The whole of this book is concerned implicitly with these questions, but some explicit views are expressed in the final chapter.

However closely or remotely the archaeologist wishes to be involved with mathematics, it is certainly possible to see over the past years a clear shift in opinion and an increasing acceptance of numerical presentation and analysis in archaeology. It is also perhaps possible to point to a few key events that have fostered this change. First and most important, the development of radiocarbon dating compelled the archaeologist to recognise that a physical scientist could produce vital information that the archaeologist himself was denied. For the first time even the most reactionary archaeologists were forced to accept the importance of the scientist for their subject. However, just as important as the dates themselves, radiocarbon dating exposed archaeologists to a whole range of associated statistical concepts that they could previously avoid: random variables, theoretical distributions, probability—in a word, confidence in a cited value. Most archaeologists now realise the importance of an estimate of confidence as an essential part of a radiocarbon date, even if they do not understand at what stage of the procedure and how this estimate is made. A fundamental change in the archaeologist's idea of 'facts' has taken place.

A second major event which produced less concern at the time but was possibly of even greater significance for the future development of mathematics in archaeology, was the joint study by an archaeologist (Brainerd 1951) and a mathematician (Robinson 1951) which formalised earlier pioneering experiments by Kroeber (1940), and demonstrated how an essentially archaeological concept (relative dating by seriation) could be formulated and manipulated mathematically.

And so more than twenty years ago, two major and quite different mathematical approaches had been associated with problems of archaeological dating: conventional sampling statistics (for radiocarbon) and less conventional 'data analysis' (for seriation). Each provided a useful solution for a given situation. However, the first could treat the problem as standard and amenable to existing statistical theory. The second required a mathematician to devise a new method, which in fact involved an *ad hoc* measure of association (Robinson's coefficient of agreement) and an *ad hoc* system for manipulating these measures.

A major difficulty with the data analytic approach in general, well seen in the Brainerd and Robinson exercise, was the need for immense numbers of repetitive, if simple calculations, requiring inordinate time and accuracy even for a relatively small problem. With the development in the 'fifties of the powerful electronic computer these difficulties suddenly receded, and data analysis has become a widespread and highly developed approach for solving problems in many subjects which, like archaeology, produce rather erratic, multivariate data.

Radiocarbon dating, then, with its attendant statistical concepts has introduced archaeologists in general to a more realistic view of science and mathematics. The computer coupled to data analysis has demonstrated a further, rather different role for mathematics in archaeology, and many other exciting approaches are under test. In some branches of the subject, notably in Palaeolithic studies, basic quantification and some more ambitious numerical techniques of data analysis have become commonplace. Altogether, it seems reasonable to claim that a firm and increasing place for mathematics in mainstream archaeology is already assured. Many basic difficulties remain to be overcome, but the first major step has been taken.

By 'mainstream' archaeology in this section we have had in mind a rather hypothetical average attitude of working archaeologists. More will be said of some techniques and terminology relevant to this attitude in the next section, but, as a general brief characterisation, the 'average' archaeologist today would appear to stress the basic facts (i.e. the material remains) and would attempt to order and then interpret these as objectively as possible. In this sense the archaeologist is a scientist, and it is understandable that he accords to mathematics a cautious but increasing welcome.

While it may be difficult to detect or characterise any such basic consensus between archaeologists, it is not difficult to see extremes on both sides of it.

At one pole, some archaeologists would still not wish to be associated with objectivity or 'science' in any real sense, especially with mathematics. Archaeology still means for them the subjective appreciation of antiquities. However, since Jacquetta Hawkes' statement of this extreme position (1968) few, if any archaeologists have seemed prepared to justify it, even if it is still quite widely held.

At the opposite extreme, a series of schools have sprung up that each claim their approach to archaeology as a new scientific discipline. Collectively these schools have been called the 'New Archaeology'. Since numerical methods are put forward as one of the chief props of this movement, and since any archaeologist who stresses the importance of quantification is liable to be thought a part of it, we must at this initial stage say something of our view of the 'new' archaeology. In brief, we find its claims greatly exaggerated and therefore dangerous. While we share some of the dissatisfaction shown by its adherents for a good deal of past and current archaeology, the proposed solution strikes us as a bizarre mixture of naivety and dogmatism. In fact, the new archaeology attempts to become scientific by seizing on one fashionable theory of scientific method and by forcing archaeological data and problems into this alien conception. Unfortunately, it seems that the New Archaeologists have not discussed their ideas with competent philosophers of science, for they often misuse the terms and concepts which they employ, and show no awareness of the great divergences of view to be found within that subject (see especially Morgan 1973). They have been willing to believe that science proceeds by the 'hypothetico-deductive' method and that archaeology must somehow do the same. Similar criticisms may be made of the acceptance by the new archaeologists of 'general systems theory' as the theoretical framework within which cultural processes are to be studied. Here again, the archaeologists concerned do not seem to have canvassed a range of

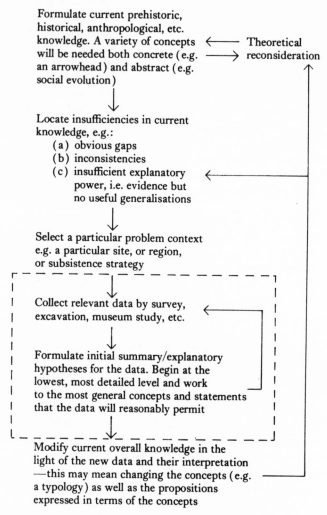

Figure 1.1. Flow chart illustrating the general conceptual framework in which the archaeologist operates. For the section within the dashed line, see figure 1.2.

experienced scientific opinion, or to have applied native critical wit in assessing the purpose and status of general systems theory, but have preferred to accept unquestioningly that a useful theory of general systems can and does exist and that it can solve archaeological problems (see chapter 13). Further naivety and lack of discussion with competent specialists is seen in their treatment of basic anthropological concepts (Allen and Richardson 1971) and in their use of statistical techniques, as will be discussed from time to time in the following chapters. However, it is the science philosophy dogmatism that gives the real character to this school.

A rather different archaeological extreme, but again avowedly scientific, is represented by the environmental determinists who choose to ignore the basic 'cultural' evidence altogether and who concentrate exclusively on a biological approach. This too seems to sacrifice the real essence of the subject, for it is in fact studying early man simply as an early animal; hardly the aim of archaeology, whether scientific or not.

1.3.   ARCHAEOLOGY: SOME BASIC CONCEPTS AND TERMS

This book cannot and does not wish to provide a further personal view of archaeological aims and methods. A wide range of texts already do this, some with distinction (e.g. Taylor 1948, Childe 1956, Willey and Phillips 1958, Chang 1967, Trigger 1968). Quantification, mathematics and computers which *are* the subject of this book, must by now be considered a part of any approach to archaeology, and it is this generality which will be stressed in the following chapters, rather than applications aligned on any given school or philosophy. Consequently this introduction will be as brief as possible.

As a summary guide to general concepts and terms, we include two flow-charts, the second an enlarged detail of the first (figures 1.1 and 1.2). It is, of course, impossible to do justice to the real complexity of archaeological research by diagrams like this. If all the links between the various empirical and interpretative levels were included, the charts would be too involved to convey any meaning at all. Figure 1.2, for example, presents no chronological aspects of empirical data. This does not mean that we are not interested in chronology and 'change', but simply that we cannot accommodate them in this diagram.

The terminology used by different authors in different parts of the English-speaking world varies considerably, and it is not always clear whether differences are verbal or conceptual. A certain amount of confusion is caused by failing to distinguish between three distinct grades of evidence: (a) the raw empirical data, (b) classes defined from such data, and (c) the interpretation of such classes in terms of 'people'. We have attempted to preserve these distinctions in the text and in figure 1.2.

Here, for the direct empirical *units* of study, we have tried to rely on terms that are those most widely used by archaeologists (e.g. *item, feature, component*). The levels at which these are depicted (1–4 on figure 1.2) are certainly arbitrary, since a more or less continuous hierarchy of units could be conceived, for instance: (1) a handle, forming part of (2) a jug, associated with other items to form (3) a pit 'lot', which forms one structural element of (4) a

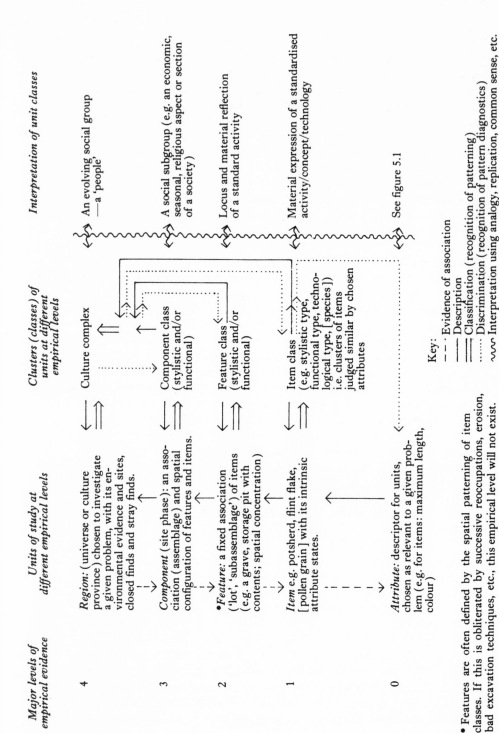

● Features are often defined by the spatial patterning of item classes. If this is obliterated by successive reoccupations, erosion, bad excavation techniques, etc., this empirical level will not exist.

Figure 1.2. Flow chart showing how empirical archaeological evidence at various levels may be classified and interrelated.

grave, which is incorporated with other finds in (5) a wall foundation, itself belonging to (6) a room, which forms part of (7) a building . . . etc., etc. For figure 1.2, possible steps in this varying hierarchy have been grouped under the broad operational levels that archaeologists have found most useful.

A correspondingly extensive hierarchy for *classes* of units could also be envisaged in the adjacent column of figure 1.2. We have chosen to record just the levels that correspond with those of the previous column. Again, we have used the regular archaeological terms for classes at these levels ('type' and 'culture complex') even though our classificatory concepts differ from those sometimes proposed by archaeologists. Following a general view of classification (see section 7.2), we regard a class as a *cluster* of related units (for instance, a 'type' as a cluster of related items), and believe that this view corresponds with general, if unvoiced archaeological opinion, more closely than do philosophies of classification conjured up by archaeologists working in isolation. These terms and concepts are discussed in detail in sections 5.2.3, 7.2 and 7.3.

The entries in the 'interpretation' column of figure 1.2 are intended merely to give an idea of the kinds of hypotheses that might be proposed, rather than as any necessary sequel to the preceding steps.

What is Mathematics?

2.1. INTRODUCTION

In this and the two following chapters the intention is to familiarise the reader successively with mathematics, with statistics and with computers. These three chapters will introduce many basic concepts needed later and will give at least some idea of the broad context within which those applying mathematical and computer methods in archaeology must work. Without some understanding of this general context it is not easy to understand or to evaluate particular procedures or experiments. Equally, without a general understanding of the nature of mathematics and the capabilities of computers it is futile to discuss their relevance to the future of archaeology.

Mathematics is undeniably a difficult subject to come to grips with. Its essence is the precise definition of new abstract concepts and their study in the most exact and rigorous way. To this end highly specialised notations are developed which to the non-mathematician, and even to the mathematician working in a different branch of mathematics, can be utterly impenetrable. In consequence while this and the following chapters will introduce a variety of important mathematical concepts and discuss them, they will contain virtually no actual mathematics. This must limit the insight which the reader without mathematical training can achieve, just as one can only learn so much about archaeology from books without field and museum experience. However there is no doubt that a useful degree of understanding is possible, and without serious difficulty, provided that the non-mathematical reader is prepared to turn over the pages a little more slowly than is his wont and to welcome and use a fair number of new concepts and attitudes. We have tried to assume no prior mathematical knowledge on the part of the reader.

Like archaeology, mathematics has many and diverse branches. Many of these will be mentioned in the pages that follow. A general distinction is often drawn between pure mathematics, studied for its own sake, and applied mathematics which exists as a tool for the solution of practical problems. The distinction is useful but should not be pushed too far. Pieces of pure mathematics often turn out to have practical applications, and many branches of pure mathematics were initially motivated by practical problems. Roughly speaking, the beginning of this chapter will be about pure mathematics and the end about applied.

2.2.   ABSTRACTION AND PROOF

Mathematics has been described as the art of giving the same name to different things. To grasp the point of this remark it is necessary to consider one of the most fundamental properties of the human mind, its ability to recognise and extract the essential similarities between objects and situations and to form corresponding abstract concepts. This happens primarily at the unspectacular everyday level, as when, for example, a child comes to recognise that there are such things in the world as cats and walks and holidays. The same process of abstract concept formation is at work when society as a whole recognises some new phenomenon such as a hippy or when a scientist introduces some new theoretical concept. It is important to distinguish between the concept itself and a word used to denote it. The former can exist without the latter, although our use of language is so developed that this is unusual.

The importance of concept formation and usage in human reasoning can hardly be overstated. Unfortunately, while your concept of a cat may be much the same as mine, your concept of a hippy or of democracy may be very different. This may not matter too much until we come to use our concepts in some process of reasoning, when the conclusions we reach will also differ. We may not even realise *why* our conclusions differ. This is an unhappy state of affairs, and one of the goals of mathematics is to avoid it by standardisation.

Mathematicians strive to isolate the essentials of the world around us. They formulate exact definitions of abstract entities which they standardise among themselves. They study the properties of these abstract entities and the relationships between them using exact chains of reasoning. The more abstract the entities, the more general the arguments. A *theorem* is a precisely stated proposition which has been proved to be true by a line of exact and fully objective argument which once understood permits no dispute. The requirement of rigorous *proof* is, after abstraction, the most fundamental characteristic of mathematics.

New abstract concepts and exact reasoning require new terminology and new and efficient notations. These are essential. While an informal explanation of a piece of mathematics can often be given in ordinary language without too much distortion, mathematical arguments themselves would be impossibly cumbersome without a specialist vocabulary and symbolism. 'Difficult' mathematical notation reflects the nature of the subject, not obscurity for its own sake.

Before some actual examples of mathematical concepts are discussed, there is a somewhat subtle point to be made. A mathematically exact proposition can only be proven to be true by an exact chain of argument from other such propositions. Precision can never be obtained from imprecision. But our actual knowledge of the world around us is rarely if ever precise in this sense. It follows that all mathematical theory is ultimately founded on definitions or assumptions (called *axioms*) which are in some degree artificial or unreal. A related point is that the content of mathematics is expanded not only by adding new assumptions and concepts and proving new theorems, but also by deducing existing assumptions from others which are more fundamental. Intuitively, as the building as a whole is more and more elaborated, so its foundations are simultaneously dug deeper and deeper.

2.3. SETS AND GRAPHS

Most mathematics has nothing to do with numbers. Rather it is about various kinds of abstract entities and the relationships between them. A fundamental entity of mathematics is that of a *set* together with its *elements* (or *members*). Intuitively a set is any well-defined collection of objects. We frequently refer to sets of people, of buildings, of apples, of ideas and so on. Abstracting away from the particular nature of the set elements, one is left with the concept itself as the object of study.

There are a number of different kinds of assertion about sets that can be made at this abstract level. One may assert that a particular object x is an element of a particular set X—conventionally written $x \in X$. One may assert that the set X is a *subset* of the set Y, written $X \subset Y$. By definition this means that every element of X is an element of Y. To refer to those elements which are members both of X and of Y one writes $X \cap Y$ and speaks of the *intersection* of X and Y. $X \cup Y$, the *union* of X and Y, is the set formed of the elements of both X and Y. It is often convenient to refer to the *null* set $\emptyset$, the set which contains no elements at all. The absence of elements does not stop the null set itself from existing. Trivially, $\emptyset$ is a subset of every other set.

The following little theorem is not untypical of set theory except in its extreme simplicity:

> *Theorem* If A, B and C are sets, and if A is a subset of B and B is a subset of C, then A is a subset of C. In symbols:
>
> $A \subset B$ and $B \subset C$ implies $A \subset C$
>
> *Comment* Intuitively this is obvious. However a formal proof must be by reference to the definition of 'subset' (see above).
>
> *Proof* To show that A is a subset of C, by the definition of 'subset' it is sufficient to show that every element of A is an element of C. Consider any element of A and call it a. (If A is the null set, then it is trivially a subset of C). Since A is a subset of B, then a must also be an element of B. But since B is a subset of C then if a is an element of B it must also be an element of C. Since a was an arbitrary element of A, it follows that every element of A is an element of C and the theorem is proved.

A more symbolic statement of this proof is:

> Consider $a \in A$ (if $A = \emptyset$ then trivially $A \subset C$)

Since $A \subset B$, $a \in A$ implies $a \in B$.

Since $B \subset C$, $a \in B$ implies $a \in C$.

Thus $a \in A$ implies $a \in C$ which by definition implies $A \subset C$.

At a very simple level the relationships between sets and their members are sometimes presented diagrammatically. Each set is equated with the area within a closed curve, and any point marked within the curve is a member of the corresponding set. Natural representations then follow for the intersection and the unions of sets. Examples of such *Venn diagrams* are given in figure 2.1. Such diagrammatic presentation is much too limited to be of any real

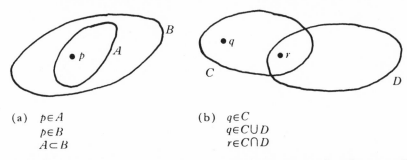

(a) $p \in A$
     $p \in B$
     $A \subset B$

(b) $q \in C$
     $q \in C \cup D$
     $r \in C \cap D$

Figure 2.1. Venn diagrams are used to portray relationships between sets and between sets and their elements. In (a) the set A is a subset of the set B and p is an element of each. In (b), r is an element of $C \cap D$, the intersection of two sets C and D. q is an element of C and is therefore an element of the union of C and D, written $C \cup D$.

mathematical value, but it does facilitate the understanding of the relationships between a few specific sets, and has sometimes been used by archaeologists and geographers for this purpose (Litvak King and Garcia Moll 1972, Haggett 1965).

In mathematics a *graph* is a set together with a relationship which may or may not exist between each pair of its elements. This is a quite different use of the word from the more informal statistical use where, for example, a diagram showing fluctuations of temperature with time is often called a 'graph'. The mathematical usage is best explained by way of simple diagrams. Suppose we represent a set by a scatter of points as in figure 2.2(a). The points might represent, for example, guests at a party. The spatial locations of the points have no significance whatsoever. Now add arrows (directed *arcs*) from one point (*node*) to another wherever one guest knows the name of another. The diagram becomes that of figure 2.2(b). This is now a graph. The graph itself is the set together with a relationship which may or may not exist between pairs of points. It might refer not to guests and knowing names, but to towns and direct rail links, or to chess players and superior playing strength, or to types of neolithic pottery and stylistic influence, or to any one of many other possibilities. When the relationship involved is reciprocal, as with towns and direct-rail links, then the pairs of directed arcs are replaced by a single line giving a *symmetric graph* similar to that of figure 2.2(c). When there are no loops in the graph, as in figure 2.2(d), then the graph is called a *tree*. If, for example, the points refer to the employees of some organisation and the arcs to the relation 'is responsible to', then a tree arises naturally.

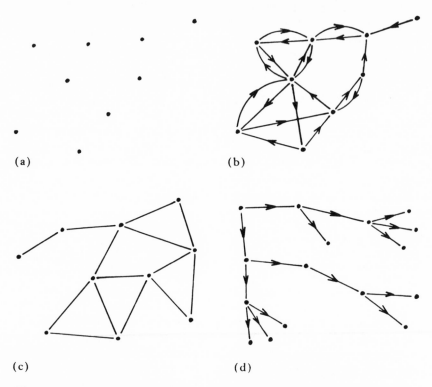

(a)   (b)

(c)   (d)

Figure 2.2. A set as shown in (a) becomes a graph (in the mathematical sense) when pairs of elements which are associated in some particular relationship are joined by a directed arc (b). A symmetric graph is shown in (c) and a tree in (d).

As with sets, the importance of graphs for archaeologists lies less in the mathematics associated with them than in the notation or representation which they provide for a wide variety of possible situations. In particular, trees are often used to present static structures such as hierarchical classification schemes (figure 9.9), and also such things as diagnostic keys and general search processes (figure 11.8).

When looking at a graph it is essential always to remember that what matters is the way the points are connected, not their spatial locations. Two mathematically identical graphs can be drawn so that they look very different. For example, one author will draw a tree growing up from the bottom of the page, while another will draw exactly the same tree growing down from the top.

2.4. NUMBERS AND VECTORS

It should be clear by now that mathematics is not at all the same as arithmetic or calculation. However, it is true that the structure and properties of the ordinary number system form a large part of mathematics. Consider the concept of a whole number, or *positive integer*, such as 3, or 258. Intuitively 3 is what three apples and three trees have in common. After 'discovering' the small integers in this way one soon arrives at the concept of an infinite sequence of integers: 1, 2, 3, 4, 5 . . . each obtained by adding one to that preceding. The force of the word 'infinite' is that in principle even larger integers could be generated indefinitely. It is, of course, possible to add and to multiply integers. Again, these are operations ultimately derived from everyday experience—a teacher will demonstrate to a child that when two apples are added to three apples, five apples result; and that four bags each containing three sweets yield twelve sweets in all.

One is soon led to discover (or invent—according to philosophical stance), other numbers beyond the positive integers. Augmenting the positive integers with the number zero gives the *non-negative integers. Negative integers* such as −3 or −6659 complete the integers. Everyday examples of negative numbers are provided by negative bank balances and negative values on a temperature scale. Both addition and multiplication are still complete in the sense that it is possible to add or multiply any two integers and obtain an integer as a result. This involves the rule, not quite intuitively obvious, that the product of two negative numbers is itself positive. For example, -2×-4 is 8.

The next step is to augment the integers with the *real* numbers, informally known as decimals: numbers such as 48.96 or 5.333. Again, the practical justification for such numbers is clear enough, and again it is easy to extend the rules for addition and multiplication to them. An interesting mathematical theorem states that, unlike the integers, the real numbers are uncountable. However the word 'uncountable' has a special meaning which cannot be fully explained here. Roughly the point is not that there are an infinite number of real numbers (which is true of the integers) but that there is no systematic rule by which all the reals can be laid out in order for the purpose of counting them. Notice that the integers are special cases of real numbers; 3 is just the same as 3.00.

After real numbers come *imaginary* or *complex numbers*. While such numbers are indeed more complex than the integers and the reals, they are essentially no more or less imaginary. The initial reason for inventing them is to fill an irritating gap in the real number system: whereas given any positive real number it is possible to find a real number which multiplied by itself gives that number, the same is not true for a negative real. For example there is no real number which multiplied by itself gives −1; that is, the square root of minus one, $\sqrt{-1}$, is not real. However the complex number system has long been a subject of major interest in its own right.

Exactly how complex numbers are defined is not important here, beyond the fact that each is a pair of real numbers and that each may be interpreted as a *vector*. At first glance a vector is merely a row or column of numbers, possibly integer, possibly real. Thus typical examples are:

$$[1, 2, -4, 0] \qquad \begin{bmatrix} 0.7 \\ -3.9 \\ 4.1 \end{bmatrix}$$

However the particular importance of vectors is that they can be used to represent geometrical points in space as will be explained in section 2.8. Thus a complex number may be regarded as a point in two dimensional space. Whilst vectors are not themselves numbers, and cannot be added and multiplied in quite the usual sense, rules for their systematic manipulation have been devised guided by their spatial interpretation. The branch of mathematics concerned with vectors and their manipulation, *vector algebra*, is of great practical importance.

2.5.   VARIABLES, CONSTANTS AND EQUATIONS

Fundamental to mathematics and to computer science is the concept of a *variable*. Intuitively a variable is something which changes from one time or context to another. Often, but by no means always, variables are described by a number. Thus the population of Britain varies with time, and the proportion of the population having dark hair varies from one locality to another.

Formally a variable has two parts; a *value*, and a name or *identifier*. It is often helpful to think in terms of a box with a label on it (the identifier) and something inside it (the value). Then a typical mathematical statement such as 'the value of x is less than zero' means that the 'box' labelled x must contain a number less than 0. As this physical analogy implies, a variable may be without a value in certain circumstances (the box is empty).

In mathematical work most variables have numerical values. However it is quite possible to have, for example, a vector variable. The object inside the box is a vector. In computer work a variable can take as its value all sorts of things—a string of letters for example. It can even take as its value another variable. Opening one box merely reveals another!

What are variables for? It is important to realise that a mathematical variable has no meaning of itself. Its meaning lies jointly in the role which it plays in a piece of mathematics and in the interpretation which the mathematician chooses to put upon it. The essential point is that one can write down statements which involve variables without knowing what the corresponding values are. In particular one can write down *equations*. The statement:

$$x = y \tag{2.1}$$

means: 'the value of x is the same as the value of y (whatever that value may be)'. A more complicated equation is:

$$2x + 3 = 1 - 4y \tag{2.2}$$

which asserts that carrying out certain arithmetic operations on the values of the variables x and y gives equal answers. In this equation $2x$ is short for $2 \times x$, and similarly $4y$ for $4 \times y$. This convention is used ubiquitously. The numbers which appear in such equations are referred to as *constants*. This term is also used of the letters a, b and c in equations such as:

$$ax + by = c \tag{2.3}$$

with the implication that on any particular occasion that we make use of the equation, these letters (but not the variable identifiers x and y) would be replaced by numbers. It is worth noting that whereas in equation (2.1) the variable value could be anything, including, say, a graph, in equations (2.2) and (2.3) they must be numbers, otherwise the arithmetic would be meaningless.

2.6.   ALGORITHMS

Consider now the equation:

$$5x - 17x = -35 - 7x$$

What is the value (or perhaps values) of x that satisfy it? A natural but mistaken thing to do is to start guessing at plausible values of x. Much better is to follow a systematic procedure by which the equation is transformed into equivalent but ever simpler forms until the answer is obvious. Thus:

$$5x - 17x = -35 - 7x$$

is equivalent to

$$-12x = -35 - 7x$$

which is equivalent to

$$35 = -7x + 12x$$

which is equivalent to

$$35 = 5x$$

which is equivalent to

$$7 = x$$

which gives what we want to know. Because it is clear that no solutions can have been lost during the manipulations of the equation, the value obtained for x is the only possible one.

It is easy enough to standardise the procedure for solving equations of this very simple kind. The result is an *algorithm*—that is, a precisely specified sequence of computations, or more generally actions, designed to bring about, or find, some desired result. Algorithms are needed frequently in mathematics. Adding or multiplying two multi-digit numbers together requires an algorithm. So does finding the square root of a number. So does finding the highest common factor of two numbers. Much more generally, so does finding an algebraic structure to satisfy certain constraints, or constructing a geometric figure with certain properties.

A simple task requiring the specification of an algorithm is that of telling an assistant exactly how to set about sorting a list of names into alphabetical order. It is easy to see that there are a number of systematic procedures that will do this, some of them being much more efficient than others. In chapter 4, in the context of digital computers, we shall be much concerned with algorithms. Again it is important to realise that an algorithm may have nothing to do with numbers as such.

2.7.   POWERS, LOGARITHMS, DIFFERENTIALS AND FUNCTIONS

The mathematical equations which find practical application are usually a great deal more complex than those so far discussed. They often involve components such as:

$$\text{(i) } n^a \qquad \text{(ii) } \log_{10}x \qquad \text{(iii) } \frac{dy}{dx}$$

and it is desirable to have at least some idea of what these expressions mean.

Powers of a number or variable are indicated as in (i). When two integers are involved, this is merely a compressed notation for multiplication. Thus:

2^2 means 2×2

18^5 means $18 \times 18 \times 18 \times 18 \times 18$

Similarly: 2.3^3 means $2.3 \times 2.3 \times 2.3$, and -2.3^3 means $-2.3 \times -2.3 \times -2.3$. It is not immediately clear, however, what meaning should be assigned to $3^{2.3}$, still less to $3^{-2.3}$. The difficulty is overcome by noticing that in the simple cases it is always true that:

$$n^a \times n^b = n^{a+b} \quad \text{(e.g. } 2^2 \times 2^3 = 2^5\text{)}$$

whatever the value of n, a and b. By extending this rule to the more complicated situations, intuitively and mathematically consistent values can be assigned to expressions such as those given. In particular $n^{0.5}$ is the number which multiplied by itself gives n: it is the *square root* of n. This conclusion is reached by considering the equation:

$$n^{0.5} \times n^{0.5} = n^{0.5+0.5} = n^1 = n$$

Other expressions for the square root of n are $n^{1/2}$ and $\sqrt{n}$. Similarly $n^{-1} = 1/n$;

to see this consider the equation $n^{-1} \times n^1 = n^0 = 1$. If it is not obvious that $n^0 = 1$, whatever the value of n, consider $n^0 \times n^0 = n^{0+0} = n^0$.

If it is true that:

$$c = a^b$$

then b is called the *logarithm* of c with respect to *base a*. In symbols:

$$b = \log_a c.$$

The immediate practical importance of logarithms is this. Suppose that for every number its logarithm is calculated for some particular base, for example 10. Then to multiply any two numbers it is sufficient to add their logarithms and find the number whose logarithm is the answer. This again follows from the fundamental rule that $n^a \times n^b = n^{a+b}$. Thus once I am equipped with a set of logarithm tables (which were compiled once and for all long ago) multiplication, which is hard, is reduced to addition, which is easy.

Of course, logarithms have other uses. Logarithms taken to base 2 are important in information theory, which is itself important for some types of automatic classification procedure (see section 7.5.3).

A *differential coefficient* is an even more subtle concept. Suppose that there are two numerical variables x and y related so that as x changes so does y. Consider any particular value of x : call it x_0. Call the corresponding value of y, y_0. Now increase x_0 by a small amount Δx. y changes by Δy. Consider the ratio:

$$\frac{\Delta y}{\Delta x} \quad \text{at } x_0$$

As Δx is made smaller and smaller it often happens that this ratio settles to a particular value, conventionally represented by the differential coefficient

$$\frac{dy}{dx} \quad \text{at } x_0$$

Thus dy/dx measures the variation of y with respect to that of x at each value of x. If x is measuring time then dy/dx is the rate of change of y at x_0. For example, if y is distance and t time then dy/dt is velocity.

The elaboration of this concept is the starting point for one of the most important branches of pure mathematics, the differential and integral calculus, which is also of immense importance in applied mathematics. Equations involving differentials, when algorithms can be found to solve them, permit the behaviour of a system over an extended time period to be worked out from its behaviour at a typical instant.

x^2 and $\log_2 x$ are both *functions* of x. That is, with each possible value of x they associate a new value. Another example of a function is that which applied to a real (decimal) number returns the nearest integer (whole number). Call this function I. Then the following equations hold:

$$I(1.446) = \ \ 1$$
$$I(3) \ \ \ \ = \ \ 3$$
$$I(-2.2) = -2$$

and so on. In an equation such as $I(a) = b$, a is called the *argument* of I, and b the *result*. A function may have two or more arguments.

A function is not the same as an algorithm though it will often be defined by reference to an algorithm. The difference is this: an algorithm specifies a course of action, often a computation, whereas a function associates values with each of the arguments to which it can be applied without indicating how those values are to be obtained in practice.

Functions are ubiquitous in mathematics. Many of them are so often required that their values have been tabulated once and for all and published for general use. Tables of square roots and tables of logarithms are perhaps the best known examples.

2.8. GEOMETRY AND DISTANCE

The concepts introduced in the preceding pages lead into a number of major branches of mathematics: set theory, graph theory, vector algebra, and infinitesimal calculus being prominent among them. An important branch of mathematics with a quite different origin is geometry. This deals with the abstract properties of points, lines, shapes and solids in space. Indeed, it deals with the properties of space itself, which in some sense we perceive all around us. Thus it is not surprising that geometry is a very old branch of mathematics dating back at least as far as the classical Greeks.

Euclidean geometry, which is the only brand which most people have encountered, has little to do with numbers or measuring. It is founded upon certain simple axioms (assumptions) and logical rules of inference and its theorems deal with such matters as the equality of two angles, or the parallelism of two lines. A typical simple theorem is that which asserts that if two pairs of parallel straight lines intersect, then the four sided figure which is formed (a parallelogram) has opposite angles equal. As always in mathematics one is assuming ideal situations: ideal straight lines of no width, and exact measurements. For no actual drawing will the theorems ever be exactly true. Thus there is something of a paradox—the truth of the theorems is unassailable within the ideal framework of mathematics but is, in practice, always less than perfect.

The lengths of lines and the sizes of angles are considered not in Euclidean geometry but in *trigonometry*. This is a much more practical branch of mathematics which enables unknown dimensions and angles of triangles and other figures to be calculated from the dimensions and angles which are known. Thus if I know how far I am from a building, and I measure the angle which the line of sight to its top makes with the ground (supposed level) where I am standing, then it is easy to calculate the building's height. Trigonometry is essential to practical surveying.

A fundamental development was brought about by the French mathematician Descartes. He demonstrated that numbers could be used to describe geometric diagrams in such a way that geometric problems could be solved numerically or algebraically. This required the crucial concept of a *coordinate system*.

Suppose that we are dealing with a large flat surface, a plane. The essence of a plane coordinate system is that with every point of the plane is associated a unique pair of numbers. The standard way of doing this (rectangular Cartesian coordinates) is to draw through some particular point, the *origin*, a pair of straight lines, *axes*, at right angles. Along each axis a regular scale is marked. Then as indicated in figure 2.3(a) each point of the plane can be associated with a value on each of these scales, and no two points have the same pair of values or coordinates. Each point, therefore, is associated with a vector with two entries. This is exactly what is done, of course, when a grid reference system is imposed in a practical context, for example upon an archaeological site. It is conventional to label the coordinate axes X and Y. Then the point coordinate variables are called x and y. Consider what it implies to assert the equation:

$$3x + 4y = 7 \tag{2.4}$$

Only certain pairs of values for x and y will satisfy this equation. Thus the equation specifies certain points in the plane and excludes the others. In fact it specifies an infinite set of points which together form a straight line (see figure 2.3(b)). Now two straight lines meet in a single point. From which we might reasonably (and correctly) infer that there is just one pair of values for x and y which satisfies simultaneously a pair of equations similar to (2.4). This is a typical if small example of a geometric intuition suggesting an algebraic result.

Roughly speaking, any algebraic equation involving two variables corresponds to a line or a curve. Any geometric relationship has a corresponding algebraic relationship. Algebraic problems can be studied and perhaps solved geometrically and vice versa. This is particularly important for the methods of data analysis to be discussed in later chapters of this book. Data analytic methods are essentially algebraic, but are largely motivated and understood by way of geometric insight.

Whilst the foregoing discussion has been in the context of a plane, that is two-dimensional space, the relationship between algebra and geometry is equally valid and useful in one and three dimensions as well. The surface of a sphere, for example, can be represented algebraically by the equation

$$x^2 + y^2 + z^2 = 1$$

where the three variables correspond to the three dimensions. The reader

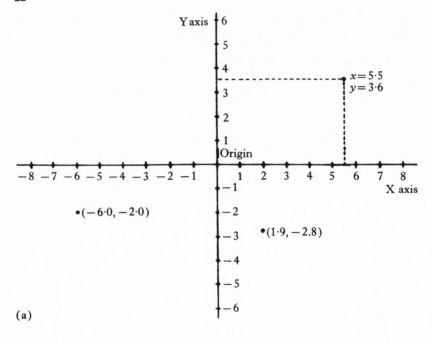

(a)

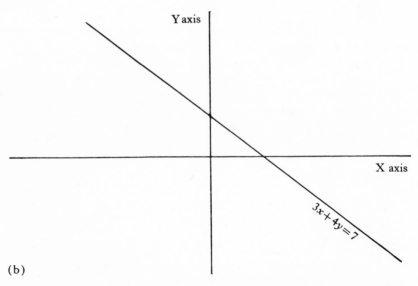

(b)

Figure 2.3. (a) A two-dimensional Carte-sian co-ordinate system. Each point is characterised by its values on the *x* axis and the *y* axis. (b) Given such a co-ordinate system, a straight line is represented by a simple 'linear' equation involving *x* and *y*.

should notice that the symmetry of the sphere is reflected in the identical treatment of the variables in the equation.

Whereas perceived space stops at three dimensions, algebra need not stop at three variables. When the mathematicians refer to four-, five-, or five-hundred-dimensional space they do not mean that such geometric monstrosities are conceivable, but that the algebraic techniques and theorems developed for one, two, and three dimensions can naturally be extended to many more than three variables. It is in this sense that a vector with twenty entries can be regarded as a 'point' in twenty-dimensional 'space'. And it is often the case that ordinary geometric or spatial intuition does help us to use many-dimensional algebra. Again this will be important in later chapters.

An important general point is that the relationship between geometry and algebra, between points and sets of numbers, is not a fixed one. Its exact form depends upon the coordinate system adopted. However, the important algebraic relationships will not depend upon the particular coordinate system adopted, just as the spatial relationship between London, New York and Moscow does not depend upon the particular coordinate system adopted for the purpose of mapping the Earth's surface.

The relationship between algebra and geometry centres on the concept of *distance*. We all have an intuitive idea of what we mean by distance. When we want to measure distances exactly we get out a ruler or a tape measure. Now, given a coordinate system, it follows from the preceding discussion that we expect to be able to compute the distance between two points if their coordinates are known. This is quite possible. If the two points are (x_1, y_1) and (x_2, y_2) in a rectangular coordinate system then the equation for the distance between them is:

$$\text{distance} = \sqrt{(x_1 - x_2)^2 + (y_1 - y_2)^2} \tag{2.5}$$

This equation for *Euclidean distance* is derived from *Pythagoras' Theorem* (see figure 2.4). Euclidean distance has a number of important algebraic properties which correspond to our intuitive notions. For example, if there are any three points A, B and C, then the distance from A to C is never greater than the distance from A to B plus the distance from B to C. Again, for any two points A and B, the distance from A to B is always the same as the distance from B to A, i.e. the order in which the points are taken is immaterial.

In fact Euclidean distance has exactly the abstract algebraic properties which define the mathematical concept of a *metric*. These properties are:

1. $d(P_1, P_1) = 0$
2. $d(P_1, P_2) \geqslant 0$
3. $d(P_1, P_2) = 0$ implies $P_1 = P_2$
4. $d(P_1, P_2) = d(P_2, P_1)$
5. $d(P_1, P_2) + d(P_2, P_3) \geqslant d(P_1, P_3)$

where P_1, P_2 and P_3 are any three points and d is the distance function. This is hardly surprising since the concept of a metric is a direct abstraction from our everyday idea of distance. It is important to realise that other distance measures may be computed, different from Euclidean distance, which also satisfy the abstract metric properties. An example is *city-block distance*, so called because it gives the distance one must cover to get from one point to another in a city laid out in square blocks. The city-block distance from the point (x_1, y_1) to the point (x_2, y_2) is given by:

$$|x_1 - x_2| + |y_1 - y_2|$$

where $|x_1 - x_2|$ means the smaller of x_1 and x_2 subtracted from the larger. As an exercise the reader might confirm that this distance function does satisfy each of the metric properties listed above.

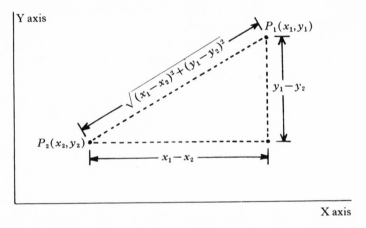

Figure 2.4. Pythagoras' theorem asserts that the area of a square drawn on the hypotenuse (the largest side) of a right-angled (90°) triangle is equal to the combined area of squares drawn on the other two sides. Since the area of a square is equal to the length of its side multiplied by itself, it follows that the length of the hypotenuse of a right-angled triangle equals the square root of the sum of the squares of the lengths of the other two sides. So to obtain a formula for the Euclidean distance between two points P_1 and P_2 given by Cartesian co-ordinates it is sufficient to draw a right-angled triangle whose hypotenuse is the desired distance and whose other two sides each have lengths involving only one of the two co-ordinates.

If property 5 in the foregoing list is altered from that given, to

5. $\max[d(P_1, P_2), d(P_2, P_3)] \geqslant d(P_1, P_3)$

where, for example, max [2, 7] is 7, then the list as a whole defines not a metric but an *ultra-metric*. This is a concept which is important in the mathematical theory of classification. Other weaker forms of metric may be obtained by varying or omitting other properties on the list.

One final important concept must be introduced in this section, the concept of *Euclidean representation*. The question here is not that of calculating the distances between a given set of points, but given a set of numbers to find a set of points in rectangular coordinates (usually in two dimensions) which have just those Euclidean distances: or if this is impossible, to achieve a close approximation. A moment's thought should make clear that this is not at all an easy problem. Roughly it is the task of reconstructing the map of Britain from a table of mileages between the important towns. In chapters 8 and 9 much will be said about this problem. Gower (1971b) has suggested that any distance capable of Euclidean representation be called Euclidean and that the term *Pythagorean distance* be used for Euclidean distance as defined above in (2.5). While we shall not adopt this suggestion, it may be helpful to the reader to mention it.

2.9. MATHEMATICS AND PRACTICAL PROBLEMS

Mathematics becomes of practical value when the abstract entities, variables and relationships which it involves can be fitted to, or interpreted as, structures or observations in the real world. A very simple example of this is the equation which relates the distance travelled by an object moving with constant speed to the time for which it has been moving. This equation is:

$$s = a + u(t - t_0)$$

where s is the distance that has been travelled at time t, u is the speed, and a is the distance travelled at the initial time t_0. If any four of the five quantities, s, a, u, t_0, and t, are specified, then the fifth can be calculated by solving the equation.

Suppose, for example, that a car is travelling at a steady 60 mph. At noon, 130 miles of the journey has been covered. How much of the journey will have been covered at 12.30? In this case $a = 130$, $u = 60$, $t = 12.5$, and $t_0 = 12$. Therefore s, the total distance covered, is $130 + 60 \times (12.5 - 12)$ which is, of course, 160 miles.

The practical importance of this equation, with the meanings assigned to the variables, is simply that it works. If a, u, t_0, and t, are known in a real situation where an object is moving with constant speed, then s will be correctly obtained by solving the equations. In practice no object ever travels at an exactly constant speed. The fit of the equation is therefore at best a good approximation.

In a context such as this an expression like $a + ut$ is sometimes called a *formula*; in this case a formula for s. When an equation or formula has wide and important application then it is likely to be called a *law*. Examples are the laws of gravitation, the laws of thermodynamics, and the laws of electromagnetism. In each of these examples the laws are sets of equations which, although enormously more complex and sophisticated than that given above, have the same kind of relationship to reality.

2.10. Mathematical Models

In recent years the word 'model' has come to be used in archaeology with a very general meaning. Some authors have used it with almost the meaning of the word 'belief'. In this book, however, we shall almost always be concerned with the much more restricted concept of a *mathematical model*. A mathematical model is an attempted specification in exact mathematical terms (usually by way of a set of equations) of the variables which characterize a real world situation or process, and of the relationships that hold between them. The purpose of all modelling, and therefore of mathematical modelling, is to learn about the properties of the situation or process modelled. The model, because it is more easily manipulated than the original, offers a cheap way of gaining information provided that its properties do indeed reflect those of the original.

There are innumerable situations in which mathematical modelling can be and has been employed. Some examples of systems suitable for modelling are: the circulation of blood through the heart; traffic flow at a busy junction; the behaviour of a spacecraft in orbit; the dynamics of a conversation between several people; the performance of a particular ocean liner in heavy seas; the learning behaviour of a rat in an experimental maze.

The distinction between a model, and a law or equation as introduced earlier, is not clear-cut. It is enough to say that models tend to be built out of one or more equations, and to be more specific and more complex than laws. Thus whereas a model might describe what goes on at a specific traffic junction, a law would be a simple assertion true for *all* traffic junctions. The nature of modelling is best understood by doing it. The following example may help in this direction and will also show in use some of the simpler concepts introduced earlier.

Suppose that a large hole is being dug by hand by a large number of labourers. Each labourer is hired by the day at a certain cost, and each does a certain amount of work in the day, measured, say, by the amount of earth shifted. A certain total amount of money is available. We would like to formulate a mathematical model in order to answer such questions as; how long will the work take? Would it get done faster if we paid more to each labourer? How should we proceed if we want to get the work done as quickly as possible?—as cheaply as possible? What factors are involved in the relationships between labourers, money, and work done?

The choice of model depends upon a number of factors: for example, how much reliable information is available, how accurately the questions must be answered, and how much trouble is acceptable in the formulation and use of a complicated model. A simple model might run somewhat as follows:

let T be the total amount of earth to be shifted

M be the total amount of money available

W be the amount of earth shifted by a single labourer in a day

C be the cost of a labourer for a day

N be the number of labourers on the job each day

D be the number of days required to finish the work

D_m be the number of days until the money runs out

Then the following equations hold:

$$D = \frac{T}{N \times W} \tag{2.6}$$

and $\quad D_m = \frac{M}{N \times C} \tag{2.7}$

If the values of T, M, W, C and N are known, then D and D_m can easily be calculated. Clearly if D_m is less than D (written in symbols $D_m < D$) then the job is not finished when the money runs out. A small complication which may be ignored is that the number of days as given by the right-hand side of the equations is not necessarily integral.

This model is unsatisfactory in several ways. It assumes, for example, that each labourer does the same amount of work each day. However its major fault is that it says nothing about the crucial relationships between the variables W, C and N. This means that it is useful only for telling how much longer the job will take, and how much it will cost, once the quantities W, C and N have been observed or otherwise obtained.

It seems reasonable to assume that the more the amount of money paid for each day's work, then the more labourers there are, and the more work they do. These assumptions can be made exact by way of the two additional equations

$$W = k_1 C \tag{2.8}$$
$$N = k_2 C \tag{2.9}$$

In these equations k_1 and k_2 are *parameters* which help to specify the exact linear relationship between W and C in the first equation and N and C in the second. To make practical use of the model values must be substituted for k_1 and k_2 which fit the equations to reality as closely as possible. Suppose that we now wish to decide how to do the job as cheaply as possible. The total cost of finishing it is: $D \times (N \times C)$. Substituting from equation (2.6) this is:

$$\frac{T}{N \times W} \times (N \times C)$$

which simplifies by cancellation to:

$$\frac{T \times C}{W}$$

The disappearance of N shows that if all that is at issue is total cost, then the number of days the work is spread over is irrelevant. Substituting for W from equation (2.8) gives the total cost as:

$$\frac{T \times C}{k_1 C} = \frac{T}{k_1} \quad \text{which is fixed.}$$

Thus in spite of the assumptions embodied in equations (2.8) and (2.9) the total cost of the job is the same whatever we make the daily rate. This may seem a little surprising. Insight can be obtained by imagining doubling the daily rate. This will produce twice as many labourers who will each do twice as much work. The whole job will therefore be done in a quarter of the time. But if twice as many labourers are paid twice as much per day for a quarter of the total time, then the actual total amount of money paid out is unchanged.

Suppose now that practical experience suggests that equation (2.9) should be modified to become:

$$W = k_1 C^{1/2} \qquad\qquad (2.10)$$

The difference is that whereas before doubling the pay doubled a labourer's output, it is now necessary to quadruple the pay to achieve this effect.

The expression for the total cost of the excavation now becomes:

$$\frac{T \times C}{k_1 C^{1/2}} = \frac{TC^{1/2}}{k_1}$$

with the implication that to minimize the total cost the daily rate should be made as small as possible.

This is nothing like the end of the story. The model as it stands is still quite obviously unrealistic. The smallest possible value of C is 0 in which case there will be no labourers and no work at all! In reality it seems likely that equations (2.8) and (2.10) should be more complex and neither independent of one another nor of time.

There is, in fact, a process of successive improvement to the model, each step increasing its complexity. This process typically terminates not, as one might at first imagine, because all the questions have been answered, nor indeed because the model has become too complicated to be worth the trouble of using it. The process terminates because it no longer becomes possible to decide with any confidence exactly which equations and which parameter values should be used in any particular application. Simple models usually have some value. Complex models with no justification for the complexity have no value at all.

The use of mathematical models in archaeology will be discussed in detail in chapter 11. There are many other topics to be covered before the strengths and limitations of mathematical modelling can be evaluated. Realistic models must often take into account the effects of chance. The theory of chance (probability theory) will be introduced in the next chapter. A model of any complexity is likely to require the use of a digital computer to extract useful information from it. Computers and computing will be introduced in chapter 4.

2.11. SUMMING UP AND CAUTIONARY REMARKS

The general power of mathematics as a means to our understanding of and control over the world around us is very great. Without it science and technology as we know them today would be quite impossible. Mathematical methods enable us to strip the world to its essentials and then extract from those essentials the useful information. Nevertheless, it is possible to be over enthusiastic, and some words of caution will not be out of place. Thus it is rather easy for a piece of mathematics on a page to look more important and impressive than it really is. The result is that the non-mathematician may be led to decipher or otherwise evaluate mathematical arguments which in fact have little practical importance (and indeed may have little mathematical importance) and which he might have done better to ignore completely.

A related point is that the desire to apply mathematical methods to a subject such as archaeology, while laudable in itself, may lead to mathematical work with only a tenuous relationship to the subject proper. This may happen when the archaeological problem has to be greatly simplified in order to attain a mathematically tractable problem. There is no doubt that some of the mathematical work inspired by archaeological problems has no immediate importance for archaeology itself. Provided that this is recognised, no damage is done and benefits may well accrue in the long run. The danger is that what is happening will not be recognised and that a true perspective on the importance of the work will thereby be lost.

Finally there is the point that mathematicians are trained to look for simple and elegant ways of stating and solving problems. They automatically seek generality. But most archaeological problems seem to involve a diversity of information and can only be solved if a wide range of background knowledge can be brought to bear. This places a severe limitation on the power of relatively traditional mathematical methods. It is by the use of techniques of statistical data analysis, and of *ad hoc* information processing by computer, that such problems can be attacked by other than purely subjective methods. This point will become clearer in later chapters.

Enjoyable and reliable non-technical introductions to modern mathematics are those of Sawyer (1955) and Bergamini (1970).

Probability Theory and Statistical Inference

3.1. INTRODUCTION

The subject of this chapter is chance and the attempts that have been made by mathematicians to formalise it and practical statisticians to make sound decisions in spite of it. Our objective is not to turn readers into competent statisticians—which would require much practical experience as well as a far longer book than this—but to survey the 'commanding heights' of probability theory and statistical inference and to lay foundations for the topics to be treated in detail in later chapters.

What is chance? What are its properties? How does one set about constructing a mathematics of chance? The man in the street is likely either to believe or not to believe in 'luck' and to leave it at that. Without pretending to be much more sophisticated it is possible to distinguish between two possible philosophical standpoints. Either certain events are essentially unpredictable, so that chance is an irreducible residue in the world that must be accepted, or chance is something we invent to cover up our own ignorance or laziness. Will it rain tomorrow? One can either see this as a question impossible to answer with certainty in any circumstances or one can take the view that if more were known about weather forecasting and all the myriad atmospheric and other factors at work then a certain prediction could be made and chance would be eliminated. In practice these two views coalesce. We all use the concept of chance to describe and allow for factors in a situation which have an effect, but which cannot be precisely identified and controlled. Whether or not the factors are in some sense irreducibly random is unimportant.

Just as the origins of geometry lie in the properties of lines, points and shapes as drawn in the dust, so the origins of *probability theory* are found in card games and gambling generally—or rather in the interesting questions that can be asked in such contexts. How likely is it that I shall be dealt all four aces? Should I double my stake every time I lose? The origins of *statistical inference* are a little less frivolous. Often statistical problems arise from situations where decisions must be made based on evidence which has been influenced by chance. Is it merely a coincidence that this run of machine breakdowns has occurred, or is there something really wrong? As with other branches of mathematics, of course, the statistical theory soon leaves its humble origins well behind; but being essentially a practical subject, it is obliged to return to them rather frequently.

The theoretical foundations of statistical inference are in dispute even among the experts, but happily this causes very little difficulty in practical work. The presentation of statistical theory to be given in this chapter, by giving prominence to Bayes' theorem, allies itself with what is still a minority rather than a majority view. We adopt a Bayesian emphasis here partly because it helps to unify techniques and concepts which can easily seem discordant at first acquaintance, and partly because it has an intrinsic importance which will be significant in later chapters.

3.2. THE FREQUENCY APPROACH TO PROBABILITY

Central to the mathematics of chance is the concept of a *probability*. A probability is a real number between 0 and 1 which is associated with a possible event. It indicates how likely it is that the event will actually occur: the larger the number the greater the likelihood. One might speak of the probability that a certain political party will win an election, or that an injury will prove fatal, or that a light bulb will fail within a thousand hours of use, or that an arbitrarily chosen seven-year-old child will be able to read to a certain standard. In all such cases an attempt can be made to quantify the probabilities involved. However, sets of numbers used as probabilities obviously must possess properties which give expression to our intuitive notion of chance and how it behaves. The means usually used to turn our intuitive ideas into exact mathematics is the idea of repeated independent trials.

Suppose that we repeatedly throw a die with six faces. On each throw, or trial, one of six events is possible (ignoring outlandish outcomes) depending upon which face falls uppermost. Thus the result of any throw is an example of a *random variable*: a variable whose value is partly or wholly determined by chance. The probability that the die will show face 3, for example, on any particular throw is defined to be the proportion of times that it shows that face in a very long sequence of throws. Bearing in mind that the die will never be perfectly shaped, this proportion might in practice turn out to be 16.2 per cent. Dividing by 100 gives a probability of 0.162. Clearly the six probabilities, corresponding to the six faces, must add up to one. An essential idea is that all the trials, the throws of the die in this case, must be independent of one another. If this conditions is not satisfied then the intuitive relationship between the frequency with which a particular outcome is observed and the probability of its occurrence on any particular occasion no longer holds. An extreme instance of this condition not being met would be to replace the actual repeated throws of the die by a repeated showing of a cinefilm of a single throw. The fact that the same face would always appear would obviously have no significance.

This frequency approach to the definition of probability is intuitively reasonable even if on closer examination logical difficulties appear concerning the exact meaning of a 'very long sequence of trials'. It does suggest basic rules which probabilities obey. Consider for example the probability of a compound event, such as the event 'face 3 or face 4'. The probability to be assigned to this event is clearly the sum of the probabilities of the two events that compose it. This is (a special case of) the *Addition Law* of probabilities. Again, if it is known that this compound event has occurred, then frequency arguments suggest that the probability that the simple event 'face 3' has occurred, rather than 'face 4', is:

$$\frac{\text{initial probability of the event 'face 3'}}{\text{probability of the compound event 'face 3 or face 4'}}$$

This is a special case of the *Multiplication Law* of probabilities.

These rules which frequency probabilities obey are analogous to the fundamental properties of distance listed in section 2.8. The analogy extends to there being alternative ways of defining, and thinking about, probabilities, such that they still satisfy the same basic rules or axioms. The motivation for such alternative definitions is not merely one of mathematical curiosity. There is a fundamental difficulty with the frequency definition. What happens in a situation where the concept of probability is needed, but to speak of repeated trials is quite meaningless? For example, what is the probability that there will be a world war next year?—that a particular scientific hypothesis is false?—that William Shakespeare and Christopher Marlowe were the same person?

3.3. PROBABILITY AND BELIEF

An alternative approach to the definition of probabilities entirely discards the concept of a repeated trial. Instead a probability is a measure of a person's (or an ideal rational man's) conviction or *belief* that a certain event will occur or that a certain proposition is true, in the light of available evidence. The rules which frequency probabilities obey are now imposed as axioms, and effectively ensure that probabilities are assigned to possible events in a consistent and reasonable manner. The main difficulty with this approach is that few people feel that they can quantify the intensity of their own beliefs with any precision, still less those of an ideal rational man. Thus, although the structure of the theory itself is mathematically clear and solid, its relationship with the real world is uncertain. The reader will already recognise this as a familiar situation. On the other hand, to relate probability to subjective expectation greatly enlarges its scope and intuitive attraction.

It is important to be clear that alternative concepts of probability do not make any difference to the computations carried out in any particular situation nor to the results obtained. The fixed rules ensure this. However a statistician who accepts the 'belief' definition will apply probability theory, and expect his results to be meaningful, a good deal more widely than one committed to the frequency approach. Thus it is the scope of the theory that is at issue, not the results that it gives. An excellent discussion of the alternative theories of probability is that of Good (1950, chapter 1).

3.4. BAYES' THEOREM

So far we have discussed only the meaning of probability, and noted some of the properties that probabilities have. The next step is to consider more carefully how new probabilities can be derived from old ones. Suppose one is in a situation where certain evidence can plausibly be explained by any one of several competing hypotheses. However some of the possible hypotheses are more plausible than others. New evidence is collected. How should one's view of the hypotheses be changed in the light of the new evidence? This is manifestly a question of very great importance. To take a rather artificial example, suppose that the available archaeological evidence in a certain region for a certain period suggests the following alternative explanations of a cultural change: (i) invasion from without; (ii) the influence of trade; (iii) internal evolution. Hypothesis (ii) is felt to be the most plausible, and (i) the least. A new site is excavated. Part way through its time span there are major changes in the typology of the structures found, indicating a discontinuity in life-style. Clearly hypothesis (i) becomes substantially more attractive.

At the heart of probability theory is the quantification of arguments such as these. This particular argument can be construed as an application of *Bayes' theorem* (sometimes called Bayes' formula or Bayes' rule) which has a fundamental, if in some respects controversial, role in probability theory (figure 3.1).

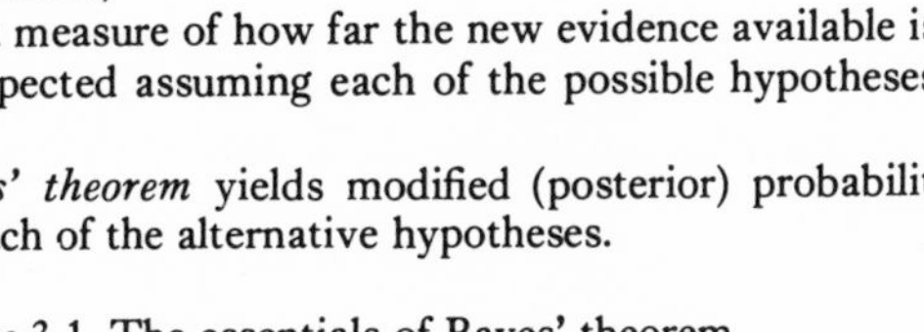

Given prior probabilities for each of a set of alternative hypotheses,
and a measure of how far the new evidence available is to be expected assuming each of the possible hypotheses in turn,
Bayes' theorem yields modified (posterior) probabilities for each of the alternative hypotheses.

Figure 3.1. The essentials of Bayes' theorem.

Call the three alternative hypotheses H_1, H_2, and H_3, and the three corresponding *prior probabilities* (on the basis of the original evidence) $P(H_1)$, $P(H_2)$, $P(H_3)$. Then because it is assumed that one and only one of these alternatives is true:

$$P(H_1) + P(H_2) + P(H_3) = 1$$

Call the new evidence E. Call the *posterior probabilities* of the three hypotheses taking into account the new evidence $P(H_1/E)$, $P(H_2/E)$, $P(H_3/E)$. The first of these, for example, may be read as 'the probability of hypothesis 1 given E'. Clearly the posterior probabilities must also sum to one.

To calculate the posterior probabilities from the prior probabilities more information is needed. Specifically we need to know the probability that E would be observed given (a) that H_1 is true, then (b) that H_2 is true, and then (c) that H_3 is true. These probabilities may be written $P(E/H_1)$, $P(E/H_2)$, $P(E/H_3)$. They will *not* sum to one. E might, for example, be extremely unlikely on all three hypotheses.

Now Bayes' theorem can be stated. It asserts that:

$$P(H_1/E) = \frac{P(E/H_1) \times P(H_1)}{P(E/H_1) \times P(H_1) + P(E/H_2) \times P(H_2) + P(E/H_3) \times P(H_3)}$$

with similar equations for $P(H_2/E)$ and for $P(H_3/E)$. These three equations can be stated simultaneously by the use of *subscript notation*. This means that instead of the subscript digit we use a letter, often i or j, and state separately the range of values the letter is to take. Using this notation Bayes' theorem takes the form:

$$P(H_i/E) = \frac{P(E/H_i) \times P(H_i)}{P(E/H_1) \times P(H_1) + P(E/H_2) \times P(H_2) + P(E/H_3) \times P(H_3)}$$

for $i = 1, 2, 3$.

By the use of another piece of notation a further compression can be effected. The symbol $\sum_{i=1}^{i=3}$ means 'add up the following expression for all the possible values of i from 1 to 3'. Using this *sigma notation* for summation Bayes' theorem becomes:

$$P(H_i/E) = \frac{P(E/H_i) \times P(H_i)}{\sum_{j=1}^{j=3} [P(E/H_j) \times P(H_j)]} \quad \text{for } i = 1, 2, 3$$

Obviously were there twenty, say, hypotheses under consideration rather than three then the number 20 would replace 3 in the above formula. The validity of the theorem would be unchanged.

The theorem has been asserted, not proved. Although it can in fact be proved very easily from the basic rules of probability, no proof will be given here. Instead we shall seek to give insight into the operation of the theorem by working out in detail the toy 'cultural change' example. Suppose that the prior probabilities of the three hypotheses are judged to be as follows: $P(H_1) = 0.2$, $P(H_2) = 0.5$, $P(H_3) = 0.3$, and that the 'conditional' probabilities relating the new evidence to the hypotheses are judged to be: $P(E/H_1) = 0.9$, $P(E/H_2) = 0.3$, $P(E/H_3) = 0.2$. Thus the figure 0.9 expresses the judgement that the evidence would very likely be observed if the invasion hypothesis were true. The task is then to perform the arithmetic indicated by Bayes' theorem and hence to derive the posterior probabilities.

Straightforward multiplication gives:

$$P(E/H_1) \times P(H_1) = 0.18$$
$$P(E/H_2) \times P(H_2) = 0.15$$
$$P(E/H_3) \times P(H_3) = 0.06$$

These values sum to 0.39. Hence the posterior probabilities turn out to be:

$$P(H_1/E) = 0.18/0.39 = 0.46$$
$$P(H_2/E) = 0.15/0.39 = 0.39$$
$$P(H_3/E) = 0.06/0.39 = 0.15$$

H_1 has the largest posterior probability which matches our intuitive expectation. The new evidence makes us now favour the invasion hypothesis.

It should be clear that only a part of the argument has really been formalised. How, it must be asked, should the prior and conditional probabilities be determined? The values assigned to them determine the posterior probabilities obtained. Is subjective judgement good enough? Alas, there is no very good answer to these questions. In fact making practical use of Bayes' theorem requires four (or five) major steps. These are:

1. Select the alternative hypotheses to be considered, the H_i.
2. Obtain the prior probabilities, the $P(H_i)$.
3. Obtain the conditional probabilities, the $P(E/H_i)$.
4. Use the formula to work out the posterior probabilities, the $P(H_i/E)$; and, possibly,
5. Select one of the hypotheses, in the light of the posterior probabilities, as 'true' (if only for practical purposes).

Of these five stages, only stage 4 is really covered by the mathematics! In spite of this, Bayes' theorem underlies much rigorous statistical inference. The subjective judgements explicit in the examples worked above are sidestepped as follows. At step 2 the prior probabilities are taken to be equal, on the argument that it is so difficult to obtain them objectively that this is the only reasonable thing to do. Any intuitive assessments of prior probabilities must therefore be used after the formal statistical analysis has been completed. Step 3 and step 1 are handled jointly. The hypotheses considered are restricted to being *statistical hypotheses*, that is mathematically stated hypotheses for which the conditional probabilities $P(E/H_i)$ can be calculated exactly. The actual statistical hypotheses considered remain a matter of intuitive judgement. Finally, step 5 is often a matter of selecting the largest posterior probability as in the example. However this is not always a reasonable thing to do. No posterior probability may be much larger than the others. There may be so many alternative hypotheses that no one of them is at all likely of itself. In such cases it may be better to be more sophisticated and less decisive, as will appear.

3.5.   PROBABILITIES AND PSEUDO-RANDOM NUMBERS

To make practical use of Bayes' theorem and the rest of the mathematical theory of probability, reliable ways must be found of associating probabilities with actual events. There are two fundamentally different possibilities. Either events can be created to fit selected probabilities or, given events of interest, a systematic attempt can be made to find the probabilities associated with them. The first alternative will be considered in this section. It is closely associated with the general idea of a simulation study. The second possibility is fundamental to all practical statistical work.

The idea of arranging events to fit particular probabilities is easy to grasp. In the interests of fairness we quite often set up situations where alternative events have equal probabilities. Commonly a coin is tossed or a pack of cards cut with just this idea of making a fair, that is equi-probable, choice between two or more alternatives. Conventionally the shipwrecked mariners, obliged to decide which of them shall next be consumed, draw lots.

If such decisions must be made not once but repeatedly, or if more complex decisions must be made, then some more elaborate procedure is needed. One or more dice might be thrown repeatedly and the values obtained associated with the choices to be made in some suitable way. From this it is a simple step to the abstract idea of a sequence of random digits, each successive digit being an independent equi-probable choice from the ten possible digits (0–9).

How can a sequence of digits be generated so that they are truly random? This is not nearly as easy as might at first appear. Strictly it is impossible. The best that can be done is to generate sequences which pass standard statistical tests for non-randomness (see section 3.13). It is correct, therefore, to refer not to random but to *pseudo-random digits* or *sequences*.

Sequences of pseudo-random digits can be generated either by mechanical or electronic devices or by suitable mathematical algorithms. A simple mathematical *pseudo-random number generator* is defined by the following equation:

$$r_n = 125 \times r_{n-1} \bmod 65536$$

Here the numbers in the sequence have values between 1 and 65535. Each number (r_n) is obtained by multiplying its predecessor in the sequence (r_{n-1}) by 125, dividing the answer by 65536, and taking the remainder. If the sequence is started with any odd number (r_0) between 1 and 65535 then successive values will appear to be drawn at random to an approximation adequate for simple purposes. It is easy to convert these values either into digits (divide by 6554 and omit the fraction part) or into numbers between 0 and 1 (divide by 65536), as is more often done.

As will appear later, pseudo-random number generators are useful in a variety of ways ranging from the design of experiments involving random sampling to simulations of complex systems with random components or sub-systems.

3.6.   OBSERVATIONS AND SCALES OF MEASUREMENT

If probability theory is to be applied to practical problems careful observations must be made on the world around us. Whilst it is natural to think of these observations as being simple measurements of one kind or another this is to over-simplify. There are several different possible *scales of measurement*. Before proceeding to a discussion of various practical statistical techniques themselves, it is appropriate to consider these different scales and the circumstances in which each is appropriately used.

Ordinary measurements, for example of weight, length or angle, are examples of a *ratio* scale. Put simply the defining characteristics of a ratio scale are: (a) that it is meaningful to speak of the difference between a pair of measurements and to compare it with the difference between another pair of measurements; and (b) the zero point on the scale is not arbitrary but really means something. A moment's thought will show that measurements of length do have these properties. But measurements of temperature on the Centigrade or Fahrenheit scale do not, for condition (b) is not satisfied. The zero point is a matter of convention. Scales which satisfy condition (a) but not condition (b) are called *interval* scales. Ratio and interval scales collectively form the *quantitative* or *numeric* scales.

On many occasions neither condition (a) nor condition (b) is satisfied. It is meaningful to rank observations but not to work with the intervals between them. Examples of such a *ranked* or *ordinal* scale are an order of subjective preference, for example of different soft drinks, or that of stratified deposits found in an archaeological excavation. In each case it is reasonable to arrange the observations in order but no more. Similarly in archaeological classification work it is sometimes reasonable to rank the similarities between artifact pairs without trying to press quantification further.

Finally a *qualitative* or *nominal* scale is one where a number of distinct observations are possible, but no comparisons at all can reasonably be made between these observations. Examples are observations of colour or material (e.g. yellow, green; flint, bronze, iron). Straightforward dichotomies (e.g. female, male) are special cases of qualitative scales. An important variant of a dichotomy, particularly in archaeological work, is a *presence/absence* observation. A typical example of such an observation is when the presence or absence of some specific decorative motif on an artefact is noted. This situation differs from the simple dichotomy because the two alternatives are no longer of equal significance. 'Presence' is much more significant than 'absence'.

The general rule is that that scale of measurement must be used which is appropriate to the observational context. It is very important neither to fail to record information which is genuinely there (e.g. to use a qualitative scale when a quantitative scale is reasonable) nor to claim a spurious sophistication of observation (e.g. by using numbers to record essentially quantitative data). The types of mathematical and statistical analysis which are appropriately and legitimately applied to a set of observational data depend very much upon the scales of measurement employed. This point will be elaborated from time to time in this and later chapters.

3.7.   SIMPLE DESCRIPTIVE STATISTICS AND EMPIRICAL FREQUENCY DISTRIBUTIONS

It may be helpful if a hypothetical data set is kept in mind for the next few sections. Suppose that a large collection of stone tools is to be studied; several hundred handaxes, say. The collection might be derived from a particular excavation, or from a particular museum, or be gathered together in some other way. Initially suppose that it is only the length of the handaxes which is of interest and is measured. In the terminology of the previous section the resulting several hundred numbers are measurements on a ratio scale.

For obvious reasons it is useful to calculate various simple quantities or *statistics* (the term gives rise to the name of the subject!) which provide summary descriptions of such sets of numbers. The commonest of these is the average or *mean*. This is defined to be:

$$\bar{x} = \frac{1}{n} \sum_{i=1}^{i=n} x_i$$

where n is the total number of observations and where x_i is the ith observation, in this case the length of the ith handaxe.

In contrast to the mean, which indicates the typical magnitudes of the observations made, the *variance* indicates the variation in the observations. It is defined to be:

$$s^2 = \frac{1}{n} \sum_{i=1}^{i=n} (x_i - \bar{x})^2$$

where $\bar{x}$ is the mean as above, x_i is the ith observation, and n is the number of observations. Intuitively the variance indicates the typical distance of the values from their mean. It is not obvious, however, why each of the terms $(x_i - \bar{x})$ should be squared. The reason can be understood by considering a very simple example. Suppose that there are only seven observations ($n = 7$) and that these have values (in order of increasing magnitude):

x_1	x_2	x_3	x_4	x_5	x_6	x_7
2	5	9	10	12	12	13

Then the value of $\bar{x}$, the mean, is $63/7 = 9$. Now consider the values of the $(x_i - \bar{x})$. There is no point in adding these values together to get a measure of the spread of the original x_i because the sum will always be zero. Those of the

$(x_i - \bar{x})$ which are negative will just be balanced by those which are positive. This follows from the definition of the mean. The least inconvenient thing to do is to square each of the $(x_i - \bar{x})$ so that all the negative values become positive. In this case:

$$
\begin{aligned}
x_1 - \bar{x} &= -7 & (x_1 - \bar{x})^2 &= 49 \\
x_2 - \bar{x} &= -4 & (x_2 - \bar{x})^2 &= 16 \\
x_3 - \bar{x} &= 0 & (x_3 - \bar{x})^2 &= 0 \\
x_4 - \bar{x} &= 1 & (x_4 - \bar{x})^2 &= 1 \\
x_5 - \bar{x} &= 3 & (x_5 - \bar{x})^2 &= 9 \\
x_6 - \bar{x} &= 3 & (x_6 - \bar{x})^2 &= 9 \\
x_7 - \bar{x} &= 4 & (x_7 - \bar{x})^2 &= 16 \\
\hline
& 0 & & 100
\end{aligned}
$$

whence the variance is 14.3. The square root of the variance is called the *standard deviation*, s. In this case $s = 3.78$.

It is often convenient to *standardise* a set of observations so that their mean becomes 0 and their variance 1. This may be appropriate, for example, when measurements have been taken in essentially arbitrary units. Standardisation is achieved by subtracting from each of the original numbers their mean and then dividing each by their standard deviation. The reader should note in passing that there is, in fact, a more efficient way of calculating the variance of a set of numbers than that used above.

The mean and the standard deviation are not the only statistics in common use. Another frequently used measure of spread is the *range*. This is defined as the difference between the smallest and largest observations. For the above figures its value is 11. Like the mean and standard deviation the range is only defined when the measurements are on an interval or ratio scale. The *median*, on the other hand, can be used to locate data which are merely ranked. If there are $(2N + 1)$ values in all (an odd number) then the median is defined to be the $(N + 1)$th value in ascending order. If there are $2N$ values, then by convention the median is taken to be the average of the Nth and $(N + 1)$th values. Thus for the above figures the median is 10. Were the value 13 discarded the median would be 9.5. Finally, the *mode* is defined to be the most frequently occurring value; in this case 12. It may be quoted even for nominal data.

If measurements are taken only very approximately, say to the nearest centimetre in the case of handaxes, then there are relatively few different values recorded and each will occur with greater or lesser frequency. In such circumstances we speak of an *empirical frequency distribution*. For a variable such as length which can in principle take any real number as its value (called a *continuous variable*) so that duplications never occur, the frequency concept really arises because observations which fall within some range of possible values are taken as equivalent. Thus in the case suggested lengths between

9.5 cm and 10.5 cm will all be recorded as 10.0 cm. Where such recording intervals are deliberately imposed, as is often the case, then the data are said to be *grouped*. Other variables are essentially *discrete* meaning that they can only take integer values. For such variables the concept of an empirical frequency distribution arises immediately. An example of a discrete variable is the number of worked flints found in a typical excavation unit. All the statistics mentioned earlier can be calculated for discrete as well as continuous variables.

The empirical frequency distribution of a continuous variable is conventionally portrayed diagrammatically by a *histogram*. An example of a histogram appears in figure 3.2. The frequency with which observations have fallen within a particular interval is expressed by the area of the rectangle drawn upon it. A different kind of diagram, a *bar diagram* (see figure 3.4) is used for frequency distributions derived from discrete variables. Bar diagrams, histograms and other diagrammatic aids to data presentation are discussed in chapter 5.

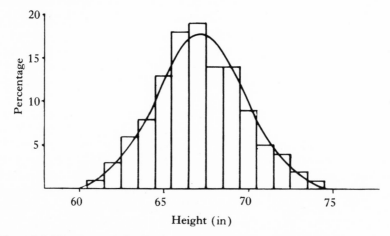

Figure 3.2. The observed distribution of the heights of 117 males, exhibited in the form of a histogram (rectangles), together with a fitted 'normal' curve (smooth curve) (Bailey 1959, 8).

When quantitative observations are prepared in empirical frequency distribution form, with the frequency of each value recorded rather than merely a long list of values, then the definition of the mean may be written a little differently:

$$\bar{x} = \frac{1}{n} \sum i n_i$$

Here n_i is the number of occasions upon which the value i has been recorded and the summation covers all values observed. The expression for the variance is similarly adjusted. Where data have been grouped a correction may be made to this formula to allow for the effect of the grouping. (Notice again that in formulae such as this the multiplication sign '×' is often omitted. Here in_i is just the same as $i \times n_i$.)

The temptation to calculate means on all possible occasions should be resisted. Not only is the result meaningless for non-quantitative data, but even quantitative data may be badly represented by the mean, for example if the data are effectively *bimodal*; that is if two substantially different values are both prominently frequent.

3.8. PROBABILITY DISTRIBUTIONS

As explained in the preceding section, an empirical frequency distribution refers to a set of observations actually recorded from some variable of interest. It is a record of the frequency with which each value has occurred. Derived from the concept of an empirical frequency distribution is another more theoretical concept, that of a *probability distribution*. A probability distribution indicates for each particular value not the frequency with which it *has* occurred but the probability that it *will* occur. If probabilities are interpreted as long-term frequencies then a probability distribution can be said to indicate the frequency with which each value will occur if independent observations could be repeated indefinitely. It follows that statistics such as the mean, median and variance (but not the range) can also be calculated for probability distributions.

Suppose that just one handaxe is selected from the total collection of handaxes postulated in the preceding section. Assuming measurement to the nearest centimetre, what is the probability that it will have length 10 cm, say? What is the probability that it will have length 11 cm?—12 cm? It obviously depends how the selection is made. Is the handaxe nearest the door chosen? Or a particularly fine specimen? Or one consciously chosen because it is 'typical'? Each alternative selection strategy will give rise to a different probability distribution for the length of the single handaxe selected. Suppose that matters are so arranged that each handaxe in the collection has exactly the same chance of being selected (not at all an easy thing to arrange, even approximately). Then this is an example of *simple random sampling*, and the probability distribution for the length of the handaxe selected, which is now a random variable, will be just the same as the empirical frequency distribution over the total collection. This is easy to see by envisaging repeated selections from the collection, each handaxe selected being replaced once it has been measured and being available for selection again.

A distribution of probability over a range of alternative events or outcomes need not refer to measurements. Thus in the context of Bayes' theorem, both the prior and the posterior probabilities form probability distributions over the set of alternative hypotheses. A more homely example of what is effectively a probability distribution is the set of odds quoted by a bookmaker for the outcome of some sporting event. There is a discrepancy with the theory however, because the 'odds' (probabilities) quoted will sum to more than one; whence the bookmaker's profit!

3.9. SAMPLES AND POPULATIONS

The idea of a probability distribution was introduced by supposing that a single handaxe was selected from a large collection and considering the probabilities associated with the lengths which it might have. This becomes more than an expository device if it is supposed that although a large collection of handaxes exist, only a few of them can actually be measured. Conclusions about the entire collection or *population* of handaxes must be made only in the light of measurements made on a small *sample* of them. The empirical frequency distribution, and the derived statistics such as the mean and standard deviation now refer only to the sample. This is not too unrealistic an assumption even in the handaxe situation envisaged. More important, the task of inferring from sample to population (in this technical sense) is the very *raison d'être* of the whole subject of statistical inference. Rarely are we content with the actual observations we have made. Almost always it is what lies behind them that really interests us. How can one draw conclusions about the total collection by a study of the sample? Intuitively, if the sample is a representative one then anything true of it should be at least approximately true of the whole collection. For example, the mean length of handaxes in the sample would presumably not differ too much from the mean length of the entire collection. The problem is how to make such inference from sample to population mathematically exact.

A quite essential requirement is that the process by which the sample is derived from the population must itself be stated in exact mathematical terms. This specification will then provide the 'ladder' by which it is possible to climb back in the reverse direction, from sample to population. If the sampling process involves no element of chance then only non-probabilistic inferences from sample to population will be possible. These will almost certainly be of very little value. For example, while it is obviously true that the length of the longest handaxe in the population is at least as great as that of the longest handaxe in the sample, this is rarely a useful piece of information. By contrast a sampling process involving the controlled use of chance, that is *probability* or *random sampling*, permits the application of probability theory. The result is that probability statements about the population become possible. Simple random sampling, in which each handaxe has the same independent chance of appearing in the sample, is the fundamental sampling process. However, a variety of more complex sampling procedures can be founded upon simple random sampling. Some of these have been studied and used in the context of archaeological excavation (see section 3.15).

That ubiquitous issue, the relationship between mathematics and reality, is prominent here. The mathematics requires that a process of random sampling takes place. This imposes strict requirements upon the actual way in which a sample is generated. In practice these requirements can only be approximated and then with difficulty. Just how does one ensure that each handaxe has exactly the same chance of appearing in the sample? Experiments have shown that it is far from sufficient to select handaxes 'haphazardly'. A sampling plan must be devised involving the careful use of pseudo-random numbers, sets of numbers chosen so that effectively they behave randomly (section 3.5). The upshot, as usual, is that to the extent that the mathematical requirements are not quite met, the mathematical results are not quite accurate. Much important statistical research concerns the quantitative relationship between inaccuracies in assumptions and inaccuracies in results.

Before moving on, it must be stressed that the handaxe example is merely one of a myriad possibilities where the sample-population relationship is possible, the former being what is available and the latter what is really of interest. In archaeology one can sample a site by excavation, or a surface scatter by a limited collection. A 'culture' may be sampled by a whole series of excavations. The composition of a bronze dagger may be sampled by drilling at a particular point. In all such cases the inference from sample to whole can only be made mathematically exact if the sampling process has, or can be assumed to have, followed an exact mathematical specification. A complication arises where the population which has been sampled is itself merely a sample of some meta-population; the handaxes are merely a sample of all those that have survived from antiquity. In fact this makes no essential difference. Inference from 'population' to 'meta-population' is possible upon exactly the same (difficult) terms as as from sample to population.

3.10. SAMPLING DISTRIBUTIONS AND ESTIMATION

Supposing that a sample has been drawn from some handaxe population by an acceptable procedure, what happens next? Consider the mean sample length. Like the length of any single handaxe selected this is a random variable. Therefore it too has a probability distribution which for obvious reasons is called a *sampling distribution* (see figure 3.3). One can imagine the sampling process being repeated over and over again, so that an endless variety of samples is generated, the sample mean varying accordingly.

Were the frequency distribution of the population known, then the sampling distribution of the sample mean could in principle be calculated. This would involve the use of probability theory and the assumption of some exact random sampling procedure. The calculation might or might not be an easy one. However in practice the population frequency distribution is not known. This is exactly the information sought from the sample.

The way out of this dilemma is essentially extremely simple. Sampling distributions are worked out not just for one population frequency distribution but for a whole range of them. It is then possible to ask the following crucial question: *which population frequency distribution of those considered gives the greatest probability of obtaining the observed sample mean value?*

The implication is that this is the population frequency distribution to be taken as true. Once the population frequency distribution has been decided upon then its mean, variance and so on can be calculated if we so wish.

In order to answer the foregoing question in any particular case, some important steps must be taken: (a) the range of alternative population frequency distributions considered must be restricted to a relatively small number judged plausible on prior grounds; and (b) ways must be found of considering whole 'families' of frequency distributions simultaneously, so that sampling distributions can be derived from them also simultaneously.

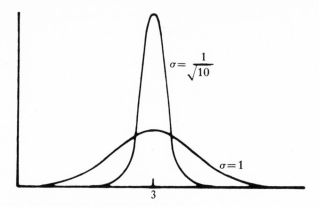

Figure 3.3. The curve of a normal distribution with $\mu = 3$ and $\sigma = 1$, together with the curve of the distribution of $\bar{x}$, the mean, for samples of size 10 drawn from it (Hoel 1962, 140).

In practice (a) remains a matter of the individual statistician's judgement. However (b) is the source of an enormous amount of mathematical ingenuity and expertise. It requires the definition of standard *theoretical frequency distributions* which are specified by mathematical formulae. These formulae typically involve one or more parameters which, as they are varied, specify whole classes of frequency distributions. Often the parameters are closely related to the statistics of the distribution. For example, a particular parameter value often specifies a frequency distribution which has that value as its mean.

Examples of theoretical frequency distributions are given in the next section. Before going into detail, however, some additional remarks should be made. It follows from what has been said that to choose a population frequency distribution is equivalent to the selection of a parameter value. In fact statisticians speak of *estimating* population parameters. The particular method of estimation indicated by the foregoing 'crucial question' is called *maximum likelihood estimation*. The term 'likelihood' is often used for the probability of obtaining a particular sample from a particular population frequency distribution.

It is appropriate at this point to refer back to Bayes' theorem. Maximum likelihood estimation can easily be seen as an example of the use of Bayes' theorem, though many statisticians still prefer to avoid the connection ('$P(E/H)$ may be called the *likelihood* of H given E. The term was introduced by R. A. Fisher with the object of *avoiding* the use of Bayes' theorem.' Good 1950, 62; his italics). All that is necessary is (a) to take the alternative population distributions to be alternative hypotheses with equal prior probabilities, and (b) to take as the new evidence E the sample itself. Maximum likelihood estimation means selecting the largest posterior probability as in the example detailed in section 3.4.

3.11. THEORETICAL PROBABILITY DISTRIBUTIONS

The population frequency distribution sought in the preceding section was a specification of the relative frequency with which certain values occur over a defined population of objects, e.g. lengths over a collection of handaxes. However in many practical instances the 'population' is to a greater or lesser extent hypothetical. Consider, for example, the set of all handaxes ever made by a certain technique, or of all handaxes that might have been made. In such instances the concept of an actual population which is sampled can be replaced for mathematical purposes by an abstract theoretical specification of the frequencies with which the observed random variable takes on particular values. Then the usual transition from frequencies to probabilities permits the identification of the hypothetical population frequency distribution with a probability distribution. In fact the formally specified distributions now to be discussed are sometimes called frequency distributions and sometimes probability distributions. We shall henceforth stick to the latter name, or merely refer to 'distributions'.

Theoretical distributions, like (numeric) random variables, are of two basic types, discrete and continuous. The former specify probabilities for variables which take on only integer values, whilst the latter deal with random variables which take real values. The distinction between integer and real numbers is effectively that between whole numbers and decimals (see section 2.4).

The *binomial distribution* is a simple and widely used example of a discrete distribution. Suppose that under certain circumstances something may or may not happen. Thus when a coin is tossed it may or may not fall heads up; when a bomb is dropped it may or may not hit the target; a person may or may not live beyond the age of sixty; a child may or may not be born a girl. Now suppose that the same circumstances are independently repeated a number of times. There are n trials, say. Then the event will occur x times, where x is some number greater than or equal to 0 and less than or equal to n ($0 \leqslant x \leqslant n$). Thus if a coin is tossed twenty times it may come down heads thirteen times. Suppose that p is the probability that the event will occur on any particular trial. What is the probability that it will occur x times in n

trials? This is the question that the binomial distribution answers.

The symbolic statement of the binomial distribution is:

$$\text{probability } x \text{ events out of } n = \frac{n!}{x!(n-x)!}p^x(1-p)^{n-x}$$

where $n! = n \times (n-1) \times (n-2) \times \ldots \times 1$. What this equation does is to specify, for each possible value of the random variable x, the probability that it will occur given the values of the parameters n and p. The mean of the distribution of x (think of it as a frequency distribution) is equal to np and its variance is $np(1-p)$.

Suppose that a 'perfect' coin ($p = 0.5$) is tossed five times ($n = 5$). The mean number of heads is 2.5 and the variance is 1.25. What is the probability that it will fall heads uppermost on just four occasions ($x = 4$)? Working from the formula this probability is

$$\frac{5!}{4!\,1!}\,(0.5)^4\,(1-0.5)^1$$

which works out to 0.15625.

There are many occasions in archaeological work when the binomial distribution might reasonably be invoked. For example it might adequately describe the process by which vessels of two different types are discarded into a rubbish pit, or that by which locations suitable for settlement in a region are or are not actually occupied. Or it might reasonably determine the proportion among blades with one-sided retouch where the retouch is to the left rather than to the right. Table 3.1 shows the results obtained when the binomial distribution is used to gauge the likely errors in observed sample proportions.

sample size	number of samples in 100			
	20	10	5	1
2000	1.4	1.8	2.2	2.9
1000	2.0	2.6	3.1	4.4
500	2.9	3.7	4.4	5.8
250	4.0	5.2	6.2	8.2
100	6.4	8.2	10.0	13.0
50	9.1	12.0	14.0	18.0
25	13.0	16.0	20.0	26.0

Table 3.1. Table indicating the errors to be expected where the proportion of some observed sample falling into a category of interest has been quoted as a percentage. Thus if the sample size is 500 then 5 samples out of 100 will yield percentages in error by more than 4.4 per cent. Notice that the larger the sample the smaller the likely error. These figures are only fully accurate if the sampling is truly random and the probability of an observation falling within the category of interest is 0.5. Other values of the probability lead to smaller errors (after Dollar and Jensen 1971, 14, table 1.1).

As the parameters in the binomial distribution vary, so does its 'shape' (see figure 3.4). For particular combinations of parameter values the binomial closely approximates to other standard distributions. Thus if n is made very large and p correspondingly small then the binomial distribution approximates more and more closely to the *Poisson distribution*. This distribution therefore applies when there are a very large number of independent

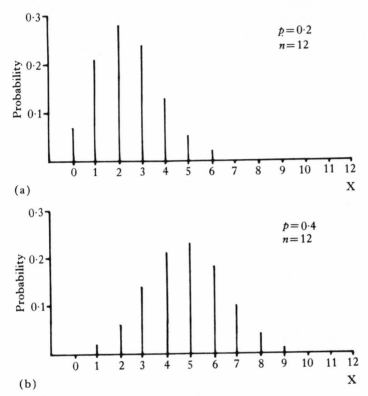

(a)

(b)

Figure 3.4. The binomial distribution for $n = 12$ and for (a) $p = 0.2$ and (b) $p = 0.4$.

trials, on each of which the chance of the event of interest occurring is very small. Its formula is:

$$\text{probability } x \text{ events in all} = \frac{e^{-\mu}\mu^x}{x!}$$

The parameter n has disappeared because it has become 'infinitely' large. The parameter p of the binomial distribution is replaced by the parameter μ whose value is the mean (and also, as it happens, the variance) of the distribution specified (figure 3.5). The reader should note this use of μ as an example of the standard convention that population parameters are denoted by Greek letters and the corresponding sample statistics by the corresponding Roman letters. The symbol e designates the important mathematical constant 2.718.

Since a radioactive atom has only a very small chance of decay in a limited time interval, the beta particle count from a quantity of a radioactive isotope follows the Poisson distribution. This distribution is therefore at the heart of radiocarbon dating for archaeological and other purposes (see section 3.19). It might also, for example, give the varying numbers of worked flints to be found in each square metre of a cleared occupation surface assuming a thin and essentially random scatter of such flints.

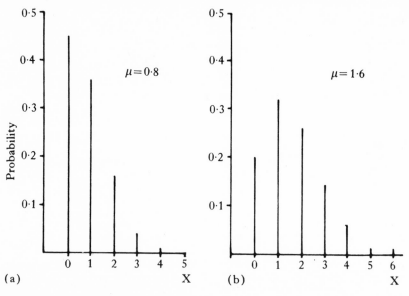

Figure 3.5. The Poisson distribution for (a) $\mu = 0.8$ and (b) $\mu = 1.6$.

Before looking at continuous distributions one other discrete distribution deserves mention. This is the *multinomial distribution* which, as its name implies, is a direct generalisation of the binomial. Whereas the binomial concerns trials with just two alternative outcomes, the multinomial concerns trials with several. It specifies the probability to be associated with each possible distribution of the outcomes of a number of independent trials over a range of alternative categories. It therefore applies when a die is to be thrown a number of times and we wish to decide how probable it is that we shall obtain some particular set of values. It would sometimes be reasonable to regard an archaeological assemblage, made up of artifacts assigned to a variety of types, as sampled from a multinomial distribution.

If in the binomial distribution the value of n is increased without decreasing p proportionately, then it approximates more and more closely to the best known and most important of the continuous distributions, the *normal* or *Gaussian*. This involves a transition from a discrete valued random variable to one that takes continuous values. Not only does the number of values which can be taken by the random variable become infinitely large—in principle this is true of the Poisson distribution—but the probability of obtaining any particular value becomes vanishingly small. It is meaningful only to talk of the probability of obtaining a value within some particular interval. For example the probability that I shall wake from sleep at exactly 07 h 37 min 48.965 s tomorrow morning is effectively zero. The probability that I shall wake between 0700 and 0800 hours is something like 0.9.

The formula for the normal distribution is:

$$\text{probability of obtaining the value } x = \frac{1}{\sigma\sqrt{2\pi}} e^{-\frac{(x-\mu)^2}{2\sigma^2}}$$

where the values of the parameters μ, σ correspond to the mean and standard deviation respectively. Curves corresponding to the normal distribution are shown in figures 3.2 and 3.3.

A very great deal of statistical theory centres upon the normal distribution. Its practical importance is that it often affords a close approximation (with a suitable choice of parameters) to empirical frequency distributions. This is predicted by certain theoretical arguments which point to the normal distribution as of fundamental significance.

Allied to the normal distribution is the *lognormal distribution*. The precise way in which this is related to the normal distribution is worth some attention. The normal distribution associates a probability with every possible value of the random variable x (as already explained this is strictly an infinitesimally small probability, but no matter). Suppose that these probabilities are transferred from the values to which they are originally assigned to the numbers whose logarithms are those values. Since every real number is the logarithm of a positive real number, the resulting distribution, the lognormal, involves values of its random variable only for numbers greater than zero. The formula for the lognormal is too complex to give here, but its shape is shown in figure 3.6. The importance of the lognormal distribution in practice is that, like the normal distribution, it will often describe an empirical distribution to a good approximation. For an archaeological example of the use of normal and lognormal curve fitting see section 5.4.5.

These are just a few of the standard theoretical distributions used by statisticians. They have all been tabulated in detail, and the tables are to be found in all mathematical libraries. The most frequently used tables are often added to text-books as appendices. The first step in many statistical analyses is to find such a distribution which will adequately describe empirical data subject to a suitable choice of parameter values. This process is often called *curve-fitting*. A great deal of statistical expertise is involved in such exercises, much of it deployed by transforming data to make them fit some standard distribution. For example, it follows from what was stated above that if we have data which are fitted by the lognormal distribution but do not wish to use that distribution and would prefer to use the normal distribution, then we simply take the logarithms of the empirical values; apply, in fact, a logarithmic transformation. Such matters are discussed in more detail in chapter 5 against an archaeological background.

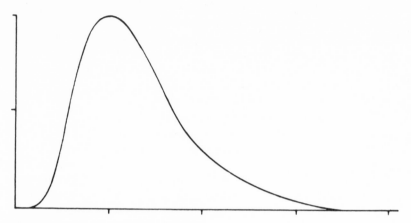

Figure 3.6. A sketch of the lognormal distribution. Note the long tail to the right.

3.12. ESTIMATION AGAIN

Something more may now be said about estimation as a statistical technique. In section 3.10 it was stated that population parameters were estimated by selecting that parameter value most likely to give rise to the sample values (or sample statistic) observed. This was maximum likelihood estimation. Simple examples can now be given which will clarify what this means in practice. Suppose that half a dozen values have been drawn from what may be assumed to be a normal distribution with standard deviation 1. The population parameter to be estimated is the mean of the distribution, μ. Suppose that the mean of the sample values is 36.9. It can be easily proved mathematically that the value of the population mean most likely to give rise to a sample mean of 36.9 is itself 36.9. The general statement is that for a normal distribution the *maximum likelihood estimator* of the population mean μ is the sample mean $\bar{x}$. Similarly, suppose that a single value has been drawn from a binomial distribution. This will be the number x of positive events in n trials. Then the maximum likelihood estimator of the population parameter p can easily be shown to be x/n. It should not be concluded from these two examples that sample statistics are always the maximum likelihood estimate of the corresponding population statistic. This is rarely so in more complex situations.

Maximum likelihood estimation is easy to understand and has a number of desirable theoretical and practical properties. However, although it is the most widely used method of estimation, it is by no means the only one. An alternative, least squares estimation, will be described in section 3.17.

Everything that has so far been said about estimation has implied that the aim has been to fix upon a particular value of a population parameter as the 'right' one. This is not really sufficient. Such a *point estimate* is bound to be inaccurate to a greater or lesser extent, and it is both desirable and possible to add to it some statement of its likely inaccuracy. If, as is usually the case, it is the mean that is at issue then the sample variance will give an idea of the potential error involved. An important and useful property of the normal distribution is that its sample mean values are also normally distributed with mean μ and standard deviation $\sigma/\sqrt{n}$ where n is the number of observations (figure 3.3). In many other circumstances sample means are approximately normally distributed. Further, two-thirds of the probability in a normal distribution lie within one standard deviation of the mean. It is good practice, therefore, when quoting the sample mean as an estimate of the population mean, to quote also the estimate of the standard deviation of this sample mean; often called in this context the *standard error*. Archaeologists are familiar with this practice in the context of radiocarbon dates. Loosely, a date given as 2320 ± 195 BC can be taken to mean that there are two chances in three that the true date lies within the confidence limits 2515 BC to 2125 BC. Such an assertion takes account only of counting variation, not of the more fundamental complications which have now arisen in the interpretation of radiocarbon dates (see section 3.19).

Quoting error limits with point estimates is virtually an example of *interval estimation*; limits within which the population parameter value must lie are derived rather than estimates of the actual value. We shall not, however, discuss these more sophisticated methods.

3.13. SIGNIFICANCE TESTS

Statistical estimation denotes inference from sample to population when the objective is to assign a value or limits to some such quantity as the population mean. A very different situation arises when the task is to decide on the basis of the sample whether or not some prior hypothesis about the population distribution should be rejected. Thus, returning to the collection of handaxes envisaged earlier, there might be reason to believe that the mean length of the handaxes in the collection was in fact 12 cm. The purpose of drawing the random sample is to check this. The mean length of the handaxes in the sample turns out to be 13.49 cm. Does this cast doubt upon the figure of 12 cm?

In fact, if the distribution is continuous, the sample mean will always differ from the true population mean. The problem is whether it differs so much that the initial hypothesis about the population mean must be rejected. This problem is solved as follows. On the assumption that the initial hypothesis is true, the probability is calculated that the sample mean would differ from the assumed population mean by an amount greater than or equal to that actually observed. In this example, what is wanted is the probability that the sample mean would be greater than or equal to 13.49 cm or less than or equal to 10.51 cm, assuming that the population mean were indeed 12 cm. The calculation requires a precise assumption about the population distribution, for example that it is normal. If the calculated probability turns out to be very small, then the inference is that something very unexpected has happened; again assuming the truth of the initial hypothesis. If the probability is sufficiently low, by convention less than 0.05 (sometimes 0.01), then we prefer to believe that the initial hypothesis is false and look round for some alternative explanation of the results.

Such a procedure is called a *significance test*. The initial hypothesis is often called the *null hypothesis*—this is because it commonly represents a conservative 'null' position that there is nothing of significance in the data. The critical figure of 0.05 or 0.01 is called the *significance level*. A significance test involves possible error of two distinct kinds. The null hypothesis may be accepted as true when it is not, and it may be rejected when it is true. The significance level fixes the probability of an error of the second kind. Generally speaking reducing the risk of one class of error increases the risk of the other. However a significance test is said to be more *powerful* to the extent that the probability of both errors can be reduced simultaneously.

Generally speaking, a significance test involves the following successive steps:

1. A null hypothesis is formulated about some population parameter or population distribution. This must be supported by assumptions about the population distribution and sampling procedure sufficient to enable sampling distributions to be derived.

2. Some sample statistic is chosen whose sampling distribution can be worked out.

3. Before studying actual observations, values of the statistic are chosen which are judged too unlikely to be consistent with the null hypothesis; this is called the *critical* or *rejection region* of the statistic (see figure 3.7).

4. If the observed value of the sample statistic falls within the critical region then the null hypothesis is rejected.

The power of a significance test depends greatly upon the decisions made at stages 1, 2 and 3. In practice there are many standard tests which are easy to use once the simple calculations required are understood. Always it is important to remember that a significance test is as much a useful 'rule of thumb' as a rigorous piece of mathematics. If observations yield a 'significant' result, this means no more than that there might well be something interesting to be found. If the observations are not quite significant, then to proceed no further is a matter of pragmatism not of theory. There could *still* be something interesting to be found in the data.

Some formal situations in which significance tests are commonly used are: (a) testing whether an empirical frequency distribution is compatible with a presumed population distribution; (b) testing whether observations are compatible with prior values for the parameters of a presumed population distribution; (c) testing the hypothesis that two samples are drawn from the same population distribution; (d) testing the hypothesis that two random variables are independently distributed.

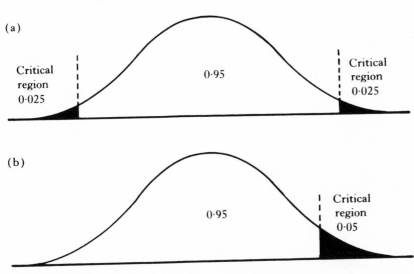

Figure 3.7. Typical critical regions for significance test. In (a) either very high or very low values of the sample statistic are regarded as significant (a 'two-tailed test'). In (b) only high values are significant (a 'one-tailed test'). Which critical region should be used in practice depends upon the context. The figures indicate probability. For both (a) and (b) the significance level is 0.05.

There are by now many examples of the archaeological use of tests of significance. Typical examples are tests for the association of two habitation features (Hill 1968); for the non-random distribution of settlements (Hodder and Hassall 1971) and for meaningful differences in posthole diameters (Brose 1970). Some discussion of the value of such exercises appears in section 3.15.

The relationship of significance tests to Bayes' theorem is an interesting one. Essentially two hypotheses are involved in a test of significance: the null hypothesis and its negation. These form the set of alternative hypotheses required for the application of Bayes' theorem. The crucial point is this: if the null hypothesis is true, the likelihood of getting the observations may be calculated, but this is not so if the null hypothesis is false. This makes it impossible to carry through the full Bayesian procedure. The concept of a significance level is introduced in order to make the best of a bad job!

3.14. Non-parametric Methods

The bulk of statistical theory concerns situations where relatively exact assumptions are made about population distributions and where estimation and significance testing is based upon these assumptions. Thus in order to test the significance of a sample mean as discussed in the previous section, it is usually assumed that the population distribution is normal. If no additional assumption is made about the population variance, then the particular test required is that called a *t-test*. Other procedures require the assumption of other distributions and known parameter values. However, it is not always realistic to assume a particular population distribution and hence methods which make no such assumption, and which are therefore called *distribution free* or *non-parametric* have been developed. These methods are particularly valuable where data have been measured upon ordinal or nominal scales (see section 3.6) and where, therefore, the more traditional and detailed assumptions about population distributions cannot be made. This is often the case in archaeological work.

A very simple example of a non-parametric significance test is the *sign test*. Suppose that a random sample of values has been drawn from some distribution about which no assumptions can reasonably be made. The null hypothesis is that the median (not the mean) of this distribution is zero. Using this null hypothesis it follows at once that a sample value will have a positive rather than negative value with probability 0.5, whatever the population distribution. Hence the number of positive sample values, x, has a sampling distribution which follows the binomial distribution with $p = 0.5$ and $n =$ the number of values in the sample. The critical region is then obviously very high or very low values of x, and this forms the basis for a very easy significance test.

The sign test should not be used when the population distribution may be taken to be normally distributed. Other tests are then more powerful. It is appropriately applied to ordinal data especially where the data are the differences between the effects of two treatments or condition, but where only the sign of the difference is known or reliable. Thus suppose that two rival excavation techniques X and Y are each tested on a number of different archaeological sites. On each site the conclusion is simply either 'X is better than Y' or the converse. Then the sign test is appropriately used to decide if an observed difference in performance between the two techniques overall, for example that X is preferred more often than Y, is 'significant'.

An important example of a non-parametric significance test applicable to nominal data is the χ^2-*test*. An example of the use of this test is to decide whether or not two classifications of the same artifacts are independent. Suppose that the artifacts being studied are graves in a cemetery and that they are classified (a) by sex, and (b) by the presence or absence of grave-goods. The null hypothesis is that these two nominal variables are independent, meaning that knowing the value of one of them for a particular burial is no guide to the value of the other. Suppose that the actual observations are as displayed in table 3.2, which is an example of a *contingency table*. The available sample of burials is assumed to be derived from a hypothetical population of possible

	male	female	sex undetermined	totals
presence	13	4	5	22
absence	7	8	8	23
totals	20	12	13	45

Table 3.2. An example of a contingency table.

burials within which, the null hypothesis asserts, the presence or absence of grave goods has nothing to do with sex. On this assumption it is not difficult to predict the entries one would expect to see in each 'cell' of the table, given that the marginal totals must be as observed. We simply divide the product of the two corresponding marginal totals by the grand total. These expected frequencies (E) can then be compared with the observed frequencies (O) by calculating the statistic χ^2 (pronounced chi-square) given by

$$\chi^2 = \sum \frac{(O-E)^2}{E}$$

The summation symbol Σ implies summation over all the cells. Now every contingency table has associated with it a number of *degrees of freedom* obtained by multiplying the number of rows in the table less one by the number of columns also less one. The table illustrated has two degrees of freedom. Further, the sampling distribution of χ^2 has been tabulated for each possible number of degrees of freedom. So it is possible to see if the observed value of the statistic is unduly large (a one-tailed significance test) and, if so, the hypothesis of independence between the two variables is rejected in the usual way. For the figures quoted the hypothesis would certainly be retained. Assuming its truth, a value of χ^2 as large as that obtained from the table (3.4 with 2 degrees of freedom) would be observed in more than 10 per cent of trials.

A χ^2-test on a contingency table is non-parametric in the sense defined earlier because no assumptions are made about the distributions of the variables involved. The test can be used on any size of table and for any number of variables, but it becomes less useful and more cumbersome as the number of variables increases. While most appropriately used with nominal variables as described, it is also applicable to ordinal or interval variables if suitable categories are imposed.

There are many other situations encountered in practical statistical work in which non-parametric methods are appropriately used. Another common example is where an empirical distribution is tested for agreement with some anticipated theoretical distribution. For a more detailed discussion of non-parametric methods and their relationship to the different scales of measurement the standard text by Siegel (1956) may be consulted.

3.15. SAMPLING AND SIGNIFICANCE TESTING IN ARCHAEOLOGICAL RESEARCH

Before moving on to consider what happens in situations where more than one random variable is involved, we should take a first look at some of the broad issues that arise when the various statistical concepts and techniques so far discussed are applied to archaeological problems. Perhaps the most important problem is that of sampling, and what the relationship between a sample and its parent population means in archaeological terms.

As has been stressed earlier, it is essential to any formal process of statistical inference that both the population sampled and the sampling process using should be precisely specified. In archaeological work these requirements lead to immediate difficulties. It is rarely easy to give exact specifications of archaeologically meaningful populations with any plausibility; and, correspondingly, it is very difficult to specify the sampling processes by which the available samples have been obtained. This is, of course, much the same as saying that in archaeology it is rarely possible to perform controlled experiments.

Nevertheless, sampling from finite and existent populations is sometimes both possible and reasonable. Thus it is perfectly realistic to make an intensive study of a small sample of artifacts drawn randomly from a larger collection itself under study as a whole (see section 9.3). However, most available collections of artifacts, for example a particular museum's handaxe collection or all surviving bell-beakers from Yorkshire, have virtually no archaeological significance in their own right. To investigate such collections by a process of random sampling is sterile as an end in itself. From the archaeologist's point of view the typical question is not so much: 'What is a statistically sound way to draw conclusions about this collection of artifacts?' as: 'Which particular collections of artifacts are archaeologically meaningful?' This crucial point will be discussed more fully in section 5.2.2.

Most discussions of the use of objective sampling procedures in archaeological work (e.g. Vescelius 1960; Binford 1964; Rootenburg 1964; Hill 1967) have been directed not at sampling populations of artifacts, but (a) at sampling an archaeological site by excavation or (b) at sampling a geographical region by excavation of some of the sites within it or by surface collection. These discussions have shown some awareness of the extensive theory of statistical sampling. For example it is recognised that the site or region must be unambiguously divided into sampling units: perhaps by some kind of gridding or by identification of all surface features. It is felt that the sampling units chosen for detailed study—to form the sample itself—must at least partly be chosen in a probabilistic manner making use of pseudo-random numbers. Further there is considerable emphasis on *stratified sampling*, in which the area to be investigated is divided into natural or convenient zones or 'strata' which are sampled independently, the results from the different strata being ultimately pooled.

Unfortunately what seems to be lacking is any real awareness of the purpose and nature of the mathematical estimation procedures which follow and complement the sampling procedures. These are typically intended, of course, to permit inference from sample statistics (count of sherds, weight of bone) to corresponding population values and associated confidence limits. Because the archaeological discussions have tended to avoid the mathematics, they have (a) looked rather too kindly upon *systematic sampling* procedures (e.g. take every fifth unit) which are virtually useless for purposes of statistical inference, and (b) tended not to face up to the inevitable limitations of sampling procedures directed at estimating population quantities. The issue, in fact, is how far it is reasonable to use a statistical sampling procedure, or to call upon the authority of such procedures, if there is no intention of carrying through the processes of statistical estimation which they are intended to promote.

We suspect that such exercises are liable to hinder rather than further real archaeological insight. Whilst estimates of total artifact counts or total food debris may indeed have important economic or social implications, most inference from the excavated part of a site to the remainder is not susceptible to statistical treatment. Statistical sampling procedures may therefore be irrelevant. Even less is possible where a small sample of excavated burial grounds or camp sites has laboriously been built up and inferences must be drawn about the cultural background from which they are derived. In such circumstances it seems quite unrealistic at the present time to expect to use formal methods of statistical inference in more than a very peripheral manner.

Essentially there are two possible ways to respond to the problem that meaningful archaeological populations are hard to specify mathematically, and actual sampling processes even more so. Either the mathematical methods can be restricted to data analysis (see section 3.20), with inference retained to the archaeologist, or the challenge can be met by trying to define realistic populations and sampling processes, accepting that the task is a difficult one and that compromises are inevitable. Rightly or wrongly much of the work so far done using mathematical methods in archaeology adopts the former philosophy. It underlies most of the practical work to be described in later chapters of this book. However, the latter approach is to at least some extent implied whenever an archaeologist makes use of a significance test; and some remarks on the use of significance tests in archaeological work will therefore not be out of place.

Typical uses of significance tests in archaeology were cited in section 3.13. In all such instances the test is essentially for non-randomness, structure, or meaning in the origin, of the observed data (e.g. is the spatial distribution of these settlements non-random?). There is no real population that has been sampled any more than there is when a die is thrown. The population is implicit in an abstract mathematical specification (the null hypothesis itself) of the data's source, which is derived from an intuitive idea of randomness or 'non-significance'. The decision to be taken is whether this 'null' source for the data is sufficiently implausible that it must be rejected in favour of some more structured interpretation.

A crucial difficulty is that the null hypothesis of randomness is frequently itself too implausible to be considered. It is inconceivable that settlements on a plain could in reality have been located at random.

> 'However, it is often unreasonable to postulate that a pattern is random; or, if not positively unreasonable, there may at least be no particular grounds for favoring the hypothesis of randomness over any other imaginable pattern' (Pielou 1969, 91).

This is a traditional problem. Almost any null hypothesis is obviously false in reality! Its sole virtue may well be that of simplicity. Nevertheless it is often appropriate to accept it as true within the body of objective knowledge until something concrete can be put in its place. The difficulty with some archaeological and related work is that this may no longer be tolerable even as an agreed fiction. It is arguable that what is needed in such work is more emphasis on estimation together with the calculation of statistics whose varying values indicate hypotheses for further study. Detailed discussions of this and related issues will be found in Henkel and Morrison (1970).

A further point worth explicit mention is that neither the statistic used as the basis of a significance test nor its associated probability level should be used as a measure of deviation from the null hypothesis. To use either of these quantities as a measure, as some archaeologists have tended, is to misuse the test procedure. Thus there is a clear logical distinction between (a) testing two random variables for independence and (b) measuring the degree of association between two random variables. The two activities should never be confused. More will be said about this in section 6.5.

3.16. Two Random Variables

In archaeology, as elsewhere, there are many situations in which random variables occur in combinations of two or more. One need only think of several different measurements being taken on stone tools, or of counts of different types of pottery sherd over a number of pottery assemblages. Indeed in archaeology such multivariate situations are greatly in the majority and most of this book is about how to cope with them. In this section an initial introduction is given to ideas that will be of great importance in later chapters with the discussion restricted in the first instance to two variables.

Just as individual observations of a single variable can be recorded, so can pairs of observations be recorded from a pair of variables. Such successive pairs of values may be expressed geometrically as points on a plane using rectangular axes as described in the last chapter. This yields a *scatter diagram* (see figures 3.10, 5.16, 5.17). The concept of an empirical frequency distribution for a random variable can be extended without difficulty to two variables; a frequency is associated with each possible combination of variable values. Thus we might record the number of handaxes from a collection having each possible combination of length and breadth measured to the nearest centimetre. Diagrammatic representations of *bivariate frequency distributions* are discussed in chapter 5. An example of a bivariate histogram is shown in figure 3.8. Similarly one has the concept of bivariate probability distributions. Some of the standard distributions, notably the normal, are easily generalized to two variables (see figure 3.9).

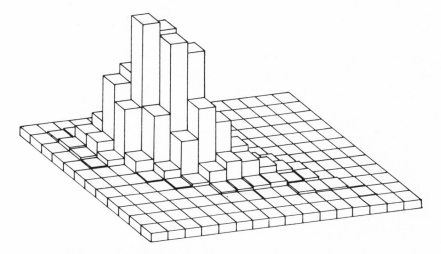

Figure 3.8. A drawing of a bivariate histogram (after Kendall and Stuart 1969, vol. 1, 21).

The principles of estimation and significance testing are unaltered by the step from one to two variables. However, the theoretical distributions are more complex and involve more parameters. This means that, for example, it is more difficult to derive sampling distributions. Consequently, less theoretical progress has been made overall.

The crucial area of investigation in bivariate situations is the relationship between the variables. The simplest and least interesting possibility is that the two variables are *independent*. Informally this means that each goes its own way quite independently of the other. Knowing the value taken by one variable on a particular occasion is no guide to the value taken by the other on that occasion. In such situations the problems are essentially univariate and are best regarded as such.

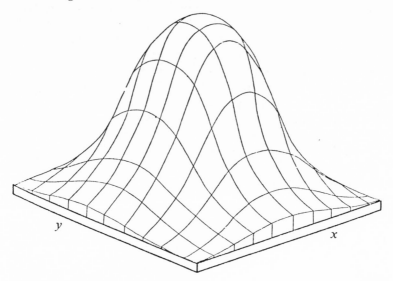

Figure 3.9. A sketch of a bivariate normal distribution. Frequencies are expressed on the vertical axis (Davies 1971, 181).

When two variables are not independent the task becomes that of capturing in numerical terms the nature of the relationship between them. Recall that the variance of a set of n observations of a single random variable x is

$$\frac{1}{n} \sum_{i=1}^{i=n} (x_i - \bar{x})^2$$

where $\bar{x}$ is the mean. The *covariance* of two random variables x and y, given as n pairs of values, is defined by

$$\frac{1}{n} \sum_{i=1}^{i=n} (x_i - \bar{x})(y_i - \bar{y})$$

where $\bar{x}$ and $\bar{y}$ are the means. The covariance can be either positive or negative. Large positive values indicate that the variables keep in step. Large negative values indicate that when one is high the other is low. Thus the covariance is a statistic which gives a general impression of how the two variables are behaving with regard to one another.

If the two random variables are standardised so that each has unit variance (i.e. a variance of one), then their covariance lies between -1 and $+1$

and is called the linear or Pearson *correlation coefficient*. The formula for the correlation coefficient, incorporating standardisation of the variables, is

$$r = \frac{\Sigma(x_i - \bar{x})(y_i - \bar{y})}{\sqrt{\{\Sigma(x_i - \bar{x})^2(y_i - \bar{y})^2\}}}$$

where, as before, the summation is over i from 1 to n.

The nature of the linear correlation coefficient can be best understood by reference to figure 3.10 (and see figure 5.16). Essentially it measures the extent to which the relationship between two variables is a linear one; geometrically, the extent to which a scatter of points can be approximated by a straight line.

Although a discussion of the archaeological use of the correlation coefficient will be deferred until chapter 6, some of its practical limitations should be mentioned immediately. Thus the linear correlation coefficient will fail to respond to a non-linear relationship, as pictured in figure 3.10(e). A zero value for the correlation should therefore never be assumed to mean independence. Conversely a strong positive or negative correlation between two variables has no causal implications by itself. For example, there probably exists a substantial positive correlation between clerical stipends and the annual number of abortions; two variables are frequently both influenced by a third. A more theoretical point is that much of the attractiveness which the correlation coefficient has on theoretical grounds is lost if the bivariate distribution sampled is not at least approximately normal. This point is often overlooked in practice (see section 6.6).

Just as the mean can be calculated both for a sample and for the parent population from which the sample is drawn, with the former being an estimate of the latter, so it is quite meaningful to talk of a sample correlation coefficient and a population correlation coefficient. If a sample correlation is non-zero, as it is almost bound to be in practice, this may merely be a sampling effect. The population value may nevertheless be zero. Where the population is, or may be taken to be, bivariate normal there exists a significance test often used to settle this point.

3.17. Regression, Least Squares Estimation and Stochastic Models

The correlation coefficient is neither the only nor the most important method of studying the relationship between two random variables. A related but more sophisticated and elaborated approach is *regression analysis*. Here the aim is not only to test or measure the relationship between two variables, but also to attempt to model it by way of a suitable equation asserting the structure of the relationship between them. In geometrical terms, the linear correlation coefficient measures the extent to which a scatter of points can be represented by a straight line, while regression analysis tries to specify the line itself.

Given two random variables y and x, a simple linear regression equation which might be assumed to connect them is

$y = a + bx + e$

In this equation a and b are parameters and e is a random variable called the *error term*. The equation asserts that given a value of x, the corresponding value of y may be derived by multiplying the value of x by b, adding on a, and

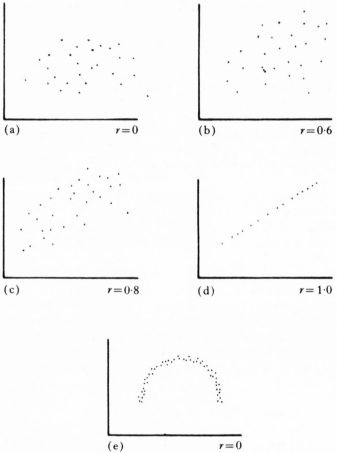

Figure 3.10. Scatter diagrams and their associated values of r, the linear correlation coefficient (Hoel 1962, 164).

then adding on an 'error', the value of e. The point of the error term is that it represents the discrepancy between the actual value of y and that obtained from $(a + bx)$. The better the model is doing its job, the smaller the error that must be invoked to make the equation hold for each particular x, y pair (see figure 3.11).

A simple application of linear regression analysis might be the prediction of a student's mark in his or her final examination (y) from that obtained at the end of the first year (x). Assuming that it seemed reasonable to use a linear model at all, the work would involve two stages: estimating the parameters in the regression equation from past records, and then using the equation as a predictor in the actual cases of interest.

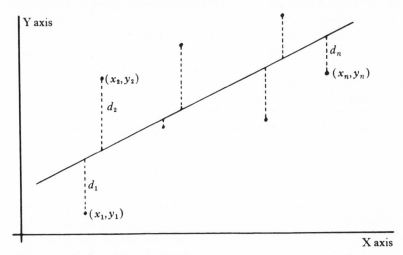

Figure 3.11. Estimating a regression line. That straight line is chosen which minimizes $d_1^2 + d_2^2 + \cdots + d_n^2$.

Parameter estimation in a regression or similar context can be based either upon maximum likelihood estimation, itself related to Bayesian methods as has been explained, or more heuristically upon the *method of least squares*. The latter technique is of great general importance. It runs as follows. Suppose that the data consist of a number of pairs of values (x_i, y_i) where i runs from 1 to n. We simply choose the values of a and b in the regression equation so that the value of the sum

$$\sum_{i=1}^{i=n} (y_i - a - bx_i)^2 \text{ which is just the same as } \sum_{i=1}^{i=n} e_i^2$$

is minimised. That is, the choice of the parameter terms is made in such a way as to minimise the sums of the squares of the error terms.

It is obvious enough why the parameter values should be chosen to minimise the error terms (or *residuals*). Intuitively the smaller these terms are, the better the model fits the available data. The terms are squared before minimisation to prevent positive and negative terms cancelling as explained in section 3.7. It can be shown that in this instance the least squares approach to estimation gives the same answers as maximum likelihood estimation. But in general, choosing parameters in a model to minimise the size of error terms is something to be done on an *ad hoc* basis when methods with more theoretical support are either too cumbersome or non-existent.

While y and e are necessarily random variables in the regression equation, x may or may not be. Indeed the values of x may be systematically chosen. This is of some importance because it means that regression analysis can safely be used much more widely than correlation analysis. x is often called the independent variable (rather misleadingly; x and y are not independent in the sense of the last section), y the dependent variable, and the equation said to express the regression of y on x. If both y and x are random variables, then it is possible to estimate the linear regression of x upon y as well as that of y on x. The two lines thus obtained only coincide in special circumstances.

The magnitude of the linear correlation coefficient and the slopes of the two regression lines are mathematically closely linked. For example, if the correlation is zero then the regression lines are at right angles and conversely. If the correlation is unity then (and only then) the two lines coincide. The general mathematical statement is that

$$r^2 = b_1 b_2$$

where r is the correlation coefficient, and b_1 and b_2 are the slopes of the regression lines, that is, the values estimated for the parameter b in the two cases. If the observations are standardised (i.e. the values of x and y are both transformed to have unit variance) then $r = b_1 = b_2$, and the slopes of the regression lines are the same and equal to the correlation coefficient.

Several attempts have been made to apply regression analysis in archaeological work. One obvious idea is to treat time as the dependent variable to be predicted from one or more observable independent variables. Thus McBurney (1967) has attempted to relate undated depths of deposit (x) in the Haua Fteah cave to absolute dates (y) using the available radiocarbon dates. Unfortunately such exercises are likely to involve dubious assumptions of linearity. In section 3.19 the application of regression analysis to problems of radiocarbon calibration will be considered. Regression analysis has been most prominent, however, in the search for clusters of variables (attribute clusters). In this context its use has been superseded by that of factor analysis (or, better, cluster analysis) to which it is related (see chapters 7 and 8).

Regression equations need not merely be linear in two variables. They can involve many more than two variables and this is often true in practical work. Further they may be non-linear, that is involving variables raised to a power such as x^2 or y^3. Similarly it is possible to define non-linear correlation coefficients which measure the success of some mathematical curve or surface in approximating data. In practice, however, it is usually difficult to work with non-linear assumptions.

A comment on the statistical use of the word 'model' is appropriate. Its use extends from well-known equations with associated standard theory, such as the foregoing regression equation, to complex equations specially constructed to meet the needs of some particular problem. In all cases, of course, some or all of the variables involved are random variables. It is the models constructed to meet particular needs which are more closely related to deterministic models as discussed in chapter 2. Models involving random variables are often said to be *stochastic*.

3.18. MULTIVARIATE ANALYSIS

In principle it is relatively easy to extrapolate from univariate and bivariate situations to those where as many as ten or a hundred variables must be considered simultaneously. Basic concepts such as that of a frequency distribution or of a significance test are unaltered. However the practical and theoretical difficulties greatly increase in multivariate situations and the methods of analysis typically used are, as will appear, correspondingly more informal and heuristic.

In a situation where many variables are being considered simultaneously it is particularly important to use a systematic notation. That in general use is founded upon the concept of a *matrix*, a rectangular array or table of numbers. A matrix may be seen as an extension of the concept of a vector. A *data matrix* might well have columns corresponding to different variables (e.g. measurements), and its rows to observation units (e.g. handaxes). The corresponding *covariance matrix* will then be a square matrix, each entry being the covariance between two variables; analogous to a table of distances between towns. Since the covariance between two variables x and y is the same as that between y and x, the covariance matrix will be a *symmetric matrix*; that is to say the value of row i and column j will be the same as that in row j and column i. The *correlation matrix* is similarly formed and will, of course, also be symmetric (see table 9.2).

Just as there exists an algebra of vectors, meaning that systematic operations upon them have been defined, so there is a *matrix algebra*. Matrices can be added and multiplied by adding and multiplying their elements in systematic and specified ways. Although almost all multivariate analysis is best described and studied by way of matrix algebra and matrix notation, to embark upon the subject here would be to become far too technical. On the rare occasions when equations involving matrices must be written we shall employ subscripted variables (see section 3.4).

This is an appropriate point to introduce an idea of considerable importance: the comparison of variation *within* groups with that *between* groups. Suppose that a measurement has been taken for each of a set of artifacts, for example the lengths of handaxes again. Suppose further that the handaxes are of a number of different types. Now the handaxes of each type will have a mean length and a variance. Therefore there will be an average variance within types. Call this M_{within}. Also the means corresponding to the different types will themselves have a variance. Multiply this by the average number of handaxes in a type and call the result $M_{between}$. Now consider what it means if the ratio $M_{between}/M_{within}$ is (i) large, and (ii) about one. In case (i) the implication is that the types are, as far as length is concerned, well distinguished. The variation between the types is much larger than the variation within them. On the other hand, in case (ii), the types are not well distinguished at all and, again just as far as length is concerned, do not seem to have any real existence. Roughly speaking, the larger the ratio the better defined the classes (see figure 3.12).

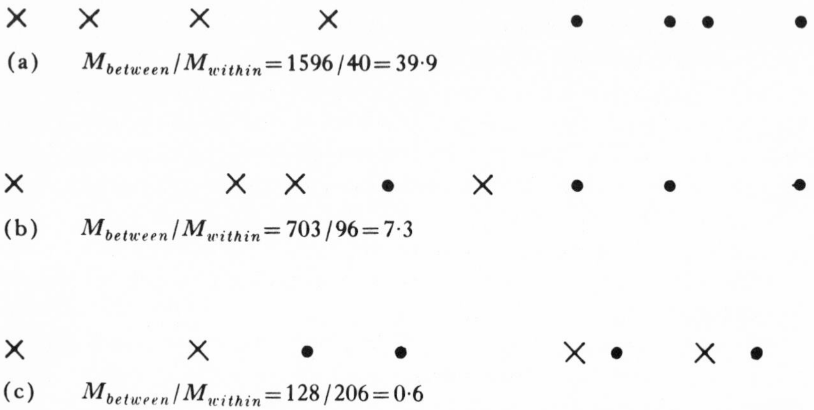

×   ×   ×   ×   •   • •   •

(a) $M_{between}/M_{within} = 1596/40 = 39.9$

×   ×   ×   •   ×   •   •   •

(b) $M_{between}/M_{within} = 703/96 = 7.3$

×   ×   •   •   × •   × •

(c) $M_{between}/M_{within} = 128/206 = 0.6$

Figure 3.12. Comparison of the ratio $M_{between}/M_{within}$ for three different linear point scatters, each made up of two sets of four points. Where the sets are well separated, (a), the ratio is large, but where they intermingle, (c), it is small.

This idea is one that has been elaborated in full mathematical detail and is the starting point for a branch of statistics called the *analysis of variance*. There exists a standard and much used significance test, the *F-test*, to decide if such a ratio (usually called an *F-ratio*) significantly differs from unity.

What is important at this point is that the study of the relationship between inter-class and intra-class variation can easily be extended, both intuitively and formally, to multivariate situations by the use of matrix algebra. It is in multivariate situations that the idea has its main archaeological application. Thus the statistical analysis by Graham (1970) of lower palaeolithic handaxes is a concrete example of just these ideas and the associated techniques being applied to an archaeological problem (see section 8.5).

3.19. RADIOCARBON DATING: STATISTICAL ASPECTS

It may be useful to end this chapter by looking at the way in which statistical methods have been used in the construction and evaluation of a particularly important archaeological technique—*radiocarbon dating*. The issues that have arisen in the use of this technique are both topical and crucially important (Olsson 1970; Clarke and Renfrew 1973). The contribution that statistical methods are making towards their resolution is therefore particularly interesting.

Most readers will be aware of the physical processes which underlie radiocarbon dating (Tite 1972). The essentials are as follows. As a result of cosmic ray activity the carbon in the atmosphere (oxidised as carbon dioxide) includes a certain proportion of a radioactive variant or isotope, carbon-14. With the passage of time this isotope decays into a stable isotope of nitrogen emitting a beta particle as it does so. Living organisms absorb carbon from the atmosphere. Once absorbed, no new radioactive isotope is formed. Hence the remaining proportion of radioactive isotope in the carbon in excavated charcoal, or wood, or bone, or other organic material is an indicator of the time elapsed since it was buried.

From the statistician's point of view it is particularly interesting that the decay of carbon-14 into nitrogen is an essentially random process. The period of time for which a particular carbon-14 atom survives before it decays is a random variable. The half-life of carbon-14 is conventionally taken to be 5568 years (a more accurate figure is 5730 years). This is the period of time needed for half of a substantial sample of carbon-14 to decay. Equivalently, it is the time taken for the proportion of carbon-14 in a carbon sample to be halved. During a small time interval the number of atoms which decay, and therefore the number of beta particles emitted, will be a random variable following the Poisson distribution. For modern carbon about fifteen beta particles are emitted per minute per gram of carbon.

Measuring the carbon-14 content of a sample in the laboratory means, essentially, observing the number of particles emitted during a particular time and relating this figure to the amount of carbon present. Since a random variable is being observed, probabilistic error limits must be assigned to the date quoted as was mentioned in section 3.12. It is worth stressing that these confidence limits should in the first instance at least be those arising solely from the essentially random nature of the decay process. The effects of possible impurities in the sample or uncertainties of calibration should be stated separately.

There are, of course, many assumptions and possible sources of error in what is in reality a complex laboratory process. One assumption has been of particular importance. Until the mid-sixties it was assumed that the radiocarbon content in the atmosphere was constant in antiquity and there was no significant evidence to challenge this assumption. However the publication of reliable tree-ring sequences, based on the bristlecone pine, has transformed the situation. These sequences stretch back some 7000 years and have carbon-14 dates associated with them (Ferguson 1969). It is therefore possible to draw calibration curves relating conventional radiocarbon dates (that is the dates that would previously have been accepted) with 'true' dates (Suess 1970; figure 3.13). 'True' dates are, in this context, those based on the dendrochronological studies and the statistical analyses which they involved.

It turns out that the conventional dates are substantially too young (that is, too close to the present) by an amount that exceeds 500 years for the earliest dates. Even more disconcerting, it appears that the same traditional date can correspond to several true dates, as the result of short-term fluctuations (lasting a century or so) in the atmospheric radiocarbon level. Given the crucial role which radiocarbon dates now play in prehistory, these results have naturally had a major impact and have been the source of much controversy.

It is now widely accepted that the bristlecone pine dendrochronology itself is essentially sound and that the conventional radiocarbon dates are indeed

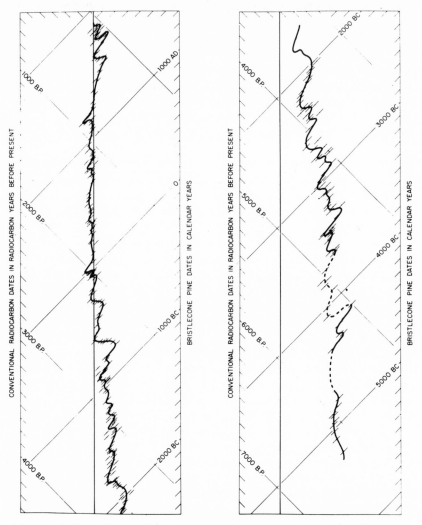

Figure 3.13. Hand-drawn calibration curves relating conventional radiocarbon dates to bristlecone pine dates. A broken line indicates scarcity of data (Suess 1970, plates I and II).

too young. This means a substantial revision of prehistoric chronology and the conclusions drawn from it. However it is still not clear whether the secondary effects, the 'kinks' or 'wriggles' in the calibration curve, have been correctly described and interpreted: the practical issue is whether or not archaeologists can ignore these kinks by the use of a 'smoothed' calibration curve possibly obtained by some form of non-linear regression analysis (see, notably, Ralph, Michael and Han 1973). One obvious possibility is that the atmospheric fluctuations are local; that those particular kinks apply only to the locality from which the bristlecone pine dendrochronology has been derived. Recently evidence suggests that this is definitely not the case. The fluctuations therefore remain ambiguous and it is reasonable to check them against archaeological evidence.

In a recent paper Ottaway and Ottaway (1972) try to do just this by considering for each of a number of archaeological 'cultures' the distribution of the corrected radiocarbon dates derived from it. By a culture they mean 'a set of dates from a single horizon at a single site' or 'dates from several culturally related sites'. They find that these distributions are systematically skewed, that is asymmetric, when the short term fluctuations ('kinks', 'wriggles') are taken into account. This is not so if a smoothed curve relating radiocarbon reading to true data is used. Reasonably enough they feel that this is evidence against the archaeological significance of the fluctuations. There are, however, problems with their analysis. For example, the number of dates available from each 'culture' is never more than twenty and often much less. Further it is not clear how far these dates used can reasonably be held to be representative of the chronological distribution of the 'cultures' themselves.

A feature of the Ottaway and Ottaway study is the way in which they respond to the technical problems of how best to present radiocarbon dates and associated confidence limits when each radiocarbon determination yields several alternative true dates. This problem is part of the more general problem of how best to present a set of radiocarbon dates for a particular culture; merely to display a long list of dates each with its associated confidence limits is more confusing than helpful.

The technique suggested by Ottaway and Ottaway and elaborated in Ottaway (1973) is to summarise the dates derived from a set of radiocarbon determinations by quoting their median, quartiles and extreme values. A simple diagram may be used for a visual presentation. The reader may need to be reminded that the median is the 'middle' value of a set of observations. The quartiles, as their name implies, are the 'middle' values (a) of those greater than, and (b) of those less than the median. Where multiple dates are associated with a particular determination then each alternative will contribute to the overall median and quartiles in inverse proportion to the number of alternatives.

The main disadvantage of this suggested procedure is that it ignores varying uncertainties in the individual determinations. This is a rather high price to pay for a simple visual summary of the data and perhaps too much attention is here being paid to convenience of study. On the other hand it is reasonable to try to work with the quartiles rather than the standard deviation given that substantially skewed distributions are to be expected. The technique may well prove useful in practice provided its limitations are understood.

Two other interesting studies relating archaeological evidence to the short-term fluctuations in the radiocarbon dating curve are those of Burleigh, Longworth and Wainwright (1972) and of Clarke and Renfrew (1972). The former compares radiocarbon date sequences to archaeological evidence at a number of sites. No discrepancies are found when the fluctuations are ignored even though discrepancies might reasonably be expected. This again suggests that the fluctuations are at least to some extent unreal.

Clarke and Renfrew in a lucid but mathematically demanding paper address themselves to the problem of how best to fit a 'floating' tree-ring chronology supported by radiocarbon dates to the main bristlecone pine chronology. Prior to their work this had been done by identifying 'kinks' in the main calibration curve, and then informally matching these kinks to the floating chronology. These authors abandon the concept of a 'kink' altogether and perform instead a modified regression analysis aimed at finding the best fit for the two data sets they consider. In spite of the fact that their methods everywhere assume linear relationships between the quantities considered, they derive reasonable results quite comparable with the outcome of the informal studies. Again the implication is that the 'kinks' in the calibration curve are somewhat insubstantial.

The issue of the significance of the short-term fluctuations in the radiocarbon date calibration curve has not yet been resolved even if the evidence tends towards insignificance. It will not be solved by purely statistical means. But statistical methods contribute to the solution of such problems by providing exact, objective and penetrating methods of analysis.

3.20. CONCLUDING REMARKS

It is worth repeating what was said at the outset of this chapter. Our aim has been less to equip the reader to use the methods we have described than to provide a conceptual framework within which their nature and sound use can be understood. Details of statistical theory and practice can be obtained from any one of scores of introductory texts. Introductions at a very elementary level are those of Huff (1970) and Moroney (1969). Texts aimed at those with rather little mathematical background are those of Bailey (1959), Cotton (1967), Dollar and Jensen (1971), and Young and Veldmann (1965). Much more mathematical sophistication is required by Hoel (1962) and Spiegel (1961). The major reference source for advanced statistical theory, in three volumes, is by Kendall and Stuart (1967, 1968, 1969).

In later chapters we shall develop in detail those of the methods introduced in this chapter which promise to be of real value in archaeological work. As earlier suggested (section 3.15), issues of sampling and formal statistical inference will be less important than more heuristic methods of multivariate data analysis. The immediate need is for methods which make only very general assumptions and which uncover hidden patterns in the data for the archaeologist to interpret. Such methods better fit the untidy world in which the archaeologist must operate even if they do also typically require large amounts of data manipulation and calculation and therefore substantial computer usage. Nevertheless the 'classical' framework of inference from sample to population must always be kept in mind. Even when not directly applicable, it provides guidelines and goals which the newer and less developed methods of data analysis badly need. Furthermore to a substantial degree it provides a general theory of logical reasoning. This will be relevant in chapter 13.

Computers. What they can do and How they are used

4.1. INTRODUCTION

In chapter 2 it was asserted that the characteristic activity of a mathematician is to provide theorems about abstract entities such as sets, lines, numbers or matrices. Also mentioned were algorithms: exactly specified procedures which mathematicians invented and used in order to find or construct particular instances of abstract entities. In its most mundane form an algorithm might merely be a detailed prescription for some minor calculation: an example is the algorithm we all use to multiply together two multi-digit numbers. An *electronic digital computer* is a machine capable of performing algorithms automatically. Given an appropriate sequence of instructions (a program) it will obey these instructions and return the results it obtains. Computers are useful because they perform algorithms far faster and more faithfully than any human can.

In order to make effective use of a digital computer one has to know: (a) what kind of tasks can be put into algorithmic form; (b) exactly how an algorithm is specified for a computer, i.e. how *to program* ; (c) how to communicate one's program (specification of the algorithm) to a suitable computer and what practical limitations there are. The aim of this chapter is to go a fair way to providing this knowledge so that the reader can judge for himself what are the issues, the difficulties, and the potentialities of computer usage. Additionally many of the terms and concepts to be introduced here will be important in later chapters.

To make effective use of a computer one does *not* have to know more than the barest minimum about the machine itself; about what is called the 'hardware'. Miracles of electronics can, fortunately, be left to the appropriate experts. At most it is sometimes useful to know a little about the general organisation of the machine or complex of machines being used; relevant remarks will be found in section 4.6. Equally, little need be known about the 'software', the complex systems programs written by experts to make life easy for the average user. It is enough to be able to call up the facilities needed (see section 4.4).

It is important to distinguish between a digital computer and an *analogue computer*. Very roughly, the difference is that whereas digital computers represent numbers by binary patterns of electronic pulses, analogue computers use actual physical quantities whose magnitudes are the magnitudes of the numbers represented. Analogue computers are much less useful than digital computers overall, but they do have a number of particular applications, for example in certain kinds of simulation work. We shall not have occasion to refer to them again.

4.2.   WHAT TASKS CAN A COMPUTER PERFORM?

It is not easy for the non-specialist to discover what tasks it is reasonable to assign to a computer. At the lowest level, gossip will tell him one day that computers are 'electronic brains' of awesome potential and power, and the next that 'computers can only do what you tell them to do' with the implication that they just help with the arithmetic. If he talks to computer specialists, the gap between these two extremes will begin to close but not all that rapidly. Some specialists will talk primarily about algorithms for solving mathematical equations, and will stress the great practical difficulties encountered. Others will talk about computers as used in industry and commerce mentioning payroll calculations, management decisions, and a variety of different kinds of data-banking. Others will talk solely of the subtleties of programming languages, or be enthusiastic about the latest advance in 'machine architecture'. Others again will indeed talk seriously about the great potentialities of computers: will speak of computers as capable of being 'intelligent', of having original ideas, of doing the 'thinking' for robots.

There are, of course, as many specialities in computer science as there are in archaeology. Even leaving aside the hard core of the subject, which is the actual design of computers and the great complexities of basic software and systems programming, divergent specialities are ensured by the diversity of possible computer applications. To a considerable extent this explains the discrepant attitudes and interests of computer specialists. Nevertheless it is undeniable that the capabilities of computers provoke the examination of deep social and philosophical questions, and it can easily happen that people within the same speciality differ fundamentally in their answers to these questions. Much the same is true of some aspects of archaeology.

In the first instance, computers are, as has already been stressed, devices for 'doing' algorithms. The mathematician finds that some task that he wishes to do in his ordinary line of work involves tedious and long calculations. It is natural first to make use of a desk calculator, and then if this is insufficient of an automatic computer. One of the first uses ever made of a digital computer was to calculate artillery tables for the US Army. Compiling astronomical tables, solving the complex equations of physics, performing long statistical calculations: these are all typical computer work.

However, although computer programming was at first the invention and tool of mathematicians, it has long since achieved an independent existence. Programmers early began to see how to make computers perform tasks which the mathematicians had not requested. Tasks, indeed, that mathematicians, as mathematicians, would never consider—keeping in mind that a mathematician is primarily interested in abstraction and proving theorems. For example, programs have been written which store and retrieve information in much the way of a card filing system, which simulate the behaviour of rats in a maze, which translate from one language into another, which compose music and poetry, which play chess, which help children learn to read, which simulate neurotic thought-processes, which analyse the results of surveys, and which classify objects into 'natural' groups. Some of these programs perform very poorly (for example the chess is mediocre and the poetry worse), but they all exist.

These applications have little or nothing to do with mathematics in the normal sense of that word—for example, with the contents of a university mathematics course. What has happened is that the concept of an exact algorithm has been extended outside the mathematical domain to link up with everyday concepts such as that of a 'plan of campaign', or a 'programme' or a 'recipe'. Further, many of these applications depend crucially on the machine's ability to store large amounts of detailed information which programs can extract and manipulate. The archaeological significance of this aspect of computers will be particularly discussed in chapter 12.

Other important concepts are those of a *heuristic* and a *heuristic program*. When trying to achieve some objective, we often have no very clear idea of how best to proceed. However there may well be definite things we can do which we are pretty sure will help. Thus if the aim is to complete a jigsaw puzzle, most people start by fitting together the side pieces; without ever feeling that they ought to prove that this is a good thing to do. Such useful 'rules of thumb' are called heuristics in this context. A heuristic program is one which involves the use of such heuristics. Heuristic programming is important in industry, and chess playing programs, for example, use heuristics to distinguish between good and bad board configurations.

A crucial idea to grasp is that the wide-ranging abilities of digital computers depend less on the physical capabilities of the machine, important though these are, than on the ability of programmers to specify complex tasks in exact detail. The question: 'Can a computer do this?' is almost always better rephrased as: 'Can this procedure be exactly specified?' Thus: 'Can a computer write poetry?' becomes: 'Can anyone specify exactly, and in detail, how to write poetry?'

4.3.   PROGRAMMING

If you want someone to do a job you must tell them what to do. The less knowledgeable and intelligent they are the more careful, precise, and comprehensive your instructions will have to be if at best error and at worst chaos is to be avoided. Computers are just lumps of machinery. Until they are told what to do they have no intelligence and only enough 'knowledge' to enable them to obey a range of very primitive instructions, the basic machine instructions. These basic instructions cover moving symbols around inside the machine (and in and out of it), and combining symbols in certain simple ways. In particular they cover the simple arithmetic operations. It is not surprising then that the first and essential requirement for a computer program is that it shall give an exact specification of what is to be done for every situation which might arise once the program is set in operation.

This may sound as if programming a computer is not only hard work, but also pointless. If programming is so much trouble, is not the programmer effectively doing the job himself anyway? It turns out that things are not quite as bad as that. Programming is indeed hard work but it is also often engrossing and enjoyable. More important, perhaps, it is nowhere near true that specifying exactly what is to be done takes as long as actually doing it. It may take a programmer a year to write a large program but it would take him a thousand lifetimes to obey it himself. It may take the machine ten minutes.

The labour of programming is alleviated in a rather ingenious way. The programming task is split into two stages, only the first of which has to be tackled by the ordinary user. He or she writes his program in a specially and precisely defined *programming language*, and then this program is translated into machine instructions by the machine itself! The reader will already understand that the machine does not do this translation spontaneously. It does it under the command of an expertly written program called a *compiler*, itself written in machine instructions.

The usefulness of the programming language to the user is that it is relatively convenient. The user's program must still be exact and comprehensive but the machine can be left to do much more on its own than would be possible were the program written in basic machine instructions. At this point something more than a little unfortunate must be admitted. There is not just one computer programming language, but literally dozens of them! There are several general-purpose languages in common use and others suitable for special applications, and these all have their own dialects. Any particular computer is likely to be equipped with compilers for several of the most common languages plus one or two local specialities. Most programmers can write programs, at a pinch, in several languages but are fully at home only in one or two of them.

The reader may wonder why computers cannot be programmed in a natural language, perhaps English. The answer is that they could, but only if the programmers were prepared to use a very small range of words and a very small range of sentence constructions. In practice the restrictions would be found arbitrary and frustrating. The user would soon come to prefer a specially defined programming language. Why cannot the programmer use whatever

English comes to mind? There are two related reasons. The range of grammatical (and ungrammatical!) constructions which the machine would need to be able to cope with would be extremely large. Further, and more important, the programmer would almost certainly assume that the machine understood certain things, or had certain knowledge, which it does not have and which no-one as yet knows how to give it.

The first requirement, then, is that the aspiring computer user must learn a programming language. Certainly the language learned should be one in widespread use. The example programs given in this chapter are written in ALGOL-60 (short for Algorithmic Language 1960) a programming language defined by a specialist international committee in 1960. ALGOL compilers have been written for almost all types of digital computer. Our use of ALGOL, rather than the somewhat more widely used FORTRAN, is partly fortuitous, partly that we find ALGOL the better designed language.

Here is one of the simplest possible ALGOL programs:

```
begin
    integer a, b, c;
    a: = read;
    b: = read;
    c: = a + b;
    print(c);
end
```

It causes the machine to accept two integral numbers, to add them together, and then to return the answer. It can be translated into ordinary language as follows: Prepare variables ('boxes'; see section 2.5) called a, b, and c which are suitable for holding integer values. Read a value from outside the computer and put it into a. Read another value from outside and put it into b. Add the values in a and b together and put the answer into c. Send back the value in variable c to the outside world.

There are a number of points the reader should note:

1. The program is obeyed from top to bottom unless there is an instruction to the contrary.

2. The **begin** and **end** delimit the program.

3. Although the layout of the program on the page is not important, almost everything else is. There are exact rules of punctuation, spelling, and terminology. If these rules are broken the program will be rejected by the machine.

4. The language has its own 'grammar'. Thus the programmer must write '*print(c)*', not '*print c*' or '*(c) print*'.

5. The first thing that must be done is to 'declare' certain variables and name them. The numbers or symbols used are stored in these variables.

6. The composite symbol ': =' means 'make the value of the variable

to the left the value obtained from the right'. It may be read: 'becomes equal to'.

7. There is a repertoire of other operations that can be requested, for example addition.

8. A distinction should be drawn between the *program* itself, the *data* needed by the program on any particular occasion (in this case two integers) and the *results* which it returns (here a single integer). The program can be used with a large number of different sets of data.

For the time being we leave aside the question of exactly how the data (and for that matter the program itself) is made available to the machine and how the machine returns the results.

This program is too minor to be very informative. Suppose the task is not merely to add two numbers together, but to find the range of the numbers in a long list of measurements. As defined in section 3.7 the range of a set of values is the difference between the smallest and the largest of them. A suitable program appears below. The line numbers shown on the left are not part of the program, but have been inserted to help the reader understand the following description.

```
 1  begin
 2     real maximum, minimum, measurement;
 3     maximum:=0; minimum:=100;
 4   marker: measurement:=read;
 5     if measurement = −1 then
 6       begin
 7         newline(1); writetext('maximum'); print(maximum);
 8         newline(1); writetext('minimum'); print(minimum);
 9         newline(1); writetext('range'); print(maximum−minimum);
10       end
11     else
12     begin
13       if maximum < measurement then maximum:=measurement;
14       if minimum > measurement then minimum:=measurement;
15       goto marker
16     end
17  end
```

The program assumes that every measurement in the input list is a decimal number between 0 and 100 and further that the end of the list is indicated by appending to it the number −1. The **begin** and **end** on lines 1 and 17 bound the program, and those on lines 6 and 10, and 12 and 16, parcel off sub-parts of it. On line 2 three variables of type real are declared, with identifiers chosen to indicate the significance of the numbers they are to hold. Ignore line 3 for the moment. The instruction on line 4 causes the next measurement to be read into the variable of that name, and *marker:* labels this instruction so that it can be referred to later. On line 5 the number just read is checked to see if it is −1. If so, then the instructions on lines 7, 8 and 9 are obeyed. These cause some output which on a page would look like:

maximum	67.89
minimum	1.23
range	66.66

Notice the important distinction between printing the letters which make up the word *maximum* and printing the number which is the value of the variable called *maximum*. If the test on line 5 fails then the instructions on lines 13, 14 and 15 are obeyed. These cause the machine to check to see if the current maximum and minimum values should be changed and if so to make the change. Then the instruction on line 15 causes the machine to jump back to the instruction to which the label *marker* has been attached, i.e. line 4.

Were values not given to the variables *minimum* and *maximum* on line 3, there would be trouble on line 14. Here the machine is asked to compare the values of the variables *maximum* and *measurement*. Were *maximum* to have no value, the machine would declare the program faulty and stop obeying it.

It is important to appreciate the significance of 'loops' such as that caused by the **goto** instruction on line 15. They enable the same set of instructions to be obeyed many times when a program is run. Were this not possible then programs would have to be impossibly long. A similarly crucial role is played by conditional instructions such as that on line 5.

These two little programs are not quite authentic. For example, getting numbers into and out of the machine involves slightly more detail than has been shown. However this is of no great importance, and it would now be natural to go on and explain all the varied instructions and combinations of instruction that can be employed in an ALGOL or FORTRAN program. But it would be inappropriate to do so. There are very many introductory manuals available which do just this, for example McCracken (1962, 1972). The small example programs given above, together with a larger example to be discussed later in this chapter, will suffice to make the essential points.

The exactness of detail required both in the actual writing of the program, and in its logical organisation, must again be stressed. Ambiguities are never pregnant. It follows that the programmer inevitably spends much of his time making and then correcting errors. Further, it is often true that a particular task can be carried out in a variety of different ways, that is, by a variety of algorithms. Some of these algorithms will be efficient and others not. The good programmer will choose between them accordingly.

4.4.   COMMUNICATING WITH THE MACHINE

It is possible (though difficult) to learn a computer language such as ALGOL from a standard manual, to write a program embodying an original and potentially useful algorithm, and to have that program published in a scientific journal for general use. It is not strictly necessary to have any contact with a computer at all. However, anyone trying to follow such a path is likely to find that the standard of ALGOL achieved is about as high as that in French learned solely by the study of a French grammar and dictionary. Further, although it is indeed appropriate to use a computer language as a language in which to publish algorithms, even here one would certainly take the program to the machine to check for errors. In the vast majority of instances, however, algorithms are programmed because there is a job to be done and only a computer has the speed, capacity and precision to do it.

There are, loosely, two means by which requirements can be communicated to a computer. One, the older method, is to code program and data on to *punched cards* (sometimes, punched paper tape). The cards are physically scanned by the machine and the information on them read. The results are returned by the machine either on punched cards or printed as text on papers by a high-speed *lineprinter* so called because it prints a line of text at a time. A typical lineprinter will print about a thousand lines of text in a minute.

In recent years a more direct and more convenient means of communicating with a computer has become widespread. The machine is used *on-line* or *interactively*. By this is meant that instructions and data are passed from the user to the machine, and results and messages passed from the machine to the user, by way of a typewriter electronically connected to the machine itself. Such *on-line terminals* even enable a user to communicate with the computer while it is obeying his program; it is possible, for example, to ascertain from a program what stage it has reached and whether additional data are needed.

On-line typewriter terminals are relatively slow communication channels and must be used in conjunction with lineprinters if the output expected from the computer is substantial. Terminals need not be physically adjacent to the parent machine. Indeed they are commonly hundreds of yards away and may be hundreds of miles away linked to it by standard data transmission lines.

Anyone using a computer will encounter the concept of a *file* of information. Derived from the conventional office or card file, the computer science concept covers any organised body of information held on a medium, such as paper or magnetic tape, which the machine can use directly. It always has a name and a defined logical structure. It may be composed of text (in English or ALGOL, for example), or of numbers, or of any sequence of symbols put together for any purpose or no purpose at all. Many different operations can be performed upon files. They may be created, destroyed, merged, searched, edited, read, printed, or obeyed as programs.

Normally an on-line user will have access to a file handling system. He will be able to create named files, typing the contents on the keyboard. He will then be able to manipulate these files at will building up a convenient file library. Some of his files will be programs and others data. Whenever he wishes he will be able to have the machine compile a program file, and run it with appropriate data files. The machine will then create files of results and add them to the user's file library. Such a file handling service is provided entirely by the machine. The user creates files by typing and then manipulates them by issuing appropriate commands and referring to files by their names. At any time he can examine the contents of a file by having it printed either at his terminal or on a lineprinter. He need know nothing of how the information is stored 'in the works'.

If an 'on-line' terminal with these facilities is not available, then the computer user will have to do much more of the work himself. Only files actually in use or to be used in the near future can be held in the computer. At other times they must be stored in some other way, and usually decks of punched cards or reels of punched paper tape are used. These are created, edited and printed on machines which are 'off-line'; not in contact with the computer. The computer can be instructed to read such paper files and can itself generate them. Large amounts of data are often kept on magnetic tapes, which again can be directly read and generated by the computer. Where files are kept and manipulated away from the machine, having a job done requires the user to specify to the human operator or to the automatic operating system what files are to be read and what is to be done with them.

The reasons why on-line interactive terminals are only now becoming widespread are instructive. Human beings type slowly. By computer standards, very, very slowly. This means that for a large computer to spend most of its time idling while one user slowly creates his data file on-line is extremely inefficient. It is far more efficient only to run actual programs—and for file handling to be done off-line by the user himself. This difficulty is largely overcome by having many people interact with the computer simultaneously. The machine turns its attention from one to the other in very much the manner of a schoolteacher attending to the queries of different members of his class, or, an even closer analogy, of a chess master playing perhaps forty opponents in a display of simultaneous chess. The machine is always fully occupied, while the user can pause for thought or a cup of coffee as often as desired. If at some instant no user wishes to interact with the machine, it carries on doing some low priority background job.

Of course, the machine does not behave in this way spontaneously. Sophisticated concepts must be developed, complex systems programs have to be written, and also some special electronics are needed. It is these requirements that have delayed the development of such 'multi-access' facilities until comparatively recent years. Large computers are now controlled by highly complex programs called *operating systems* which themselves administer the flow of work through the machine and communicate with perhaps scores of on-line users simultaneously. Thus when a user switches on an on-line terminal, it is part of the operating system which will identify him as known to the system and will then accept his instructions.

It should be added that on-line computer usage remains a costly business and it is a matter of controversy whether the facilities offered to the user justify the expense.

There are some other more sophisticated ways in which a user can communicate with the computer. The most important of these concern *visual* or *graphical input* and *output*. Thus quite commonly an on-line terminal consists not of an electric typewriter but of a keyboard together with a *visual display unit* : essentially a small TV screen which shows both what the user types and the machine replies. Most installations of any size possess a *graph plotter* of some kind. This is a peripheral machine connected to the computer which draws line diagrams under program control. Although rough diagrams can be drawn by use of a lineprinter these are very crude in comparison.

Equipment is sometimes available which enables the programmer to have the machine draw dynamic line diagrams on a visual display: effectively on a TV screen. This can be an extremely effective way for a programmer to supervise the behaviour of his programs, and to study the results it provides. It is possible to go further, and create a cine-film from the display for projection in the normal way.

Input to the machine can also be handled graphically. A user can himself draw a line diagram or modify a diagram drawn by the machine, and have this graphical communication read by the machine. For some applications this is much more convenient and appropriate than typing. More will be said about this in chapter 12 in the context of computer-based data banks and their potential uses in archaeology.

4.5.   AN EXAMPLE: COMPUTER PLOTTING OF DISTRIBUTION MAPS
Practical experience is essential for a full understanding of computers and their capabilities and limitations. Such experience the reader must obtain for himself. All that can be done here is to discuss a realistic example of what it is like to conceive, write and test a computer program, indicating the successive stages of the process and the practical problems likely to be encountered.

Suppose that the objective is to have the machine draw distribution maps. An example would be an outline map of England and Wales showing (a) Iron Age and (b) Saxon settlement sites. Drawing such maps is often a moderately tedious business which it seems reasonable to try to automate. What is needed is a small 'utility' program available to anyone who wishes to use it. If we were really serious we would probably make use of a graph plotter (see above) but for the purposes of the example it will suffice to exploit the ordinary text printing facilities in a crude but effective way.

The first requirement is an exact specification of the task. This usually involves, in the first instance at least, being relatively unambitious and making the task as simple as possible. Complications can always be introduced later. Here the exact requirement might reasonably be a computer program which given: (a) a specification of the boundary of a region (the outline of England

and Wales); (b) the coordinates of a number of points (settlement sites); and (c) a classification of these points and a symbol associated with each class (distinguishing Iron Age from Saxon), will draw the boundary on the lineprinter output, and appropriately locate symbols within it.

Since the use of a graph plotter has been ruled out the machine has no way of actually drawing lines. It can only print letters of the alphabet, digits and punctuation marks. Hence drawing the boundary means distributing asterisks, say, over the paper in such a way that they give a suitable effect. Specifying the boundary then means specifying the coordinates of all the points upon it. If the dimensions of the actual plot are fixed at fifty typewriter rows by fifty typewriter columns, for example, then the coordinates of a point, on the boundary or otherwise, will be an ordered pair of integers each between 1 and 50 inclusive. The alternative symbols required under (c) can be letters of the alphabet.

There is little difficulty in establishing the broad structure of a suitable program. It falls naturally into five parts:

1. Declare and initialise working variables and a suitable *array*; that is, a matrix of variables here to be used to build up an internal representation of the map to be generated.

2. Read the boundary point coordinates and place corresponding values in the array.

3. Read the symbol to be used for a set of non-boundary points.

4. Read the coordinates for a set of non-boundary points.

5. Print the actual map.

Control of the machine is initially in (1), moves successively to (2), (3) and (4), repeats (3) and (4) as often as is specified, and then finally moves to (5).

An actual program listing (ICL 1960A ALGOL-60) is shown in figure 4.1(a). The part structure is marked by the successive labels READ OUTLINE, READ SYMBOL, READ POINTS and PRINT MAP. Values are inserted into the array MAP in accordance with the following code:

-1 blank
0 an asterisk
1 the letter A
2 the letter B
3 the letter C

Notice that this program can cope with up to three different types of non-boundary points, to be represented by the symbols A, B and C. Suitable invented data for the program are shown in figure 4.1(b) and the corresponding program-generated map in figure 4.2. As one might expect from so simple a program, the result is very crude. A much more sophisticated piece of computer mapping using a graph plotter is shown in figure 4.3.

The reader should not imagine that even a program as simple as this can be written and run on the machine without setbacks. Errors are the rule, not the exception. Assuming that on-line facilities are available, the first step is to

```
'BEGIN'

'INTEGER' X,Y,SYMBOL;
'INTEGER' 'ARRAY' MAP[1:50,1:50];

'FOR' X:= 1 'STEP' 1 'UNTIL' 50 'DO'
'FOR' Y:= 1 'STEP' 1 'UNTIL' 50 'DO'
  MAP[X,Y]:=-1;


READ OUTLINE:

X:=READ;  'IF' X=0 'THEN' 'GOTO' READ SYMBOL;
Y:=READ;
MAP[X,Y]:=0;
'GOTO' READ OUTLINE;


READ SYMBOL:
SYMBOL:=READ;
'IF' SYMBOL=0 'THEN' 'GOTO' PRINT MAP;

READ POINTS:

X:=READ; 'IF' X=0 'THEN' 'GOTO' READ SYMBOL;
Y:=READ;
MAP[X,Y]:=SYMBOL;
'GOTO' READ POINTS;


PRINT MAP:

'FOR' X:=1 'STEP' 1 'UNTIL' 50 'DO'
'BEGIN'

NEWLINE(1);
'FOR' Y:= 1 'STEP' 1 'UNTIL' 50 'DO'
'BEGIN'

'IF' MAP[X,Y]=-1 'THEN' SPACE(1);
'IF' MAP[X,Y]=0 'THEN' WRITE TEXT('('*')');
'IF' MAP[X,Y]=1 'THEN' WRITE TEXT('('A')');
'IF' MAP[X,Y]=2 'THEN' WRITE TEXT('('B')');
'IF' MAP[X,Y]=3 'THEN' WRITE TEXT('('C')');

'END'

'END'

'END' OF PROGRAM
```

```
  8   25
  9   25
  9   26
 10   27
 11   27
 12   27
 12   28
 13    .
      :
      :
      :
      . 20
 12   21
 11   22
 10   23
  9   23
  9   24
  8   24
  0
  1
 15   19
 14   22
 16   25
 19   22
 23   27
 24   16
 26   16
 27   15
 29   16
  0
  2
 23   20
 27   41
 29   31
 31   36
 32   31
 34   23
 35   26
  0
  0
```

(a)   (b)

Figure 4.1 (a) A simple ALGOL-60 program (ICL 1900) for plotting distribution maps, and (b) some of the data for the program.

type a file which is the program itself. Then a second file is created containing simple test data, invented data sufficient to test all the different parts of the program. After this the ALGOL compiler is called to compile the program (translate it into basic machine instructions). Almost certainly the compiler will find that the program has syntactic errors; an omitted semi-colon, an undeclared variable, a misspelled command word. The programmer must pin down exactly what the errors are, and edit the program file accordingly. It is often only after several cycles of error correction that the compiler announces that it has succeeded in translating the program. The compiled program can then be run, that is, the machine is instructed to obey it. More errors will now appear. These will be not in the grammar, the syntax, of the program, but in its logic or organisation. Such errors will either bring the program to a full stop (e.g. an attempt to divide by zero) or will cause erroneous or more likely, chaotic results. Thus the function of the test data is not merely to 'exercise' each part of the program but to generate results which can be checked independently by the programmer. More than one set of test data must normally be run in order to ensure that the program is really doing what it should.

Correcting *programming errors* can be an extremely frustrating business. Whilst most errors, especially syntactic ones, can be diagnosed and put right quite quickly, some can remain baffling for days on end. This is true even when full use is made of automatic aids to error detection. At worst one may be obliged to simulate the machine itself, and laboriously perform by hand all

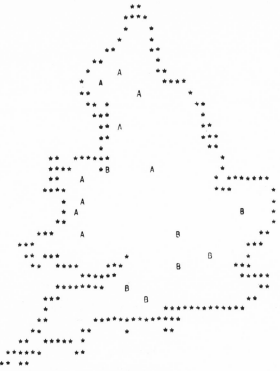

Figure 4.2. The map printed by the program of figure 4.1(a) given the data of 4.1(b).

the operations required by the program until the mistake stands out. Even then it is possible to deceive oneself. The scope for subtle mistakes sometimes seems endless, especially when one is a novice programmer. Complex professionally written programs (such as compilers) are commonly found to have minor errors even after they have been distributed to users and are in everyday use. Successive versions of such programs are issued, each version correcting some of the errors surviving in the previous version. Thus the amateur should never be too confident that he has finally got his program doing just what he intended!

Once a program has been adequately tested it can be put to the use for which it was intended. In almost all cases, but especially if the program is to be used by a number of people, the program and its use must be systematically described or documented. *Documentation* covers such matters as how the program is organised, how to organise the data for it, and how to interpret the results which it yields. Information is also needed about how long the program takes to process the data, how much memory store it occupies in the machine, and what, if any, special peripheral machinery it requires. These are matters

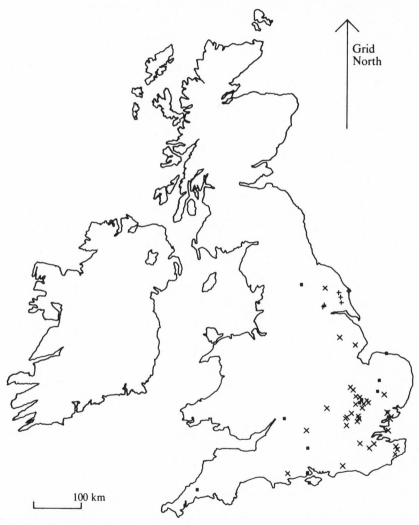

Figure 4.3. A distribution map obtained using a computer and a graph plotter (Wilcock 1971, 480).

we have not previously discussed. The point is that although computers operate at very great speed and can store large amounts of information (programs, data, etc.) it is always possible to find programs which stretch one or other or both of these capabilities. In any case very few programs have time and storage requirements which are actually negligible. Hence any computer user must be aware of how much time and store he can reasonably use on the machine available to him, and how much of these quantities his program is likely to use on a given occasion. Very often the user will find that he must state in advance absolute limits in the amount of machine time his program will use, and the amount of output text he will generate. Then if these limits are exceeded, perhaps in consequence of a programming error, the machine will terminate the program automatically.

The program described above is, of course, very simple. It is easy to think of possible improvements and extensions. Some obvious ones are: (a) extend the program so that it can generate several maps with the same outline but different distributions; (b) extend the program so that it can automatically convert a coordinate system convenient to the user into its own mapping coordinates; (c) cope with situations where several points (possibly with different symbols) should be superimposed; (d) enable text to be written on the map; (e) avoid the use of the large array (which is wasteful of machine storage); (f) use a graph plotter; (g) enable the program to draw its data from a permanent machine-based data bank rather than from outside. Very many computer programs are such that the more effort put into their writing, the more useful and clever they are. But in practice there comes a point at which the possible gains are not worth the effort which must be expended in procuring them.

It may well seem that if getting a program to work is so much trouble, it would be simpler to plot one's distribution maps by hand. Probably it is fair to say that if a suitable program is already freely available, then it makes sense to use it if there are a number of maps (or just scatter diagrams) to plot with a fair number of points on each. This is certainly the case if the data are already on the machine, as implied in (g) above (Wilcock 1971). In addition, eliminating programming errors is not just a time-wasting nuisance. It means that whatever the program is about, one is *obliged* to get the detail right. If the program is a theory of how some system operates (and some of the most important programs are) then that theory has to be made detailed and precise. Bad theories cannot be made to look good by elegant hand waving. These points will become clearer in later chapters as detailed examples of computer work are discussed.

4.6.   GETTING ACCESS TO A COMPUTER

In practice the first problems the intending computer user has to solve are how to learn to program and how to get access to a machine. These two problems are not quite independent since there is little point in learning the language SNOBOL, say, if the only machine available has no SNOBOL translator.

Most readers of this book are likely to be working in a university environment. These days all universities provide a general *computing service*, although, of course, procedure and facilities vary greatly from one university to another. A typical computing service will include regular courses in the locally favoured programming language, usually supported by very limited access to the machine for the purpose of practical tuition. Manuals for the most widely used languages may be bought in any bookshop. Application to the service centre will probably obtain access to the machine and its supporting facilities together with a reasonable quota of actual computation time (there are complications here; for example, the maximum amount of machine storage used may be limited as well as the amount of computing time). The actual mode of access could be: (a) a personal on-line terminal (very unlikely); (b) access to a terminal not too far away, perhaps in the computing service building itself; (c) access to off-line card-punching machines etc., with the right to hand in card decks (i.e. program + data) to be run, the results being available for collection a few hours later.

A combination of (b) and (c) is common. The amount of use that a user can make of the machine (and what if anything he must pay for it) will depend upon his seniority and experience, the kind of work he is doing, and his persuasiveness! It will also depend, of course, upon the size of the computer installation (which may well involve several computers each itself composed of a variety of sub-units) and the load upon it. Help with data preparation, for example card punching, is often possible.

An important part of any computing service is the advice given on programming and general machine usage. The inexperienced programmer and system user will find himself threading a maze of complex and often apparently incoherent detail. Without competent guidance there is a real risk that he will never emerge. Guidance is also needed on the contents and use of the library programs available. Any computer installation has a library of useful programs available for general use. These will range from simple editing programs and pseudo-random number generators (see section 3.5) to packages of programs for use by specialists in statistics or mathematical programming or numerical analysis. The archaeologist will find many programs in such libraries which will have at least some relevance to the problems that interest him. Some of these will, of course, be discussed in later chapters.

Most potential computer users, whether in a university or not, will find themselves negotiating access to a large computing installation in the manner described. However there is an alternative: to buy one's own. This is not quite as unrealistic as it may at first appear. Computing devices range from electronic pocket calculators costing a few tens of pounds, to computers costing several millions, or, most recently, networks of computers costing tens of millions. The range is continuous and hence there is a machine to fit everyone's budget. Whether that machine will do the jobs required depends on the nature of the jobs. An archaeologist thinking in terms of relatively simple statistical calculations may well find that a table-top mini-computer will serve his purpose, especially if the alternative is fighting a large installation a mile away. But if he can attach an on-line terminal to a large central machine the mini-computer may seem very limited in comparison. For advanced work, access to a large machine is essential.

4.7.   MATHEMATICS, STATISTICS AND COMPUTER SCIENCE

It is appropriate to end this chapter by recapitulating briefly the relationships between mathematics, statistics and computer science. These relationships are not always well understood by archaeologists, and where false or over simple perspectives exist, misunderstandings and mistaken evaluations are liable to result.

The starting point is pure mathematics, which may be seen as a communal (among mathematicians) exercise in exact abstract reasoning leading to new and deeper understanding of the abstract logical properties of reality. Mathematical procedures and conclusions can be applied to practical problems, for example building a bridge or planning a space-flight, where the practical problem can be matched to some pre-existing or specially developed piece of theory. The application process, unlike mathematics itself, is informal, depending a great deal upon the expertise and intuition of the applied mathematician.

A branch of pure mathematics is probability theory, the mathematical theory of chance. Closely related is mathematical statistics which links probability theory to applied statistics, a solidly practical subject concerned with the collection and interpretation of detailed information, usually numerical, about problem situations where chance factors make interpretation particularly difficult. The statistician must be able to understand problems put to him by workers in other disciplines who may know no mathematics of any kind. He must decide the best way to formulate these problems in statistical terms and then try to solve them with appropriate techniques. He must know how to allow for chance, avoiding both the assumption that no inferences are possible and the converse error that whatever first appears to be true is true.

Algorithms are exactly specified procedures by which certain results may be calculated or, more generally, certain goals achieved. They are important in all branches of pure and applied mathematics. They are particularly important in statistics. Computers are machines which may be programmed to perform algorithms very rapidly and reliably. Computer science, now a quite distinct subject from mathematics, concerns the design and use of computers including the design of the extremely complex systems programs which make computing easy for the average user.

Just as computer science is no longer merely a branch of mathematics, so the algorithms which computers are programmed to perform are no longer solely concerned with numerical calculations. Applied computer science is now concerned with general information processing, whether or not that information is expressed numerically.

Whatever else archaeology may or may not be, it certainly involves the collection, collation and interpretation of large amounts of detailed information. This immediately suggests that archaeologists should pay most attention to the methods of applied statistics and general information processing, recognising that pure mathematics involves too much abstraction to hold out much promise of being directly useful. Just what this attitude means in practice will be examined in detail in the following chapters, commencing in the next chapter with easily posed but difficult and extremely important questions of basic quantification. In the next and succeeding chapters a central aim will be to identify the data analytic methods appropriate to each type of archaeological problem. It is the limitations of the theory of data analysis, as much as the limitations of archaeological theory, which make this such a difficult task.

Finally it may be useful to suggest further reading on computers and their applications. Unfortunately the subject is now so broad and contains so many specialisations that it is impossible for anyone to write a balanced and authoritative overview. Elementary but correspondingly limited little books which introduce computers and some of their applications are those by Hollingdale and Toothill (1965) and by Laver (1965), and most books on programming, for example those by McCracken (1962, 1972) cited above, have some kind of general introduction. Particularly relevant here, of course, is the very useful introduction to computers written by Chenhall (1971b) specifically for anthropologists and archaeologists. However for a wide view of what is going on in computer science it is probably best to browse through the proceedings of the latest international computer science conference (Freiman 1972; especially volume 2) or the series of volumes *Advances in Programming* (Rubinoff 1972). Useful texts on statistical computing, notably on programming computers to perform multivariate statistical analyses of the kind to be discussed in later chapters, are those by Cooley and Lohnes (1962), Veldman (1967), and Davies (1971).

PART TWO
Data Analysis

The Initial Quantification of Archaeological Evidence

5.1. INTRODUCTION : WHY QUANTIFY?

It seems worth stressing at the outset of this chapter that quantification is in no way alien to traditional archaeological procedure. Some information regularly used by archaeologists is inherently quantified: not only the evidence from the natural sciences, such as counts of pollen grains, proportions of trace elements in metals and so forth, but more 'purely' archaeological statements, that one type is larger or smaller than another, more frequent in this assemblage than that, equally involve quantification in a real sense. If there is a contrast between quantification and a traditional approach it is in the degree of precision rather than in the approach itself.

Any archaeologist consciously or unconsciously considers only some of the evidence that is conceivably relevant; he emphasises some and plays down some. If he quantifies, he has to realise, admit and specify these choices, and the first reason for quantification is that it exacts this kind of specificity. A second purpose is that once quantified, archaeological information may be presented clearly, comprehensively and concisely in tables and diagrams. A third major reason is that quantification leads to numerical (e.g. statistical or computer-orientated) techniques of proven value in assessing and analysing archaeological data. If these hesitant links between archaeology and mathematics can be strengthened in the future, one clear pathway for the disciplined development of the subject will have been opened.

Some hints of how this future development could proceed are given in chapters 11–13. However, this section of the book (chapters 5–9) examines a more traditional approach to archaeology and simply attempts to make this approach more explicit and rigorous by quantification. The present chapter deals with the preliminary translation of archaeological material into a descriptive, numerical language that can provide a starting point for its presentation and analysis.

5.2. GENERAL FORMAT : UNITS AND ATTRIBUTES

5.2.1. *The data matrix.* The basic format for presenting quantified information in archaeology as in other subjects is a table or matrix, where units of concern are listed and described by their scores on a number of variables (see section 3.18). Archaeologists, in common with other data analysts, often refer to variables as *attributes*, a convention that we will follow from here on. It is as a table, then, that data will normally be recorded, first on suitable data sheets and subsequently on cards, tape or disc for direct use by a computer.

Archaeological units listed in any one table must be comparable and most often will represent one of two major empirical levels: either single items, often artifacts (level 1 on figure 1.2), or associations of items from features or components (levels 2 and 3 on figure 1.2). Attributes chosen to describe items will tend to be dimensions that are directly measurable, or characteristics that may be recorded as present or absent. For associations (lots or assemblages), attributes will usually be classes of items that may be recorded as present or absent, represented by a proportional count or summarised by simple statistics (e.g. mean and standard deviation).

The obvious problems involved in drawing up this kind of table are to decide how much information to include and in what form.

5.2.2. *The choice of units : meaningful populations and samples.* Deciding which units to study, whether quantitatively or not, is really equivalent to defining the scope and purpose of a piece of research. The units will be chosen to represent a general or a more specific problem area, and for precise results it seems instructive to relate this choice of units to the statistical concepts of sample and population introduced in sections 3.9 and 3.15: the concept of population should help in defining the scope and content of a problem; the concept of sample should help in deciding how much of this general context to consider, and in assessing how legitimate it may be to generalise from specific evidence. Even more important, any realistic discussion of these concepts will emphasise how archaeology relates to and differs from other disciplines where quantification is better understood and established.

A good. deal has been written about archaeological populations and samples (e.g. Vescelius 1960, Binford 1964, Rootenburg 1964, Ragir 1967), but, as Cowgill (1970) points out, much of this ignores the real problems involved. The main difficulties arise from:

(a) The complex, ever-changing character of any human society and its territory that together must be considered the source of meaningful archaeological populations.

(b) The partial and erratic reflection of (a) by material remains.

(c) The partial and erratic survival of (b) through time.

(d) The partial and erratic discovery of (c) by chance and design.
Standard statistical inference would aim to proceed from (d) to (a), i.e. from samples to populations via mathematical understanding, or models relating each stage to its predecessor. However, the links between these stages are in no sense 'standard' and a rather different rationale for disciplined inference in

archaeology is required. This remains to be devised. Meanwhile it may be instructive to consider some general distinctions that have been found useful in subjects that involve some of the archaeologist's sampling problems.

Geologists, who must often deal with the partial survival of evidence (after erosion, for example), have found it useful to distinguish between a *sampled population* and a *target population* (cf. Krumbein and Graybill 1965, 149). The distinction is emphasised between two situations, the first where generalisation from sample to sampled population may be based on statistical theory either because the scientist himself has chosen the sample in a theoretically valid manner, or because it is reasonable to act as if such a sampling procedure has taken place; the second where any generalisation must be based on expertise and common sense, since the relationship between sample and target population is not under the scientist's control and cannot reasonably be specified mathematically. (b) and (c) above both illustrate stages of sampling that the archaeologist cannot control or yet model mathematically. The geological analogy is especially relevant for level (c). The best evidence that the archaeologist can hope to sample rigorously, then, is at this level (c), already twice removed from the source of ultimate target populations, but still potentially able to reflect definite human societies.

To discuss sampling at level (c), it is necessary to envisage how relevant populations may be delimited. Technically, a population is merely a set, and it is not difficult to delimit sets of archaeological units that a statistician would accept as populations for sampling and study (see section 3.15): for example, all of the sherds of pottery of all ages buried in a specific hillfort; all of the bronze axes housed in museums in England. If a suitable random sampling strategy could be devised, the statistician would be able to estimate parameters (and associated confidence limits) for the populations concerned: ratios of one defined type to another, population mean and variance of maximum length, and so on. As stressed already in section 3.15, this kind of statistical exercise will only lead to interpretations of archaeological importance if the populations sampled are archaeologically meaningful: the above examples would not have this meaning, since they are not related, even informally, to target populations of interest at levels (b) and (a) above; rather, they represent uncertain mixtures. What the archaeologist really wants to study are not populations related to current political or environmental boundaries or to his convenience, but to past human groups.

In archaeological contexts other than prehistoric, this requirement presents no real problem: valid groups for study may be defined directly from literary or ethnographic sources. The prehistorian, however, does not have this direct access: he has to start from an arbitrary frame of reference in which he may search for meaningful groups. This has been done traditionally by classifying items into 'stylistic types' and then by studying the distributions and associations of such types (see chapter 7.3). It is assumed that stylistic patterning will delimit a hierarchy of culture-complexes which will in turn reflect 'peoples' (level 4 in figure 1.2), that is to say, sources for target populations of value. For the sake of clarity, it may seem worth distinguishing verbally between an arbitrary initial framework and any meaningful groups defined within it. If population is reserved for the latter, *universe* might be used for the former. (In standard statistical parlance, universe and population appear to be interchangeable.)

Archaeological populations at level (c) then (as distinct from universes) could be such sets of units as 'houses of the early Bandkeramik complex', or 'graves of the Marnian Culture', or 'Romano-British kilns'.

Whatever strategy for investigating such populations may be followed, it will be impossible to claim that the available material is a statistically random sample of what has survived. Figure 5.14 provides a typical example of the capriciousness of archaeological samples.

A similar difficulty confronts the social scientist generally. Often the difficulty and its statistical consequences are simply ignored, but statisticians working in this area have found it necessary to distinguish between a sampling situation and a *case-study* situation; for the latter, the investigator may delimit a meaningful population or set to be sampled, but he cannot possibly devise a statistical sampling strategy for it (cf. Lohnes and Cooley 1968, 169). This is the usual archaeological situation as well: the archaeologist may be able to delimit a meaningful 'people' by classifying material remains or from literary or ethnographic evidence; he cannot pretend to obtain a random sample of its relevant surviving material. For practical purposes, this distinction is equivalent to the geologist's distinction mentioned earlier: a case study would be a representative but non-random sample of a delimited but inaccessible target population.

This discussion of meaningful populations and non-random samples leads to important general conclusions about statistics in archaeology. The archaeologist is dealing primarily with case-study situations: he can select material, for example a site, that is relevant to a meaningful target population, but he cannot establish mathematical links between the two. The situation must be treated as one where a finite population is studied *in toto* and where, consequently, probabilistic methods, like significance tests, are of limited relevance (see Hills 1971, M. G. Kendall 1971). Statistical procedures will be used to describe and summarise data and to suggest hypotheses, but not to estimate parameters of hypothetical parent populations, the context for standard statistical theory. Probabilistic considerations will not be ignored completely: for example, tables like 3.1, and certain kinds of simulation (see chapter 11) are able to provide a most useful informal indication of the confidence to be placed in descriptive statistics computed for samples of a given size; but for the immediate future, most emphasis is bound to reside in more informal, heuristic procedures like those dealt with in following chapters.

The scope for random sampling and its associated concepts in archaeology, then, must not be exaggerated. The most obvious contexts would be at a further fifth stage in the 'descent of evidence', beyond (a)–(d) so far considered. For example:

1. the known surviving material relating to a universe or a target population at level (d) may be too copious to study completely; a random sample of suitable size could then be taken (cf. the samples of handaxes discussed in section 9.3).

2. Material from a previously unexplored site may be required (i) to relate it to other comprehensively excavated sites, or (ii) to provide source material for a general regional classification of items. Some form of random sampling from the site would then be appropriate, if it could be devised.

It is important to point out that site-sampling like this would be dealing with very limited aspects of a site as such. If the site is to be studied as a functioning component (a settlement, a cemetery, etc.) there seems to be no place for random sampling since there is no population (set) to be sampled, but rather a cultural entity or 'system'. In this more usual situation, professional etiquette dictates that no unthreatened site will be excavated completely, but otherwise, excavation will be as complete as finance allows and ignorance of the type of site requires. Investigation of an entity like this will be quite different from the random sampling of a population. Each site will be treated as a unique problem and investigation will proceed sequentially—for instance from an initial regular grid of trial trenches or by working out from features recognised before excavation begins. Stratified sampling, sometimes proposed as a probabilistic alternative to simple random sampling, is not relevant to the initial excavation of a site, since useful strata have not yet been recognised. Sampling of populations that have been stratified by excavation will involve sets of items (like pollen grains, or pottery sherds). In the terms followed in this section, this sampling will thus be to reduce the evidence available for level (d) by selecting a sample at a further level (e).

To return to the practical task of choosing units for tabulation in a quantitative archaeological study. The first aim will clearly be to delimit a topic for study and a valid archaeological context (target populations) to which the units will refer. This will almost certainly involve a classificatory exercise: new data must be compared with old, and any existing classes (of items, features and components) assessed and modified in the light of the new data. Without this preliminary study, new material cannot be integrated into a wider, meaningful context.

It may be feasible to tabulate all of the relevant units both old and new for this kind of classificatory exercise, but a valid sampling strategy for newly discovered material will often be required. This will be true of any site producing large quantities of potsherds, and/or flint artifacts. The intention will be to assign the vast bulk of material to classes defined from the sample.

Examples of units tabulated in this way for attempts at classification by quantitative methods would be Clarke's set of British beakers, where a convenient sample was provided by all the surviving complete pots (Clarke 1964,

1970), or the handaxes discussed in section 9.3, where random samples of the relevant universe were taken. As will become clear, these and similar attempts have not yet been able to provide adequate classifications and keys, but they help to elucidate the classification process. Traditional taxonomies (e.g. type-lists) are also necessarily created from samples of the relevant material, but unfortunately the nature of the samples and the universes for which they are intended are rarely if ever specified.

Once a classificatory framework has been established for items (at level 1 on figure 1.2), it will be possible to tabulate associations of items. The operational units will now be defined at levels 2 or 3 ('lots' or 'assemblages'), and the attributes will be provided by the classes of items (types, species, etc.). Using these descriptions it will be possible to classify the lots and assemblages and to establish the overall framework for study. Examples of tabulated units in this context would be: for level 2, grave lots or metal hoards described by their content of types (cf. the many seriation studies discussed in chapter 10); for level 3 the Palaeolithic assemblages discussed in sections 5.3.2, 5.4.3, 8.3, 8.4, and 9.5.

It seems important to separate conceptually all these general classificatory studies from more specific studies that operate within an established taxonomic framework and that seek to investigate single aspects within and between the classes defined. At the item level, this kind of investigation is familiar from os-teological studies where variations within known species are investigated by means of selected measurements. A more specifically archaeological example is Orton's study of variation in the diameter of Romano-British pots within and between accepted taxonomic groups (Orton 1970). The analysis is based on lots of pottery assumed to represent different kiln firings.

These examples emphasise that different tables of units and descriptors will be required for different archaeological investigations of the same available set of data.

For the examples so far cited in this section, a specific table has been set up for the given investigation. However, it may often seem desirable to tabulate and store in the computer a more substantial body of data from which subsets may be chosen both for classificatory and for more specific studies. This leads to the concept of a data bank.

The setting up of a large scale data bank entails many theoretical and prac-tical pitfalls: great amounts of time are required to record the information on cards and so great care is needed in deciding just how the information should be listed. For preliminary classificatory studies especially, where small samples of units may need to be described in great detail, an all-purpose data bank would seem irrelevant. Further, it is at least arguable that specific very large-scale projects in archaeological data recording should not be initiated until more experiments with different forms of recording and analysis have been completed, and until outstanding problems of sampling and classification in archaeology have been substantially resolved (cf. Whallon 1972a, 37). These issues will be discussed in more detail in chapter 12.

For most of the discussion that follows, the units tabulated will refer to a specified problem and a specified range of analyses. Such a table could have been derived as a subset from a suitable data bank if one existed, and for data bank analysis, the first step would usually be the choice of a subset of information like the raw data matrices discussed in the following chapters.

The definition of the units of study, then, represents a first major stage of archaeological research; the choice of attributes to describe them represents a second.

5.2.3. *The choice of attributes.* Although artifacts and their attributes provide the starting point for most empirical research in archaeology, it must be admitted that methods of study, whether intuitive or quantitative are highly unsystematic and controversial. The main difficulty stems from the contrast between what the archaeologist sees as different aspects of an artifact (basically material, size, shape and surface treatment), and the quite other factors that conditioned its manufacture. The archaeologist wishes to deal with the latter but is confronted with the former (see figure 5.1). Other difficulties are specific to the kind of artifacts being studied, whether of pottery, stone or metal: each category (and others) have their own character so that a method of study suited to one may not necessarily suit the others. Some experimental and ethnographic studies are beginning to throw considerable light on the significance and interpretation of artifact attributes, and much further work of this kind may be hoped for in the future (cf. for chipped stone tools: Semenov 1964, Bordes 1967, Bordes and Crabtree 1969, Newcomer 1971, Gould *et al.* 1971, White and Thomas 1972, Hester and Heizer 1973; for pottery: Friedrich 1970; for metalwork: Lowery *et al.* 1971). However, this kind of enlightenment deals with a rather different problem than the description of objects and their capture into a system where they may be manipulated via such formal descriptions. This is a general scientific problem, not just confined to archaeology.

The basic distinction between attribute and attribute state follows general practice and terminology in data analysis (cf. Jardine and Sibson 1970, 3). Two concepts are concerned: (a) mutually exclusive general descriptive terms such as 'colour', 'material', 'maximum thickness'; and (b) the actual descriptive terms applicable to units or parts of units, e.g. 'brown', 'made of flint', 'maximum thickness 20 mm'. It is convenient to use the term *attribute* for (a) and *attribute state* for (b). Phrased another way, (b) will represent a specific score on (a); or, in the mathematical terminology for variables introduced in section 2.5, (a) would be the identifier of a variable, (b) its value. 'Attribute' has been used in both senses by archaeologists, leading to serious confusion.

It would probably be misguided to suggest fixed rules of procedure for setting up descriptive attribute lists. It is more important that a clear purpose for any such list be defined first, and that the list be then set up with this purpose

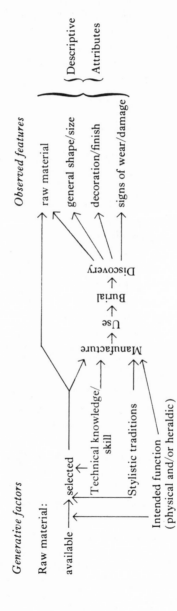

Figure 5.1. Artifacts: the status of descriptive attributes.

and the given material in view. The archaeologist may be interested in one underlying aspect of his material only, and may feel that he can select one or a few attributes *a priori* as those relevant to this aspect. On the other hand, he may not believe that this direct link can initially be made, or he may wish to set up a more comprehensive descriptive system so that several underlying aspects and their interaction may be investigated together.

Some archaeologists have doubted whether comprehensive, general purpose attribute lists like this are feasible:

'There is virtually an infinite number of attributes connected with any item, and it is physically impossible to take account of them all, or even more than a small percentage of them. . . . To insist that we be aware of all or most attributes is untenable, for whatever the attributes described, each of them can be further divided into a nearly infinite number of additional attributes' (Hill and Evans 1972, 250).

We do not accept this viewpoint, and believe that the theoretical 'impossibility' may be avoided quite simply in practice: first, by preserving the clear distinction between attribute and attribute state (see above); second, by avoiding redundancy (i.e. by omitting attributes that merely reflect others in a slightly different guise); and third, by common sense, by not going out of the way to look for irrelevance and obscurity. If a general morphological description of artifacts is thought necessary, it does not seem at all unreasonable to attempt this with a well-designed attribute-list, as some practical examples in the next section demonstrate. Multivariate methods are then able to deal comprehensively with such overall descriptions (see especially chapters 7–9). This does not mean that specific problems cannot be posed and solved by considering few, perhaps even one relevant attribute. However, the smaller the number of relevant attributes considered, the more subjective the exercise is likely to appear. Choice of just a few attributes is sometimes excused by the claim that a specific hypothesis is being tested. This may appear a valid approach, but with such eclecticism it is difficult to escape the most regular of all archaeological pitfalls: the delusion that evidence, sought out perhaps unconsciously to support a preconception, is somehow providing an objective test. The difficulty of setting up specific hypotheses and testing them objectively in archaeology is stressed in chapter 13. By considering more rather than fewer relevant attributes, this trap at least may be avoided.

A rather different and perhaps less soluble problem with descriptive attributes is the range of hierarchical levels at which these may be conceived. Size, for instance, might be regarded as a suitable attribute as given by volume or weight; but 'length', 'width', 'thickness', could also be regarded as attributes themselves. Or, for decoration, a dot or an arc could be regarded as a presence/absence attribute, but so could a recurring complex motif made up of combined dots and arcs (cf. Shepard 1956, 259 ff.). Superficially, it might seem simplest and most reasonable to reduce different morphological aspects to the lowest feasible descriptive level: on the one hand this may give a semblance of objectivity, and, on the other, such low level attributes may be assumed to reflect only one of the aspects of the generative process (e.g. either function *or* tradition and nothing else).

However, the supposed objectivity may be illusory since the more 'parts' that are defined, the more difficult it may be to record structural relationships between them; and each action of the craftsman, however simple, was almost certainly conditioned by a combination of generative factors (see figure 5.1). From this point of view, it could be argued that the most realistic description of artifacts would be given by attributes defined at the highest and not the lowest possible level of the hierarchy.

One possible approach might be to define low level attributes but then to group them mathematically into attribute *factors* of some kind (cf. Benfer 1967). This mathematical approach involves the difficulty of distinguishing between 'statistical' and 'meaningful' correlation (see chapters 6 and 7), and also the general difficulties of factor analysis (see chapter 8), but it is worth consideration.

Another suggestion has been to look for analogies in outside disciplines to throw light on possible structural relationships between artifacts and their attributes. Deetz (1967, 87) developed and illustrated this approach, using linguistic analogies for the 'structure' of arrowheads. He was criticised on certain details by Hymes (1970) and, in general, it may seem preferable to tackle the problem more directly than by reference to outside disciplines which have not yet solved such structural problems themselves.

In discussing a specific project where complex artifacts had to be studied, Doran (1971a, 427) suggested the following course of action (the problem refers to graves and their contents from the La Tène Iron Age cemetery of Münsingen-Rain, Switzerland): (a) define a few broad categories of objects (fibulae, rings, swords and so on); (b) for each category of object define a hierarchical decomposition of the object into parts (for example a fibula consists of coils + bow + foot + pin, and so on); (c) define a set of decorative and structural motifs (for example 'diamond', 'split leaf', 'tapering segment') noting instances where one motif is part of another or where two motifs can reasonably be said to be similar; and (d) for each part of each object take characterising measurements and record the structural and decorative motifs present.

In spite of the large subjective element apparent in (c) above, it was maintained that intuitively assigned similarity relationships, crude but realistic, make better sense than a mathematically pleasing but unrealistic policy of treating all motifs as independent and equal. It was, however, added that if conclusions were found to depend critically on uncertain intuitive judgements, then these conclusions must also be regarded as uncertain.

If it proves difficult or impossible to decide between competing levels for attribute definition, a feasible solution at present would be to set up a number of alternative attribute lists and to make use of them all. A technique suited to this situation is 'constellation analysis' (see chapter 8.4).

Despite the difficulties that have been mentioned so far in this section, and while admitting that much experiment and refinement are needed, it has been found in practice that a suitable descriptive level for item attributes has often been found. Some examples are given in section 5.3.

Just the same general problems arise when describing assemblages: the difficulty of deciding a suitable level at which to define assemblage attributes (i.e. detailed versus generalised types), and the difficulty of describing relationships between constituent types, especially where spatial configurations are involved. Little advanced work in this sphere has yet been attempted and far more basic research is required, but the quantifier must at least attempt to reflect all aspects of an assemblage that would be judged relevant to his problem.

Finally, it is worth emphasising that, at the assemblage level also, there is really no need to shrink from defining alternative descriptive systems for the same material, even if they should appear at first sight to conflict with each other. The analytical technique described in later chapters, constellation analysis, is specifically designed to facilitate the assessment and coordination of such diversity.

5.2.4. *Attribute states and their codification.*

When a suitable set of attributes has been defined, units may be described by their score or state for each attribute. The kind of score recorded will depend on the way in which the relevant attribute is measured, that is to say, on the kind of scale used (see section 3.5).

Measurements on a numeric scale should be recorded exactly as they are made (in millimetres, angles, etc.). It may prove necessary before analysis to convert these values into proportions, or to coarsen the intervals of measurement, but these and other transformations are best performed by the computer from the raw data. Measurements on the other (non-numeric) scales require codification of some sort: i.e. although the states may be recorded by numbers these will not be arithmetic values. Ordinal, ranked scores will naturally be recorded by their agreed rank (e.g. the nth archaeological level in a sequence will naturally be scored n), and the ordinal nature of this attribute noted.

The main problem is set by the so-called nominal scales. One regular solution is to regard each state of the attribute as an independent attribute itself and to score this on a present/absent basis. However, the presence/absence scale still sets problems, especially if arbitrary numerical values are given initially to the two states (e.g. 0 and 1) and are later used during analysis. This implies equal importance, a numerical 'reversibility' for presence and absence states which is unjustified. (See also sections 6.2, 6.5 for further consequences of this transformation from a qualitative to a presence/absence scale.)

Often in practice this problem will be avoided by counting presences and treating the counts as the basis of analysis. In this form, or as proportions, they may be treated as numeric values. These problems are dealt with in more detail in the next chapter. Initially, it is safest to record presence/absence information by a non-numeric symbol (e.g. +, −) so that confusion will be avoided.

A further problem is set by conditional attributes. For example, in recording decoration on artifacts a first attribute may simply record decoration as present or absent. If decoration is present it is relevant to have further attributes for the presence of simple and complex motifs, but if not, the question: 'What kind of decoration?' is irrelevant. It is useful in this context to have a 'non-applicable' symbol of some sort. The same symbol may then also be used for uncertain or incomplete information, as often occurs in archaeology. Here again, the use of 0 as a score is likely to cause confusion (and has certainly done so in at least one major archaeological analysis).

A great deal of further work is required on the treatment of nominal attributes, and on the mixing of metric and nominal information, but possible solutions will appear later in this and the following chapters. At the moment it is probably most important to stress that the choice of units, the definition of an attribute list and the applicability of analytical methods must all be considered as part of the same problem, each stage conditioned by the others.

5.3. QUANTIFIED DESCRIPTION IN ARCHAEOLOGY

5.3.1. *Introduction.* In selecting the following examples an attempt has been made to cover, however briefly, the main range of empirical material and to emphasise cases where quantification has been a means to a defined end that can be considered in later chapters.

5.3.2. *Chipped stone tools.* Attempts at the quantitative description of chipped stone tools and debitage have proliferated since the late 'fifties, but little consensus has yet been achieved. The inherent difficulties are obvious: the unfamiliarity of modern man (including most archaeologists) with the manufacture and use of tools of struck stone, and his remoteness in all aspects from prehistoric groups that used such tools; the natural intractability of stone; the large quantities and vast morphological range of these artifacts; and complications due to resharpening and re-use of existing tools.

In studying material deposits, geologists and botanists have long since based their descriptions on the percentages of the different species which the deposits contained. Since the turn of the century at least, archaeologists have attempted to follow this approach, substituting types for species. It is perhaps not surprising that major advances in this area have often originated in Scandinavia, where collaboration between archaeologists and botanists has been particularly strong and of long standing (cf. Madsen *et al.* 1900, Johansen 1919, Troels-Smith 1937, Mathiassen 1939). However, the best known development of this approach is probably that devised by F. Bordes and his school at Bordeaux. Two slightly different approaches have been followed, one for the Lower and Middle Palaeolithic (Bordes 1950, 1961), the other for the Upper Palaeolithic (Sonneville-Bordes and Perrot 1953, 1954–56; Sonneville-Bordes 1960).

The Bordeaux method is essentially pragmatic, based on experiments with flint tool production and on a search for patterning in prehistoric flint artifacts, i.e. the definition of types. Bordian types are defined at various hierarchical levels, but emphasis is placed on a fairly detailed classification. Because it is so deeply rooted in the type concept, this aspect will be discussed more fully in chapter 7.

As in all similar studies, the broad aim is to assign each artifact to a defined type, and then to describe any assemblage quantitatively by the count or percentage of each type found in it. For the Lower/Middle Palaeolithic, other categories of information cutting across the type-list are also recorded (e.g. technological details about the form of the butt, the nature of retouch, etc.). This second set of information is quantified in the form of assemblage indices, or proportions of artifacts possessing such technological features. Summary typological indices may also be defined from a higher level grouping of related types. All this information provides a direct and comprehensive quantified description of an assemblage that may be represented graphically and used as a basis for interpretation and comparison, either by the visual inspection of suitable graphs (as in Bordes' own approach, see section 5.4.3), or by multivariate analytical techniques to be described later—or preferably by both.

In the terms of attributes discussed earlier in this chapter, Bordes' approach concentrates on one qualitative attribute to describe flint tools: morphological type, with a large number of alternative states.

For Lower and Middle Palaeolithic assemblages Bordes has a basic type attribute with 83 states (ten biface types, plus 63 other tool types, plus eight core types, plus unretouched, non-Levallois flake, plus unretouched, non-Levallois blade). This attribute is supplemented by conditional attributes for some of these states: butt type, a six-state qualitative attribute for unretouched flakes and blades, and a Quina-retouch attribute: a conditional presence/absence attribute for certain types (some points and racloirs).

The Upper Palaeolithic attribute system concentrates on the one *type* attribute with 93 states (Sonneville-Bordes and Perrot 1954–56). However, it is relatively straightforward to add technological attributes if required (see Azoury and Hodson 1973, and section 9.5). In the terms of section 5.2.3, this approach is clearly concentrating on an extremely high level of attribute definition. By having so few attributes at the item level (basically one), it is in practice possible to describe assemblages and tools in the same operation: one stroke on a worksheet (or at most two or three strokes) are enough to describe each artifact, and when each artifact has been dealt with in this way, the number of strokes entered for each attribute-state immediately provides an equivalent count at the assemblage level.

The Bordes' system for describing European Palaeolithic assemblages represents one of the major archaeological achievements of past decades. It is essentially practical allowing the archaeologist's natural judgement, backed up by experimental knowledge, full play in the areas where these are most relevant and speedy: in the visual assessment of complex morphological patterning. It resorts to quantification at the level where visual appreciation breaks down, i.e. when dealing with numerous whole assemblages of such complex items. The system in practice allows a skilled and trained archaeologist to deal with a realistic amount of material in a finite time. As a method it is adaptable to widely differing problem areas, e.g. to material from North America (Irwin and Wormington 1970).

However, it is possible to question details of this approach in principle and as applied to specific study areas. To take the latter first, one ambiguity has been the intended scope of the two main systems (whether for southwest France, for west Europe, for Europe, or for Europe and the Middle East). In other words, a clear target population or universe for application of the classificatory systems has not been defined, but this would be essential if a type-list is intended for comparative studies.

Another difficulty has been the need to concentrate interest on a particular level of a taxonomic hierarchy when a hierarchy clearly exists. For example, Bordes himself has a detailed hierarchical classification for handaxes (or bifaces) which themselves represent a class or type at a first taxonomic level. Five further levels are then recognised, e.g.: (1) *biface*; (2) *plat*; (3) *d'aspect cordiforme*; (4) *régulier*; (5) *allongé*; (6) *à talon*. A similar hierarchy is recognised for other major classes, for example side-scrapers (racloirs), points, end-scrapers (grattoirs), burins, etc. For simplicity and perhaps for the lack of suitable computerised techniques, Bordes has tended to concentrate on one or two levels of these hierarchies, when all could, and perhaps should, be considered during analysis.

Again, and perhaps for the same reason, relatively few cross-classifications have been used, especially in Upper Palaeolithic studies, where technological features and alternative classifications could be allowed more play.

These relatively minor criticisms of details of the Bordian approach could be overcome by fitting type-lists to more clearly defined target populations and by using computerised, multivariate techniques to study more taxonomic levels of types and more cross-classifications. However, a general difficulty would still remain. This approach relies heavily on fixed, detailed type-lists for the description and presentation of data. But, to anticipate chapter 7, if the type concept is to have much value, it must allow types to be reassessed and if necessary changed as evidence about the target population for which they are intended itself changes. The long-term, fixed, detailed type-list is simply not flexible enough *a priori* for progressive archaeological research.

In spite of these specific and general criticisms, the two Bordian systems have undoubtedly allowed great advances to be made in Palaeolithic studies.

Many attempts have been and are being made to provide a workable alternative; some of these are discussed later in this and in other chapters. None of these alternatives has yet been able to match the Bordian system for feasibility or for producing demonstrable results.

To summarise, this first approach to the description of flint tools relies on the definition of major tool classes, types and sub-types in an extensive hierarchy. Each tool is then ascribed to the relevant class or classes. This information provides the groundwork for assemblage description, but it may be amplified by further technological and typological attributes cutting across type-lists.

It must be emphasised that this approach was elaborated for the general comparison of total assemblages from occupied caves and shelters where an 'assemblage' is defined by its association with a visible level or stratum (not of course with an arbitrary 'spit'); however thin, any such level could represent deposition over a day or a millennium. Where short term occupation can be guaranteed, at open settlements like Pincevent (Leroi-Gourhan and Brézillon 1966, 1972), or at kill sites, a suitable type-list may prove useful, but an adequate description of the assemblage will involve spatial distinctions and relationships, and a different descriptive system than the simple statement of the proportion of type by feature.

Here, as for settlements of any period, adequate quantification presupposes not only the recognition of valid levels, but the horizontal definition of features and/or activity areas (level 2 of figure 1.2). For each of these, a decision has to be attempted about its likely duration and functional consistency. These are largely problems that refined excavation technique and the skilled study of organic remains are already helping to resolve and where great advances have been made over the past decades. Clearly, in those rare contexts where evidence of this precision is available, interpretation via quantification will be on a quite different footing than where the jumbled effects of successive occupation, even if by related groups, have to be dealt with. The potential of quantification in these circumstances has still to be investigated (see also section 6.5).

A second quantified approach to the study of flint tools accepts an intuitive first classification of flints into major artifact classes (e.g. bifaces, endscrapers, tanged projectile points), but is reluctant to accept more detailed 'types' defined on the same basis. Instead, descriptive attribute lists for these tool classes are devised and, it is hoped, studied by valid quantified methods. In some instances this approach is expected to reveal types, which may then be taken as attributes for studying assemblages (Australian axes and choppers: Tugby 1958; end-scrapers: Sackett 1966; British handaxes: Hodson 1971; cleavers from an African site: Cahen and Martin 1972). In other similar studies it has been hoped to describe assemblages directly by summarising the scores of their constituent artifacts on these attributes (e.g. British handaxes: Roe 1964, 1968). In another similar study, Benfer (1967) has hoped to elicit independent aspects (*factors*) of projectile point morphology and key attributes that may be correlated with temporal and cultural effects.

These attempts, which will be discussed in later sections, were not necessarily successful, but the aims were clearly defined. In some other studies, attributes for tool classes have been defined without a very clearly stated purpose, although presumably it was hoped to discover something by studying the frequency distributions of attribute scores, or the estimated statistical associations between pairs of attributes (projectile-points: Fitting 1965; Upper Palaeolithic tool classes from a French cave: Movius *et al.* 1968, Movius and Brooks 1971; projectile points: Binford 1963b). Where they exist, analytical developments of these projects will be discussed later: only the attribute lists themselves will be dealt with in this section.

As for artifacts in general, the major aspects of flint tools to be described by attributes are size, shape and surface finish. For flints, the latter may be seen as the result of primary flaking, secondary retouch or polishing, resharpening, and wear. The natural attributes to describe size and shape are measurements of dimensions and, possibly, angles. Measuring flint tools is not easy, but various aids to measurement have been devised from simple combinations of plasticene, wooden blocks, rulers and protractors (Bordes 1961, Cruxent 1965, Sackett 1966, Movius *et al.* 1968, Wilmsen 1968a) to an automated, direct recording system for projectile points that uses a sonic grid to provide coordinates for salient tool features (Irwin *et al.* 1971, see figure 12.4).

The attribute list for British handaxes devised by Roe (1964, 1968) is a good example of attempts to record size and shape by linear measurements and ratios (see figure 5.2). Six attributes are measured for all handaxes; a seventh is conditional. One linear measurement (length) is available, with weight, to record *size*; the other measurements are converted into ratios, expressing aspects of *shape*. All attributes are recorded on the numeric scale, as they are measured. In practice it has been found that one of the pointedness ratios is not entirely satisfactory: the basis for the ratio B_1/B_2 is not determined by the other recorded attributes, so that the outline of any specific tool may only be approximately recovered from them. Again, it is probably preferable to make the further pointedness measurements on all rather than on some of these artifacts. Roe (personal communication) has in fact modified this attribute list since his early publications.

Bordes (1961) uses a similar range of handaxe measurements and ratios or indices. However, these are not intended to help in a search for types, but to provide a key for attributing handaxes to types that have previously been discovered by inspection. The contrast between a classification and a key is discussed in chapter 7.

In several other studies, measurements of a similar kind have been converted initially from the numeric scale on which they were measured to a nominal scale. The relevant range of measurement has been split into relatively few divisions (often only three) and each attribute-state recorded as a separate attribute on a presence/absence scale (e.g. Fitting 1965, Sackett 1966). Not only is the accuracy of the original measurements debased but even the ordering between the three states is lost. This sacrifices at the outset any pretence at the subtle recording of size and shape, and cannot be expected to compete with pattern recognition carried out by a trained human eye.

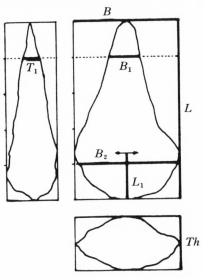

Figure 5.2. Size and shape of handaxes: the descriptive system used by D. A. Roe. Measurements taken: W = weight; B = breadth; L = maximum length; Th = maximum thickness; L_1 = height of maximum breadth; T_1 = thickness near tip; B_1 = breadth near tip; B_2 = breadth near butt. (T_1 and B_1 are measured at $L/5$ from the tip, B_2 at $L/5$ from the butt). Attributes used for analyses are: (1) W; (2) L; (3) B/L; (4) Th/B; (5) B_1/B_2; (6) L_1/L; (7) T_1/L (only listed for 'pointed' implements, where $L_1/L < 0.35$). (Roe 1968.)

Another alternative for the description of shape has been to suggest as attribute states a series of idealised templates against which tools may be matched (e.g. Tugby 1968, Binford 1963b). However, this is hardly logical if the attribute list is intended as an aid to taxonomy: if shape types (which the templates really are) can be defined intuitively, the intuitive type concept as such is accepted and a search for types via a complicated attribute-list would appear circular.

A comprehensive attribute-list for flint tools must include information about techniques of primary flaking and the nature and location of retouch and wear patterns. Attempts have been made to quantify some of this information (Binford 1963b, Sackett 1966, Movius *et al.* 1968, Cahen and Martin 1972). Here again, there has been a tendency to express information on a nominal scale even where the attributes imply specific measurement: for example, the extent of retouch or the curvature of a working edge. However, it is likely that some of the technological information would have to be expressed in qualitative or presence/absence form.

On the whole, it is difficult to assess the value of the attribute lists that have been proposed for major classes of flint tools: the lists are only a means to an end and must be judged by their performance. Unfortunately the methods used to analyse the more ambitious attribute-lists have been rather naive and do not provide a fair test of the descriptive approach as a whole (see section 7.4.4).

A third approach to studying assemblages of flint tools by quantitative methods has been advocated: this takes all the tools of an assemblage and studies them collectively by the same attributes, mainly measurements of length, edge angles, or ratio of width to length. For example, Wilmsen (1968a, 1968b, 1970) recognises the existence of such diverse tool classes as end-scrapers and projectile-points, but describes assemblages made up of these and all other tools by average dimensions, such as length. This procedure would hardly be considered for material with which archaeologists are more familiar. The average length of metal tools from a modern household, for example, where knives and forks, hammers and chisels, shovels and hedge-clippers were all lumped together, would clearly seem meaningless, but this is equivalent to the indiscriminate measurement of all prehistoric flint tools from a given assemblage and their summarisation by collective indices.

5.3.3. *Pottery.* The quantitative study of pottery presents many of the problems that have just been discussed for flint tools. Major differences are: (a) the fragmentary nature of the evidence—complete artifacts are now an exception; (b) the greater emphasis generally placed on decorative rather than functional attributes when seeking a detailed taxonomy; and (c) the greater freedom given to the potter than the flint knapper so that an acknowledged 'norm' may be closely repeated or consciously rejected according to the whim and skill of the potter. If a wheel or mould is used during manufacture, virtual duplication of forms may be achieved.

For the archaeologist it is inherently simpler than with flints to distinguish decorative from functional attributes and to allow cross classification, or a hierarchy, that treat these aspects separately. In many instances it is possible in fact to ignore one or other aspect and to concentrate directly on function, *or* style as given by size and general shape, *or* decoration.

As with flint-tool studies, most quantitative studies of pottery have accepted the definition of pottery types or classes by archaeological intuition and experience, and quantification has been directed to the study of assemblages of these types (e.g. Brainerd 1951, Robinson 1951, Brown and Freeman 1964, Hill 1968, Longacre 1968, Orton 1970). This corresponds with the first approach for flint tools just described, where artifact taxonomy is carried out by eye, but assemblages are studied and interrelated by quantification.

Corresponding with the second approach, some attempts have been made experimentally to distinguish detailed *types* via attribute lists. Clarke (1962, 1970) has studied complete or restorable British beakers in this way. As with several of the flint studies mentioned, 'shape' attributes given on a numeric scale were converted into three or four non-ordered presence/absence attributes, so foregoing the sensitive description of shape. Other attributes dealt with position of decoration and decorative motifs.

An attribute list for sherds of coarse pottery from the Juntunen site (a 'late Woodland' settlement) was devised for taxonomic purposes by McPherron (1967). Of a total of over 100 000 sherds recovered, 4 750 only were considered sufficiently significant for analysis. McPherron contrasted continuous variables with 'discrete' attributes: the former being defined for lip thickness, body thickness and outside diameter at the lip. However, some of the 'discrete' attributes, e.g. angles, were not inherently discrete (or more precisely, as he treated them, unordered multistate attributes) but were simply *coded* into this form. A distinction between nominal and numeric variables would perhaps have been more useful. Decorative motifs were dealt with by defining fifteen basic motifs which could be scored as present or absent. Techniques of decoration (e.g. incised, stab and drag), details of the tools used, general vessel finish and many other details make up a comprehensive descriptive scheme for the coarse pottery. McPherron also listed the provenance of pottery, a tentative type designation and the occurrence of carbonised material. It is worth quoting from McPherron's thoughtful discussion of his Juntunen pottery (1967, 55): 'It should be noted that an additional category "indeterminate" or "no decision possible" should be appended to the list of categories [states] under nearly every attribute. It was found that this was one frequently used in the analysis.'

As for most of the flint tool studies, these attempts to define classes of pottery or 'types' via an attribute list are interesting from an experimental point of view, but could not be accepted as a basis for description at the assemblage level (see also sections 7.4.3 and 7.5.3).

Soudský's quantified study of European Neolithic material was also designed to deal with sherds of decorated, coarse pottery, although here the purpose seems to have been the direct description of assemblages of sherds by counting the presence of various traits, rather than the discovery of types (Soudský 1967, 1968). A hierarchy of motifs was defined, from simple elements (dot, arc, etc.) to combinations of these into more complex patterns. For each sherd recorded, detailed information on local and general provenance was also listed on punched cards. This was a pioneering attempt initiated in the mid-fifties, to set up a comprehensive data bank. As such, it was perhaps over-ambitious: not all of the available sample of sherds could be dealt with in this detailed fashion (the duplication of so much locational information for each sherd would now be considered unnecessary), and relatively little of the recorded information seems to have been used so far. In fact, assemblages appear to have been described directly by proportions, 'indices' of only five decorative attributes: a practical and workable system, but one that is not really related to the very detailed list of attributes. However, far more comprehensive treatment may be expected in the Bylany monograph, now reported by Soudský (1973) to be in press.

Quantified studies of pottery at the assemblage level have tended to accept intuitive types of whole vessels or parts of vessels. For example, the important study of Brainerd and Robinson started from deposits represented by counts of types. A basic difficulty here is the distortion that may be introduced if many small fragments from the same vessel are counted separately because they are of the same 'type'. Of course, conjoined sherds may be treated as one item, but, especially with coarse pottery, it is often impossible to decide whether sherds of the same type belong to the same vessel or not. As a solution, weighing rather than counting type representation has been suggested, and results of the two methods compared (Solheim 1960). In a different context, the relative size of sherds from different features at a site has been used to infer human traffic: McPherron's 'trampling index' (1967, 254).

The study of wheel-made pottery from Romano-British kilns in London by Orton (1970) starts by organising the data into a form corresponding with Palaeolithic assemblage description, where general tool classes are measured separately (cf. Roe's handaxe approach mentioned above). Orton's assemblages are 'lots' of pottery sherds assumed to be related to one or more distinct firings of a kiln. Conventional major classes of vessel are studied separately (for example, shouldered jars, beakers), and the variation of, say, rim diameter is compared over different lots, so that conclusions about the consistency and production characteristics of the industry may be drawn. Each lot of sherds, then, may be characterised initially by the proportion of major types in it and by the sizes of these types. The treatment of these data goes beyond comparable Palaeolithic studies.

It is perhaps worth remarking that descriptive quantification of animal bones from archaeological sites presents many of the same problems as pottery, and that some of the same solutions have been suggested (for example, weighing rather than counting related fragments, and the need to recognise and interpret a 'shattering index'; see, e.g., Uerpmann 1973). However, the definition of classes for bones (species) is clearly a rather different problem than the definition of classes for pottery (types).

5.3.4. *Metalwork*. From some points of view, metalwork provides one of the best kinds of material for experiments in quantification: objects are usually found complete, and since they are made by specialists in a highly controllable medium, the craftsman's intention is likely to be more clearly and consistently revealed to the archaeologist than with stone and clay artifacts. However, few quantified studies of the morphology of metal tools have so far been attempted.

The authors have used one small set of metalwork artifacts for testing methods of cluster and scaling analysis: bronze brooches or fibulae from the Swiss Iron Age site of Münsingen (Hodson 1968, see section 9.1). These have proved useful for test purposes since a great deal is known about their context. Several of these experimental studies have dealt with shape only, as described by ratios of measurements, or by angles (Hodson 1970), although qualitative information about decoration has also been used in other experiments (Hodson, Sneath and Doran 1966). Here, measurements were converted into *ordered* multi-state attributes by a coding system described by Sokal and Sneath (1963, 76) for situations where quantitative, qualitative and incomplete or uncertain information must be accommodated. This splits up the range of a numeric scale into a number of intervals or states as for the studies on flints and pottery criticised above, but the order between the states is preserved by suitable coding, and the accuracy of measurements is preserved by dividing the range into more intervals (say five to eight, rather than three to four); in other words an attempt is made to preserve most of the information given by numeric measurements. The subsequent analysis of these data (see section 9.1) provided results that could be assessed by independent criteria, and which suggested that this method of coding could produce realistic results.

Assemblages of metalwork or of mixed pottery and metalwork will naturally be described by counts of relevant types once these have been defined. One frequent situation is the description of graves by their contents for seriation or other studies. Here the presence or absence of each type in each grave has provided a convenient basis for investigation, e.g. at Münsingen (Hodson 1968; see sections 10.3 ff.).

For features with large quantities of material also, the simple presence/absence of categories has sometimes been used (Bordaz and Bordaz 1970, True and Matson 1970), or advocated (Kerrich and Clarke 1967), but proportional counts are really required. The situation is not very different from the description of pollen spectra according to the species represented: *presence* of a single pollen grain would mean little. Similarly in archaeology, the intrusion of one alien fragment into an assemblage could completely distort the description if presence/absence is used. Difficulties involved in using proportions seem minor compared with this basic flaw.

5.3.5. *Summary and conclusions.* From these examples it is clear that different areas of study present similar problems in primary quantification. For describing lots or assemblages, the most general approach has been to accept 'types' that have been defined by eye at a general or a more detailed level ('tool classes' or 'primary types' respectively). The content of assemblages has then been described by one or more of the following categories of quantified information for each assemblage:

1. Counts (or the presence/absence) of items attributed to primary types.

2. Counts of items attributed to major tool classes.

3. Dimensions or other attributes (a) summarised over major tool classes, or (b) more comprehensively described over major tool classes.

4. Counts of artifact attributes that cross-cut defined types.

Various combinations of these categories of information have been used: for example in the studies discussed above, Bordes for Middle Palaeolithic assemblages combines 1, 2, and 4; Brainerd and Robinson for levels with pottery, Hodson (Münsingen) for graves, use only 1; Roe for assemblages of handaxes uses 3(a); Orton for lots of pottery sherds, 2 and 3(b).

Another aspect of primary quantification has been the attempt to describe artifacts individually so that primary types could be deduced from such descriptions e.g. for flint tools Tugby 1958, Sackett 1966, Hodson 1971, Cahen and Martin 1972; for pottery Clarke 1962, McPherron 1967; for metalwork Hodson, Sneath and Doran 1966, Hodson 1970. Some of these studies have shown a tendency to underestimate the difficulty of the problem and, especially for size and shape aspects, to debase the scale of measurement beyond the point where realistic results could be expected (Tugby, Clarke, Sackett). All these attempts must be regarded as experiments only in numerical taxonomy, which have not so far been able to provide a basis for the description of assemblages. However, future developments may make this approach more feasible (see chapters 7 and 9).

Attempts to by-pass the definition of types or classes of tool (e.g. Wilmsen 1968) and to describe assemblages directly by the attributes of all artifacts taken together do not seem to provide a realistic alternative.

A final point about the description of assemblages is obvious but of such importance that it bears repetition: any count of items is first and foremost dependent on the consistent recovery of such items from the archaeological deposit. If sherds or flakes are to be counted, it is necessary to fix a lower limit to the size of items counted in keeping with the techniques of excavation (and sieve size) in use. This is especially true if proportions are to be calculated: it may well be preferable to exclude whole categories of items from a count, especially if the products of old excavations are being studied (e.g. microliths from Upper Palaeolithic assemblages, Hodson 1969), rather than to pretend that a complete picture has been obtained after incomplete recovery at the time of excavation.

5.4.   PRELIMINARY ORGANISATION AND PRESENTATION OF DATA

5.4.1. *Modification of raw data before presentation and analysis.* The last sections have described how basic archaeological information may be expressed by symbols or numbers so that it is ready for mathematical treatment. The data may have been recorded directly in the form of a table with ordered rows and columns, or in a looser form with information labelled and listed as it was most easily collected. Here the first stage is to assemble the scattered data into a more ordered table.

Before any further study, it may also be necessary to modify parts of the table so that it becomes meaningful as a whole: so that values entered in the various rows or columns are comparable. Clearly, if some attributes were measured in inches and others in millimetres they would have to be modified. Similarly, if categories of material from large and small assemblages are listed by raw counts, it may be helpful to convert these values into proportions or percentages so that comparisons may be made. Changes from one symbolic code to another, from one scale to another, the amalgamation or elimination of poorly represented categories, the search for obvious errors, and many other forms of data screening may be necessary at this stage. Most of these operations are very simply (and accurately) performed by the computer and should not normally be carried out by hand where more than a trivial amount of information is concerned.

5.4.2. *The direct visual presentation of primary data.* A table of quantified data prepared by the conventions just described will effectively condense a mass of information into a small space. However, the more information systematised and assembled in this way, the larger and fuller the lists and tables, the more difficult it becomes to make use of this potential wealth. Even a single row of figures extracted for study may mean little when taken as a whole. The following sections describe how quantified information in this form may be appreciated by simple, visual presentation. Basically, the numerical values entered in the cells of a table are represented on a diagram by lines, shaded areas or by distances proportional to their size. Figure 5.5 (Bohmers 1962) which will be discussed in more detail during this chapter, shows how a large table of numerical values may be translated into direct visual terms. By a suitable presentation of such visual images, general patterns may be revealed from the mass of primary detail. In the following account, for consistency, data will be assumed to have been organised into a table with rows representing units (often artifacts or assemblages) and columns representing attributes.

5.4.3. *Bar charts and their development for special purposes.* The simplest and most familiar representation of quantified data is the bar chart, where each 'bar' corresponds to a count of units. In the conventions just described, such a chart will often represent a single row of a data matrix with each cell represented by a bar of appropriate length, cf. figure 5.3. Often, as here, archaeologists blur the distinction between a bar chart and a histogram by drawing the 'bars' as rectangles.

As presented in section 3.7, the feature of bar charts that is usually stressed by statisticians and that distinguishes them technically from histograms (section 5.4.4) is that they are intended for discrete rather than continuous attributes. An equally important distinction needs to be drawn within bar charts between those intended for (a) qualitative, and (b) ordinal and numeric attributes. For (b), the ordering of the bars in the chart is fixed by the ordering of the attribute states; for (a) it is not. In figure 5.3, for instance, the ordering of the bars is quite arbitrary (this does not necessarily mean illogical). This distinction is especially important for cumulative bar charts or graphs (see below).

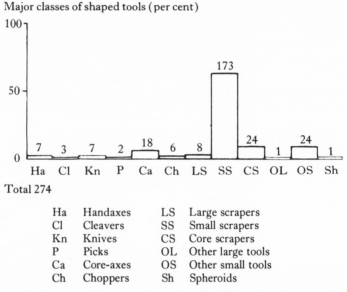

Major classes of shaped tools (per cent)

Total 274

Ha	Handaxes	LS	Large scrapers
Cl	Cleavers	SS	Small scrapers
Kn	Knives	CS	Core scrapers
P	Picks	OL	Other large tools
Ca	Core-axes	OS	Other small tools
Ch	Choppers	Sh	Spheroids

Figure 5.3. Bar chart for major classes of shaped tools from Floor B 2/59/4, Kalambo Falls. Bars are drawn as adjacent rectangles (Clark 1964).

This characteristic of many bar charts, the need to impose an order on the categories where none may be justified, is irritating but unavoidable. It is perhaps less obtrusive in the pie chart alternative (figure 5.4). This requires categories to be represented as proportions of a stipulated total, but is really equivalent to a bar chart. However, many archaeological situations involve a rather large number of categories which may not always be represented in the units for which comparative diagrams are required. Pie charts are clearly not suited to either of these difficulties (numerous categories, categories with zero entries).

The principles underlying the bar chart have proved so useful in archaeology that a number of developments have been introduced. These are designed so that (a) more than one set of bar charts may be co-ordinated on one diagram and compared, and (b) so that a given ordering between these sets may be preserved. F. Bordes' 'cumulative graphs' are a good example of

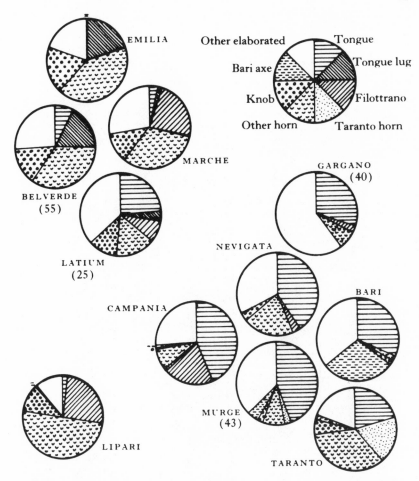

Figure 5.4. Pie charts showing regional differences in the relative frequency of handle types on pottery of the Appennine Culture. Sample size given when less than 150 (Trump 1958).

the first intention. The problem is to take complex bar charts from a number of contexts and to preserve as much information as possible on one diagram. Bohmer's solution is to arrange a whole series of direct bar charts into one diagram (figure 5.5, top 31 rows). This allows a detailed comparison between separate aspects of the different assemblages, but a comparison between assemblages as a whole is difficult. One possibility is to convert the bar representation into a line joining the tops of the bars. This adjustment allows one bar chart to be superimposed on another and facilitates overall comparison (figure 5.6, bottom). However, values are naturally concentrated in the lower part of the graph and confusion results, especially if more than two sets of information are superimposed in this way. The convention usually

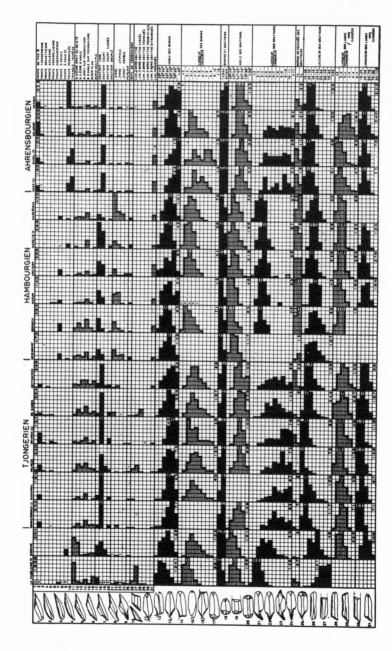

Figure 5.5. Eighteen assemblages of flint tools as presented by A. Bohmers. At the top of the diagram bar charts record the percentage occurrence of thirty-one 'types' (illustrations in the panel refer to this type-list). Below, histograms present measurements and measurement ratios for certain general classes of the material (Bohmers 1962).

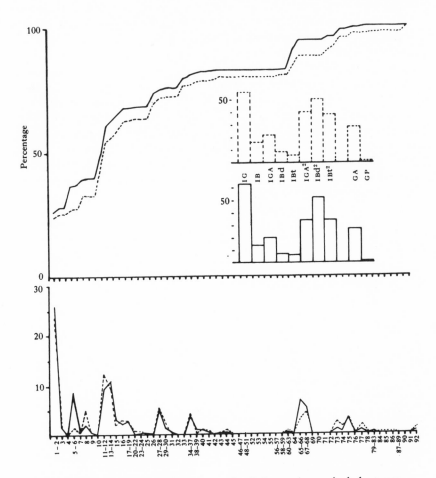

Figure 5.6. Comparison between two
Aurignacian assemblages from south-west
France: Lartet (lines) and Poisson
(dashes). The presentation is based on a
standardised list of 92 types. This
detailed information is presented as
cumulative graphs (above) and by
frequency polygons (below). The inset
bar charts represent (a) indices of tool
classes made up by amalgamating
detailed types (e.g. IG includes types
1–15, IB 27–44, etc.), and (b) two
general indices amalgamating culturally
diagnostic types (GA, Groupe
Aurignacien, is made up of types 4, 6,
11–14, 32, 67–68; GP, Groupe
Périgordien, is made up of 45–59, 60–64
and 85–87) (Sonneville-Bordes and
Perrot 1953, 129).

followed by the Bordes, then, is in effect to add each bar to the previous one and to graph cumulative values (figures 5.6 and 5.7). As a result, two or more original bar charts may be effectively combined into one diagram without too much overlapping, and an overall impression of the total relationship between them is given. Further, since the ordering of 'types' along the abscissa is not random, but corresponds to a grouping into major classes, and since the same type list and the same ordering are used in all related studies, the general shape of the graph gives an immediate indication of the kind of assemblage concerned (provided that the convention is understood). Of course, no simple, direct presentation of complex multivariate data can be a substitute for the types of analysis described in later chapters, but as an initial presentation and as a simple heuristic device, Bordes' conventionalised cumulative graphs have in the past proved of great value in studying the European Palaeolithic and will no doubt continue to do so.

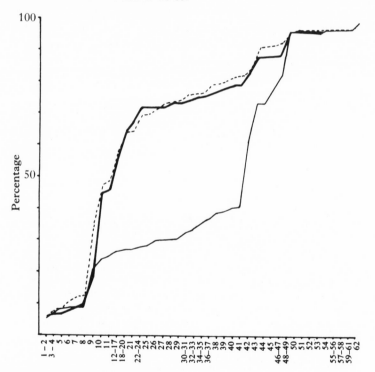

Figure 5.7. F. Bordes' cumulative graphs. A comparison between three Mousterian assemblages: from Moustier level J (fine line), Ermitage (thick line), and Ferrassie level C (dashes). (Bordes 1954.)

This presentation does, however, have definite disadvantages: the most obvious is the disproportionate visual effect of differences between counts at the beginning and the end of the cumulative sequence (Bohmers 1962).

Nevertheless, if one diagram is intended at the same time (a) for each assemblage, to record direct percentages of numerous categories (e.g. of 93 types); (b) to provide a general summary of the profile for these counts; and (c) to allow up to five assemblages to be presented together in this way, it is difficult to suggest any alternative to the Bordes' 'cumulative graph'. The conventional extension of the bar graph to include a separate bar for each assemblage for each category (as advocated and illustrated by Kerrich and Clarke, 1967), would in this instance produce a sequence of 465 adjacent bars of various lengths and intensities, and would fail to achieve any of the above three aims with clarity.

Perhaps it is too much to expect one diagram to achieve all these intentions. The restriction to five or so assemblages is, in any case, too drastic for general comparative studies. Starting from the basic Bordes' descriptive system, an obvious approach would be to record the relevant raw counts of items on cards and then to use the computer (a) to calculate a variety of percentages and indices, (b) to produce bar charts at general and specific levels of type definition (and cumulative graphs, if desired), and (c) to produce dendrograms and scaling diagrams showing clustering and general inter-relationships between overall assemblages (see sections 7.2.4 and 9.5).

A second development of bar charts is the convention used by pollen analysts and others to represent counts of items from a whole series of *ordered* contexts: for example from levels in a stratified deposit. Here, for each level, the bars are effectively turned sideways and spaced out along a line. The tips of corresponding bars from successive levels are joined and the original bars eliminated, so forming new graphs that trace the change of each category through time. A similar representation for material from successive archaeological levels is shown in figure 5.8. Here, the intention is to emphasise development in time and not to bring out total relationships between different assemblages. A similar and more regular archaeological convention for this kind of information is the 'battleship diagram' familiar from seriation studies in the United States (figure 10.5), although it is important to note that in many of these studies, this kind of representation is not intended for material in a known order, but as a heuristic device for establishing such an order (see chapter 10).

All these developments that, in effect, combine sets of bar charts from different sources, depend on uniformity of the values from these sources. Representation of *percentages* is the obvious and regular convention. If percentages are used, it is important to include in the diagram the size of the sample for which the percentages are calculated. For instance in figure 5.8 it is vital to realise that 'percentages' are plotted for assemblages containing as few as three items. Only if such totals are given, as they are in this example, is the reader able to assess the likely significance of the presentation.

5.4.4. *Histograms.* Although some of the diagrams just discussed are at times

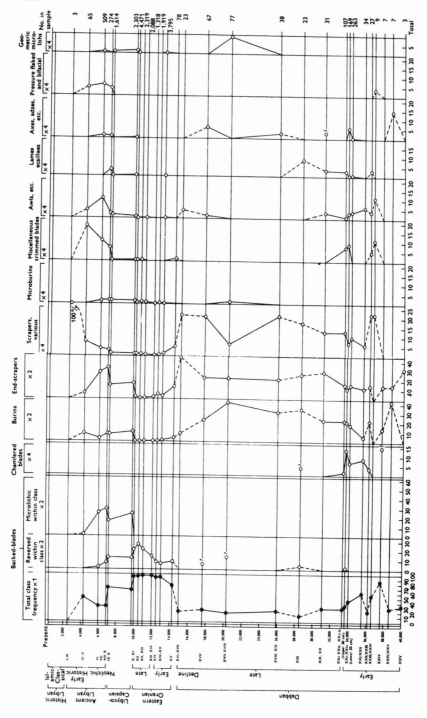

drawn to resemble histograms, this format essentially reflects a different concept: a representation of the frequency of different measured values of one continuous numeric attribute (see section 3.7). This contrast is seen clearly in Bohmer's diagram (figure 5.5), where, in spite of a superficial similarity, the top part of the diagram is concerned with bar charts, the lower part with histograms. Figure 5.9(a) shows a typical simple histogram for lengths of

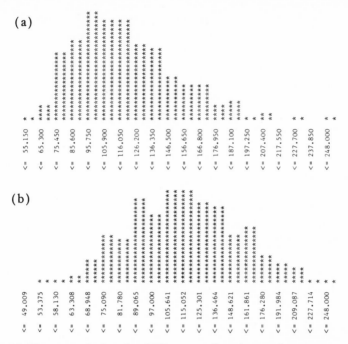

Figure 5.9. Histograms for lengths of 488 British handaxes. Plotted (a) from raw measurements in millimetres, and (b) from a natural logarithmic transformation of these measurements. The histograms are produced by the computer lineprinter and counts are represented by symbols rather than by strict 'areas'. The 488 implements represent a random sample of D. A. Roe's total measured sample of British handaxes (Roe 1968).

handaxes from a range of sites in Britain. The total range of relevant lengths is split into a chosen number of intervals and a count is made of the number of measurements falling into each interval. These counts are then represented by the size of the shaded areas on the diagram. An important difference between

Figure 5.8. General summary of the sequence at Haua Fteah (Libya) as presented by McBurney (1967). This representation is closely related to conventions used by pollen analysts to emphasise changes in the relative frequency of single-item classes through time. Except for chamfered blades, dotted lines refer to percentages calculated from an overall total of less than thirty (see totals on right).

this and many bar charts is that the ordering of the shaded areas is not arbitrary but an essential feature.

An obvious practical problem with histograms is to decide how to group values: how many divisions to make along the baseline. It is, of course, possible not to group values at all and instead to mark the position of each score as a dot or line relative to a continuous, exact scale. This would be equivalent to one-dimensional scaling (see p. 270) or to a one-dimensional scatter diagram (see p. 130). This alternative form of representation is not often found useful: as soon as two or more units have the same value, concessions have to be made to accuracy and clarity. As the number of units and tied values increases, this approach soon breaks down. Second, it is often only by grouping values that the general characteristics of an attribute are revealed. As a possible indication of the number of intervals to choose when drawing a histogram for n units, a rule of thumb given by Huntsberger (1962) may prove useful: he suggests the empirical formula $k = 1 + 3.3\log_{10}n$, where k is the number of classes. However, there is no reason to take such formulae too seriously (cf. Blalock 1960, 30). For large sets of data the choice of class-size and boundaries is not so critical. Usually, however, not more than ten to twenty divisions are found necessary.

As for bar charts, archaeologists and others have developed this basic histogram format so that information from more than one source may be represented together. Bohmer's juxtaposition of sets of related histograms has just been mentioned (figure 5.5). A similar convention has been established by Waterbolk and Butler (1965) for presenting information about trace-element quantities in metal artifacts of the Copper and Bronze Ages of Europe (figure 5.10).

For some purposes it is convenient to represent cumulative values on a histogram and to construct a 'cumulative frequency polygon'. Orton (1970) has used this convention to represent the variation in rim diameters from hypothetically different firings of a Romano-British kiln (figure 5.11). The cumulative representation of a frequency distribution like this allows multiple presentation on one diagram (as with Bordes' cumulative graphs), but, because the ordering of values on the x-axis is not arbitrary, it involves a generality that is absent from Bordes' convention.

The cumulative representation of values as in figure 5.11, then, has certain advantages, especially where a comparison between more than one graph is the main interest. However, the shape of a single graph is less easy to appreciate in cumulative form and cumulative presentation should not be followed without good reason.

5.4.5. *The study and interpretation of histograms.* As discussed in the last section, the histogram reflects a key concept in studying data by statistical methods and some further ramifications must be discussed, however briefly. To recapitulate ideas introduced in chapter 3, much of conventional statistical analysis is involved in assessing the relationship between an empirical frequency distribution, when actual data are plotted as a histogram, and a theoretical probability distribution which may be exactly specified by a mathematical equation, and which consequently has known properties. In practice, a relatively small number of theoretical distributions have been found to reflect, in an idealised form, patterns that arise frequently in everyday life when repeated events are counted or measured. The purpose of linking empirical data to a given theoretical distribution like this is that additional properties may subsequently be assumed for the data than those directly measured.

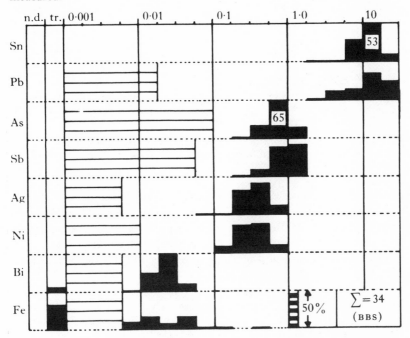

Figure 5.10. Conventions developed by Waterbolk and Butler (1965) for representing the overall metal content of a given group of prehistoric bronzes. A histogram is drawn for each element sought during spectrographic analysis. The histogram intervals are based on a logarithmic scale for percentage values. Hatching indicates a segment of the scale where 'presence' rather than a quantity is recorded. Plotted here are 34 analyses of bronzes from the Wilburton Fen Hoard, Cambridgeshire.

Some attempts to fit archaeological data to the normal and other theoretical distributions will be cited later. However, in archaeology, a histogram will usually be studied more informally, often in the hope of discerning that mixed populations or groups are represented. For example, figures 5.12 and 5.13 both suggest that two distinct groups of units are concerned: for figure 5.12 heavy and light bangles; for figure 5.13 small and large postholes

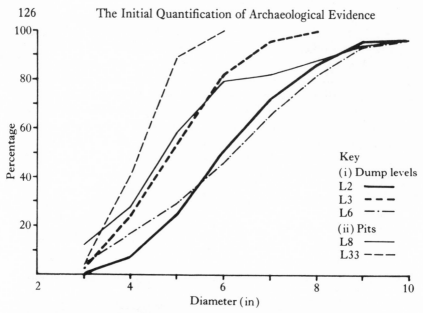

Figure 5.11. Cumulative frequency polygons comparing the rim diameters for one functional pot type in different deposits of wasters at a Romano-British kiln site in London (Orton 1970).

(presumably associated with two types of structural element).

Just how valuable or 'significant' is such an informal indication of bimodality likely to be? Because of the sampling problems outlined in section 5.2.2, here, as in so much archaeological investigation, rather than attempt a mechanical but spurious test of significance, it is probably more realistic to

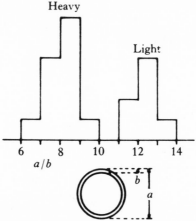

Figure 5.12. Nineteen plain bronze bangles from Münsingen. The histograms shows the existence of two stylistic types, heavy and light (Hodson 1968).

accept this kind of indication for what it is: a direct presentation of the existing evidence, able to suggest grouping or other effects of provisional interest, to be tested against existing evidence from other sources and against future evidence of the same nature. Figure 5.14 shows how an informal hypothesis of bimodality (for the proportion of racloirs in Mousterian assemblages in France) required reconsideration after further evidence had accumulated. Such marked bimodality (or multimodality) as seen on figures 5.12, 5.13 and 5.15(b) is rare but of great interest when found. More often, the separation, even provisionally, of archaeological units into two or more groups will depend on the cumulative effect of less obvious patterning in several variables, and as such will be tackled by cluster analysis (see chapter 7 and especially figure 7.2).

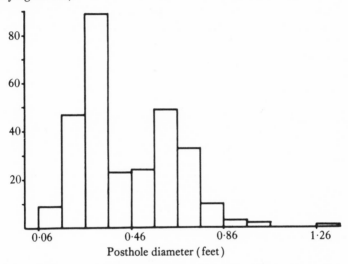

Figure 5.13. Histogram of posthole diameters from the Summer Island site (Lake Michigan). Two types of structural support are suggested (data from Brose 1971).

Another use of histograms would be to indicate marked *skewness* of raw values, and the effect of simple transformations on such irregular data. Figures 5.9(a) and (b) show this effect for the lengths of a sample of British handaxes. A regular transformation (by taking logarithms) results in a far more symmetrical frequency distribution. In many forms of analysis it is useful to have data that are symmetrically distributed and this informal presentation would suggest the logarithmic transformation of these handaxe values before such analyses are carried out. A similar effect is produced by the logarithmic transformations of trace element data, figure 5.10.

More formal attempts have been made to fit archaeological data to the normal or to related distributions. Vértes (1965) has given a worked example, with the calculations, for fitting a normal curve to the mean and standard deviation of the lengths of flint blades from a Neolithic hoard at Boldogkőváralja (Hungary). He also showed how a special form of graph paper ('probability paper') may help to judge the normality of an empirical frequency distribution. On this paper, values on the x-axis are transformed so that a normal distribution, plotted cumulatively, will give a straight line. Vértes concluded from a visual comparison of the graphs that the lengths of the blades in the hoard could be drawn from an underlying normal distribution. However, this seems to be an exceptional result for empirical archaeological data: raw measurements taken by archaeologists rarely produce such symmetry. Even in this example there are perhaps doubts, since 565 blades are said to have been found in the cache, but only 390 are plotted. The more usual plot for raw artifact dimensions or indices is skewed, like figure 5.9(a).

In the same study, Vértes (1965) investigated such a skewed distribution to see whether in fact a normal distribution could be hidden by the scale of measurement of the artifacts. He fitted logarithmic rather than raw values to the corresponding normal distribution, and, again after visual assessment, claimed an approximate fit.

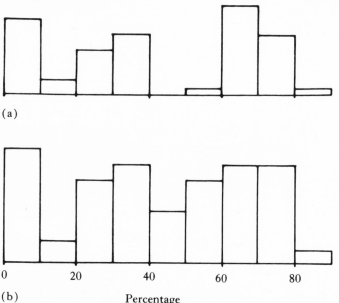

Figure 5.14. Histograms for the proportion of racloirs ('side-scrapers') in Mousterian assemblages. Intervals on the baseline refer to racloirs as a percentage of the total content of retouched tools (excluding handaxes) in the assemblages studied. (a) The evidence from 48 assemblages studied by F. Bordes in 1953. A clear division is suggested between sites with more or less than 50 per cent racloirs (i.e. *Charentian* and *other* Mousterian assemblages). (b) The evidence available from 88 assemblages in 1970. The pattern has changed drastically (Bordes 1953, Bordes and de Sonneville-Bordes 1970).

Since most frequency distributions of measurements and ratios of archaeological attributes turn out to be skewed, they will tend to approximate a lognormal rather than a normal distribution. McBurney (1967) has published an
attempt to fit forty-one sets of measurements and ratios of palaeolithic
material at Haua Fteah to log-normal distributions (in each of the forty-one
tables published, *iterative* seems to be a misprint for *cumulative*). He concluded that: 'Taken as a whole, it would appear that rather more than half the
characters can be reasonably described by log-normal curves, and the
remainder, although diverging to some extent, do so far less markedly than
from normal (Gaussian) forms.' This confirms the general finding that
frequency distributions for dimensions and ratios of artifact classes tend to be
skewed.

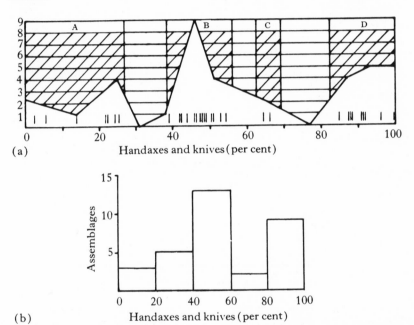

(a) Handaxes and knives (per cent)

(b) Handaxes and knives (per cent)

Figure 5.15. Two alternative ways of
presenting the same data. The ratios of
handaxes and knives to handaxes, knives
and small scrapers in thirty-two African
Acheulean assemblages. (a) As
published by L. R. Binford; this shows
the exact ratio for each assemblage as a
stroke on the baseline. The remainder of
the diagram with shaded areas, polygon
and vertical divisions represents an interpretation of this distribution (Binford
1972). (b) A more conventional histogram for the same data. A basic bimodal
structure is suggested.

These examples of curve-fitting are interesting, but perhaps a little remote
from regular archaeological situations, where an informal approach to
histograms and frequency distributions will often be more in keeping with the
data available and the conclusions desired.

5.4.6. *Scatter diagrams.* The third direct diagrammatic method of presenting data is the scatter diagram. Here, two attributes are taken to define the *x* and *y* axes of a coordinate system (see section 2.8) and each unit is located, as a dot, by its score on these two attributes. If very many points are involved, it is possible to group values for each attribute (equivalent to the histogram treatment), and to represent the density of points by differential shading of the grid that the grouping defines. The direct two-dimensional scatter diagram provides information from two points of view: first, relationships between the units are shown by their relative positions on the diagram: second, the relationship between the two attributes is shown by the overall pattern of the dots.

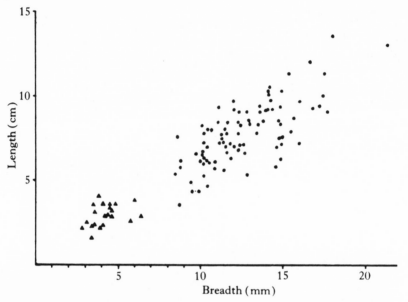

Figure 5.16. Scatter diagram for the length and breadth of a general class of flint tool from Corbiac (south-west France). Two clusters (types) within this general class are indicated: Gravettes (dots) and micro-Gravettes (triangles). The concentration of the overall distribution close to a line from the origin to the upper right corner shows that the two attributes, length and breadth, are highly correlated ($r = 0.88$). (Bordes 1967.)

These two aspects are well illustrated in figure 5.16. Here, from a rich level at Corbiac, flint artifacts of a given morphological category (straight-backed, pointed blades) are plotted against two size attributes, length and breadth. It is assumed that all of the flints of this category are plotted. The dots fall into two groups or clusters: the first of short, narrow, the second of long, broad blades, with a marked discontinuity between them. This suggests that two 'types' or 'sub-types' are represented and these correspond with the Gravettes and micro-Gravettes of the Sonneville-Bordes/Perrot Upper Palaeolithic type-list (1954–56). At the same time, it is clear that the dots are confined to a restricted part of the quadrant; they fall close to a line from the origin to the right hand corner. This shows that the two dimensions length and breadth are, in this sample, closely related or correlated (both in fact reflecting 'size'): on the whole, a broader point is also longer. By contrast, the handaxe plot (figure 5.17) shows no such clear relationship between the two attributes.

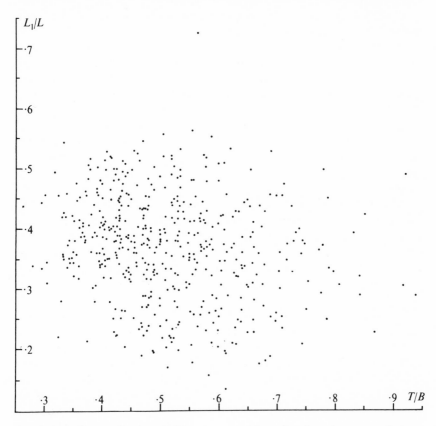

Figure 5.17. Scatter diagram of 488 British handaxes plotted against relative thickness (T/B) and pointedness (L_1/L), see figure 5.2. There is virtually no evidence for clustering or correlation ($r = -0.21$). D. A. Roe's data (Hodson 1971, 43).

Many, if not all, of the analytical methods described in chapters 7 to 9 represent an extension of these two concepts, clustering and correlation, into situations where a scatter diagram with more than two attributes (axes) is required, and consequently where the simple visual appreciation of a two-dimensional diagram is impossible.

This basic kind of two-dimensional scatter diagram may be used to recall some of the concepts introduced in section 2.8 and vital for the following chapters. As well as the direct visual assessment of a scatter diagram, it is possible to express the relationships between the various points, or between the two axes, in more precise mathematical terms. On figure 5.16, it would be possible to measure with a ruler the distance between any two dots (representing artifacts); this *distance* between two points is an expression of the *difference* in size between two artifacts. A convenient, regular way to represent such mutual distances between whole sets of units is in a symmetrical matrix like a mileage chart (e.g. table 9.13).

For the values plotted on the scatter diagram, however, it is not only possible to measure distances with a ruler; given the scores on each axis it is possible to calculate the various distances using Pythagoras' theorem without constructing a diagram at all (see figure 2.4). It is also instructive to realise that a Euclidean ('Pythagorean') distance may be found by the same two operations (ruler and calculation) in three dimensions as in two. For more than three attributes (or dimensions) the algebraic calculation is still possible and valid even though a visual geometric representation is no longer possible. It is thus feasible to calculate distances in multi-dimensional space, i.e. where units are described by many attributes.

It will be obvious that an exact representation according to this model will require as many dimensions as there are attributes. However, this dimensionality may be limited by the number of units (n) involved. If there are less units than attributes, the space involved will have ($n - 1$) dimensions (the distance between two units may be represented in one dimension, three in two and so on, however many attributes are concerned).

5.4.7. *More than two dimensions.* As will be shown in later chapters, various indirect methods are available for plotting multi-dimensional information not in the number of dimensions required for an exact presentation, but in fewer dimensions: often, in fact, as a two-dimensional scatter diagram. These stratagems involve transformations of the original variables and the loss of some information which may or may not be redundant. For three dimensions, direct plotting is still possible either by constructing a model in three dimensions, or by a perspective presentation (cf. figure 8.7), or by using different sized symbols (e.g. dots, arrows) to represent this kind of depth. For example, on figures 9.6 and 9.25 (C2 and C8) arrows are drawn proportional in length to scores on a third axis. They point right for positive, left for negative values. Such diagrams are quite feasible where relatively few units are involved, especially if the third dimension is in some sense less important than the first two (as it is in principal components analysis, see section 8.2). It is even possible to represent a fourth dimension on a scatter diagram by adding a further directed line at right angles to a third dimension pointer. An alternative solution that can accommodate any number of dimensions is to plot each unit as a graph (Andrews 1972) rather than as a point on a scatter diagram. However, these representations all become cluttered as the number of units increases and the entire visual effect of the diagram is then lost.

If three attributes are variables of constant sum, i.e. if they are proportions or percentages of a collective total, then a three-pole triangular graph is possible. This kind of presentation is discussed in detail by Koch and Link (1971, 171) and has been used by archaeologists (e.g. by Meighan 1959, Laplace 1968, Ihm 1970, Isaac 1972, Laville and Rigaud 1973; see figure 5.18).

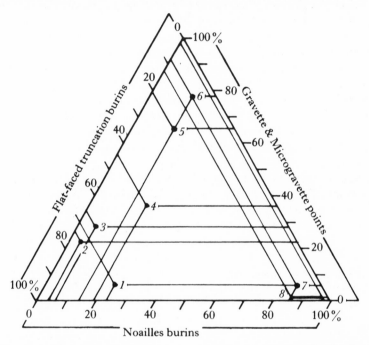

Figure 5.18. Three-pole coordinate system for three attributes of constant sum. A series of Perigordian V levels from sites in south-western France are plotted relative to three diagnostic tool classes. These were extracted for study from the total tool inventory, and form the basis for the calculation of percentages. The assemblages are: 1, 2, 5, 6 Flageolet I, levels V, I V, V I I and V I; 3, 4 Les Jambes, levels 3 and 2; 7 Roc de Gavaudun, layer I I; 8 Abri du Facteur. (For 8, the exact percentage of flat-faced, truncation burins could not be calculated and the possible range is shown by a thick line). Assemblages 7 and 8 are clearly separated from the others on this evidence (Laville and Rigaud 1973).

All of the attributes discussed so far have been assumed to be measured on a numeric scale. If there is also qualitative information it is possible to use different symbols (or different colours for the same symbol) for the attribute states and to add a further 'dimension' to the scatter plot in this way: equivalent to the use of different symbols for different categories of material on an archaeological distribution map. Here again, it is theoretically possible to have a whole series of sets of symbols corresponding to different attributes so that each unit on a scatter diagram is represented not by one dot but by several symbols; but again, the complication will tend to spoil any direct visual impact. On the whole, if a large number of units are to be plotted it is difficult to represent more than two numeric and one qualitative attribute on the same scatter diagram. This means that where three or more metric attributes are involved, direct plotting of values will normally require more than one scatter diagram—in fact one for each pair of variables concerned. This is equivalent to $n(n-1)/2$ diagrams where n is the number of variables. Although a computer is able to generate sets of scatter diagrams in this way rapidly and simply and either display them on a cathode ray tube or print out any plots requested (see sections 4.4 and 4.5), the archaeologist would tend to be confronted with more rather than less complexity, and at the same time the more general interplay between groups of attributes is still not represented, only that between pairs of attributes. This is the situation that multivariate methods described in the next chapters attempt to tackle.

For certain special problems it may prove possible to devise other stratagems than those so far mentioned for the direct presentation of multi-dimensional data, but attempts to establish such conventions should not be made lightly. For example, Roe has suggested plotting handaxes on diagrams that accommodate three variables (1964, 1968). He divides one of the attributes into three divisions and then produces a standard two-way scatter diagram for each of the three groups of handaxes which result from this division. This places great stress on, first, the selection of one variable for priority and, second, the divisions into which it is split. All further diagrams are conditioned by these decisions, but neither is really convincingly justified in Roe's accounts.

The direct diagrammatic presentation of data by the methods discussed in these last sections is of great importance. All of the methods presented in chapters 7 and 8 really develop out of the concepts seen at their simplest in bar charts, histograms and scatter diagrams.

Measures of Similarity and Correlation

6.1. INTRODUCTION

Much of an archaeologist's work consists in judging relative similarities or differences between material remains, whether at the level of artifacts, assemblages or whole complexes. This judgement provides the basis for the ordering and classification of material which itself forms one of the essential links between discovery and interpretation. Numerical estimates of resemblance and correlation play an equally prominent role in the quantitative analysis of archaeological data, and it is appropriate to devote a chapter in this book to them.

Some basic aspects of distance and correlation were introduced in sections 2.8 and 3.16, and were recalled in the last chapter in connection with scatter diagrams. This chapter will carry on from that point and will discuss first measures of distance or similarity, and then measures of correlation, as quantified estimates of the relationships seen visually on a scatter diagram. First, however, some justification and reservation must be expressed as a prelude to treating the intuitive concepts of similarity and dissimilarity as numerical concepts of proximity and distance.

In practice, numerical values have to be placed on the similarity or dissimilarity between units. Because distance is a widely used and understood mathematical concept, it is natural to concentrate on distances, and, if necessary, to transform 'proximities' to distances by a simple manipulation (for example by subtraction from a constant). But how realistic are such manipulations for the direct concepts of similarity and dissimilarity? How realistic for archaeological material is the geometric model where distances are accepted as a fair representation of dissimilarity, and are manipulated arithmetically? It is important to realise that these problems exist, and that there are and can be no simple, agreed answers. As in so much statistical work, supposedly standard procedures require detailed justification in every application, and an archaeologist should not be too surprised to read a statement like the following from highly experienced mathematicians:

'From the point of view of data analysis, the prescription of a distance function will generally be a trial and error task in which the use of some general techniques needs to be aided by insight, intuition and good luck' (Gnanadesikan and Wilk 1969).

One fairly basic principle is that if numerical dissimilarities are to be treated as distances, they should satisfy the relevant mathematical rules for a metric (see section 2.8). Several of the operations discussed in the next section are designed to observe these rules when transforming a similarity to a dissimilarity, a proximity to a distance.

However, one further general problem must be mentioned. When a series of such distances have been calculated, it may prove very difficult to decide which scale of measurement the values represent. Since an exact number will be placed on each dissimilarity, often calculated to a number of places of decimals, it will be tempting to assume that a truly numeric (ratio) scale of measurement is involved, and to manipulate the values arithmetically (working out averages of selected distances, for example). Many multivariate methods, it is perhaps fair to say most, assume that a distance function is associated with a scale of this precision. There is a good deal of controversy about the propriety of applying such analytical methods when this scale assumption is not specifically justified. One solution is to restrict analysis to those procedures that consider only the relative ordering of distances and not their absolute values; i.e. to consider that similarity or dissimilarity is always measured on an ordinal scale unless clear proof exists to the contrary (cf. Sibson 1972). This approach is theoretically attractive, but has proved to be rather restrictive and sometimes unhelpful in practice, as will be discussed in later chapters.

One reasonable precaution would seem to be that if numerical dissimilarities are to be considered, then data should as far as possible be prepared in a form where the calculation of a given distance function may be expected to produce values with numerical (ratio) properties. Unfortunately little work appears to have been done to assess this approach for different, standard forms of data. Nor is it clear just how misleading is likely to be the application of some standard multivariate procedures when these precautions have not been taken, and when the measurement scale of dissimilarities/distances is possibly or certainly ordinal rather than numeric. Helpful discussions of some of these basic problems will be found in Gower (1966, 1967, 1971c, 1972).

6.2.　Some Useful Measures of Distance and Similarity

The calculation of Euclidean distance (d) and its chief characteristics have already been described (in sections 2.8 and 5.4.6). It is a measure of great importance since it has a direct intuitive interpretation and is simple to compute. It necessarily forms the basis for many computerised classification programs.

However, there are inevitably some difficulties in using d with empirical data. A first difficulty is the relative scaling for the various attributes scored: if one attribute were measured in inches and another in millimetres the value of *d* would clearly make nonsense. Such an obvious anomaly is not likely to arise in practice, and could be rectified immediately by conversion to one scale or the other. However, if one measurement were length and another weight, or an angle or the number of excrescences, there will be a similar imbalance in the scale of the attributes which cannot be rectified by any obvious conversion. Or if measurements are all to the same scale but vary within quite different limits (measures of length and breadth and thickness of long, thin objects such as swords, for example), a direct Euclidean distance might seem unreasonable.

Both of these scale problems are regularly dealt with by standardising scores on each attribute: in effect by dividing all scores by the standard deviation of the attribute concerned (see p. 39). Such standardisation is a regular procedure in many kinds of data analysis; usually scores are at the same time expressed as deviations from the relevant mean (so that in other words each attribute has zero mean and unit variance), although clearly the location of the mean makes no difference in the calculation of *d*. Of course, if the scores are all counts expressed as percentages (for example of types in assemblages), a form of standardisation will already have been imposed on the data. Additional standardisation, as described above, would then have the effect of making each attribute contribute equally to the general pattern of distances, whether it was sometimes common or always rare. This may or may not seem desirable, according to the problem concerned.

Other methods of standardisation may be used, such as division by the range rather than the standard deviation of an attribute. A well known disadvantage of the range is that it gives undue weight to isolated extreme values; an advantage is that, if differences between scores on any attribute are divided by its range, they will automatically fall between 0 and 1, a feature exploited in the Gower coefficient (see below). Taking logarithms is another possible way of standardising scores when different attributes are measured on different segments of the same scale: this would arise in archaeology in the sword example quoted above, or when trace-elements and major constituents of alloyed metals are considered together, or, often, when measurements are expressed as proportions of other measurements. A practical difficulty with logarithms is that values of 0 may occur where quantities, angles, etc. are measured. Since it is not possible to convert zero into a logarithmic scale, it is necessary to add a small constant to all values before transformation. It is worth adding that all these transformations from raw scores for analysis and back to raw scores for interpretation are extremely tedious to carry out by hand but are trivial for the computer.

So far in discussing Euclidean distance, all attributes have been assumed to have been measured on a numeric scale. Values on an ordinal scale (ranks, preferences, for example) would simply be treated as though they were metric, which could be more or less objectionable according to the attributes concerned. Qualitative attributes present a further problem. Presence/absence attributes are regularly scored as 1 and 0 and then treated as though they were on a metric scale. The obvious dangers of this practice (e.g. of assuming an unjustified reversibility of presence and absence) have already been mentioned. Multi-state qualitative attributes are again regularly converted to a series of presence/absence attributes and each scored 1 or 0 (e.g. by Cahen and Martin 1972).

There seems to be no general agreement about the propriety of this expedient, although most authorities have clear doubts. One obvious inconsistency is the effective increase in the distance calculated between two units when they differ on any attribute converted in this way (see table 6.1). It would, of course, be trivial to modify a computer program so as to eliminate

attribute 'material'	a flint	b chert	c obsidian
tool 1	1	0	0
tool 2	0	0	1

$$d^2 = 1^2 + 0^2 + 1^2$$
$$d = \sqrt{2}$$

Table 6.1. The effect on Euclidean distance of converting a multi-state attribute to a series of dichotomous attributes. The distance between two different units on the one attribute 'material' becomes $\sqrt{2}$ rather than $\sqrt{1}$.

this effect. If qualitative attributes only are defined for a study, this problem may not seem so important since one of the similarity measures discussed below could be chosen. However, d has so many computational advantages and is so suitable for some general purpose iterative procedures such as k-means cluster analysis (see section 7.5.4), that the problem of the arbitrary 0, 1 treatment of presence/absence and qualitative attributes is important. This seems to be a field where much more comparative study is required (cf. Williams and Dale 1962).

Missing or conditional scores, of course, cannot be so easily forced into a convenient format for calculating Euclidean distance. Much can be done in the original definition of attributes and choice of units to avoid these dilemmas, but it may still be necessary to fall back on one of the less convenient but clearly more appropriate similarity coefficients discussed below.

A quite different and even more general problem is set by the nature of relationships between the attributes defined. Euclidean distance proceeds as though all the attributes were independent. But in an empirical situation, some attributes are bound to be linked to (correlated with) others, and the validity of the direct Euclidean space model may be suspect. Discussion of this problem will be postponed until after the section on measures of correlation between attributes. However, in anticipation, it may be mentioned that if desired, such correlations *can* be totally compensated in calculating a distance. In practice, such total compensation may or may not seem appropriate.

Although Euclidean distance has not been used widely in archaeological research, we ourselves have found it practicable and satisfactory especially in studying relationships between assemblages of types (e.g. Doran and Hodson 1966, Hodson 1969, Azoury and Hodson 1973, Newcomer and Hodson 1973; cf. Daniels 1967, Ammerman 1971). It also provides a convenient basis for some general structure-seeking computer programs, like *k*-means cluster analysis, to be discussed in later chapters.

6.3.   OTHER MEASURES OF DISTANCE AND SIMILARITY

In the previous section, archaeological units were considered as points in a space where distances may be measured, at least conceptually, by a ruler. In that context, scores have been considered as measurements, and Euclidean *distance* represents a natural expression of *difference* between the units. However, in archaeology (and in many other social sciences), scores on attributes are often clearly not measurements: they may be statements of presence or absence, or counts of such presences, perhaps expressed as percentage occurrence. In such situations, the initial squaring of differences, as in Euclidean distance, where large differences are effectively emphasised at the expense of small, may be thought inappropriate. It is quite possible simply to sum absolute differences rather than squared differences between scores, giving a measure called the city block metric (see section 2.8). Here too, preliminary transformation or standardisation of the attributes would often be appropriate. The Robinson coefficient of agreement is a special case of this distance: it effectively totals the percentage differences between defined categories (types) for pairs of archaeological assemblages. In this form these differences would conform with the rules for metric distance even if they are clearly not Pythagorean. The maximal difference between any two units is 200 per cent. By subtracting any calculated distance from 200 an equivalent measure of similarity or agreement is achieved, i.e.:

$$S_{R_{ij}} = 200 - \sum_{k=1}^{a} |P_{ik} - P_{jk}|$$

where P is the percentage representation of attribute k in assemblages i and j. In this form this coefficient has been used in a number of seriation and other studies since Robinson's initial formulation of 1951 (e.g. Freeman and Brown 1964, Johnson 1968).

An even simpler equivalent to a similarity coefficient for presence/absence data has been used by D. G. Kendall (1969, 1971). This in effect simply sums the number of attributes (here 'types') common to any two units (here 'graves'). For the specific Münsingen cemetery application, where there is no great variation in the number of types per assemblage, this measure proved adequate.

Texts on numerical taxonomy (cluster analysis) regularly include long lists of possible distance and similarity measures (Sokal and Sneath 1963, Cormack 1971). Some of these are designed for measuring the difference between populations using the dispersion of the scores for constituent units as well as the average population values (see Mahalanobis distance, section 8.5). Others attempt to weight rare or common attributes on the assumption that one or the other is more important (cf. Gower 1970). However, some other measures simply attempt to deal as effectively as possible with data from different sources and of different kinds. Three of these must be mentioned: the Simple Matching Coefficient, Jaccard's Coefficient and Gower's Flexible Coefficient. The latter, particularly should prove of great value in archaeology.

In discussing similarity coefficients calculated from nominal attributes it is conventional and useful to refer symbolically to the four possible combinations of states by the letters a–d. (See table 6.2.) These letters represent counts of associated states for any two units. This is, of course, similar to the contingency table illustrated in section 3.14.

		unit 1	
		+	−
unit 2	+	a	b
	−	c	d

Table 6.2. Conventional lettering for counts used when calculating the similarity between two units (e.g. b = the number of attributes scored 'absent' for unit 1 and 'present' for unit 2).

The *Simple Matching Coefficient* S_{SM} (Sokal and Sneath 1963, 133; Hodson, Sneath and Doran 1966) is suited to qualitative data and to situations where conditional and missing values cannot be avoided. Attributes are scored as present, absent or non-applicable ($+$, $−$, $/$). For any two units, the number of positive *and* negative matches is counted and expressed as a proportion of the valid comparisons made (i.e. referring to table 6.2, $S_{SM} = (a + d)/(a + b + c + d)$). This means that S_{SM} will always lie between 0 and 1, and subtraction from 1 will give a measure of dissimilarity rather than similarity, if desired, again lying between 0 and 1. In fact, a more usual distance transformation would be $\sqrt{(1 - S_{SM})}$ since this gives a distance suitable for a wide range of subsequent analyses (Gower 1972). Judicious use of the 'non-applicable' symbol allows for missing data or irrelevant attributes (usually where a condition has been set by a previous attribute and already scored as non-present); no comparison or count of comparisons is recorded when either unit scores 'non-applicable' for a given attribute. If too free a use is made of this 'non-applicable' facility, the Euclidean property of the distance transformation just given may be upset, but this is probably not a serious threat in practice.

Quantitative attributes *can* be accommodated as well as qualitative in calculating S_{SM}; the range of the relevant attribute is split into a reasonable number of divisions (in the archaeological example to be quoted, these varied between five and eight) and a suitable combination of + and − for the various divisions allows the relative magnitude at different points of the scale to be preserved. However, this is an extremely cumbersome procedure, and where both qualitative and quantitative attributes are needed, S_G below seems more suitable.

This measure, S_{SM} with the non-applicable facility for conditional data and with suitable coding for quantitative attributes, was used for experimental analyses of fibulae (Hodson, Sneath and Doran 1966; see section 9.1). It performed very satisfactorily, but the large number of states for quantitative attributes meant rather tedious data preparation. In addition, this treatment effectively weighted quantitative against qualitative attributes according to the number of divisions into which each was split. This could be justified on empirical grounds since the effective weighting corresponded with the subjective assessment of reliability of the various attributes. In other experiments this effect was eliminated by dividing the calculated similarity for one attribute by the number of attribute states defined. But on all grounds, this approach could certainly be improved.

The Simple Matching Coefficient gives equal weight to negative and to positive scores, and so is not basically suited to simple presence/absence information. In many situations it would clearly be more sensible to count only agreement scores in assessing similarity. *Jaccard's coefficient* S_J is designed to do this: negative matches are ignored in counting agreements and in counting valid comparisons for the divisor. In the conventions of table 6.2, $S_J = a/(a + b + c)$. An equivalent though more obscure formula for $S_{J_{ij}}$ is:

$$S_{J_{ij}} = \frac{\sum_k \min (r_{ik}, r_{jk})}{\sum_k \max (r_{ik}, r_{jk})}$$

where $\min (r_{ik}, r_{jk})$ stands for the element, either 0 or 1, that is the smaller of numbers r_{ik} and r_{jk}, and max for the element that is larger. Bordaz and Bordaz (1970) who quote the formula in this notation, used this measure for assessing the relationships between assemblages, 'lots', which were described by features of constituent potsherds. Before further analysis, the Jaccard similarities were transformed into suitable distances by a logarithmic adjustment, $d_{ij} = -\log S_{ij}$, similar to that suggested above for converting S_{SM} into a distance. In this form, the Bordaz refer to it as the 'Tanimoto distance function'.

A straight Jaccard coefficient was also used by True and Matson (1970) to estimate similarity between preceramic sites in Chile. Here the attributes are said to be mainly bead and lithic artifact 'traits' as distinct from traditional artifact types, although it is not clear in the preliminary report what proportion of the artifacts are represented once, or more than once, or not at all by this descriptive system.

In both of these analyses the assessment of similarity would seem highly conditioned by the size and homogeneity of the assemblages concerned. It is likely that large or slightly mixed assemblages will have most traits represented at least occasionally. Counts of types or traits represented as percentages are likely to provide a better basis for the comparison of settlement debris than a simple record of presence (see section 5.3.4).

	values of attribute k			
unit 1	+	+	−	−
unit 2	+	−	+	−
score_{12_k}	1	0	0	0
weight_{12_k}	1	1	1	0

Table 6.3. The Gower similarity coefficient: calculation of the score and weight for the similarity between two units on one presence/absence attribute k.

A coefficient that is able to cope satisfactorily with all the different kinds of data discussed so far has been devised by Gower (1971c). In fact it combines three options equivalent to S_J, S_{SM}, and a city-block metric standardised by the range, for the three basic kinds of data encountered: presence/absence, qualitative and quantitative attributes respectively. The formula is:

$$S_{G_{ij}} = \sum_{k=1}^{a} S_{ijk} \Big/ \sum_{k=1}^{a} W_{ijk}$$

S_{ijk} represents a score for each attribute (between 0 and 1); W_{ijk} a weight set to 0 or 1 according to whether the comparison is considered valid for attribute k. The scores and weights are assigned as follows:

(a) For presence and absence, see table 6.3. Compare the Jaccard coefficient discussed above.

(b) For qualitative attributes (including alternatives): $S_{ijk} = 1$ if the attribute states for the two units i and j are the same, and 0 if they differ. W_{ijk} is always 1 unless this attribute is non-applicable (missing data, or a conditional attribute ruled non-applicable by the score on a previous attribute). Compare S_{SM} above.

(c) For quantitative attributes with values x_1, x_2, ..., x_n on attribute k:

$$S_{ijk} = 1 - |x_i - x_j|/R_k$$

where R_k is the range for attribute k. The weight W_{ijk} is again 1 except in the 'non-applicable' conditions mentioned in (b). Gower suggests that other normalisers than the range could be used if desired, although this is the most obvious.

This coefficient requires careful coding of the raw data so that, effectively, the computer can recognise the three kinds of attribute. As a preliminary to scaling or clustering procedures it would seem ideally suited to archaeological data.

One other supposed measure of similarity must be mentioned since it has been used in archaeological work: the linear correlation coefficient r (Witherspoon 1961, Thomas 1971, figure 1(a)). As discussed in section 3.16, this coefficient is designed for attributes and as such will be described in the next section. It is unsuitable for assessing similarities since in this context it effectively standardises scores by the mean and standard deviation of each unit's set of scores. This will become clearer when the properties of r are discussed in the next section.

6.4.   MEASURES OF RELATIONSHIP BETWEEN ATTRIBUTES

The basic concepts involving the relationship between two attributes have been introduced in earlier chapters (see sections 3.16–18 and 5.4.6). There, to recapitulate, a distinction was drawn between the related concepts of regression and correlation: regression concerns predicting a value on one attribute given the value on another and involves a regression equation; correlation concerns the accuracy with which such a prediction may be made and involves a coefficient such as the linear correlation coefficient r. In the following sections, r will be discussed further, and some coefficients for non-numeric data will be introduced.

The basic formula for calculating r has already been given in section 3.16. An alternative version is:

$$r = \frac{\Sigma xy}{Ns_x s_y}$$

where x and y represent scores measured as deviations from their respective means, and s_x and s_y the standard deviations of attributes X and Y. From this formula it will be seen that high values of r will result when high departures from their respective means occur for both variables together (Σxy); also that the standard deviations of the attributes are involved. In effect, scores of units on the attribute are standardised (see section 3.7). Other raw-score formulae are available for calculating r, and some desk calculating machines give r automatically, although for a reasonable quantity of data it is worth using a computer.

Values for r lie between -1 and $+1$ and are positive when values for both variables increase together, negative when one increases as the other decreases. Often the direction or sign of r will depend on an arbitrary decision. To take an obvious example, which also illustrates the sort of context where r is regularly used: the depth (attribute X) of a set of artifacts could be measured from a baseline upwards or from the ground surface downwards; the relative width of the artifacts could be expressed as a ratio (attribute Y), length/breadth or breadth/length. If r is used to measure how closely the relative depth or age of the tools is related to their relative width, four different sets of data and four different calculations could be made. Assuming total correlation, two calculations of r would give $+1$, two -1. In other cases, for direct measurements or counts, this problem does not arise.

Given that the sign of r may be arbitrary and that values will lie between 0 for no linear relationship and -1 or $+1$ for total relationship, what do intermediate values, say an r of 0.25, 0.5 or 0.75 signify? It is possible to assess r by considering it in another guise: as r^2. r^2 in fact represents the proportion of the variation in one attribute accounted for by its linear dependence on another, and as such is likely to be more patently meaningful in many archaeological situations where r itself has been calculated for convenience, or as part of a more general computer analysis.

As suggested in chapter 3, a regular significance test for r is available and tables are published for given r and given sample size with a null hypothesis of no correlation in an assumed parent population. Often, a computer program is designed to indicate when 'significant' values of r are reached according to this test, and it is natural and regular to publish matrices of correlation coefficients with an indication of significance (e.g. McBurney 1968, Brose 1970). Unfortunately, a number of restrictive assumptions (especially about the frequency distribution of the attributes) have to be met if this test is to have much value. In many archaeological situations when r is used, these conditions are not remotely approximated. The most regular and obvious departure from the normality assumption is when there are many extreme and relatively few intermediate values for an attribute. This happens regularly where counts of categories are made and where such categories are often absent from many of the samples: values may concentrate around 0 with just one or two positive counts, and yet very high r (positive or negative) will result for pairs of such attributes. This is clearly true in McBurney's table for Ali Tappeh (1968, table II) where one attribute (percentage occurrence of the mollusc *Cyclotus*) has correlations of $+1$ or -1 with nine of the other thirty-one attributes, including radiocarbon date, even though it was found in only four of the twenty-three deposits on which the calculations were based. Other difficulties with r may arise if measurements are made on heterogeneous material: negative correlation between length and breadth, for instance, could appear as positive if basically distinct small and large types of tool were taken together. Even the simple conversion of counts to percentages would often be sufficient to make nonsense of the 'significance' of a value for r calculated on the assumption of normality (see below).

In other words, reliance on a stereotyped significance test as the chief means of assessing r is unsatisfactory. A scatter diagram of the data for the two attributes on which any r is based will usually reveal such dangers, but where many attributes are concerned, all of the relevant scatter diagrams cannot be inspected. Practical ways of studying large matrices of correlation coefficients will be mentioned later (see especially section 8.2).

A final warning about r already mentioned in the last section concerns its use as a measure of similarity between units rather than of linear correlation between attributes. It will now be clear that r is concerned with values measured as deviations about a mean and standardised by the relevant standard deviation. If for the formula above, X and Y are thought of as scores on units, these will be expressed as deviations from the mean scores of each unit X and Y and these will have been standardised by the standard deviations of such scores. Any distance or similarity estimated between X and Y after such transformation will have little meaning.

A general difficulty in archaeology, as in some other subjects (geology, palynology) occurs when r has to be estimated from data expressed as percentages. A very regular situation is for assemblages described by their content of types. Cowgill (1970) has discussed this difficulty, although the detailed likely effects over a range of typical archaeological situations remain to be worked out. Induced correlation will tend to be negative because as one value increases others must decrease, and this effect will be more pronounced where the number of categories is small. As the number of categories increases the effect is likely to decrease, and there is no reason to imagine that, in the palaeolithic studies quoted in this book, distortions of r from percentage presentation are serious compared with all the other sampling and analytical errors that are known to operate.

However, it would be reassuring to be able to base this hope on statistical theory or simulated experiments rather than intuition. General and specific consequences of percentage presentation, not necessarily concerned only with r, will be found in Chayes and Kruskal (1966), Mosiman (1962), Koch and Link (1971, 168), Gower (1967, 23).

6.5. MEASURES OF CORRELATION AND ASSOCIATION BETWEEN NON-NUMERIC ATTRIBUTES

This section discusses estimates of association between attributes that are measured not on the numeric scale for which r is designed, but on ordinal, qualitative, or presence/absence scales. For the ordinal scale, the problem is relatively straightforward conceptually and practically, because the situation is basically a weaker form of the correlation situation just discussed. Two regular coefficients are available: the Spearman rank correlation coefficient r_s, and Kendall's *Tau*. Only the former need be presented in this chapter.

The *rank correlation coefficient* may be calculated by the same formula as r itself, although when ranks are used rather than a numeric scale, a simpler formula produces the same result:

$$r_s = 1 - \frac{6 \Sigma (X_i - Y_i)^2}{n(n^2 - 1)}$$

where X_i is the rank of x_i, Y_i the rank of y_i and n is the number of observations. Like r, r_s will fall between -1 and $+1$ and will have a similar general meaning.

An example where this coefficient is appropriate is in comparing the ordering of assemblages given by a stratigraphy, with ordering inferred from seriation (using different categories of information as a basis for the seriation). Table 9.14 gives a series of such rank correlations for assemblages at Ksar Akil (Azoury and Hodson 1973). This table in fact reports, in a very simplified form, how closely changes in different categories of material are related with time.

Rank correlation plays an important part in studies where exact measurement is impossible and where, in a sampling context, assumptions of normality may be unrealistic. It could well prove of far more value in archaeology than it has done so far.

In passing from ordinal to nominal data, the problem of association becomes rather less straightforward. Archaeologists have regularly involved themselves in estimating association between qualitative attributes, and in fact a mystique of 'attribute analysis' has grown up which apparently attempts to solve general problems of classification by starting from such estimates. The classification aspects of this approach are criticised in the next chapter, and some preliminary difficulties have already been mentioned: the failure to distinguish between attribute and attribute state, and between different scales of measurement. A further difficulty stems from the failure to distinguish between measures of the *significance* and measures of the *intensity* of association (see section 3.15).

Archaeological situations where a measure of association might seem useful could be such as the following. In a given palaeolithic assemblage of a hundred tools, three attributes might be considered of interest:

    1. the technology of the blanks on which the tools were made, whether (a) Levallois, or (b) non-Levallois;

    2. the material of which they were made, whether (a) obsidian, or (b) flint;

    3. the general class to which they belong, whether (a) scraper, (b) burin, or (c) point.

To what extent were these three attributes related? For example was technology (1) more closely associated with (2) raw material or (3) a functional end product? Was choice of raw material (2) more closely associated with (1) technique of production or (3) end product? To answer this question three estimates of association are required between 1 and 2, 1 and 3, 2 and 3. (The same example could apply to pottery with (1) representing technology: handmade or wheel-made; (2) material: grit or shell tempered clay; (3) functional shape: bowl, cup, storage jar. Here interest could centre on whether technology (1) were more closely associated with (2) a kind of clay or (3) an end product, and whether the type of clay (2) was more closely associated with (1) intended technology or (3) end-product. Again, three measures of association would be required). An equivalent, but possibly more interesting situation could be envisaged at the feature rather than the item level of study: for instance, the investigation in a cemetery of relationships between social status and burial ritual. Here three equivalent attributes could be (1) burial rite: cremation or inhumation; (2) sex: male or female; (3) grave design: simple trench/pit, stone setting or mortuary chamber. Again, a suitable measure of attribute association would be useful for investigating these and the many other qualitative features of graves in a given, large cemetery. A similar artificial example was given in section 3.14 to illustrate a significance test for independence.

Various potential measures of association have been proposed and are discussed in standard texts (e.g. Blalock 1960, Dollar and Jensen 1971). *Phi* is one of the best known. The formula for its calculation may be given by referring to a table of counts like table 6.2 although now with *attribute* substituted for *unit* in the row and column headings. (In other words, *a* will now represent the number of units with attributes 1 and 2 present, *b* the number of units with attribute 1 absent and 2 present, etc.). With these symbols,

$$phi = \frac{bc - ad}{\sqrt{(a + b)(c + d)(a + c)(b + d)}}$$

Phi is in fact equivalent to the correlation coefficient *r* for two attributes where the only admissible scores are 0 or 1. Like *r* and r_s, the squared value of *phi* allows intermediate coefficients between 0 and +1 or −1 to be given a clear, direct interpretation (for the proportionate reduction in error in estimating *y* knowing *x*, as against not knowing *x*, see above, and for more detail Costner 1965).

However, these advantages of *phi* apply only when the relevant attributes are dichotomies, like attributes 1 and 2 in the above artificial examples: it presents considerable difficulties when more than two states are involved, (as with attribute 3 in the artificial examples). Here, the upper limit of *phi* is no longer +1 as it is for dichotomies, and so the basic standard of comparison between a series of these measures is lost. In archaeology, multistate attributes are so regular that *phi* appears too restrictive for wide general use.

A modification of *phi*, Cramer's V^2, is available for the more general situation (Blalock 1960, 230), and has been used with archaeological data by Sackett (1966). V^2 is calculated as:

$$V^2 = \frac{\chi^2}{N \min (r - 1, c - 1)}$$

i.e. χ^2 divided by the number of units times the smaller value of (rows −1) or (columns −1). (For the calculation of χ^2 see section 3.16.) As discussed in the next chapter, we have grave doubts about the general context in which Sackett uses these coefficients, especially when they are used for attributes that are really numeric (see section 7.4.4). However, even in an acceptable context, the value of this measure is doubtful: it admits no clear interpretation for values between 0 and 1, and in a major discussion of these coefficients, Goodman and Kruskal state quite unequivocally 'we have been unable to find any convincing published defense of chi-square-like statistics as measures of association' (1954, 740). A number of measures not based on χ^2, and possibly of more practical value are in fact suggested by these authors. Their *lambda* would seem relevant but we do not know of any archaeological applications.

More recently, a further range of coefficients has been provided by Information Theory, and some of these have been used by ecologists and archaeologists for classification (see section 7.5.3). These measures again were really developed and are intended for dichotomous attributes (cf. MacNaughton-Smith 1965).

It is important to stress that in this exercise the 'significance' of the various associations has not been discussed, but only their intensity. However, the χ^2 value calculated incidentally in computing V suggests a significance test approach, and Sackett does quote χ^2 values as a test of significance of association in his study. Strictly speaking, this probabilistic use of χ^2 assumes (a) that the investigated sample is a random sample of a parent population, and (b) that a null hypothesis of 'no *a priori* association between attributes in that population' is realistic. In most empirical situations in archaeology, certainly in Sackett's study, neither of these assumptions seems realistic, and the χ^2 value, highly dependent as it is on the size of the sample, is perhaps misleading rather than helpful if taken as any more than a very uncertain hint of the confidence to be placed in a measured association. It is interesting that this χ^2 approach led Sackett to the rather drastic steps of amalgamating attribute states and abandoning the accepted levels of significance (1966, 376).

This emphasis on χ^2 in case-study situations where a measure of the *intensity* and not of the supposed *significance* of association is required is more serious in those studies where no other measure of association is attempted, and where χ^2 is used in its stead (e.g. Binford 1963a, Fitting 1965, 1968). Further comments on the contrast between a test of significance and a measure of association are made on pp. 58 and 168.

A related but distinct situation is involved if each attribute *state* is treated as a presence/absence attribute in its own right, and if a measure of association is then required for pairs of these simpler 'attributes'. In the above artificial example, this would be equivalent to transferring interest from relationships between 'material' and 'type', to relationships between 'flint' and 'point'. At first sight this may seem to be a useful, general approach with a wide potential, since it is possible to reduce almost all data to presence/absence form if a really determined effort is made. However, very serious difficulties follow. The basic attribute (material, technology, functional class, etc.) will apply to all units studied, and a symmetrical relationship may be expected between these attributes (e.g. the degree of association between stone type and functional type is equivalent to the association between functional type and stone type). When the attribute is split up into its 'states' however, this symmetry disappears. For example, the association between *point* and *flint* posited above would not be symmetrical with the relationship between *flint* and *point*. Expressed in percentage form, 100 per cent of points may be of flint, but only 10 per cent of the flint tools may be points. This general situation is portrayed in figure 6.1. Here, v could represent 'material' and i 'flint'. It is quite possible to force such information into coefficient form: for example, the number of co-occurrences of two features relative to their total number of occurrences would give some idea of their relationship. A formula for this calculation is discussed below. This would perhaps be simpler, and more comprehensible as a measure of association than a χ^2-based coefficient. However, any of these expedients seems to be brushing the essential difficulties aside.

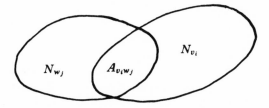

Figure 6.1. Diagram of the 'association' between two states (i, j) of two qualitative attributes (v, w).

N_{v_i} = number of occurrences of state i of attribute v. $A_{v_iw_j}$ = number of co-occurrences of v_i and w_j.

Fortunately, there may turn out to be few standard archaeological situations where such a coefficient is absolutely necessary. It would be required for the archaeological technique of 'matrix analysis' were this a valid approach, but this is seriously questioned in section 7.4.3. In his 'matrix analysis' of British beakers, Clarke (1962, 1970) based his published results on straight counts of co-occurrences of attribute states rather than on coefficients. This clearly weights common attribute states heavily against rare ones in estimating association, and because of the great range in the frequency of different states, is quite inacceptable. Clarke mentions (1970, 472) that on the advice of a mathematician he did carry out some other analyses using a coefficient of association, but simply states that the two sets of results were not very different. Referring to figure 6.1 this coefficient would be calculated for two states v_i and w_j as $A_{v_iw_j}/(N_{v_i} + N_{w_j} - A_{v_iw_j})$. This is, in effect, a formula for calculating the co-occurrence of two attribute states as a proportion of the total occurrence of both states. A glance at figure 6.1 shows why the last term is subtracted from the divisor.

In another empirical study, of Arikara ceramics, Deetz (1965) converted his qualitative data to presence/absence form, constructing pairs of asymmetric tables of percentage co-occurrences for each pair of attribute-states, which he called 'column percentage-grams' and 'row percentage-grams'. Deetz was evidently attempting to assess the intensity of association between pottery attribute-states in three successive phases of the Medicine Crow site on the Missouri River, hoping to show that 'association' decreased through time. Such a decrease, he believed, would be related to a change in social organisation at the site. These anthropological assumptions have been severely criticised (Allen and Richardson 1971). Deetz's treatment required the visual assessment of complex histograms created from his percentage counts. Using all of the information collected, this procedure did not in fact produce the effect hoped for, since the histograms for the earliest and latest phases were very similar (Deetz 1965, figure 13(a)). Undeterred, Deetz then looked for, and found, some categories which did support his convictions. A measure of association could perhaps have been calculated for the various pairs of pottery attributes (rather than attribute-states) in each of the three levels separately, and these measures compared with each other. However, it is difficult to think that this whole formulation has much general archaeological relevance.

Some of the difficulties entailed in estimating association between presence/absence attributes may be avoided either by comparing *counts* of presences of features using *r* or the rank correlation coefficient, or, especially in taxonomic studies, by manipulating the units rather than the attributes, i.e. by following what is often referred to as a *Q* rather than an *R* approach. This would apply to some of the studies where assemblages or 'lots' have been described by item *attributes* (such as decorative motifs on sherds) rather than by item classes (such as types of pottery). If a measure of association between such attributes *is* unavoidable, a proportionate measure might prove adequate.

Sherds and design motifs have been mentioned specifically since, in addition to Deetz' study just cited, some other well-known quantitative studies have dealt with data in this form. Longacre's studies of Carter Ranch (1968) have also attempted to infer social structure from the distribution of pottery motifs within a site. In view of the comments of Allen and Richardson (1971) and of Longacre himself (1968, 100 n. 6), these original social interpretations would probably not be taken seriously today. However, the general treatment of sherd and motif distributions requires comment. A good deal of emphasis has been placed on 'non-randomness' in the distribution of design motifs and other elements at sites (see notably Binford and Binford 1968, 85). However, once again, a null hypothesis of statistical randomness in a parent population seems rather irrelevant. In any case, the fact that sherds with given design motifs will often come from the breakage, in one or several locations, of complete pots, means that a realistic null hypothesis would *expect* the distribution of certain design motifs to be clustered and non-random. The intensity of association of given design motifs with each other or with different parts of a site, or both, would have to be established by more rigorous numerical techniques than those followed in the above studies. Once established, various possible reasons for the clustering would have to be considered: individual potters' styles, chronological styles, distinct styles associated with different functional vessels, differences in the size of sherds in different locations: these, and other factors, could all lie behind the secondary effect of differential association of stylistic features within a site or between sites, and would all have to be considered.

The recognition of patterning (as distinct from 'non-randomness') in the spatial distribution of archaeological units is an important problem, and one that is receiving considerable attention (cf. Hesse 1971a, 1971b, 1973; Dacey 1973; Whallon 1973). Although a number of interrelated problems are involved, the most basic is how to define distinct spatial units that may be incorporated into a regular analytical framework (i.e. that may be tabulated with other features, described by their contents and interrelated). The physical boundaries that usually define features (level 2 of figure 1.2) are now absent: they may have disappeared with time or perhaps they never existed (for instance if the associated activity involved a point source and a scatter rather than any bounded structure).

The imposition of a regular, arbitrary grid and recording counts of item classes per grid square might give some indication of 'association' between these classes, but it will clearly be a poor substitute for the recognition of true spatial patterning.

The archaeologist can achieve a great deal here by the careful excavation, recording and plotting of his data (e.g. Leroi-Gourhan and Brézillon 1966, 1972; Brézillon 1971). The human eye will then be able to pick out quite complex regularities in the distribution of single classes (clustering of various shapes and sizes, clines, etc.), and it will be able to compare these effects between different categories. Many of the numerical methods discussed in chapters 7, 8 and 9 are in fact simply attempting to transform data described in more than two dimensions into two-dimensional form so that they may be plotted and assessed in this way. Because spatial patterning may involve irregular shapes, and because it is two-dimensional, it will require very sophisticated numerical procedures indeed before judgement by eye can be bettered. It is valuable to look for such methods but not to imagine that they can be replaced by stereotyped tests of significance and the imposition of grids: these both involve unwarranted assumptions about the data and their structure, and could not in any case detect spatial patterns of varied, irregular shape and size.

After this digression on the definition of 'features' that have been and may be used as the basis for studying associated material, something further must be said about the interpretation of the measures of association themselves.

6.6.   THE INTERPRETATION OF CORRELATION AND ASSOCIATION,
       AND SOME FURTHER MEASURES

The interpretation of numerical dissimilarity or distance between units is
reasonably straightforward. However, the interpretation of correlation or
association between attributes is a little more complex. Very often correlation
coefficients, like distances, will have been calculated merely as a first stage of a
general multivariate analysis (see chapters 7 and 8). However, such analyses
are only as reliable as the correlations on which they are based; their interpretation also will depend directly on the 'meaning' that may be given to such
correlations. In other contexts, one or at most a few estimates of correlation
could be the end result of an analysis. From several points of view, then, the
archaeological interpretation of correlation is of real importance.

To take r first. While tests of significance for r as an estimate of correlation
may occasionally be valid in archaeology (i.e. if it is reasonable to assume random sampling of a bivariate normal distribution), r will generally be used
heuristically and various values considered and compared, starting with the
largest and working downwards until no obvious interpretation is possible.
For large correlation matrices, this could be facilitated by a hierarchical
linkage analysis (see chapter 7; cf. also Parks 1966, Hills 1969).

If units are at the item level (e.g. artifacts), and if attributes are
measurements or ratios of measurements, high positive correlation between
them will mean that units with a high score on one attribute will generally
have a high score on the other. Strong negative correlation will mean the
reverse: high values on one attribute will imply low values on the other. Just
how interesting the discovery of a high correlation will be, depends entirely on
the nature of the two raw attributes concerned. If they both represent direct
measurements, and if there is much difference in the overall size of the artifacts, high correlation will not really cause surprise: larger objects will
automatically tend to have larger dimensions on more than one attribute. This
effect is seen in figure 5.16, where r for length and breadth of the plotted tools
is 0.88. An example where very high correlation would be expected is for the
length and weight of a sample of British handaxes (see table 9.7). Similar high
correlations (not tabulated) result for length:breadth (0.80), and
length:thickness (0.81). For this reason, where the absolute size of units
varies a good deal, it is reasonable to convert most measurements to proportions of one chosen 'size' attribute. They should then represent *shape*
relationships rather than simply *size*. Roe's other handaxe attributes listed in
figure 5.2 would be of this kind. The one 'size' attribute may then be included
in or excluded from any further analysis according to whether both size and
shape are of interest or simply shape.

What now, if high correlation is found between such ratio attributes? This
may still have a trivial cause. For example, in describing the shape of complex
or even relatively simple objects by ratios of measurements, one attribute will

often be largely, if not entirely linked to another. A handaxe with a pointed tip will automatically tend to have a maximal width closer to the base than a handaxe with a blunted tip; i.e. in terms of figure 5.2 the ratio attributes L_1/L and B_1/B_2 would be expected to show strong correlation, as in fact they do ($r = 0.76$). This does not mean that in such cases either attribute may be subsequently ignored. The absence of total correlation shows that some units do not fall into the general pattern detected.

When such natural correlations have been assessed, more 'interesting' correlations may still remain. These will often be connected with general effects; the passing of time, for example, may affect two basically independent attributes so that they both show related trends. The crucial relationship is between each attribute and time, but this results in correlation between the measured attributes. Several high correlations between the fibula attributes discussed in section 9.1 appear to be of this kind. Other similar effects could be geographical or ecological clines, or social clines reflecting age, wealth or status.

In the experimental sciences, such independent variables would often be segregated or controlled by the design of experiments so that attention could be concentrated on one at a time, as well as on their overall effects. In archaeology, the nearest approach to this kind of control is probably to work with well-documented data from sites where known 'independent' variables, like time, may be isolated and controlled (cf. Rowlett and Pollnac 1971, and the studies of Münsingen and Ksar Akil mentioned in chapter 9). Often evidence of 'independent' variables like this can be coded and included as contextual evidence in a data table, ready for use in correlation or other investigations. Possible ways of integrating such evidence into numerical studies will be mentioned below in connection with assemblages.

Some of the most interesting and useful quantitative studies in archaeology have in fact started out from correlations between assemblage attributes, notably from correlations between pairs of tool types in palaeolithic assemblages. Here again, the basic meaning of a high positive correlation between two types will be that they tend to be well or poorly represented in the same assemblages. High negative correlation will mean the opposite: where one is frequent the other will be rare, and vice versa. High positive correlation does not of course necessarily imply that the *absolute* rarity or frequency of the correlated types is the same, only their *relative* rarity or frequency. In this context of assemblages also, high correlation may often be an artifact of the method used for preparing data and estimating correlation. For example, the absolute rarity of any category, its absence from all but a few relevant assemblages, will automatically tend to produce large values of r. This effect has already been mentioned in connection with McBurney's Ali Tappeh study (1968), where several correlations of $+1.0$ were cited for rare categories (see p. 144). Further correlation artifacts (negative correlations) have been discussed for percentage data, the usual form of presentation for assemblages (see p. 145). Assuming that these induced effects have been allowed for, remaining strong correlations between categories in a group of assemblages should prove of archaeological interest.

One obvious reason for correlation between two artifact types in this context would be that the 'types' were not in fact distinct in any meaningful sense: that they were the result of 'dissection' rather than 'classification' in the terms of chapter 7. This could be true if an arbitrary dividing line were drawn between straight and offset dihedral burins, or between straight, concave and convex racloirs, or between tools and micro-tools: Gravettes and micro-Gravettes, for example. Provided that the frequency distributions of the alleged distinguishing features supported these typological divisions, this effect could be discounted and another reason for correlation would be sought. Figure 5.16 (after Bordes 1967) shows such confirmatory evidence for the distinction between Gravettes and micro-Gravettes for one site at least, although we do not know of similar evidence to support the subdivisions of dihedral burins and racloirs.

As for artifact attributes, non-redundant correlation between artifact types could be related to various general effects. Obvious possibilities operating singly or together could be: *time* (correlated types becoming jointly more frequent or rare as time went on); *function* (the types performing the same detailed function or forming constituents of a combined tool-kit (Binford and Binford 1966)); *culture* (the types sharing stylistic features characterising one human group); *economy* (the types required for different functions but connected with the same general economy); *environment* (types suitable for diverse tasks but in the same environment—snow shoes and thick gloves, for example); the possibilities are in fact extremely diverse. If a given general effect of this kind is known to operate and may be quantified, its effect could perhaps be controlled, or removed by suitable numerical adjustments (the experimental control situation introduced above in connection with correlation between item attributes).

It must be admitted that little work has been attempted along these lines by archaeologists. One possible approach would be to attempt to remove the effects of a controlled independent variable, such as time, before correlations or other relationships were investigated. A relevant analogy would be the biological study of dimensions of a given species when age effects need to be removed. Delaney (1964) has demonstrated a regression technique for removing such effects. Another possible approach, which has been attempted in archaeology, is to remove the effects of an assumed general causal variable, such as time, *after* correlations between the other attributes have been calculated. A possible procedure here is to calculate a *partial correlation coefficient* (Blalock 1960, 333). McBurney and Callow (1971) suggest this approach, and provide an archaeological example where a series of such coefficients have been calculated. Their example is rather difficult to follow, and a more direct example will be given first.

At Ksar Akil, a sequence of early Upper Palaeolithic levels shows a clear development of types and technologies through time. It is possible to calculate the correlation between various types from their proportional representation in the different assemblages (Azoury and Hodson 1973; see section 9.5). Some of these types may be expected to be functionally and stylistically independent and yet to demonstrate strong correlation through their joint relationship with 'time'. It would seem reasonable to attempt to remove these time effects using the evidence of stratigraphy, i.e. to calculate the direct correlation between any type or attribute and time (represented by depth of deposit or level number), and to use this correlation to adjust the correlation calculated between the types or attributes themselves. The formula for calculating the partial correlation coefficient is:

$$r_{ij.k} = \frac{r_{ij} - r_{ik}r_{jk}}{\sqrt{(1 - r_{ik}^2)(1 - r_{jk}^2)}}$$

The symbol $r_{ij.k}$ represents the (linear) correlation between attributes i and j when the (linear) effect of k on both is compensated. In the palaeolithic context this could mean, for instance, the correlation between the relative frequency of end scrapers and splintered pieces in given assemblages when time effects are removed. As a practical example, values of $r_{ij.k}$ between these two and other pairs of types at Ksar Akil, with and without allowance for time effects (controlled by stratigraphy) are given as table 6.4. It will be seen that the first correlation (a) is considerably reduced, while others are increased.

	i	j	r_{ij}	r_{ik}	r_{jk}	$r_{ij.k}$
a	endscraper (ES)	splintered piece	0.83	0.73	0.70	0.65
b	dihedral burin	truncation burin	0.81	0.02	−0.28	0.85
c	backed piece	points	0.77	0.25	−0.11	0.83
d	ES on retouched blade	dihedral burin	0.83	0.42	0.02	0.90
e	ES on retouched blade	denticulate	0.65	0.42	0.25	0.62

Table 6.4. Partial correlation coefficients between types at Ksar Akil when time effects (k) are eliminated.

McBurney and Callow's application to material from Cotte St. Brelade, Jersey, concentrates on two aspects of the stone industry relative to time (given by cumulative thickness of deposit). The two aspects are: (a) raw material preference, and (b) gross metric characteristics of the industry. The intention appears to be to control for time effects when estimating the correlation between various aspects of (a) and (b). Unfortunately, the definition of categories for (a) and (b) are not kept separate (e.g. measurements on different categories of artifact, core, tool, etc. are separated according to material of which the artifacts are made). It is not surprising that the resulting table of partial correlation coefficients appears confusing and that relationships are quoted for such attributes as 'mean size of quartz per piece' relative to 'quantity of quartz per level', adjusting for the correlation between '? time and quantity of quartz per level' and '? time and mean size of quartz per piece'. More instructive perhaps would have been a partial correlation between 'quantity of quartz per level' and 'size of tools per level', adjusting for the effect of time on each.

In spite of the rather unsatisfactory application of the partial correlation coefficient here,* the idea of using this measure is important, and it could possibly prove of value in future archaeological studies. Other possible, though by no means trouble-free, methods of dealing with major effects will be discussed in chapter 8 under principal components and constellation analysis.

It is now possible to return to the problem posed earlier in this chapter: that of calculating distances between units when statistical correlation between attributes has been established. It will be recalled that in the general model treating data as points in space, the calculation of d depends on the Pythagorean theorem where reference axes (representing attributes) are considered at right angles to each other. Once we know that some attributes are in fact correlated, we may wish to eliminate these effects and to define another kind of generalised distance where the covariance matrix is used during computations so as to eliminate the cumulative effect of correlated information (Gnanadesikan and Wilk 1969, 617; Cormack 1971, 326). Here, distances turn out to be equivalent to Euclidean or 'ruler' distances in a space where reference axes are inclined to each other at an angle reflecting the correlation between the relevant pairs of attributes. The computation of such distances is tedious but quite feasible by computer.

However, as these authors and Gower (1970) emphasise, it is difficult to justify such a wholesale elimination of all statistically correlated information, since, as the above discussion has suggested, statistical correlation may arise from all kinds of primary and secondary effects which it would be quite unreasonable to discount: often, in fact, the analysis will be intended to reveal just such effects. There is no simple solution to this problem, but various general precautions may be suggested. The initial choice of attributes for any study should be made with care so that automatic correlations are avoided (i.e. alternative ways of measuring the same quantity should not be admitted). Second, it is probably always worth calculating and studying correlations between attributes even in an exercise where distances are the prime concern. Principal components analysis, described in chapter 8, provides a suitable method for investigating correlations over the whole of a given range

---

* Much more interesting results have now been presented by McBurney (1973).

of attributes, and for defining new uncorrelated, descriptive attributes should these be required.

A special situation arises when the units of a study are known to belong to quite different groups, even if they are described by the same attributes. In this case, it is possible to use this prior knowledge of grouping to determine which attributes discriminate between the groups, and if desired, to base any measure of distance on this discriminatory evidence. This approach results in a specific measure of distance, *Mahalanobis D^2*, with interesting properties, which will be discussed, with discrimination in general, in section 8.5.

One regular criticism of attempts to analyse archaeological data mathematically is the alleged impossibility of weighting evidence according to its 'importance'. Mahalanobis distance provides one clear example where different categories of information (attributes) *are* given differential weights according to their importance (for discriminating between defined groups). Provided that 'importance' can be specified in this way, it will almost certainly be possible to devise a suitable quantified scheme for weighting evidence in any data analytic context. The essential difference between intuitive and mathematical weighting is that the latter must be justified explicitly. Prior weights are not regularly attempted in data analysis because it is very difficult to justify them by objective argument.

Automatic Classification. Taxonomy and Typology

7.1. INTRODUCTION

This chapter is concerned with methods for transforming the unmanageable mass of individual units that form the basic archaeological record into a coherent body of information. 'Archaeologists consider phenomena almost exclusively as members of a class, or as they say, instances of a type' (Childe 1956, 6). At first sight the problem is straightforward: related units must simply be grouped together into classes or types and these classes used as the basis for subsequent discussion. And yet, this superficially straightforward task has proved one of the most time consuming and contentious aspects of archaeological research. Even if Chang's claim (1967, 71) that 80 or 90 per cent of the archaeologist's time is taken up in classifying his material is exaggerated, it would be foolish to brush aside the real difficulties faced at this very first stage of research. The inherent stumbling block is the complexity of the apparently simple concept of '*related* units'. However, this difficulty has been magnified by the stolid refusal of many archaeologists to define what they mean by 'class' and 'type', or by their providing a definition that does not really correspond with their practice. It is understandable that many archaeologists have felt sceptical about traditional approaches to typology, and that they are looking for more objective methods of procedure.

Archaeologists, of course, are not alone in their difficulties with classification: many biologists and other scientists have found themselves in a similar quandary. A recent, quite general response has been to look for clearly defined, numerical procedures for grouping units into classes: *numerical taxonomy*. Specific methods of numerical taxonomy are still disputed, but at least 'classification' has been discussed openly, and important distinctions have been made between different stages and aspects of the classification process. Attempts are being made to introduce some of the specific procedures of numerical taxonomy into archaeology and these form the basis for the present chapter. However, before discussing these attempts in detail, it will be necessary to summarise general concepts of classification which have been emphasised in works on numerical taxonomy. These seem to be fundamental to classification in any subject: for archaeologists they provide a terminology and a framework in which both traditional and numerical methods may be discussed and assessed. It seems far more preferable for archaeologists to start out from this basis than to attempt to deal with archaeological classification in isolation (e.g. Dunnell 1972).

7.2. NUMERICAL TAXONOMY: GENERAL CONCEPTS AND TERMINOLOGY

Although a subject of relatively recent interest, numerical taxonomy has already produced a large literature. In a recent review, Cormack (1971) estimated that more than a thousand papers on the subject were appearing annually. However, most of these deal with specialised applications and procedures: the general philosophy behind the approach may be found in *Numerical Taxonomy* by Sokal and Sneath (1963), which represents the first major landmark in the subject. A more recent critical review by Cormack (1971) has just been mentioned. These two publications form the basis for the following summary of major aspects of 'classification'. Unless stated to the contrary, quotations are from Cormack's paper.

7.2.1. *General definitions*. 'A classification, as usually understood, allocates entities to initially undefined classes, so that individuals in a class are in some sense close to each other.' A first basic distinction is made between *classification* in this sense and *identification* or *assignment* where a new entity is placed in one of a number of already defined groups. A further immediate distinction needs to be emphasised between classification and *ordination* where units are located in a series. Archaeologists refer to ordination in one dimension as *seriation* (see chapter 10).

7.2.2. *Dissection*. A further major distinction is made between classification and *dissection*, 'according to whether entities in one class are or are not required to be distant from entities in another'. A *class* is something more than an arbitrary division of material: 'Two basic ideas are involved: internal cohesion and external isolation. Sometimes isolation is stressed . . . sometimes cohesion . . . more usually both are included. . . . All collections may be dissected, not all classified. . . . Classification may be a technique for generating hypotheses, dissection not. . . . In most cases, dissection does not serve any purpose. . . . We want to cluster only if clusters exist.'

7.2.3. *Purpose of classification*. Two main purposes are generally stressed: the summarisation of data for descriptive purposes and a means for generating fruitful hypotheses. For example: 'to arrive at a useful description of the sample and to discover unsuspected clusterings which may prove to be important' (J. L. Fleiss and J. Zubin quoted by Cormack).

7.2.4. *Terminology*. In numerical taxonomy, the classes to which entities are assigned are called *clusters* and the entities *units* or *OTUs* (*operational taxonomic units*). The units are described by their scores on attributes (see section 5.2.3). Distinctions are drawn between different kinds of clusters. They may be required to be disjoint, or they may overlap (i.e. units may belong to more than one cluster). The latter are sometimes called *clumps*. Often a *hierarchy* of clusters is sought, rather than one level of clustering. 'In a hierarchy, the classes (clusters) are themselves classified into groups, the process being repeated at different levels to form a tree.' The tree may be represented diagrammatically as a *dendrogram* (cf. figures 9.9–11). The branches do not represent genetic descent but affinity between the units. A continuous hierarchy may be created by dividing the sample into progressively smaller groups, a *divisive* strategy or by gradually combining units into larger groups, an *agglomerative* strategy. Alternatively, a hierarchy may not be sought, but rather a direct division of the sample into a given number of clusters, a *partition*.

7.2.5. *Natural and artificial classes.* One of the most important distinctions made by numerical taxonomists is between (a) classes that have been defined because their members are similar, and (b) classes that have been defined because their members possess given characteristics. With classes of the first type, each member will share with each other member a large number of characteristics in common, but no one characteristic *has* to be possessed by all members, although of course it may be. Classes defined in this way are called *polythetic* and are regarded as natural. Classes of the second type, where each member *must* possess one or more characteristics, are called *monothetic* and are regarded as artificial. This contrast is discussed very fully by Sokal and Sneath (1963).

7.2.6. *Classification and keys.* A clear distinction is made between constructing a classification and a *key* to that classification. A key is a procedure by which a new unit may be assigned to an appropriate established class. Keys are probably most familiar from botany where their use for identifying plants is commonplace. Typically, classes themselves are defined on a wide range of features: the key simply emphasises those features that distinguish one class from another (Sokal and Sneath 1963, 58, 75; cf. Pankhurst 1970).

7.2.7. *Mathematical considerations.* The concepts discussed so far are all concerned with the general approach to classification whether a numerical approach is followed or not. When numerical procedures are attempted, it becomes necessary to define terms like 'sample', 'affinity', 'cluster' and 'hierarchy' with mathematical precision and then to find algorithms in keeping with these definitions. Since alternative definitions are possible, a variety of procedures result, but these problems may be ignored in this general discussion. However, it is probably necessary to point out that the nature of the collection to be classified is recognised to vary fundamentally. Some authors have been mainly concerned with the classification of units which are themselves samples drawn from populations in the statistical sense. The ultimate aim of the study is to classify the populations. A good example is the classification of tribes in India (e.g. Rao 1971). The book by Jardine and Sibson (1971) on *Mathematical Taxonomy* is largely concerned with this situation.

A rather different and more general situation occurs where the data have not been 'sampled' by accepted statistical procedures but are regarded *as* the population or the best available reflection of it (see section 5.2.2). This leads to important differences in possible approach. M. G. Kendall (1971, 359) comments:

> 'In a number of cases we know the whole population—for example if we try to classify British towns. Furthermore when we do have a sample, it is usually not a random sample . . . and so probabilistic tests of significance seem to us for the most part inappropriate.'

Even without such statistical connotations, the clear definition of the sample of units to be classified, and a statement of the universe or target population to which it is supposed to refer are vital.

7.3.   TRADITIONAL APPROACHES TO TAXONOMY

The general comments of the last section should provide a background and terminology for discussing traditional approaches to classification in archaeology, the theme of this present section. By traditional will be understood non-mathematical.

There do seem to be some definite differences in approach to classification between Old and New World archaeologists, and opinions from the two areas will be discussed separately.

For the Old World, Gordon Childe provides a suitable introduction: he is not only generally recognised to have been one of the great practitioners of archaeology, but he was prepared to discuss his methodology at length in *Piecing Together the Past* (Childe 1956). The page numbers quoted here refer to this book. Childe operated at two basic taxonomic levels: 'cultures' and 'types'. His definition of a culture was clear: 'a recurrent assemblage of archaeological types' (e.g. pp. 15, 33). He adds that types are found repeatedly associated together just because they result from the behaviour pattern standardised within one and the same society. This, in essence, was Childe's methodology for proceeding from raw data via types and then cultures to 'people'.

He made three important points about classification at the culture level:

1. 'Not all types to be assigned to a culture need occur in every assemblage constituent of that culture' (p. 33).

2. 'Least of all is an archaeological culture characterised by a few type-fossils. Yet these type-fossils are the sole marks by which a

culture can be recognised and distinguished from another' (p. 34). It is interesting that he added: 'the archaeological concept of a culture is largely statistical' (p. 34), and 'no doubt a quantitative element must enter into any definition of a culture' (p. 122).

> 3. 'The totality of genetically related cultures constitutes the simplest case of what I propose to designate a *cycle* (of cultures) or culture cycle. A more objective definition would be: "All cultures characterised by the same families of types belong to the same cycle"' (p. 142).

Point 1 above hints at a polythetic rather than a monothetic approach to classifying cultures. Point 2 draws a clear distinction between the elements (types) that make up a class (culture) and those that distinguish it from others (type-fossils). This is the distinction between the formation of a classification and a diagnostic key discussed above. Childe's type-fossils provide the key to the class. Point 3 illustrates two stages in a hierarchy: cultures and culture-cycles. Childe also cited a hierarchy with more ranks suggested in a similar context by Pittioni (Childe 1956, 142).

When he came to the concept of type itself, Childe was less explicit, and perhaps a little evasive:

> 1. 'The individual members of each (type) . . . exhibit certain common features, repeated in . . . all members of the class. Archaeologists consider phenomena almost exclusively as members of a class, or as they say, instances of a type. They ignore that it is the particular peculiarities, accidental or intentional, that in fact distinguish each specimen' (pp. 5–6).
>
> 2. 'We accordingly sort our data into functional groups . . . then in each functional group we still recognise a vast number of different types' (pp. 14–15).
>
> 3. 'Things once lumped together as a group representing a single type are broken up between a growing number of types . . . each more concrete, defined by more and more distinctive characters' (p. 6).
>
> 4. 'An arbitrary element must enter into the discrimination of types. If statistical analyses are to be conducted co-operatively by several independent workers, the unit types must be very narrowly defined. The total number of types will then become embarrassingly large. Alternatively, using somewhat broader definitions, there would arise so many borderline cases on which no two classifiers need agree. . . .' (p. 81).
>
> 5. 'Many types, indicative of highly significant cultural behaviour . . . are useless for classifying cultures though of prime importance in describing them. Other phenomena, less significant in themselves . . . are found to be confined to a single horizon in several stratified sites and to a limited continuous area. Such phenomena have been used since de Mortillet as type-fossils to define archaeological periods and

cultures' (p. 33). 'The significance of a type as a type-fossil is proportionate to its improbability. Unluckily there is no reliable criterion for determining that by inspection. Still less can cultural probability be measured by a mathematical formula' (pp. 35–6). 'To be diagnostic of a culture a type should be (1) capable of ostensive definition (its formal features being reproducible diagrammatically) (2) exclusively associated with two or more similarly defined types, and (3) distributed in accordance with a recognisable pattern' (p. 126).

6. 'Types are just creations of individuals that have been approved, adopted and objectified by some society' (p. 9).

The first quotation suggests that the classification of types is monothetic: 'common features represented in all members of the class'. 2 and 3 suggest a hierarchy: functional class, followed by more and more detailed types. However, 4 seems to imply that the whole procedure is rather hit and miss. 5 draws a distinction between different types of type while 6 establishes a direct link between the archaeological concept of type and its 'meaning' in human terms.

From some points of view, Childe's systems of classification for types and cultures are similar. This is especially true for hierarchies. However, in other respects, the approaches seem to differ, and, on the whole, the system for types seems much less incisive, and rather disquieting (4 above). Virtually nothing is said about the 'features' that describe or identify types (1 above); no suggestion is made of diagnostic features, for example, which would be equivalent to the type-fossils at the culture level.

Childe's approach has been stressed because it is probably the fullest account of traditional archaeological method ever attempted in the Old World. Many Old World archaeologists today, if they could bring themselves to describe their methodology, would probably approximate Childe's account.

Another major, and in many ways, contrasting approach to classification in the Old World is represented by F. Bordes and his school. He has essentially attempted what Childe rather briefly dismissed as the 'narrow definition of unit types'. The chief aim is the description of total Palaeolithic assemblages by quantitative means, especially by counts of types (see sections 5.3.2 and 5.4.3). However, the types themselves are recognised by eye without recourse to quantification. Measurements are taken for some groups of artifacts, notably for handaxes (bifaces), but basically to assist in attributing tools to defined types, i.e. as part of a diagnostic key (Bordes 1961, 50).

Bordes does not seem to give a specific definition of 'type' as such, but comments that the existence of types is suggested both *a posteriori*, after the examination of assemblages, and *a priori*, since tools were manufactured for specific uses even if we do not know what these uses were. He remarks also that modern tools are highly standardised, and that this was true of tools from Acheulean times onwards (1961, 77). 'A group of highly standardised artifacts' would perhaps provide the essence of Bordes' concept of type. One important element of Bordes' approach is that of a hierarchy already discussed. Another is the implication of a polythetic rather than a monothetic system of classification: a basic division of handaxes into thick and thin is suggested, but this feature is not expected to be inviolable. This may be seen explicitly from the heading in the main key to handaxe classification: 'II bifaces épais (exceptionellement plats)' (Bordes 1961). Most of Bordes' types, in fact, seem to correspond closely with polythetic clusters in the terms of the last section: they are clearly thought of as groups of objects both internally cohesive and externally isolated. Relatively few types seem intended as dissections, although, in our opinion, a defect of the Bordes approach is the lack of a clear distinction between clustering and such dissection.

In the New World, classification and 'the type concept' have been much more fully discussed, although often in the rather narrow context of potsherds. Thomas (1972a) gives useful summaries of and references to the controversy, for such it often is.

One body of opinion seems close to attitudes just mentioned for the Old World. Heizer (1967) for example, refers to a type as a 'homogeneous group of artifacts', and Ford (1954, 54) remarks that 'variation in actual artifacts tends to cluster about a mean that may be regarded as the central theme of the type'. Shepard's concept of a 'cultural type' (1956, 309) is again similar, although she regretted in 1956 that this concept of the 'thirties had fallen out of favour. She emphasised the tentative, heuristic nature of such types: 'a tentative hypothetical class to be re-examined, corrected and amplified from time to time as evidence accumulates . . . it is a category in the process of formulation instead of a fixed standard of reference' (1956, 315).

A change of emphasis is provided by Krieger when he restricts 'typology' to the definition of types that have a proved historical significance (1944, 273). This is equivalent to restricting type to 'type-fossil' in Childe's terminology. It is interesting that Krieger's sample description of such a type-fossil (of projectile point) also is clearly couched in polythetic not monothetic terms: e.g. 'stem: *usually* concave . . . ; edges *commonly* ground; base: *usually* concave *but* grades into a straight line . . .; blade: edges *essentially* straight *but* may be irregular . . . ; etc.' (Krieger 1944, 281; our italics).

Rouse's approach to classification differs rather widely from all those discussed so far in this chapter, and involves:

1. A change of emphasis from groupings of units to groupings of attributes (or rather, presumably, attribute-states: in the terminology of data analysis followed in this book Rouse's *dimension* would seem to correspond to attribute, his *attribute* to attribute-state). A type is a diagnostic group of attributes, 'the attributes which characterise the class' (Rouse 1970, 8).

2. A contrast is made between classification based on many or all features of the units ('analytical' classification, resulting in analytical types), and classification based on a conscious choice by the archaeologist of a few

features ('historical' classification into historical types). The latter are suggested to consist of a 'pattern of attributes which was implicitly or explicitly recognised by the people who made and used the artifacts' (1970, 9).

3. Rouse has introduced the concept of a mode, described as: (a) 'Any standard, concept or custom which governs the behaviour of the artisans of a community. ... Such modes will be reflected in the artifacts as attributes' (1960, 313); and (b) 'Modes are formed by classifying the features belonging to a single dimension such as tempering material, shape or design, and abstracting the diagnostic attributes of each class in that dimension' (1970, 9).

To Rouse, a type is thus not a class or a cluster of objects in the terminology of section 2, but a diagnostic key (point 1). Rouse's second point draws the important distinction between classifications or rather partitions based on many attributes, and partitions based on few. However, the implication that the latter are somehow closer to ancient peoples and their intentions is less obvious. The more general empirical view is that for any group of units, there are as many possible partitions as there are possible discrete or 'modal' attribute states shared by two or more units. Classification attempts to reduce this mass of primary groupings by recognising clusters of units which share similar states not of single attributes but of many attributes. One view of efficient classification would be to minimize the number of classes or types relative to the number of attributes considered. For example, if type A defined on shape is the same as type B defined on decoration (the same in terms of the units which each type represents), the archaeologist will naturally group the units into one type. This general type could then have both functional and stylistic significance. Speculation about specific versus general intention in the mind of the maker seems misplaced.

Rouse's use of the word 'mode' (point 3) again raises doubts. At times it seems equivalent to diagnostic attribute 'state' or 'modality' (3(b) above), at others to the direct interpretation of empirical evidence into an 'intention of ancient man'. Some of these ambiguities arise from the lack of an accepted terminology for classification by archaeologists. We have attempted (in section 2) to suggest terms accepted in other disciplines which could be so used.

Before passing on to attempts to classify archaeological material numerically, it is probably worth seeking some common ground between the varying points of view which have been cited (and also the very many that have not). In essence, the intuitive class or type in archaeology seems to correspond closely with what was discussed in section 7.2 as a polythetic cluster: a subset of units judged by their attributes to show internal cohesion and external isolation. In traditional archaeology, relationships between units (similarity or difference) are intuitively judged over a wide range of observed, but usually undefined, characteristics, each of which may well reflect a mixture of generative impulses (intended function, available technology and materials, stylistic tradition, etc.; see figure 5.1). If it is possible *a priori* to relate some observed attributes to specific impulses of this kind, it may well be possible, at the beginning, to divide the total range of descriptors into groups ('constellations') and to set up a distinct classification for each. Metal tools, for instance, are regularly cross-classified in this way by their metal content, their shape, and their decoration (see sections 9.1, 9.2 and 9.4). Such distinctions are often brought out by a hierarchy (cf. Childe), with functional classes subdivided into stylistic types. However, the real problem usually occurs when it is necessary to search for useful clusters at a detailed stylistic level: i.e. when it is necessary to define clusters of units such that cluster members are stylistically closer to each other than to members of other clusters when judged by most or at least a representative sample of their observed attributes. Many archaeologists do seem to think of types as such 'groups of standardised units'.

First of all then, any class or type must represent a morphological whole of some sort. To define such a 'type' it would be possible:

1. To enumerate all the constituent members considered; after all, this is what the type represents.

2. To summarise them by quoting an average score and a dispersion for each of their relevant attributes.

3. To list those key attributes that distinguish one cluster from other known clusters, but that do not necessarily describe it.

To restrict the term 'type' to this last rather special 'diagnostic key' sense (Rouse) seems rather misleading.

A second major requirement often demanded of a type is that it should have 'demonstrable historical significance'. This requirement may only be satisfied at a second stage of a two-stage procedure: the first involving the definition of hypothetical types, the second their testing (cf. Thomas 1972a). Shepard, as quoted above, has emphasised how contextual evidence available for defining and testing types is constantly changing. In fact, specialised types have often been used in the past (quite justifiably in our opinion) not to be tested by contextual evidence, so much as to establish this evidence (e.g. concordant distributions of functionally related but stylistically divergent types implying two phases of occupation, or seriation studies where the occurrence or varying proportions of types in assemblages is used not to test for chronological validity of the types so much as to establish the chronological sequence). The empirical solution to this circularity has been, in fact, to insist that provisional types ('ostensive' to Childe) should be as distinctive as possible: that is to say, defined over the widest possible range of relevant attributes. This is related to the distinction between dissection and classification brought out in section 2.2, and also to Childe's rather imprecisely expressed but clearly understood idea of the significance of a type being 'proportionate to its improbability'. If an ostensive type is defined over the widest possible range of attributes and represents a cohesive, isolated group, it is *a priori* most unlikely that it will not have some definite cultural significance. There seems no very good reason to exclude this as a type simply because its significance is not yet revealed. On the contrary, the value of such heuristic types can hardly be exaggerated. Where a distinctive type like this is concerned, testing for 'validity' is not likely to be so much a stage in its definition as in its interpretation.

To summarise then, it may seem representative of a wide spectrum of archaeological opinion and practice to define a type as the mean of a group of standardised artifacts. Standardisation may be judged overall, or over a given aspect only (e.g. functional, technological, stylistic); however, it would be expected that the more attributes included, the more significant any type would be and the simpler the total classification.

At the level of cultures or, rather, complexes, Childe's definition ('a recurrent assemblage of archaeological types') would probably be generally accepted. Some of these types would be diagnostic, key types (Childe's type-fossils) useful for discriminating one complex from another. Others would be useful in understanding the complex as a whole. Types would of course include sites, structures and economic features, as well as simpler artifacts.

It is always possible that given data may not form natural clusters at all: they may reveal continuity rather than discontinuities. If this is shown to be so, it is clearly better to admit it, and to locate units or assemblages in a spatial configuration (such as a scatter diagram) rather than to dissect them into artificial clusters. However, it is probably fair to say that in most empirical situations, both clustering and ordering are there to be found and interpreted.

Referring back to section 2, and to general aspects of classification, the main confusions in archaeological taxonomy have been between: (a) clustering and ordination or seriation (both sometimes called 'typology'); (b) dissection and classification, the product of both being called types; (c) classification and the key to a classification; (d) attribute and attribute-state; (e) whether any given feature is or is not required to be found in every member of a class (monothetic versus polythetic classes); (f) classification of units into groups or attributes into groups; (g) whether types can be fixed once and for all, or whether their definition will change as the universe for which the classification is intended changes. Whether numerical procedures are attempted or not, it seems reasonable to hope that archaeologists could be specific about such basic elements of their trade.

7.4. Attribute Analysis

7.4.1. *Introduction.* However brief and selective the commentary just given on non-numerical classification as practised by archaeologists, it has probably been sufficient to demonstrate disagreement and an absence of clear statements about classification as understood by archaeologists. It is not surprising that many archaeologists have felt that defined numerical procedures should be investigated in the hope of bringing some discipline into this morass of intuition and claimed expertise. The rest of this chapter attempts to describe and illustrate the main numerical approaches that have been used to divide archaeological units into classes. All are considered by us as experimental and most as unsound numerically and inappropriate archaeologically. However, by forcing archaeologists to specify their data and procedures they have already performed a valuable service and must continue to do so. Some of the methods do now seem to be approaching what is required of them.

7.4.2. Spaulding's approach. The first serious attempt to find a rationale for numerical typology in archaeology was made by A. C. Spaulding in 1953. He attempted a definition for 'type' that could be accepted on archaeological grounds and that at the same time could be formulated mathematically. His definition of an artifact type was 'a group of artifacts exhibiting a consistent assemblage of attributes whose combined properties give a characteristic pattern'. He continues: 'This implies that, even within a context of quite similar artifacts, classification into types is a process of discovery of combinations of attributes favoured by the makers of the artifacts, not an arbitrary procedure of the classifier.' The difficulty was to find a numerical approach, an algorithm, that would lead to the segregation of units into types corresponding with this definition. Spaulding took a very natural step: 'There seems little doubt that the best approach to these problems involves a search of statistical literature for appropriate methods' (1953, 305). Here was the real difficulty: no 'appropriate statistical methods' existed. Probably the only paper of real value to Spaulding at this time would have been T. Sørensen's in the Danish journal *Biologiske Skrifter* for 1948. But this would have required an immense search. Spaulding was looking for his method a decade before Sokal and Sneath's *Numerical Taxonomy*. Even so, in these conditions, wide consultation with practising multivariate statisticians might have proved more profitable than a search of the literature.

The method that Spaulding did choose from the literature was the χ^2 test of significance between pairs of dichotomous (in fact alternative-state) attributes (see sections 3.14, 3.15, 6.5). For any such pair, assuming that they were independent and that the units were a random sample from an enumerated population, the test would enable the archaeologist to reject the null hypothesis of 'no statistical association' in the assumed parent population between the two attributes at a given level of confidence. Spaulding concluded that a 'significant association' of this kind demonstrated the existence of a type.

It is perhaps unfortunate that Spaulding's formulation has had such an influence in New World archaeology. The definition of a type as a 'non-random attribute cluster' has in fact become a major element in the mythology of the 'New Archaeology' (e.g. Watson *et al.* 1970, Hill and Evans 1972). Not only is the significance test approach to case-study classification misleading (see sections 3.15, 5.2.2, 6.5, and cf. Robinson and Brainerd 1952), but the whole emphasis on attribute association or correlation draws attention away from the real meaning of 'type' or 'class' or 'cluster' which is concerned with 'discreteness' or 'modality' whether in one attribute or in many. This contrast will become clearer in the following discussion.

Apart from this, in our opinion, basic misconception, the major difficulties of Spaulding's original approach then involve:

1. χ^2 as a suitable measure of association, for this is what would be required (see sections 3.15 and 6.5).

2. The fundamental difference between statistical association and archaeologically meaningful association (see section 6.6).

3. The extension of this approach to deal with more than a very few attributes. After all, Spaulding's own definition included 'assemblage of attributes whose combined properties . . .'

4. The extension of the approach to deal satisfactorily with numeric attributes (e.g. to measurements, ratios and general size and shape descriptors).

5. The requirement of polythetic grouping.

Spaulding did not really deal with any of these immediate complications. The remaining experiments discussed in this section represent attempts to deal with one or two of these five specific objections, although not with the basic objection: that attribute clusters are not the essence of types.

7.4.3. *'Matrix Analysis'*. Although the term 'matrix analysis' could refer to any number of analytical procedures, it has become associated in archaeology with a procedure first suggested and practised by Tugby (1958). This attempted to deal with difficulties 3 and 4 above. Spaulding's definition of type was accepted in its essentials (Tugby 1958, 27) and an attempt was made to define such types from a sample of 135 Australian stone choppers and axes. The description of these specimens involved a number of continuous measurements (length, width, thickness, weight, edge curvature estimated by a radius, etc.). Although most of these were rejected before attempting the analysis, the radius variable was retained and simply split into three 'categories', i.e. states. The inadvisability of this procedure has already been emphasised in section 5.3.2 and will be discussed further below. Other attributes were mainly qualitative multistate (surface: flaked, hammered or cortex retained, for example); no attempt was made to retain variables expressing general shape or size, surely a rather drastic step.

The first stage in the analysis was to record in a symmetric matrix the number of times each trait occurred with each other. These counts were used directly as measures of association between traits. Clearly this was no answer to the first objection above, and simply ignored the need for a measurement of association altogether. Common traits would automatically be 'associated' more highly with other common traits than with rare. Spaulding's χ^2 measure, although inappropriate, was clearly better than this. There then followed a 'matrix analysis' of the kind suggested by Brainerd and Robinson for recovering a seriation of units (see chapter 10). This was inappropriate for distinguishing disjoint clusters or types, and should have been used with a coefficient of some sort (such as Robinson's, see section 6.3) and not with raw counts. However, Tugby felt that he was able to distinguish the existence of two major and three minor 'percepta'. Whether these were finally regarded as 'types' is not apparent.

Clarke's 'matrix analysis' of British beakers followed exactly the same sequence of rather dubious steps as Tugby's. Quantitative attributes were debased into non-ordered categories, and direct counts of the co-occurrence of such categories and traits were recorded in a matrix (Clarke 1962). This was then 'ordered' on the Brainerd and Robinson principle for seriation. The chief interest of Clarke's exercise was the use of a computer program to carry out this procedure, even if the procedure itself was inappropriate. Clarke too claimed that this series of steps was able to produce a meaningful classification of beakers. It could not be claimed that 'matrix analysis' had dealt satisfactorily with difficulties 3 and 4 of the original Spaulding approach. Difficulties 1, 2 and 5 were not considered, nor the basic contrast between attribute clusters and item clusters.

7.4.4. 'Attribute cluster analysis'.

Further attempts, more closely related to Spaulding's original approach have been made to improve upon some of its more apparent difficulties. Sackett (1966) spoke of 'attribute cluster analysis' as a promising approach. This was demonstrated on a sample of Aurignacian end-scrapers. Sackett attempted to deal with the first objection above (χ^2 as a measure of association) by using not χ^2 itself but a χ^2-based measure, Cramer's V^2 (Sackett 1966, 368; see section 6.5). Unfortunately this question is closely linked to the problem of association between attributes that are not simply two-state, but fully quantitative. Most of Sackett's attributes were in fact in this form. Once again, Sackett split the range of a given continuous measurement into divisions and treated each division as a state of an unordered multistate attribute. It seems worth illustrating in more detail some of the pitfalls of this procedure. Figure 7.1(a) and (b) illustrates possible scatter diagrams of the relationship between two attributes length and breadth when judged by different units, say endscrapers. For simplicity, the attributes are almost completely correlated.

A glance at the scatter diagrams would show that, judged on this information, in figure 7.1(a) there is one cluster, in 7.1(b) two. Unfortunately, attribute cluster analysis as followed in Sackett's approach (and by Tugby and Clarke) could not reveal this. First of all breadth and length would be split into a number of ranges, perhaps three, as indicated on figure 7. A measure of association would then be calculated between each pair of attribute-states. Very high association would be found between L_1 and B_1, L_2 and B_2, and L_3 and B_3 for both situations (figure 7.1(a) and (b)). Provided that the sample were large enough, these associations would be statistically 'non-random'. It would therefore be concluded that three statistically significant 'types' had been discovered: short, narrow; medium, medium; and broad, long. The types would be a direct artifact of the method.

This example illustrates two important points: the *démarche* of splitting up the attributes into categories or states and 'associating' them is likely to be often, as here, a roundabout and inefficient way of discovering that the attributes are correlated. The more important point is that such correlation between attributes has nothing to do with clustering. This is one instance of our basic objection to the general Spaulding approach. Sackett himself realised some of these difficulties and dangers. He realised, for example, that much of the clustering he discovered was 'mechanical'. But to claim from such misguided results that 'this fundamental pattern [*sic*] is either obscured or even grossly distorted in the end-scraper typologies currently used in Upper Palaeolithic systematics, presumably because the largely intuitive operations employed in their design are incapable of systematically controlling the subtleties of multiple attribute variation' seems a little ironic.

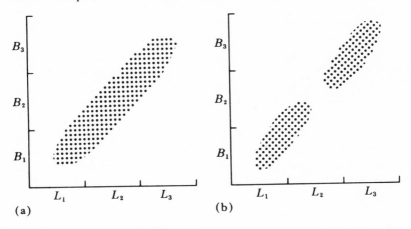

Figure 7.1. The danger in 'attribute analysis' of splitting a single numeric attribute into a series of discrete attributes.

It is important to emphasise that 'attribute cluster analysis' as practised by archaeologists has nothing to do with cluster analysis in the sense used in works on numerical taxonomy and as outlined in section 2 of this chapter. Ecologists have developed various forms of 'inverse cluster analysis' to find clusters of attributes rather than units. However, the attributes here are the presence or absence of given species in zones or quadrats: more equivalent to the archaeological level of assemblages than artifacts. Some of these methods will be discussed in the next section.

Benfer (1967) suggested a more promising use for clusters or 'factors' of attributes than direct artifact typology: groups of related attributes might be used to indicate independent key attributes of a given set of artifacts; this knowledge could then perhaps help in the search for 'types' at a quite distinct, later stage of analysis. These problems of attribute relationships will be resumed in the discussion of factor analysis in the next chapter.

It will be clear from this section that we do not accept 'attribute analysis' or 'matrix analysis', as practised by some archaeologists, to be a valid approach to taxonomy or, really, to anything else. They appear to run counter to both intuitive archaeological classification and to theoretical taxonomy as discussed by numerical taxonomists, and they embody specific statistical misconceptions.

7.4.5. *Conclusions.* Before proceeding to numerical taxonomy in detail, it is perhaps worth recalling the main general features of taxonomy as seen in both the traditional and this new approach.

The essence of a type, (or class, or cluster) is discreteness or modality shown by some units relative to others. This modality may be expressed by one attribute or many, and the attributes may be qualitative or quantitative. For very simple items, plain undecorated rings for example, a taxonomy could be based on one attribute only: diameter. Provided that modality in the measurements were indicated (by a simple histogram), a type would correspond to each mode. If three discrete groups of diameters were indicated, it would be obvious to define three types of rings. Very likely these would turn out to have a real archaeological significance (they could for example represent finger rings, bracelets and anklets), whether this could be proved by available contextual evidence or not. These types would be no less valid than any other simply because they were recognised via only one attribute: the units would be simple enough for this to classify them adequately. Practical examples of this situation would be the types of bangle and post hole implied by figures 5.12 and 13.

For more complex items (or assemblages), an adequate classification whether of one defined aspect, or overall, will generally need to consider more than one attribute, since an adequate description of any one aspect will require a number of descriptors. Here, individual attributes may imply different modalities (in terms of constituent units), or modality may only be detectable via the interaction of more than one attribute. For example, in figure 7.2 bimodality may only be seen by considering both attributes together: either one by itself would imply no clustering. For more than two attributes, the scatter diagram representation cannot be extended (see section 5.4.7). If this kind of modality is to be detected in multivariate data, other techniques are required. The human eye can doubtless sometimes detect multivariate clusters of this kind, for instance when they are concerned with shape patterns in a small set of artifacts. It will not be able to detect this kind of modality from overall contents of assemblages. For both of these multivariate situations (conflicting modality within sets of attributes, or multivariate modality), numerical taxonomy hopes to provide a solution. 'Attribute analysis' clearly cannot.

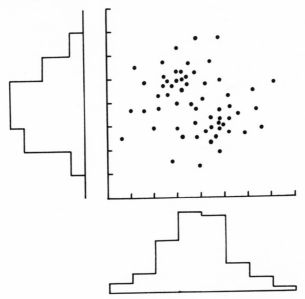

Figure 7.2. Bimodality detected only when more than one attribute is considered. Neither attribute by itself hints at the existence of two groups.

7.5. NUMERICAL TAXONOMY IN ARCHAEOLOGY
(CLUSTER ANALYSIS)

7.5.1. *General strategies.* In section 7.2.7 it was pointed out that different mathematical interpretations could be placed on the general concepts of 'relationship' and 'cluster'. These differences of detail, combined with alternative search strategies have led to a bewildering variety of procedures in cluster analysis. In discussing these techniques it is probably simplest to deal with the main alternative search strategies first, since these are readily appreciated in a general archaeological context. Suppose, for example, that there is a definite sample of artifacts to classify; say 300 handaxes laid out on a table (a situation which F. Bordes set himself in a published case study (Bordes 1961, 50)). How would an archaeologist classify the specimens into groups? The following procedures, with counterparts in numerical taxonomy, would all seem feasible:

    1. After looking at the whole range of material, the archaeologist might start by placing together handaxes that were most alike. First one pair would be formed, then a second; or the first pair might be enlarged, and so on, with groups gradually building up until what was judged a suitable number of

classes or types had been constituted. More than one stage in the sequence might be judged suitable, with varieties or sub-types, then types, then classes being defined. This is an 'agglomerative' strategy with corresponding search procedures in numerical taxonomy. Objects would probably be judged 'alike' over their total morphology rather than by selecting one apparently diagnostic attribute, and so the procedure would be polythetic. The archaeologist would probably then look to see which features were the ones separating the different 'types' at the various levels (a diagnostic key to the classification).

2. A second strategy would be to survey the objects as a whole and pick out what appeared to be the most striking attribute that showed clear variation: perhaps the presence of an S-twist, or large size, or 'refinement'. The collection would then be divided into two by this criterion. Each of these groups would then be surveyed and divided into two by further features judged diagnostic, and the process continued until a suitable number of groups had been reached. This is a divisive strategy: in fact monothetic divisive, since each subdivision is made on a single feature only. There is no need to look for a diagnostic key since this is given automatically by the procedure (the key feature which has split off each group at each level).

3. A third strategy would be to survey the 300 handaxes briefly and to pick out a suitable number of provisional, distinctive type specimens, say five or ten. Each of the remaining specimens would then be compared with these, and grouped with the one to which it was most similar. After all the specimens had been located in a group, each group in turn could be surveyed, and, if necessary, a more representative type-specimen selected. Further study might suggest interchanging some specimens between groups. Before long, the archaeologist might hope to have a series of stable groups or 'types'. This is equivalent to a re-allocation or relocation procedure.

4. If strategies 1 and 2 were followed, the archaeologist might find that after a certain number of rigid combinations or divisions of existing groups had been performed, the location of certain specimens might seem anomalous. He could then combine the technique of 3 with 1 or 2, reassigning specimens between groups at given levels to make the groups more homogeneous. If this were done, the rigid hierarchy of 1 or 2 would be broken: the grouping could no longer be represented by a continuous branching tree (see the next section). For strategy 2 in fact the procedure would no longer be monothetic at all and would become rather polythetic divisive. It is likely that much intuitive archaeological classification involves reallocation of this kind.

A search strategy, then, is clearly a major part of any classificatory procedure whether numerical or intuitive, and it will be convenient when discussing numerical procedures to group them according to the strategy followed. This is, however, mainly a practical rather than a theoretical consideration. Given (a) a suitable rationale for estimating relationships between individual units (in numerical terms an adequate distance function, see sections 6.1–6.3 and 6.6), and given (b) an adequate measure of the homogeneity of classes (a valid clustering criterion), it is in principle enough simply to enumerate all possible partitions of a set of units, to evaluate the clustering criterion for each, and to pick out for use the grouping with the best criterion score. In practice, of course, such total enumeration is quite impossible for more than fifteen or so units, and an economical search strategy becomes essential.

In this situation, a logical procedure for finding a hierarchical sequence of clusters is sometimes substituted for a precise definition of the qualities that clusters at any given hierarchical level should have: the clusters are simply justified by the reasonableness of the procedure that has found them (e.g. average-link cluster analysis, see below). Such clusters may well carry less conviction than those where both an efficient search strategy and a clear definition of the homogeneity of clusters are involved.

The question of alternative possible criteria for good clustering may be envisaged intuitively by imagining a number of handaxes grouped into a series of classes: is a given handaxe in a class because it is very like one other, a few others or all other members of that class? As this criterion is varied, so the overall classification of handaxes will vary. The archaeologist may complain that such questions complicate what is essentially simple and straightforward. Whatever procedures are followed, will not archaeologists always arrive at substantially the same classification for the same set of specimens? As archaeologists, we would like to think so, but we are bound to have doubts. One specific test of this hope produced from different archaeologists widely differing classifications of the same small sample of specimens (Hodson, Sneath and Doran 1966; see section 9.1 and figure 9.5). Usually this kind of embarrassment is avoided by restricted access to material and by the reluctance of archaeologists to change existing classifications.

The question remains an important one: how should an archaeologist classify 300 handaxes; how did Bordes deal with them? It should be possible to answer these questions, but the answers given by archaeologists would probably be diverse enough themselves to require classification.

The numerical approaches to be described are able to demonstrate what kinds of classifications may result when some different definitions of class are combined with different search techniques.

7.5.2. *Agglomerative hierarchical procedures.* The general strategy for this approach was described in the last section; however, many detailed differences are possible (cf. Cormack 1971, 330). Most of the procedures start from a matrix of similarities or distances, like a mileage chart, recording relationships between each pair of units. This is repeatedly scanned during the procedure and units 'similar' to existing cluster members are successively joined to them, until all units and clusters have fused into one. This kind of structure may be exactly represented by a tree or dendrogram. Each unit starts at the tip of a twig. Twigs gradually form branches until all are joined in the trunk (see figures 9.9–11).

Different trees will result from different estimates of similarity or distances. These have been discussed in chapter 6. They will also result from different rules for cluster formation. The simplest of these procedures is known as *single-linkage*, or *nearest neighbour*, cluster analysis. Here, at each successive stage of the hierarchy, a search is made for the closest pair of previously unlinked units, and a fusion is made between them. If the units are already included in clusters, the clusters fuse. A cluster of this kind corresponds with a consistent, simple notion of clustering: at every level of the hierarchy, every unit assigned to a cluster is more like one other member of that cluster than any member of any other cluster. Single-link clusters may be, in fact, like chains, with each member similar to its immediate neighbours (or neighbour if it is the end of the chain), but not necessarily similar to any other members. The two ends of any chain may be quite distinct.

Single-linkage clustering is of great importance because it is the only direct, hierarchical procedure that satisfies what some mathematicians regard as essential requirements for numerical clustering (Jardine and Sibson 1971). For instance, cluster formation depends only on the relative ordering of similarities not on their absolute values: whether Euclidean distance, or squared Euclidean distance, or the logarithm of either were taken as the estimate of relationship, the resulting tree would be for all practical purposes the same. This is not true for most other kinds of cluster analysis. From a practical point of view also, single-linkage is very simple and rapid to perform: fast, efficient, algorithms have been developed that avoid storing a complete similarity matrix between all the units, so that practically, very large numbers of units may be clustered by this method (Gower and Ross 1969, Sibson 1971(a)). A reasonable number of units may even be clustered by hand, provided that a preliminary similarity matrix may be calculated.

Unfortunately, chain clusters are not necessarily 'homogeneous' in the sense that is required empirically, and this method has been found unsatisfactory in ecology and archaeology (Hodson, Sneath and Doran 1966, Hodson 1970). Figure 9.9 demonstrates the lack of structure and uninformative chaining of the kind that this method regularly produces. Similar unsatisfactory chaining is seen in the single-linkage result for African cleavers published in Cahen and Martin (1972, figures 10 and 12). (These authors refer to single-linkage as '*méthode du minimum*'.) Nevertheless, because the method is so straightforward, it may well be worth attempting single-linkage with any new set of data rather than reject it out of hand.

A hierarchical agglomerative procedure that finds tight clusters is *complete-linkage* or *furthest neighbour* clustering: as the hierarchy is developed, a unit is allowed to join a cluster only if its similarity with all cluster members reaches the required value. This procedure is not as acceptable as single-linkage from some theoretical standpoints. In particular, the content of clusters at a given level of the hierarchy is dictated more by the configurations at previous levels than by any criterion for optimal, disjoint clustering. However, as for single-linkage, the procedure does depend on the order of similarities only and not on their absolute values and so has some theoretical advantages. Although it was one of the first methods of cluster analysis to be suggested (Sørensen 1948) it has not become popular with practising taxonomists, and there have been few archaeological applications. Cahen and Martin (1972, figure 14) have published a result from this procedure (which they refer to as *'méthode du maximum'*).

Johnson (1968) claimed to recognise complete-linkage clusters by the positioning of values in a similarity matrix that had been ordered for seriation (cf. Tugby 1958, Clarke 1962, Whallon 1973). Except in unusual circumstances (a linear ordering of clusters), the two-dimensional pattern seen in a similarity matrix could not possibly reveal clustering in three or more dimensions, which is the regular situation in archaeological taxonomy. It could certainly not reveal a complete linkage hierarchy of the sort given by a valid clustering algorithm. Since well-tried algorithms for all of these procedures are readily available (e.g. Wishart 1969), it would seem unnecessary as well as misguided to attempt to divine clusters via a matrix ordered by a one-dimensional seriation technique.

An agglomerative hierarchical procedure that has found favour with archaeologists and biologists and that also avoids chaining is *average-linkage* cluster analysis (Hodson, Sneath and Doran 1966; Hodson 1969, 1970; Johnson 1968; True and Matson 1970: see figure 9.11). This avoids chaining by allowing a unit to join a cluster only if its average similarity with all existing members reaches a specified level. Because of undoubted mathematical objections it is probably not a procedure to be used for a final result (Hodson 1970, 307), but it may well prove useful for suggesting a provisional result for improvement. An illustration of this strategy is given below for faience beads (see section 9.4).

Another way to avoid chaining but to remain mathematically respectable at the same time, is to allow clusters to overlap, i.e. units to belong to more than óne cluster at the same level of a hierarchy (Jardine and Sibson 1968). This leads to obvious complications and archaeological applications so far are disappointing (Hodson 1970). A result for the trial sample of fibulae is included (figure 9.10). Allowing one member only of a cluster to overlap already causes sufficient complexity to prejudice its value. In addition, chaining has not been greatly reduced.

None of these agglomerative procedures appears very satisfactory, and it could well be asking too much to expect a rigid hierarchy to be both useful and mathematically irreproachable.

7.5.3. *Divisive, monothetic procedures.* Procedures that successively divide classes by a single attribute at each stage have not until recently received much attention from archaeologists: any monothetic procedure would seem counter to the intuitive definition of types (cf. the quotations from Childe, Bordes and Krieger in section 7.3) and to the basic philosophy of numerical taxonomy (Sokal and Sneath 1963). However, ecologists have consistently followed this approach for classifying quadrats of land by the species present (or inversely, species by their co-occurrence in quadrats), apparently with satisfactory results, and recently Whallon (1972b) and Peebles (1972) have advocated this approach for archaeological taxonomy.

The basic principle with monothetic divisive methods is to find, at each point where a division is to be made, that dichotomous attribute most highly correlated with other attributes still showing variation in the group. The units in the group are then split into two according to their score on this dichotomous attribute (in ecology by the presence or absence of the relevant species). The degree of correlation or association between one attribute and the rest tends to be measured by summing χ^2 values (in one guise or another) calculated between each given attribute and the others that are relevant. The clusters themselves are successively subdivided by this procedure and the 'significance' of each subdivision assessed by further χ^2 calculations. When this value is judged insufficient, subdivision on that branch is terminated. Cormack (1971, 344) comments on this particular approach to clustering (association analysis) and related developments, and emphasises difficulties in using χ^2-based measures as measures of association (see pp. 58, 148 and Cormack 1971, 328). Here again, clusters at any level in the hierarchy are defined by previous clusterings and the algorithm for finding them, rather than by any general criterion for the homogeneity or goodness of clusters.

Whallon's archaeological applications of 'association analysis' dealt with Owasco pottery from the Late Woodland period (c. 1000–1300 AD). Slight differences in the classification resulted from varying the minimal number of associations between attributes considered, and between different χ^2 functions used to measure association. Whallon was satisfied that 'the resemblance between the statistically generated typology and the standard typology of Ritchie and MacNeish is striking', although this claim is hardly borne out by the published comparative table (Whallon 1972b, table 4). Attributes used by Whallon were not only presence/absence, but also qualitative multistate, and dependent. This is a departure from the ecological situation of independent dichotomous attributes (presence of species in a quadrat) and would seem to make detailed discussion of χ^2 as a probabilistic measure superfluous.

Whallon is enthusiastic about the value of this approach for archaeologists, but we remain to be convinced for several reasons:

1. The technique is basically restricted to material that can be adequately described by presence/absence or alternative state attributes. Whallon's extension of the method to multistate dependent data adds complications and still does not allow quantitative attributes to be accommodated.

There cannot be many archaeological situations where quantitative attributes can be entirely ignored. And so, even if the method were theoretically and practically sound, it would be extremely restricted in application.

2. We are not convinced by Whallon's dismissal of the polythetic approach to archaeology. His criticism of the Spaulding–Sackett method and his practical demonstration of its failure with this material are most interesting, but have no relevance to a discussion of polythetic methods or numerical

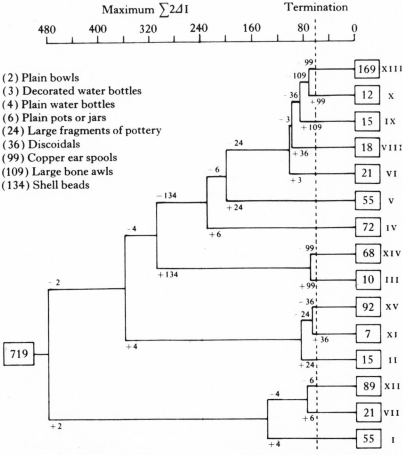

Figure 7.3. Monothetic classification of burials from Moundville (Alabama). Divisions are made successively according to the presence or absence of single attributes (− and + on the diagram). For example, the first major division depends on the presence or absence of attribute 2, 'plain bowls'. Division was terminated when fifteen clusters had been defined (Roman numerals); each cluster box then shows the number of burials assigned to it. $\Sigma 2\Delta I$ refers to the measure used to assess the strength of association between one attribute and the remaining relevant attributes (Peebles 1972).

taxonomy. Whallon's statement (1972b, 16) that 'it is clearly impossible to produce a tree-type classification scheme from these (Sokal and Sneath) methods' is manifestly incorrect. Nor does Whallon acknowledge the difference between classification and the formation of a diagnostic key. Rather than compare his procedure with the non-method of attribute analysis, he should really have compared his 'association analysis' with an accepted polythetic procedure (single-linkage or k-means, for example). When Lambert and Williams (1966) did compare these two approaches in ecological situations with true presence/absence data, the results were judged very similar. If anything, these authors inclined towards the agglomerative polythetic procedure which they used.

In a recent, related study, Peebles (1972) substituted a more acceptable measure of association (taken from Information Theory) for the χ^2-based measure used by Whallon. Figure 7.3 reproduces Peebles' dendrogram. He evidently had to exclude a good deal of the available evidence so that the monothetic divisive algorithm could be followed, but claimed that results were surprisingly good. Once again, a method that could cope with all of the relevant scales of measurement would seem preferable.

7.5.4. *K-means procedures*. The hierarchical algorithms discussed in the last two sections seek a continuous structure in classification: one cluster is always derived directly from, and contributes directly to another as the hierarchy proceeds. This has the advantage that a simple, branching tree represents the whole classification. However, once formed, a cluster can never be broken and its members redistributed with units from another branch. This can lead to anomalous situations for all but the single-link procedure, which has in any case been shown to be unsuitable for most kinds of archaeological data.

The idea of reviewing a classification at any step in the hierarchy, and, if it seems appropriate, reallocating individuals to other groups is intuitively reasonable (see section 7.5.1), and may be implemented in computer programs. These methods involve characterising any cluster by the average value of the scores of its members on each relevant attribute, i.e. by its *centroid*. This recalls Ford's definition of an archaeological type quoted in section 7.3. If, on inspection, a member of one cluster is found to be 'closer' to the centroid of another (i.e. is judged more typical of it), it will be reallocated. New centroids for the two clusters have then to be calculated. A complete run through the data, reallocating units where judged necessary, is called a *re-assignment pass* in the literature (e.g. Friedman and Rubin 1967). A marked practical advantage of the procedure is that relationships between all pairs of units do not have to be calculated, still less stored in the computer for reference. Only relationships between individuals and the current cluster centroids are of concern. This immediately lifts any rigid limit to the number of units that may be clustered in one analysis. (It is impractical to store similarity matrices for many more than 250 or so units, certainly for 1 000.)

A second feature is that for some of the regular measures of distance, this reallocation procedure is equivalent to an attempt to maximise some definite and appealing criterion for good clustering: that is to say, a mathematical formulation for the intuitive clustering concept of 'internal cohesion versus external isolation'. An alternative and more stable basis for the reallocation of units between clusters is thus suggested: a unit will be reallocated if the global criterion of clustering is consequently improved. A complete run through the data testing each hypothetical reallocation against the global criterion is referred to as a *hill-climbing pass*. After a number of such passes through the data a stable partition is reached where the criterion cannot be improved by reallocating any single unit to any other cluster.

The most regular measure of relationship between a unit and cluster centres so far is Euclidean distance (see section 6.2). The equivalent clustering criterion being maximised, or rather minimised, is *sum squared error* (SSE): the procedure is effectively attempting to minimise the total sum of squared distances between each unit and the centroid of the cluster to which it is assigned. A basic mathematical relationship establishes that this is at the same time equivalent to maximising the sum of squared distances between the cluster centroids. Thus the two intuitive features of effective classification, internal homogeneity and external isolation are embodied in this one numerical criterion. Usually this value is expressed as a proportion of the total sum of squared distances between each unit and the centroid for the whole sample.

Provided that Euclidean distance seems to be an appropriate measure of relationships within the data, this approach has obvious attractions. If other estimates of distance between units and cluster centres (or cluster 'profiles' if the data are qualitative) are preferred, it is possible to improve the homogeneity of clusters by reassignment passes, even if it is not clear which, if any, global criterion of clustering is being maximised.

Unfortunately, a serious difficulty is involved in attempts to maximise mathematical criteria by this kind of iterative computer procedure. (A similar difficulty will be encountered with non-metric multidimensional scaling, see section 8.6.) The re-assignment or hill-climbing algorithm may find a stable partition where it is impossible to improve the clustering criterion by moving any single unit into another cluster, and yet the partition may be far from the best possible. Since the direct algorithm can deal with only one unit at a time, the large-scale reshuffling needed to effect an improvement is impossible: a local not a global optimum will in fact have been found.

One regular solution is to start from a number of different provisional or even random clusterings, and after a number of stable partitions have been found by reallocating units, to pick the best of the resulting local optima in the hope that this is close to, or perhaps equivalent to the global optimum. Of course, it is never possible to be certain that a global optimum has been found (cf. for multi-dimensional scaling section 8.6). Experiments with the sample of thirty fibulae showed that a 'best' result at the six-cluster level was achieved only three times out of twenty-four by 'hill-climbing' from different random partitions. Some of the stable partitions that resulted were clearly far from optimal (Hodson 1971, table 1). As the number of units increases, so the likelihood of finding a true global optimum will decrease.

With ingenuity it is possible to devise stratagems for assisting in the search. One such that has proved satisfactory with archaeological data is described by Ball (1967) as the Singleton-Kautz algorithm (Hodson 1971, and see sections 9.1–4). An outcome of this algorithm is a series of 'best' results, with corresponding clustering criteria, for partitions at all levels from two to a required maximum. This information should give a valuable indication of a significant level of clustering. That is to say, by studying the relative homogeneity of clusters at successive levels, and by producing a graph for this clustering criterion against numbers of clusters defined, a clear level of clustering should be revealed if it exists. The solid lines in figures 9.12 and 9.18 show graphs of this kind.

In the ideal situation, such a graph would show a progressive drop for two, three, four clusters until the 'real' number of clusters was reached. The graph would then flatten as no further clear discontinuities were reflected by the clustering criterion. This idea of looking for a natural break in the data by plotting a graph of successive distortions and seeking a change in the slope of a graph will recur in the next chapter in discussing multidimensional scaling and principal components. Cormack (1971, 341) remarks that 'reaching a decision on the basis of a discontinuity observed in the data is well known to be a hazardous procedure. If the [relevant] set E is unique, then it is all that can be done. If E is in any sense a sample from a larger population, then the number of clusters or dimensions suggested by the first analysis can be treated as a hypothesis to be tested by new data'. The result of running such a replication in an archaeological context will be described for handaxes in section 9.3.

A further stratagem has been suggested (by J. MacQueen, see Ball 1967) and employed in an archaeological context to help interpret this kind of graph. The idea is to establish a comparable graph for certainly *non*-clustered data as a yardstick for the data concerned. The procedure is to 'randomise' the given data by dissociating scores on attributes from the units to which they belong. In effect, the values in each column of a matrix of units (rows) by attributes (columns) are randomly shuffled and the cluster analysis repeated on this new, non-clustered data. If repeated sufficient times, this procedure should make it possible to have a good idea of the significance of the clustering criteria calculated for the data in their original form. Table 9.5 provides the results of six such randomised tests for the thirty fibulae. Their clustering characteristics are consistent and differ markedly from the real result. Unfortunately this useful yardstick requires a great deal of computation; in fact each randomised trial is equivalent to a complete analysis. For large data sets this is clearly impracticable, and it may only be possible to run one or two randomised comparisons. However, judging by the result for the thirty fibulae, even one such comparison is likely to be helpful (cf. figures 9.12 and 9.18).

This problem of knowing how many clusters should be considered for a given body of data is clearly of great importance. Usually the archaeologist will have independent information to help in this assessment: evidence of space or time patterning for example; but it is preferable if at all possible to have some clear indication of clustering from the data themselves as a hypothesis to test against this independent archaeological evidence. One of the attractions of this k-means approach is the availability of internal tests for potential clustering even if these tests are still not highly developed. Similar tests for hierarchical clustering have been proposed, for example, by Sparck-Jones (1970) who demonstrates them on the same trial set of thirty fibulae.

So far, k-means procedures have been discussed in the fairly straight-forward context of Euclidean distance and related measures of clustering. However, theoretical reasons have been put forward for preferring a more complex approach that locates the units in a transformed 'discriminant' space, and that deals with Mahalanobis distances in this space (see section 8.5). The theoretical attractions are first, that Euclidean distance is very sensitive to the scale of the original measurements made on the data. This problem of scaling has been discussed already and will be recalled in the next chapter. Second, Euclidean distance ignores correlations between the attributes on which the measurements are made. Mahalanobis distance and discriminant space on the other hand provide conditions where linear transformations of the original data have no effect, and where intercorrelations between attributes are accom-modated. Friedman and Rubin (1967), who advocated this approach, were able to show that for a given set of trial data (Fisher's famous iris data) their procedure could produce a better clustering than those achieved by other methods.

Calculation of Mahalanobis distance requires the prior knowledge of 'groups' to which units may be assigned. Distances between group centroids or between units and group centroids may then be calculated using the knowledge of correlations or rather covariances, within these groups. In cluster analysis the *groups* of discriminant analysis (see section 8.5) are provided by a partition into provisional *clusters*. It is possible then to proceed, as before, by reassignment of units between clusters if a cluster member is judged closer (in terms of Mahalanobis distance) to an alien cluster than to its own. Unfortunately, the computations involved are heavy. This is even more restrictive for the procedure actually proposed by Friedman and Rubin, where a discriminant criterion is involved and where this is constantly reassessed during a hill-climbing procedure (rather than by reassignment using Mahalanobis distance).

Reasons have been proposed earlier why it might *not* seem desirable to eliminate the cumulative effect of correlated information in archaeological studies, and a good deal of uncertainty surrounds the whole problem. However, since in one of the few clear tests that have been made (on the iris data) Mahalanobis distance did produce a better result than Euclidean distance, and since discriminant space provides useful coordinates for plotting clustered units (see, e.g., figures 9.8(c), 9.17, 9.23, 9.24), this approach has been provisionally adopted as a regular procedure for clustering archaeological data when continuous variables are concerned. The k-means approach followed has been to reach an optional partition by Euclidean distance and then to modify this result by reassignment using Mahalanobis distance.

This more economical procedure reproduced the best iris result reported by Friedman and Rubin (using their discriminant criterion). The same procedure may of course be used to 'improve' a provisional cluster result provided by any other method. The faience beads example (section 9.4) represents such a modification of a partition suggested by average linkage. It has turned out in some cases that no reassignments are in fact suggested at this second stage of reassignment, especially when relatively many attributes are involved in the study.

To detect a suitable level of clustering for this discriminant approach, Friedman and Rubin suggested again looking for a discontinuity in the graph of clustering criterion versus the number of clusters. More recently Marriott (1971) has proposed a general criterion derived from characteristics of multivariate normal distributions, although he does not claim that this would rate all multimodal distributions as such (see section 9.3). He also makes the point that this kind of approach may well tend to find clusters of equal size and to split what are in effect simple clusters into two roughly equal parts.

K-means procedures in general have obvious attractions for the archaeologist: the possibility of analysing realistic quantities of data, and the emphasis on cluster *means*, thus making available information about the attributes of clustered units and facilitating the search for a key. In contrast, agglomerative hierarchical procedures lose this information in the process of calculating a similarity matrix. The reallocation side of k-means makes it possible to modify clusterings suggested by another approach, if necessary introducing features of discriminant analysis (i.e. resolving some problems of scaling and intercorrelation, if this is desired, and providing a key): however, reallocation procedures as such will not guarantee anything like an optimal solution for a given clustering criterion, unless the starting configuration is already close to a global rather than a local optimum. The complete k-means procedure described earlier (based on the Singleton-Kautz algorithm) may well avoid this problem, and it is quite feasible where a relatively small number of clusters are of interest. The search for a large number of clusters will tend to increase computation rather drastically, as will the occurrence of a large number of attributes, although here, the prior reference of raw data to principal axes (as described in the next chapter), provides a practical solution (M. G. Kendall 1971).

7.5.5. *Possible ancillary, or alternative approaches for cluster analysis.*
Contrasting methods for discovering clusters have been suggested from time
to time. One of these is to project the units onto a scatter diagram and to look
for clusters in the plot (Solomon 1971). If the data are not highly dimensional
(if there are few attributes, for example), or if the clustering is very marked,
plotting units via multidimensional scaling, or principal components (or coordinates) could well produce a very satisfactory result by itself. These
procedures will be described in the next chapter as versatile, general
procedures for 'looking at' data. However, it seems preferable where
taxonomy is the main interest, to carry out a special purpose cluster analysis
of the kind described in this section as well as a general dimension-reducing
analysis, so that the rather different information provided by both methods
may be combined (see figure 9.23).

Another ancillary procedure, to be described in the next chapter, is relevant to cluster analysis if it is desired to separate out attributes and to produce
special purpose rather than general taxonomies. Although little experimentation has yet been carried out, the 'rotational fit' technique described in section
8.4 would allow various subsets of attributes to be defined as constellations,
and compared against each other, against the whole set of attributes, and also
against contextual evidence (such as geographical location, stratigraphy,
associated faunal and floral remains). Final subsets of attributes could then be
chosen to search for taxonomic clusters. This could well become an accepted
preliminary to any archaeological cluster analysis and will be discussed
further with examples in chapter 9.

On the whole, relatively little published numerical work by archaeologists
has been clearly directed to establishing a taxonomy as such, even where it has
claimed to do so. Most of this work has already been reported in section 7.4.
One further series of analyses of material from the Juntunen site are of great
interest for some aspects of data preparation and quantification, but the
procedures used for taxonomy were not of the kind described in this chapter.
'The main purpose was to obtain types with approximately the same
characteristics as those currently popular among archaeologists'
(MacPherron 1967, 71). Hence traditional types were accepted at the start of
the analysis and diagnostic features derived and studied for consistency. Some
of the examples in chapter 9 show how types consistent with traditional
requirements may be obtained without starting out from them (e.g. the
Hallstatt swords). These results imply that numerical taxonomic methods,
suitably adapted to archaeological problems, should be able to provide
valuable classifications for the archaeologist.

7.6. Summary and Conclusions

Taxonomy has been discussed at length in this chapter since it is so basic to
archaeological research. The archaeologist is regularly faced with the task of

classifying great numbers of highly complex items. We do not believe that intuitive classifications by archaeologists are necessarily invalid. On the contrary, the visual appreciation of complex morphological patterning is a major human ability which it would be perverse to discount. It is certainly naive to suppose, as several archaeologists have done, that a relatively simple numerical technique will provide a better classification in this difficult context. However, it is also clear that the innate abilities for pattern recognition that archaeologists may possess are rarely controlled sufficiently for consistent, communicable classifications to result.

In this predicament, numerical taxonomy has a dual function: first, by making explicit the whole series of different concepts involved in 'classification', it should help the archaeologist to channel his natural abilities for recognising morphological patterns into a more constructive approach, so that consistent, communicable classifications are produced. Two obvious lessons which the traditional archaeologist may learn from numerical taxonomy are the need, before any classification, to define the universe for which the classification is intended, and also to make precise his views of 'type' or 'cluster'.

The second broad function of numerical taxonomy will be to provide classifications in those areas where unaided pattern-recognition can make no headway: for example, in classifying whole series of assemblages, each containing very many diverse items, or in classifying unfamiliar or complex items where conflicting classifications or no classification at all have been proposed. Although many of the numerical procedures used by archaeologists in the past to classify their material appear misconceived, procedures are now available which seem adequate for most situations. Examples of these are given in chapter 9.

Other Methods of Multivariate Analysis

8.1. INTRODUCTION

This chapter deals with a variety of methods for analysing multivariate data. Some of them, for example principal components and discriminant analysis, are procedures that have been known for many years but that have only become really practicable with the development of fast computers. Others, like non-metric multidimensional scaling, are the direct result of the power of digital computers, and have only been developed during the last decade. These newer methods tend to proceed by iteration, progressively maximising some goodness of fit criterion, like the k-means procedures discussed in the last chapter. Although the computer programs themselves may be highly complex, it is not too difficult to appreciate intuitively what they are doing, or for this to be described in comprehensible and accurate language (Kruskal 1971). The more traditional methods, on the other hand, depend on a body of mathematics (matrix algebra, see section 3.18) with a conventional notation and standard procedures that are very difficult for the uninitiated to follow, even when the mathematician goes out of his way to be helpful (e.g. Gower 1967). However, even here there is usually a fairly simple aim behind the mass of detailed symbolism. In this chapter we will try to concentrate on these aims and show how they relate to standard archaeological situations.

These procedures are all closely linked with ideas of space, distance and dimensions, introduced in chapter 2 and at the end of chapter 5. A first basic idea is to consider archaeological units as points in a space, where distances between points are taken to reflect differences between units. The configuration may then be considered a direct representation of the raw data. In section 5.4.7 we discussed how this geometric model may be treated algebraically and calculations performed in a space of more than three dimensions.

A second basic idea involves referring the configuration to coordinate axes. It is generally convenient for axes to be at right angles to each other; also further, that they should meet at the centre of gravity of the configuration (readily achieved in data analysis by subtracting attribute scores from their respective attribute means, see p. 137). However, the whole system of axes may be considered free to rotate around this fixed point and its location, for reference purposes, is at choice.

A geographer's globe provides a simple analogy: cities are located as dots on the surface of the globe so that distances between the dots exactly reflect distances on the ground. In a sense, all the essential information about the location of the cities is given by this configuration. However, it is convenient to be able to refer to places by a grid reference and so an arbitrary system of longitude and latitude has been agreed. The whole grid system could be thought of as lines on an artificial transparent globe covering the real globe, and free to rotate independently of it. It has proved convenient to fix this artificial globe so that one basic reference axis passes through Greenwich, but this decision was quite arbitrary. In much of this chapter, archaeological units are equivalent to cities on or within the globe. They are fixed relative to each other in a unique configuration by their mutual distances, but the position of a system of reference axes is at choice. Several of the methods discussed in this chapter are primarily concerned with making a choice of this kind.

A further basic idea involves 'simplification' by reducing the number of dimensions below those required for a direct representation of the raw data. Such a direct representation could require a separate dimension for each attribute considered. In palaeolithic studies, where attributes are often 'types', the original configuration may thus have not far short of a hundred dimensions. In this situation, the archaeologist is often looking for a structure of some kind, that is obscured by this complexity. In practice, many of these dimensions may prove to be (a) highly correlated, in fact providing the same information about the underlying structure sought; or they may (b) provide very little information, being made up of little more than the 'errors' that would be expected from inaccuracies of identification and measurement, vagaries of survival and so forth. By combining the duplicated information of (a) into new, summary dimensions ('components', 'factors') and ignoring the dimensions involved in (b), it may well prove possible to find a configuration for the original units or points that is much simpler than the starting configuration but that sacrifices little, if any, information about the structure of interest. Figure 8.1 illustrates a simple example of these concepts where three-dimensional raw data embody a one-dimensional structure.

If the number of attributes can be reduced in this way to a few important dimensions, it may be possible after all to produce a physical model or scatter diagram that can be appreciated visually, or at least to have a much simpler body of transformed data to deal with. As may be expected, it is often difficult to strike a fair balance between simplification and distortion. However, all of these approaches provide a measure of distortion (a proportion of the total variance or 'spread' sacrificed by the reduction in dimensionality). In any analysis it is clearly important to pay as much attention to this measure as to the result as a whole.

Before passing on to distinct procedures, the problems of relationships between population and sample, and of theoretical distributions, must be recalled, and related to multivariate studies. Corresponding with a theoretical frequency distribution for one variable, for example the normal distribution, it is possible to consider *joint* distributions for more than one variable (see section 3.16). Figure 3.9 represents a bivariate normal distribution. It will be observed that for each value of *x* there corresponds a whole series of values for *y*, which together represent a normal distribution. As here, the spatial model for a bivariate frequency distribution requires three dimensions. A convenient

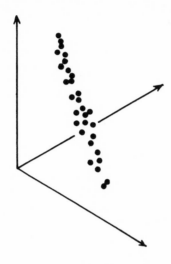

Figure 8.1. A basically one-dimensional structure seen in three-dimensional data. The three co-ordinates could be numeric attributes, the dots archaeological units located by their scores on them.

two-dimensional representation is to consider such a distribution projected onto the plane defined by *x* and *y*, with 'frequency' represented by density like the shaded contours on a map. Figure 8.2(a) represents a bivariate normal distribution according to this convention. The contours represent ellipses of equal density or frequency. The joint frequency distribution for three variables could not be represented in the convention of figure 3.9, but in the convention of figure 8.2(a) it would look something like figure 8.2(b), in fact an ellipsoid, rather like a squashed rugby football. As for studies of one variable, some procedures in multivariate statistics assume that the units investigated represent a random sample of one or more multivariate normal populations. For the reasons given in section 5.2.2, archaeological interest will centre on multivariate methods where such assumptions are not made. It may often be helpful to think of the units as roughly representing an ellipsoidal swarm of points in space, but the analogy will not have the precision that it would in the truly multivariate normal case.

The different methods described in this chapter result partly from different assumptions that the investigator wishes to make about his data, especially about the various scales of measurement used and kinds of relationship considered (linear or non-linear, for example), partly from different purposes: general purpose simplification versus simplification or

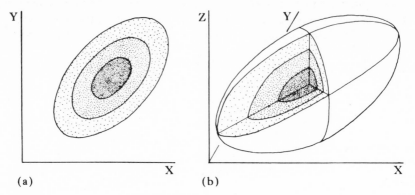

Figure 8.2. Schematic representation of bivariate (a) and trivariate (b) normal distributions.

transformation to emphasise a given structure already suggested for the data (e.g. to emphasise discrimination between two or more known groups). In all cases, however, an attempt is made to condense into few dimensions data originally described in many.

8.2.   PRINCIPAL COMPONENTS ANALYSIS

Like most multivariate techniques, *principal components analysis* may be discussed either in geometric or in algebraic terms. It is perhaps most easily introduced geometrically, but the method itself is essentially algebraic.

Suppose that, as explained earlier, a large number of points have been located in a multidimensional Euclidean space. Each point represents an artifact, assemblage or other unit. The space is essentially defined by a set of orthogonal axes together with the usual concept of distance. The origin of the axes is assumed to be at the centroid of the point scatter. The purpose of a principal components analysis is to find a new set of orthogonal axes, with the same origin, which have certain desirable properties. The chief of these is that the first new axis is along the direction of greatest spread of the point scatter, the second along the direction of greatest remaining spread and so on. There will be as many new axes as there were old. The new axes are called (unstandardised) *components*.

Often it will turn out that with very little distortion the points can be accommodated in the space defined by the first few components, and the remainder may be ignored. It is perhaps fair to say that this is usually the case for archaeological data. Figure 8.3 shows how variance is redistributed in this way in specific examples.

Algebraically, an axis corresponds to a variable. Principal components analysis therefore involves finding a new and often smaller set of variables linearly related to the old set (and orthogonal). A very important property of the components or new variables is that they are uncorrelated. It is possible, therefore, to regard the analysis as exploiting any correlation between the original variables so as to replace them by fewer and uncorrelated variables. If there are strong intercorrelations between the original variables, the first few components may be able to summarise them very effectively.

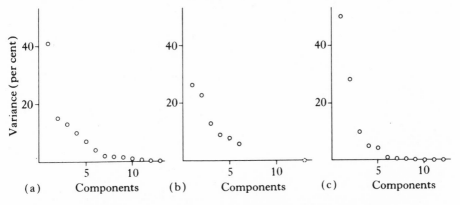

Figure 8.3. Principal components. Three empirical graphs of the percent variance accounted for by successive components. (a) Thirty La Tène fibulae described by thirteen attributes (see section 9.1.). The first component accounts for considerably more variance than the rest. (b) Thirty-two Acheulean assemblages described by thirteen types (data in Binford 1972, see section 8.3). Most variance is accounted for by the first *two* components which are of comparable importance. (c) Thirteen assemblages at Ksar Akil described by seventeen types. Most variance is accounted for by the first three components, each of successively less importance (see section 9.5).

In archaeological work it is often true that many of the original variables or attributes are correlated because of some underlying effect that is not being measured directly by them but only indirectly. The obvious effect of this kind in archaeology is time, and it often turns out that the first component obtained in an analysis does correspond to the passage of time as reflected through different raw attributes. Other general effects could be environment, function and so forth. The principal components analysis, then, may not only summarise data measured on many correlated dimensions by means of a few uncorrelated dimensions: those new dimensions may be directly interpretable in archaeological terms and may reveal effects that were hidden in the mass of unordered raw data.

The foregoing description of principal components analysis is, of course very sketchy. In particular nothing has been said about *how* the new axes are found. We shall now go into a little more detail, with the non-mathematical reader especially in mind, but with no pretence at being rigorous or comprehensive. For mathematicians, accounts of principal components analysis are given in all general textbooks on multivariate statistics, and in comparative accounts such as those by Gower (1966) and Krzanowski (1970).

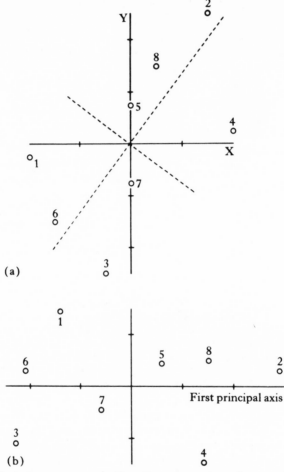

Figure 8.4. Principal components. Artificial example to illustrate the effect of the Principal Components transformation. The eight dots could represent archaeological units, the *x* and *y* coordinates numeric attributes such as length and breadth. The first Principal Axis or Component of (b) is found by rotating one of the original axes so that it passes closest to the points.

Consider an artificial example involving the variables length and breadth, as shown in figure 8.4(a). This is clearly related to the actual example reproduced as figure 5.16. The measurements of the units are expressed as deviations from the mean score for each attribute rather than raw scores, so that the original axes meet at the centre of gravity or centroid of the points. The disposition of the scores shows that the two attributes length and breadth are highly correlated. The first principal component is found by rotating the reference x (or y) axis so that it passes closest to the points on the diagram (dashed line on figure 8.4(a) and of 8.4(b)). More exactly the sum of the squared perpendicular distances from each point to this component is minimised. The second component has to be at right angles to the first (i.e. orthogonal) and since only two dimensions are concerned here, its position is fixed by the first. It is now possible to refer to any point on the diagram by its projection onto these two new axes.

In this artificial example, it is obvious that far more variation is now expressed by the first component of figure 8.4(b): in fact this new component (really representing 'size') would by itself reflect almost all of the information given by the original two attributes, length and breadth.

It is clear from this discussion and illustration that the units have remained fixed relative to each other: it is simply the position of the reference axes that has changed (cf. the analogy of cities and grid references suggested above).

Algebraically a component is represented by a linear equation relating it to each of the original variables. The above artificial example with data on two original variables x and y, length and breadth, would be referred to components by two equations of the form:

$$p = ax + by$$
$$q = cx + dy$$

The first of these verbalised would be: the score of a unit on the new component, p, equals a multiple a of its original score on length x, plus a multiple b of its score on breadth, y. The variance in the sample would be redistributed so that it was concentrated in the first component.

A principal components analysis basically consists of calculating the weights a, b, c, d, which are reported as a table. Usually the components are represented as columns and the original variables as rows: each entry will then represent the contribution of an original variable to a component (e.g. table 9.4(a)). This means that the components may be interpreted directly in terms of the original variables.

The calculations involved in maximising these combined weights for each successive component are extremely tedious and were simply not practicable even for modest quantities of data before the development of computers. In mathematical terms they require the calculation of the *eigenvectors* (or *latent vectors*) of a covariance or correlation matrix. Related to each of these eigenvectors is an expression of how much variance it represents (its *eigenvalue* or *latent root*). This is usually expressed as a percentage of total variance: only the roots and vectors for the first few components are generally reported. (The calculations involved with the simple artificial example may be followed by referring to Hope (1968, 42) who works with these specific values.)

A key feature of principal components analysis is that there is only one solution for a given set of empirical data. However, the form in which the data are presented is critical. As in many other situations already discussed, variables may well be measured originally in different units; different components will then result from different transformations of the raw variables. The most regular approach is to standardise each attribute (dividing by its standard deviation, see section 3.7), and effectively to find components via a matrix of correlation coefficients. This procedure will be illustrated later in this section. However, this is not the only, or necessarily the best way to proceed. If the scores are in percentage form (for example, assemblages described by tools), finding components via a correlation matrix is equivalent to giving equal importance to each category whether frequent or rare (or, rather, whether its variance is large or small). This may or may not seem desirable. At all events the standardisation of attributes during a principal components analysis should be carefully considered and not regarded as automatic.

Before proceeding to an archaeological example, an important variant of principal components must be mentioned: *principal coordinates analysis*. Unlike principal components analysis, which starts from direct scores of units on variables, a principal coordinates analysis starts from distances between the units. In other words, it is possible to find principal axes and to locate points on these via a distance (or similarity) matrix of the sort described in the last chapter. Eigenvectors of this matrix (suitably transformed) give the direct location of the units on principal axes. In this form the analysis has been called principal coordinates analysis by Gower (1966). This alternative approach may save computation time when there are few units and many attributes, but a more important practical advantage is the ability to proceed via a choice of distance or similarity measures; for example via the simple matching coefficient or the other measures discussed in chapter 6. This may make it possible to find principal components for data measured on mixed qualitative and quantitative scales, or with missing and conditional values where the calculation of any given correlation or association coefficient between attributes would be inappropriate. Where complete, continuous data are available, principal coordinates analysis via standardised Euclidean distances and the transformation given by Gower (1966, 1967) will produce exactly the same final configuration as principal components analysis via a matrix of correlation coefficients. However, as described earlier, a distinct advantage of the latter approach is that it provides information about attributes as well as units.

The following description of a complete principal components analysis should help to show how the procedure leads to results of relevance to archaeology. The same thirty fibulae used for the taxonomic experiments mentioned in the last chapter have been analysed in this way. Thirteen shape attributes are concerned (see figures 9.1–3 and tables 9.1–2).

Correlation coefficients are first calculated: table 9.3 (see sections 3.16 and 6.4). Latent roots and vectors for this matrix are then extracted by a standard computer library program (see table 9.4(a)). Each successive column represents a component. The lower rows in the table indicate the proportion of overall variance reflected by successive components. It will be seen that the first accounts for 40 per cent and the first two for 56 per cent. Upper rows record the weights by which each original attribute must be multiplied in order to obtain a particular component score. They are scaled so that they may in fact be considered as correlations (×100). These values may be plotted for pairs of components to show these relationships visually (see figure 9.6 for the first three, i.e. the most informative components). It will be seen for example, that attributes 1, 8 and 12 are located together, as would be expected from their high basic intercorrelation (see table 9.3). Attributes located far out from the centre of the configuration (i.e. with large positive *or* negative values) are those important for its structure and interpretation. Attributes close to the centre (i.e. with small positive or negative values) are not playing much part in the two-dimensional 'summary'. This stage in the analysis in fact provides one kind of direct summary of the information in the correlation matrix, and permits a low-dimensional representation of this summary.

Each of the thirty fibulae may now be considered relative to the components: its original standardised score on each attribute is multiplied by the relevant component 'weight', and the sum of these thirteen values gives a combined score for each unit on each component. These scores may in turn be taken as coordinates locating the fibulae on a scatter diagram where the x and y axes are chosen pairs of components (see figure 9.8(a) for the first two components).

Although a principal components analysis is often carried out as ancillary or preliminary to further analyses, it generally provides extremely useful information by itself. In this example, the first component may be seen from table 9.4 to be related to several original attributes, but most markedly to 2, 3, 8, 12 and 1. The negative correlation of bow height simply means that a low-scored (i.e. high) bow goes with a high-scoring (i.e. short) foot, etc. This component, then, represents a contrast between two extremes; basically fibulae with high bows and short feet and low bows and long feet. This may be seen visually by comparing the fibulae located to the left with those to the right of figure 9.8(a). Since this one component accounts for about half of the variation in the whole sample, this trend may be assumed to have a major importance. Comparing the trend with known contextual information it is clear, in fact, that it is reflecting change in time from one basic style of fibula to another. It is possible that this is not only a stylistic but a functional change, related perhaps to increasing thinness of material worn, but there is not enough direct contextual evidence to check this for this fibula sample.

The second component is heavily influenced by one attribute: length of catch-plate (value of −0.95 in table 9.4(a)). This component is, by definition, uncorrelated with the first, and figure 9.8(a) shows this effect in operation: fibulae with short catch-plates (low down on this figure) are not consistently at one or other end of the first component. They show a definite but quite different pattern: short catch plates at both extremes; long catch plates only towards the centre and the left. Contextual information again shows a chronological relationship, slighter than the first and not linear but circular: catch-plates are at first short, become longer and then shorter again.

The third component, accounting for 14 per cent of the variance, is quite strongly associated with the length of the spring (i.e. the number of its coils). Long springs are a rare feature, only occurring on fibulae nos. 2 and 14. A separate component has evidently been required for this feature and these fibulae.

This example gives a good idea of the versatility of principal components analysis. It has provided:

1. A diagrammatic summary of the relationships between attri-butes (figure 9.6).

2. A diagrammatic summary of the relationships between units, fibulae (figure 9.8(a)).

3. The indication of a major trend behind the raw data (40 per cent of variance accounted for by the first component), and of the attributes prin-cipally involved in this trend (high negative and positive values in the first column of table 9.4(a)).

4. A general transformation of the data where 92 per cent of the variation is compressed from thirteen attributes into six, and where the new attributes are uncorrelated.

The diagrams mentioned under 1 and 2, apart from their intrinsic interest, provide a useful basis for plotting the results of other kinds of analysis, es-pecially cluster analysis. The information from 3 will be discussed further in the chapter on chronological seriation, because this is one of the inter-pretations that may be placed on an ordering of units derived from the first few components. 4 provides a basis for further numerical analyses: for the rotational fit program to be discussed in section 8.4 and, perhaps more dubiously, for some versions of factor analysis discussed in the next section.

In view of its versatility and value, it is surprising that principal com-ponents analysis has not been used more widely in archaeology. The method seems especially well suited to the investigation of palaeolithic assemblages (Hodson 1969 and see section 9.5).

Borillo and Ihm (1971) have studied archaic Greek statues using principal components analysis and a form of principal coordinates analysis. They generalise these methods slightly in order to deal with incomplete data.

White and Thomas (1972) have also used principal components analysis as the major technique for investigating variation in dimensions of flakes produced by different flint knappers on different occasions and from different villages in New Guinea. Unfortunately a misunderstanding of the technique led to errors in interpreting the results. It was not realised that the attribute weights on a component are rather like correlations, so that high negative values and positive values are both important. In this study, insignificant positive values were in fact given more weight than large negative values (+0.18 for *width* on component 2 was taken as diagnostic instead of −0.91 for *edge angle*, leading to the complete misinterpretation of this component). Since this enquiry was largely concerned with discrimination between known groups of flakes, it seems in any case that canonical variate analysis should perhaps have been used as well as, or rather instead of principal components and univariate *t*-tests (see section 8.5). These most important field data would certainly repay further multivariate analysis.

Although it is such a useful method it is important to remember that principal components analysis starts from covariances or correlations between attributes, principal coordinates analysis from dissimilarities between units, and that they will be subject to the complications discussed for these measures in chapter 6: the disproportionate effect of extreme values, changes which result from slight changes in the sample analysed, effects of presenting data in percentage form. All these difficulties may be carried over directly from the bivariate into the multivariate situation.

8.3.   FACTOR ANALYSIS

Principal components analysis has clear aims and it produces a unique result for a given body of empirical data. *Factor analysis*, on the other hands, covers a rather wider and less straightforward range of approaches, each of which may well produce a quite different result. Since factor analysis has already become one of the most frequently used multivariate methods in archaeology it will be necessary to say something of its background and of the reasons why such alternative results may be expected.

In most of the archaeological applications to be discussed, factor analysis has been used implicitly or explicitly to find clusters of attributes. These clusters have been interpreted as:

1. 'Kits' of tools, where tools are the attributes of the study and their relationships have been judged by their co-occurrence in selected Mousterian assemblages (Binford and Binford 1966).

2. 'Zones' of sites where the zones are groups of Marnian sites judged similar through shared cultural characteristics (Rowlett and Pollnac 1971).

3. 'Types' where each type represent a group of artifacts related by their attribute scores (Glover 1969).

4. Clusters of pottery types, related by their co-occurrence in rooms at the Broken K Pueblo (Hill 1968).

In these and other archaeological examples then, 'factors' are generally considered as clusters, usually of attributes, although not exclusively (e.g. 2 above).

This is a rather different concept of factor analysis than that held by the psychologists who instigated and developed the method. In psychological studies, the analyst is seeking to investigate presumed general aspects of personality, such as intelligence, aggression and so forth, but he cannot isolate and measure these directly. He is forced to invent and apply tests that measure diverse aspects of personality at one and the same time. His basic assumption is that the score of a subject on any given test is made up of two distinct parts: one that reflects a combination of the general effects in which he is interested; a second that reflects performance specific to that test alone and in which he has no interest (for example the ability to manipulate triangles as distinct from any general visual, or comprehensive ability). Factor analysis was intended to separate these two aspects in the data, to discard 'specific' effects and to allocate 'common' effects between a number of general factors of personality.

The usual mathematical formulation of this model is

$$x_i = l_{i1}f_1 + l_{i2}f_2 + \cdots + l_{ik}f_k + b_i s_i + e_i$$

The f, s, and e are assumed to be random variables, all independent, with f and s having unit variance. The number of factors, k, is less than the number of attributes. A rather clumsy verbalisation of this equation is: the score x_i for any unit on any attribute i is made up of the sum of a series of factor scores together with a specific score and an error score. Each factor score is calculated by multiplying the value f of the factor in question for that unit by a loading l_i associated with the attribute. The specific score is calculated by multiplying the specific value, s_i, for the attribute for that unit by an associated weight b_i. Various algorithms have been proposed for fitting actual data to this model. Clearly they are not primarily intended to provide 'clusters' of tests.

The archaeologist is concerned to know, then, (a) whether the model and algorithms devised in this psychological context *are* able to provide him with 'clusters' of the kind he requires, (b) whether there are archaeological contexts closer to the psychological situation for which the model was intended, than the search for clusters.

Three main stages are involved in carrying out a factor analysis. It must first be decided how many general effects or factors are relevant. Then the information considered relevant to these factors ('common' variance) must be separated from what is considered irrelevant ('specific' and 'error' variance). The third stage involves distributing this common variance between factors according to a predetermined idea of the structure of mental performance (for example, according to whether general factors are assumed independent or correlated, whether tests are expected to measure performance on a few general factors only or on many, etc.).

Mathematical procedures tend to carry out the first two stages together (cf. Lawley and Maxwell 1971). Assuming that the data are a random sample from a multivariate normal population, it is possible, though difficult, to estimate by maximum likelihood methods, best fitting solutions for successive numbers of factors and to test whether a significant improvement has been achieved by the addition of each extra factor. The solution consists in allocating common variance between the individual tests (their *'communalities'*) and in estimating weights, or 'loadings' for each test on each factor, rather like the principal component weights discussed in the last section. In any solution, these weights, the communalities and the original correlation matrix between tests are interdependent, and the analysis is conducted so that the communalities (i.e. the amount of variation in each test attributed to general as distinct from specific effects) is maximised for a given number of factors.

However, the weights or loadings provided by this maximisation are not unique: the third stage is required to decide between any number of alternative transformation of these weights. In geometrical terms, the attributes have been located in a space with the number of dimensions equivalent to the number of factors. Each factor is regarded as an axis in this space, to which the attributes are referred. However, the orientation of these reference axes is arbitrary and rules are required to 'fix' them in some agreed way (cf. the geographer's globe analogy, p. 188).

A major choice is whether the reference axes originally calculated to be at right angles to each other (orthogonal, uncorrelated) should remain so during this rotation, or whether they should be allowed to become oblique (in the latter case they would be considered correlated to some extent). Other rules are required to decide the kind of final relationship preferred between factors and attributes. The structure most usually fitted is 'simple structure' as suggested by Thurstone (1947) which assumes that tests (attributes) will fall into distinct groups with loadings that are high on some factors, moderate to low on others and negligible on others. Computer programs have been devised to produce a best result from a given matrix of factor loadings in keeping with these rules. Such a mathematical artifact may or may not be considered a natural way to transform a given body of factor weights in a given situation.

The derivation of the original loadings, based on the separation of specific from common effects, the estimation of communalities and the choice of the number of factors to consider, has proved a far more difficult task. Efficient procedures for maximum likelihood estimation do now exist, but in the past and, generally still, various short cuts and rules of thumb have been developed to achieve an acceptable result with a reasonable amount of computation. It is these methods that have been used so far by archaeologists.

One of these, the *centroid* method, was developed before fast computers became available. It is discussed in some texts on factor analysis, although without great enthusiasm. Daniels' analysis of Transvaal Middle Stone Age sites followed this approach (Daniels 1967). A main 'factor' was rotated by hand to fit and test informally an existing archaeological hypothesis for the ordering of the sites.

A more regular approximation is to start from a principal components analysis, and to use the weights of attributes on the first few components (e.g. table 9.4(a)) as the factor pattern matrix (Binford 1972, Rowlett and Pollnac 1971). This is then rotated to conform to a chosen structure, usually 'simple structure' as fitted by the *Varimax program*. This approach will be illustrated on a trial example (see below). Various rules of thumb have been suggested in this context for deciding how many factors to consider (i.e. components to rotate): a jump in the eigenvalue curve, an eigenvalue of a given size (H. F. Kaiser suggested any eigenvalue greater than 1 as relevant), percentage of variance accounted for (e.g. 80 per cent). In this approach there has been no attempt to conform to the basic factor analysis model since no distinction has been drawn between 'common' and 'specific' variance: all of the variance concerned in principal components is considered 'common'.

Thus, although principal components analysis and factor analysis start from very different assumptions and with very different aims, the main difference in practice often hinges solely on a rotational procedure applied to loadings for attributes to provide what it is hoped will be a more direct interpretation for them.

There is much difference of opinion about the relevance of the whole factor analysis model to practical situations. For example, Gower suggests that 'the reason for obtaining meaningful results when using factor analysis in these situations [where the sample is not a random sample of a homogeneous population] is that the results obtained are often very close to the results obtained by a principal components analysis' (1966).

If clusters are really required rather than a principal components summarisation, the whole factor analysis model may seem inappropriate or at least unnecessary. For example M. G. Kendall (1971, 359) remarks:

> 'In spite of extreme cases which have been adduced, we usually have something like no more than fifty variables and it is easy to display the correlation matrix and to pick out the clustering almost by hand without any further mechanical methods. This I find in practice is quicker and just as effective as using principal components and going to oblique factors.'

Some of these points may be clarified by a fairly simple factor analysis of this kind (which would perhaps be better described as 'Varimax component analysis'). The same set of thirty fibulae may be considered. The analysis starts from the first stage of the principal components analysis reported in table 9.4(a).

To choose the number of factors to consider, Kaiser's eigenvalue criterion mentioned above suggests four. This is equivalent to deciding that only the information given by the first four dimensions or components of the principal components analysis will be considered. In a true factor analysis, an attempt would have been made to ensure that the rejected information was concerned only with 'specific' and 'error' effects so that all the information of interest would in fact be retained, but clearly in this procedure this has not been attempted. Instead, as much information as possible has been condensed from thirteen into these four dimensions by the principal components procedure.

The attributes are now considered as vectors in this four-dimensional space and an attempt is made to rotate the reference axes (the components), fitting them to a given structural model so as to make this configuration of the attributes more interpretable. If only two factors were being considered, this would be equivalent to taking figure 9.6 as locating the attributes (ignoring the arrows for the third dimension), and then rotating the coordinate axes in some way to make them more closely related to the attributes. This is the stage where quite different approaches are possible but the general intention is to rotate the axes so as to pass through groups or clusters of attributes. The Varimax program frequently used was applied here (cf. Cooley and Lohnes 1962, 179). It reports a transformation or rotation of the axes so as to keep them orthogonal (independent) and to maximise the variance of factor loadings by columns. This means creating loadings that are as close to 1.0 or 0.0 as possible, and in fact grouping attributes with given factors. The end result is a table of weights (table 9.4(b)) derived from, and representing an orthogonal transformation of table 9.4(a). They may again be considered roughly as the correlation ($\times 100$) of an attribute with a factor.

Looking at the factor loadings for each of the thirteen attributes in turn, it will be seen that some are now closely associated with just one factor (attributes 1, 4, 5, 6, 8, 12 and 13), others are strongly associated with one and less strongly with a second (3, 7), others are less strongly associated with two or perhaps more (2, 9, 10, 11). Looking down the column of factors, each except 2 has at least two attributes highly associated with it. The rules of the Varimax criterion have clearly been observed and much of the information redistributed according to its 'model'. This result is represented diagrammatically as figure 9.7(b).

An attempt may now be made to interpret these four factors. The highly associated attributes suggest: (1) a foot-length factor (I on figure 9.7(b)); (2) a foot-end factor (II); (3) an element-plus-coils factor (or a width factor as seen from above: III); (4) a bow-plus-coil profile factor (IV). In general terms, these could possibly be seen as the various parts of the fibula that could vary as units independently of each other. The secondary attributes generally associated with more than one factor complicate the interpretation and do not obviously add very much.

As a further step in the analysis, it is now possible to calculate a score for each fibula on each of these factors; this would allow the fibulae to be described or plotted relative to pairs of factors, e.g. foot-length and bow-and-coil profile, figure 9.8(b). Unfortunately, with more than two factors, a comprehensive plot is not readily available.

This example illustrates the kind of result that Varimax rotation of principal component axes for attributes may be expected to produce. The attributes have been divided into groups with main and secondary constituents (the secondary members often overlap), and a possible interpretation of these clusters may be given.

However, this is a rather roundabout, complex procedure when compared with cluster analysis as described in the last chapter. It is not obvious, for example, what purpose is served in a search for clusters by rejecting a given proportion of relevant information in the correlation matrix *before* Varimax clusters are sought.

Since the correlation matrix of relationships between the attributes is the starting point for this whole process it might seem more reasonable to apply a method of cluster analysis directly to the correlation matrix (as suggested above by M. G. Kendall, and cf. Parks (1966), Thomas (1971, figure 1b)). To provide a comparable result with the Varimax clusters, an overlapping method would be appropriate. For thirteen attributes only, the double linkage procedure is very simple to carry out by hand and is sufficient to provide a comparison with the Varimax result (see figure 9.7(a)). Here, there is a hierarchy of clusters to choose from, but the best comparison with the Varimax clusters would be at about the 0.65 level. At this level there are some similarities (e.g. a cluster with attributes 1, 8 and 12 is the same as factor I), but also marked differences.

Without going into great detail, the most obvious of these is the creation of Varimax factor III from attributes 7 and 13. This implies a relationship, a bipolarity, between the size of the foot-element and the number of coils (large element/few coils; small element/many coils); but the basic absolute correlation between these attributes is no greater than 0.41 (see table 9.3).

This is a disturbing effect, but one that is bound to arise if data are forced to fit a model (here 'simple structure'), that is likely to be too rigid or fundamentally inappropriate.

To summarise the results of this practical example of a factor analysis, or rather a Varimax component analysis: clusters of attributes have been suggested by this procedure although by a roundabout sequence of steps. The factors can be interpreted, but the suspicion is strong that the mathematical artifact produced and interpreted may be a particularly distorted version of the evidence. It perhaps stresses the importance of keeping an eye on the starting point of the analysis (the correlation matrix).

Various other general studies have stressed the danger of accepting a factor analysis result because it is plausible. Almost any body of data if required would produce Varimax factors that would correspond to a certain extent with simple structure, but this would not mean that the exercise in any way made sense (Armstrong 1967, Armstrong and Soelberg 1968).

The discussion of factor analysis so far has been concerned with, in effect, clustering attributes or variables. However, as mentioned earlier, the same computer programs have been used in an 'inverse' form to suggest clusters of units: for instance 'sites' by Daniels (1967) and Rowlett and Pollnac (1971). This seems to misapply the basic factor analysis model: as Gower points out (1967, 2), the idea of separating specific from common effects in this context is difficult to accept (cf. also Maxwell 1971). With so many other methods of cluster analysis available, it seems unnecessary to call on factor analysis to cluster units.

The best known applications of factor analysis in archaeology are probably those in Binford and Binford (1966) and Binford (1972). Both deal with Palaeolithic data where assemblages are described by the percentage occurrence of a range of tool types.

The earlier study by Binford and Binford (1966) dealt with a selection of sixteen Mousterian assemblages of Levallois facies, mainly from the Middle East (Jabrud and Shubbabiq), although with one assemblage from Europe. This would in no way be considered a representative sample of the general industries under consideration and it is important to stress that any results reported would refer to this particular group of sites only, and not to the 'Mousterian of Levallois facies'.

The greatest interest of the Binfords' study is the archaeological hypothesis advanced to explain differences between Mousterian assemblages. This places the emphasis on one possible cause for their differences, function, as opposed to the more conventional interpretations, 'tribal' or chronological. For example, the frequency of Upper Palaeolithic types in some Mousterian assemblages would be given only functional but no chronological significance (Binford and Binford 1966, 249). Many archaeologists would no doubt prefer a hypothesis that allowed functional, chronological and perhaps stylistic ('tribal') and environmental factors all to play differential roles in interpretation of these assemblage differences, but this is a matter of archaeological judgement rather than the numerical analysis itself, which is the main concern here.

The clusters or 'kits' of tools for interpretation were suggested by a 'factor analysis'. Forty of Bordes' types were taken as attributes describing the assemblages. Although the precise method of factor analysis is not stated, it appears that a matrix of correlation coefficients was first calculated from the percentage counts of tools. This effectively gives equal weight in the analysis to types that are very poorly and very well represented overall. The total numbers of tools on which the percentages were calculated are not given for the Shubbabiq assemblages, and so it is difficult to judge whether forty attributes treated in this way provide a realistic description of them.

The Binfords next report 'factor loadings' for each of the forty attributes on five factors. It is unfortunate that no details of the procedures are given, other than the number of a computer program at a local computer installation. The choice of the number of factors is critical, but no reason for the choice of five is given. It is again not stated whether the reported 'loadings' are derived without rotation or from oblique or orthogonal rotations, and since the basic correlation matrix is not published, there is no possible way of assessing the reported numerical results.

The general doubts about factor analysis reported earlier, added to the unrepresentative sample of sites used for this analysis and the lack of detail given on the methods followed, make it difficult to have any confidence in interpretations of the specific results. However, this paper advocated serious multivariate analysis for such data and provided new, enlightened ways of considering clusters of types in Mousterian contexts, once such clusters could be obtained.

Binford's second reported factor analysis deals with thirty-two African Acheulean assemblages described by Kleindienst's general tool-classes (twelve in all). This analysis is more explicit: raw data and the particular version of (factor) analysis are specified: Varimax orthogonal rotation (presumably of principal components, although Binford states that the matrix of correlation coefficients itself was rotated). This then appears to be the same procedure as that used above for the fibulae. Unfortunately, the small correlation matrix of each tool class against each other, which represents the key stage in the analysis is not included. Again, this stage has effectively given equal weight to each type whether frequent or rare, well or not so well delineated (e.g. to the classes 'handaxes' and 'other small tools').

The choice of the number of 'factors' to create in this analysis was clearly not easy, as the curve reconstructed from Binford's figures shows (figure 8.3(b)). The really big jump in the values comes after the *second* dimension, but 50 per cent of the cumulative variance might be considered a rather drastic reduction. However, because of this marked indication of two-dimensionality, and since the computer program presumably gave as a by-product information necessary for a principal components plot of attributes on these two 'factors' before rotation, it would certainly have been worth while considering and publishing this two-dimensional result. Kaiser's more generally followed decision rule suggests four factors. Binford chose to consider five, allegedly because of a jump in the eigenvalue curve, although the actual plot (figure 8.3(b)) shows that this is not convincing.

The need to make an arbitrary choice of this kind emphasises for factor analysis, here as elsewhere, Lawley and Maxwell's comment in discussing this very point (1971, 38): 'It should always be kept firmly in mind that, except in artificial sampling experiments, the basic factor model is, like other models, useful only as an approximation to reality, and it should not be taken too seriously.' Unfortunately, this choice of the number of factors is critical since from this decision onwards the rotational procedure will be constrained to redistribute correlation between five dimensions.

Binford goes on to suggest interpretations for his five factors and he plots the thirty-two assemblages relative to three of the possible ten pairings of factors. He then attempts to incorporate these results into his own views of 'association' claiming a fundamental distinction between 'associational patterning' and 'association':

> ' "Associational patterning" simply refers to the recurrent association between two things, although the frequencies of these things may or may not vary in a related fashion. Association says that A tends to co-occur with B, but it does not imply that the frequency of A varies in a related fashion with the frequency of B' (Binford 1972, 145).

We find this distinction obscure; certainly it cannot be reconciled with mathematical concepts of association. In fact, the general impression conveyed by Binford's paper is that a method intended to simplify data has resulted in greater and unnecessary complication.

It will be clear throughout this section that our attitude to factor analysis, as so far used in archaeology, is not very favourable. The whole idea of rejecting 'specific variance' as redundant or irrelevant does not seem to fit the standard archaeological situations where factor analysis has been applied. If clusters are wanted, this distinction seems misguided, and it is not clear why any information whether 'common' or 'specific' should be rejected *a priori*. It would almost certainly make better sense to emphasise the 'simplification' aspect of these studies, basically achieved by a principal components transformation, and to omit reference to 'communalities', 'specific' effects and the other perhaps misleading aspects of a model which is neither obviously relevant nor rigorously applied.

8.4. ROTATIONAL FITTING AND CONSTELLATION ANALYSIS

Rotation has been a basic concept in the approaches just described: the principal components transformation rotates the system of axes so that the first corresponds to the axis of maximum point scatter. In factor analysis rotations attempt to fit axes to an external model like 'simple structure'. Rotation forms the basis of the methods discussed in this section too, but instead of manipulating reference axes for one configuration of points (representing archaeological units), two different configurations of the same set of points are considered; one is held fixed and the other effectively superimposed and rotated around a common origin until the best overall fit between the corresponding points is achieved. The sum of distances remaining between these pairs after fitting, provides an estimate of the overall difference between the two configurations. Orthogonal reference axes for each configuration are necessary for calculations but are not involved in the interpretation of results. In the geographic globe analogy, rather than rotating latitude and longitude to fit cities, two alternative representations of the location of the cities would be available, and one would be rotated to fit the other.

An even simpler illustration of the idea in two dimensions rather than three is given by figure 8.5(a). It shows how one configuration of three points (represented as a triangle) is fitted to another by rotation or reflection. Here,

the configurations are in fact identical and no residuals between corresponding points remain to be measured. If one triangle were slightly distorted (as
for figure 8.5(b)), fitting would proceed as before, but the 'best' combination
of rotation and reflection would now leave a measurable distance between
each pair of corresponding points: in the formulations of this section, due to
Gower (1971a), the sum of these squared distances would represent the
'difference' between the two triangles, ignoring their original, arbitrary orientation. Gower (1971b) calls this measure of fit or misfit M^2 (rather than R^2 as
he originally proposed, Gower 1971a). The relevance of this formulation to
archaeology is fairly obvious: the points A, B and C of figure 8.5 would be units
such as artifacts or assemblages; the dotted lines would represent differences
between these units calculated by one set or constellation of attributes, the
solid lines differences estimated by another. The residual M^2 would represent
the difference between the two constellations of attributes as shown by the
three units A, B and C.

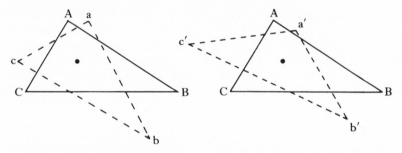

Figure 8.5. Rotational fitting. (a) Three points (shown as a triangle) are located by one constellation of descriptors in positions A, B and C, and by a second in positions *a*, *b* and *c*. Rotation allows a perfect fit. (b) Here, the same three points are located by a third constellation of descriptors as *a'*, *b'* and *c'*. Rotation will not now achieve a perfect fit, and residual distances between equivalent points may be cited (M^2). (After Gower 1971.)

Although this simple, artificial example refers to the rotational fitting of
two-dimensional configurations only (the triangles), the method is applicable
to configurations in three dimensions (cf. the geographical analogy), and in
multidimensional space, and it is in this context that the real power and versatility of the approach may be appreciated.

Gower himself (1971a) illustrates the method with anthropometric data,
where the constellations are different parts of the skull (each part described
by a whole series of up to sixteen measurements), and the units are distinct
early and recent hominid populations. However, Gower also suggests a wide
variety of other theoretical and practical situations where rotational fitting is
relevant. By combining Gower's procedures and suggestions with ideas put
forward by Wish and Carroll (1971; see section 8.6), it has been possible to

implement a general sequence of steps that represent a flexible data analysis package and that may collectively be termed *constellation analysis* (see figure 8.6).

In brief, units are first related to principal axes for each constellation of attributes (i.e. one configuration for each constellation). Next, each resulting configuration is fitted to each other and the relevant series of M^2 values are

---

1   Read in data: A ($n \times v$)
2   Transform data, e.g. from counts to percentages: B ($n \times v$)
    For each i in turn ($i = 1, 2 \ldots c$):
3   Stipulate a subset (constellation) of p attributes and form a reduced data matrix C_i ($n \times p$)
4   Compute a principal axes transformation of each C_i leading to E_i by either:

| (a) | or | (b) |

| Principal coordinates analysis | Principal components analysis |

4.1 Compute matrix of similarity coefficients between units based on the p attributes: D ($n \times n$ symmetric)

4.1 Compute matrix of correlation coefficients between attributes of this constellation Δ ($p \times p$, symmetric)

4.2 Compute principal axes of D. Coordinates for units on these axes are given automatically: E_i ($n \times p$)

4.2 Compute principal axes of Δ: Δ^* ($p \times p$)

4.3. Plot scatter diagram for p attributes on first few principal axes of Δ^*

4.4 Refer units to the p principal axes of Δ^*: E_i ($n \times p$)

5   Plot scatter diagram of units referred to first few principal axes of E_i.
6   Decide the number of dimensions q in which the principal axis configurations will be studied. This will depend on the dimensionality revealed at stage 4.
    (At this stage, there are c principal axis configurations for the n units, each stored in the computer as a matrix E_i^* ($n \times q$); $i = 1, 2 \ldots c$.)
7   Scale each configuration E_i^* to have equal 'spread': F_i ($n \times q$).
    For each pair of scaled configurations $F_i F_j$ (i.e. for $F_1 F_2$, $F_1 F_3$, etc.):
8   Fit F_j to F_i by rotation and reflection, transforming it to F_j^{**}. If desired, plot a scatter diagram for units after the rotation.
9   Compute residuals M_{ij}^2 remaining between each pair of fitted configurations F_i and F_j^{**}.
    (Steps 8 and 9 provide a matrix of distances between pairs of constellations: G ($c \times c$, symmetric).
10 Compute principal axes of $G : H$ ($c \times c$). This locates the C constellations in a principal axes configuration.
11 Plot scatter diagram of constellations referred to first few principal axes (i.e. first few columns of H).

Figure 8.6. Sequence of major steps in a constellation analysis. Capital letters refer to the chief matrices used, letters in brackets give the size of these matrices (rows × columns): n = number of units, v = total number of attributes, c = number of constellations, p = number of attributes defining a given constellation (in this diagram it is assumed that $p < n$), q = number of dimensions in which the constellations are compared.

calculated. Finally, these M^2 values are treated as distances and are referred to principal axes to give a final diagram summarising relationships between the constellations (see figure 8.7). The necessary calculations are all given in Gower (1966) for the principal axes transformation and Gower (1971a) for fitting by scaling, rotation and reflection. All three steps make extensive use of the same numerical procedure (latent roots and vectors of a real symmetric matrix) which is a standard library item in any research computer.

The entire procedure will be illustrated in section 9.5 by a palaeolithic example where the units are total assemblages of flint artifacts from stratified levels in the rock-shelter of Ksar Akil (Azoury and Hodson 1973; see also Ammerman and Hodson 1972, Newcomer and Hodson 1973). As illustrated in these examples, the method is especially suited to the study of assemblages where the same constituents may be classified in different ways: palaeolithic

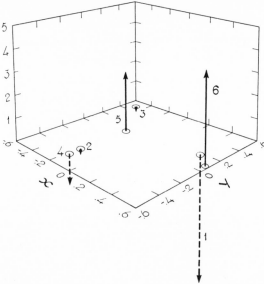

Figure 8.7. Constellation analysis: the six constellations plotted represent some different categories of evidence available for studying thirty-five Late Palaeolithic assemblages in Italy: (1) nine burin types, (2) nine end-scraper types, (3) eighteen types of backed blades and points, (4) six types of laterally retouched blades and scrapers, (5) seven denticulate types, (6) location (longitude/latitude). (Types refer to classification of G. Laplace.) The assemblages are first located in a series of configurations, one for each constellation; for (6) this is virtually a map of the relevant sites. These six configurations are then compared with each other by rotational fitting, and distances (M^2) between them are derived. This diagram represents these M^2 distances referred to principal axes (three axes are needed to accommodate up to 74 per cent of the total variance). It is clear that constellations 2 and 4 have provided similar information about the sites; the burins (1) contrast with all of the other tool groups; geographical location contrasts with all tool constellations. (Modified from Ammerman and Hodson 1972.)

tools may be considered according to technological groupings (the blank and butt type of tools, for example), or stylistic groupings, or supposed functional groupings, and this cross-cutting information for sets of assemblages compared. Or, alternative approaches to typology (or 'attribute analysis') may be compared when applied to the same set of assemblages. The approach has proved particularly revealing when studying alternative hierarchies of tool types.

Although these published applications have so far been confined to one main problem area, the method itself has a very wide potential relevance to many aspects of archaeology. Wherever different aspects of a set of units may be considered, a constellation analysis should prove worthwhile. In the study of artifacts, for example, different kinds of attribute may often be defined *a priori*, some referring to technology, some to decoration, some to function (see chapter 7): or different functional parts of artifacts may suggest a separate study for each as well as integrated studies (the blades and hilts of swords, for example). It would also be possible to study contextual evidence for artifacts and to compare, for example, the geographical or climatic location, or the localisation in a site of artifacts or their attributes, as well as their typological affinity. By splitting up and recombining attributes into a number of different constellations like this, it should prove possible to quantify many of the relationships that would otherwise remain hypothetical.

No doubt many extensions of the basic 'fitting' idea will develop during the next few years. One obvious approach would be to consider the relationship between rank orderings of distances between points in alternative configurations, rather than their direct Euclidean distances. This would simply involve calculating the rank correlation coefficient between the ordering of all pairs of distances between points estimated from any two different constellations of attributes. Where the metric properties of the estimated distances are in doubt (see p. 136), this could well prove a more acceptable as well as a simpler estimate than one derived from more detailed rotational fitting. This less restrictive formulation would relate to the non-metric multidimensional scaling approaches discussed later in this chapter.

8.5. Discrimination, Canonical Variates and D^2

The methods discussed in this section are designed for the situation where units are already divided into valid groups: handaxes grouped according to their site of origin, or morphology; or groups of raw material, such as flint, known to come from specific prehistoric flint mines. Discriminant analysis is intended basically to discover and emphasise those attributes which discriminate between such known groups, and to assign fresh, ungrouped units to one or other using this knowledge. For this latter purpose, the statistical model regards each group as a random sample from a known population: all of the units are described by the same range of attributes. The populations are assumed to be multivariate normal with identical variances and covariances. The centroids themselves of course differ.

Discriminant analysis was first developed for *two* groups, where the units are described by a number of attributes. A linear function of the attributes is found, involving multiples for each attribute (as in the definition of principal components), which, using a threshold value, divides the points into one or other class with a minimal likelihood of misclassification. Tests have been devised to decide whether the assumptions behind the model are justified (e.g. tests for the homogeneity of group covariances). It is also possible to calculate the likelihood of misclassification if a new unit is assigned to one or other group by calculating its score on the discriminant function.

Among the many ramifications and developments concerned with the discriminant function, two are of direct interest in archaeology: the extension of these discriminant concepts to deal with more than two groups (*canonical variate analysis*); and second, distances in the space defined by discriminant functions (Mahalanobis distance or D^2). For more than two groups, a series of discriminant functions or canonical variates are in fact required, one for each additional group (or for the number of attributes, if this is less than the number of groups -1). The functions are calculated by a procedure similar to principal components so that each successive canonical variate accounts for the maximum possible separation between group centroids. As with principal components, it is hoped, and is often found, that the first few canonical variates account for most of the inter-group variance. This allows the group centroids and individual units to be plotted in a space of reduced dimensions, often two dimensions as in figure 9.8(c), 9.17, 9.20 and 9.23, so that interrelationships between the groups may be appreciated visually.

In fact these successive canonical variates define a new space: the space defined by the original attributes and their scores is transformed so that discrimination between groups is emphasised. This transformation is of great interest since it overrides the original linear scaling of the attributes: for example, whether measurements were recorded in centimetres or inches or both, and whether scores were standardised or unstandardised or both, the configuration in discriminant space will be the same. At the same time, the duplication involved with correlated attributes is eliminated by this transformation. This gives unusual interest to distances measured in this space. Euclidean (Pythagorean or 'ruler') distances in this space in fact correspond to Mahalanobis distances in the original space. These were mentioned without serious discussion in chapter 6. Their invariant properties (insensitivity to linear transformation and suppression of correlated effects) may now be appreciated. Mahalanobis distances may be calculated from the raw scores by operations using the matrix of covariances within groups. These are extremely tedious to carry out by hand, as are all discriminant calculations, and were not practicable for realistic quantities of data before the advent of the computer. A straightforward account of the mathematics involved, with simple examples is given by Hope (1968, 23, 102, 125; see also Gower 1966, 1967; Friedman and Rubin 1967).

A first question of obvious interest to the archaeologist is the appropriateness of using any of these transformations and distances when data are in no sense a random sample of populations, with multivariate normal distributions and equal dispersions around group means. This doubt is especially relevant when 'groups' are 'clusters' suggested by one of the procedures discussed in chapter 7. Opinions of specialists would no doubt differ, but, as in other situations of data analysis already discussed, representation of units in discriminant space for descriptive and heuristic purposes and the calculation of Mahalanobis distance between group centroids or between units for similar purposes, seems quite acceptable.

A second question would concern the appropriateness of Mahalanobis distance as a general measure of relationship. Even where prior groups are not defined, a measure of distance with some D^2 properties may be calculated by substituting an overall dispersion (covariance) matrix for the pooled within-group dispersion matrix usually employed. Such distances would have the noteworthy properties of true D^2 mentioned above: insensitivity to prior

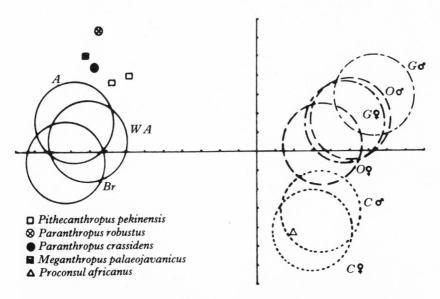

□ *Pithecanthropus pekinensis*
⊗ *Paranthropus robustus*
● *Paranthropus crassidens*
▬ *Meganthropus palaeojavanicus*
△ *Proconsul africanus*

Figure 8.8. Canonical Variate analysis of tooth measurement (for the permanent first lower premolar) from different primates. Eight measurements were taken for each tooth. The circles enclose 90 per cent of the sampled populations (from which the canonical variates were calculated). A = Australian, Br = British, WA = West African, C = chimpanzee, G = gorilla, O = orang-outang. Symbols represent problematic fossil finds. The first canonical variate (horizontal axis) clearly separates the human from the non-human populations and locates all of the fossils except *Proconsul* with the former rather than the latter (Ashton *et al.* 1957).

linear scaling and to intercorrelations in the data. However, it is by no means clear that these effects should be eliminated in situations where discrimination is not the intention. This is a general problem already touched on in chapter 6 and recalled in chapter 7.

One of the earliest and most interesting examples of a comprehensive canonical variate analysis dealt with the discrimination between groups of primates, using measurements on teeth (Ashton, Healy and Lipton 1957). A particular problem was the relationship of the groups *Proconsul* and *Pithecanthropus* to apes and modern humans respectively. A number of measurements were made on teeth and a separate canonical variate analysis

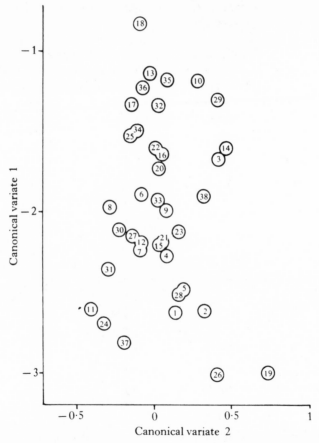

Figure 8.9. Canonical variate analysis of 4 800 British handaxes from thirty-eight site locations in Southern England (D. A. Roe's data). The handaxes from each location are treated as a group and each group mean (i.e. the 'average' handaxe for each group) is plotted. The two co-ordinates (the first two canonical variates) represent the original attributes (see figure 5.2) combined in such a way that the best separation between the groups is achieved (Graham 1970).

performed for each tooth. The plot of results for one tooth, (the permanent first lower premolar) is reproduced as figure 8.8. The circles represent the spread of values around the average for primate groups in the space defined by the first two canonical variates. The symbols represent single problem examples. The first canonical variate (horizontal axis) clearly separates apes from humans, and locates *Proconsul* with the former, *Pithecanthropus* with the latter. The canonical variate weights or coefficients included in the original publication show which measurements were most important for discrimination on this and subsequent axes. The second canonical variate (vertical axis) mainly distinguishes between the chimpanzee and the other apes, but also serves to separate the *Proconsul* specimens from modern man.

Since this study, canonical variate analysis has become a regular procedure for studying differences between multivariate populations where measurements of teeth or bones are concerned (e.g. Higham and Leach 1971, Rightmire 1971), but another interesting application has studied the trace-element content of populations of flint from different prehistoric mines and other sources (Sieveking *et al.* 1972).

The first direct archaeological application of the method appears to be Graham's study of handaxes from sites in Southern Britain (Graham 1970). Using data supplied by Roe (1964, 1968, and see above section 5.3.2), Graham treated the available handaxes from each of thirty-eight sites as a sample of a homogenous population, and derived canonical variates: these indicated which raw attributes discriminated best between the sites, and they provided coordinate axes against which the thirty-eight sites could be plotted in summary form (figure 8.9). In spite of some minor anomalies in the data which Graham mentions (the lack of scores on some attributes for some handaxes), and in spite of the unsatisfactory nature of all assemblages of British handaxes, this study is of the greatest interest.

Another field of application of discriminant analysis is in k-means cluster analysis, where 'groups' are not known *a priori* but are suggested by an initial cluster analysis of the units concerned. Once clusters have been suggested, it is possible to treat these as 'groups' of units and to derive canonical variates to discriminate between them (Friedman and Rubin 1967). This approach was discussed briefly in the last chapter and will be illustrated with examples in the next.

8.6. NON-METRIC MULTIDIMENSIONAL SCALING AND RELATED PROCEDURES

The methods so far discussed in this chapter investigate relationships between units by starting from two main premises: differences between units are treated as distances in a space with definite and familiar properties (i.e. as 'ruler' distances); second, relationships in the space are expressed as linear equations and are investigated by the branch of mathematics known as linear algebra. The calculations involved are extremely tedious, but the computer makes light of such work even where large quantities of data are concerned. During the last decade, methods have been developed to approach similar situations in data analysis from quite different, and much less restrictive starting assumptions. The results from these analyses are presented for convenience as configurations in geometric space (scatter diagrams), but the original relationships within the data are referred only to an ordinal scale, and they are not investigated by searching for the linear dependence of one attribute on another. These new methods also make full use of the computer; but instead of merely increasing the size of a problem that may be tackled by existing traditional methods, the procedures represent a new departure stimulated directly by the computer.

The most generally available and familiar of these approaches is *non-metric multidimensional scaling* ('non-metric' being usually omitted in descriptions). A general description of this approach has been written specifically for archaeologists by one of its leading exponents (Kruskal 1971), and the method has in fact been used widely in archaeology for general purposes (Doran and Hodson 1966; Hodson, Sneath and Doran 1966; True and Matson 1970; Ammerman 1971; Johnson 1972), and as a specialised approach to seriation (see chapter 10).

The impetus for developing this approach came from psychometric studies where raw data are often in the form of personal reactions to stimuli: for example, judgements of the relationship between sounds or colours under various conditions. Clearly in this situation, similarities or differences are not likely to have the property of a numeric scale but may only be ranked. Several authorities, for example Sibson (1972), imply that this is not an exceptional but a regular situation in many kinds of data analysis. At the same time, certain kinds of structure suggested to be involved in human perception and, again, in other data analysis contexts, would not seem suitable for linear description: 'perception' as related to appreciation of the colour circle provides an example, and in fact, psychologists have postulated a number of specifically non-linear models such as a 'radex' or 'circumplex' whose names alone suggest this non-linear character. As an alternative to the use of *metric* multidimensional scaling (e.g. principal coordinates analysis) for investigating low-dimensional structure, Shepard (1962) and Kruskal (1964a, b) suggested a revolutionary approach which avoids the obvious inappropriateness of any metric or linear assumptions. We shall discuss their basic ideas.

First, they consider only the rank order of similarities ('proximities' as they call them), rather than their exact numerical value. This frees the data from an assumed, but possibly unjustified, exact scale of measurement. Second, units are located in a space of given dimensions so that the rank ordering of distances in this space corresponds as closely as possible with the original ordering of their raw distances. Third, a measure of stress is calculated, reflecting how far this resultant ordering departs from the raw ordering. It is the behaviour of this stress measurement for configurations set up in few dimensions that is intended to reveal the underlying dimensionality of the data. As in some previous approaches, a result is calculated for alternative numbers of dimensions and a shoulder sought in the curve of stress versus dimensionality (cf. the curves for clustering characteristics in k-means cluster analysis, figures 9.12 and 9.18, and the eigenvalue curves in principal component analysis, figures 8.3(a)–(c)). If the dimensions for any configuration are sufficient, it is of course possible to achieve zero stress (one less dimension than the number of units, or if fewer, the number of attributes, provide this critical figure). However, if the data are generated by an underlying structure in one, two or a few dimensions, the stress for configurations at this dimensionality should be obviously smaller than for comparable data where no such underlying structure exists. In fact, it is only the 'noise' in the generating process behind the data and in their measurement that should in theory prevent finding zero stress for the true dimensionality. In a practical situation, provided that this noise is not overwhelming, it would seem reasonable to expect a markedly low stress value where a low-dimensional linear *or* non-linear structure is involved. Consequently, even where the raw data are suspected to be genuinely metric, this approach might be chosen in preference to traditional methods because of this potential ability to indicate non-linear structure.

To balance these obvious theoretical advantages, there are at present undoubted practical difficulties with multidimensional scaling. It has, in fact, proved extremely difficult to achieve a 'best' configuration with the search-strategies available. As for k-means cluster analysis (see pp. 179–84) an iterative approach is necessary, and local rather than 'global' optima are generally found. The strategy has been, for a given number of dimensions, to start from a number of different, often random, configurations and to 'improve' each by iteration, until the stress cannot be reduced further. That configuration with lowest stress is then chosen as the result. Since the iterative procedures themselves are rather time-consuming even with a fast computer, and since in general results are required in a choice of dimensions, the number of units that can be considered is severely restricted. For seriation based on multidimensional scaling, where a two-dimensional result only is sought (see chapter 10), calculations have proved possible for up to 150 units or so. However, where configurations in a sequence of dimensions are required from, say, five down to one, it is doubtful whether any computer installation would at present encourage the analysis of more than fifty units. Another disadvantage is that the problem of local optima has proved extremely tiresome for low-dimensional configurations, especially for results in one dimension, and it has proved difficult to find a realistic stress value for one dimensional results. For a method that requires such a realistic estimate as a basis for any interpretation of structure, this is a serious defect. Again, if the original scale of measurement is genuinely metric (in many archaeological studies of morphology, or where occurrences are counted, this could well be so), debasement of the scale to rank values could potentially sacrifice important information.

Again, simple non-linear structures *may* be found by linear methods in many practical situations: for example a basic circular structure would be recovered by principal coordinates analysis if two dimensions are considered. The appearance of the plot would indicate immediately the existence of the underlying structure (cf. the non-linear time effects revealed for Ksar Akil, section 9.5).

Non-metric multidimensional scaling, then, has great theoretical attractions, and it has undoubtedly proved itself in the archaeological applications quoted above. However, this does not mean that it may yet be considered as a more desirable replacement for principal components and related analyses. Unfortunately few practical comparisons between the two approaches appear to have been made. In one such comparison by Gower (1971a), which analysed M^2 distances from rotational fitting, principal coordinates analysis appeared to provide a more acceptable result. Far more experiments of this kind are needed before the relative merits of the two approaches in archaeology will be clear.

An interesting recent development of multidimensional scaling is *individual difference scaling*, the corresponding computer program being called INDSCAL (Wish and Carrol 1971). The new feature of INDSCAL is that it does not merely scale a single set of dissimilarity or similarity data, but generates a scaling based on several comparable data sets, indicating how this common scaling is related to each individual set. This facility is particularly valuable for psychological data, where regularly a range of data sets is obtained from a range of experimental subjects. Individual difference scaling is not non-metric, being based on a linear assumption relating scale distance to the similarity data. However, a quasi-non-metric version is said to be available.

Wish and Carrol (1971) have advocated the use of INDSCAL in the study of archaeological data, suggesting that the individual similarity matrices might be defined from different categories of unit attribute. In unpublished experiments we have used INDSCAL in this way to study the Hallstatt Sword data described in section 9.2, but have found the technique cumbersome and not illuminating. While further archaeological experiments with INDSCAL would certainly be justified, our own strong preference is for constellation analysis, or perhaps for simpler rank correlation methods suggested above.

We have mentioned only a small part of the exploratory work which has been carried out in the general area of non-metric scaling. Interesting and useful variant procedures have been developed by Shepard and Carrol (1969) and Lingoes (1970), but as yet little or no attempt has been made to apply them to archaeological data. One of the great tasks of the next decade will be to develop and evaluate all these procedures and to reduce the present heavy computational requirements associated with them. It should also prove possible to compare this whole class of techniques with potential developments of traditional methods such as 'generalised principal components' (Gnana-desikan and Wilk 1969), which are themselves still in their infancy.

Data Analysis in Archaeology. Some Examples

In chapters 5–8, different sets of data and different numerical techniques have been introduced piecemeal, and it may still be difficult to envisage what would be understood as a comprehensive quantified analysis of actual data. This chapter attempts to fill this gap by discussing very briefly some complete analyses that have been carried out by one of the authors (F.R.H.) on what are considered typical sets of data. Some of these individual analyses have already been mentioned, but hardly related to a genuine archaeological context, or to each other. Now an attempt will be made to draw some of these analyses together and to relate them to what may be considered a range of typical archaeological situations and problems. Mostly the analyses deal with well-known and either fully published or readily accessible data.

9.1. LA TÈNE FIBULAE FROM MÜNSINGEN

A small sample of thirty bronze fibulae (safety pin brooches) has been used in a variety of experiments to test out available numerical techniques of classification (figures 9.1 and 9.2). Raw data for this sample are given in table 9.1. All of these artifacts, except two included for comparison (figure 9.2), are from the same Iron Age cemetery of Münsingen, near Berne, Switzerland.

The context of the Münsingen objects provides useful information for checking suggested taxonomies and seriations. Objects are often associated with others in closed grave groups, and the distribution of graves within the cemetery (figure 11.6) follows a pattern that is disturbed by social effects (preferred locations for children, women and men, and possible family or even 'tabu' effects), but that primarily reflects a linear extension through time. This context, and mechanical scale drawings of all of the fibulae and other artifacts from the site, are presented in a republication of the finds which are themselves housed and available for study in the Bernisches Historisches Museum (Hodson 1968).

In spite of the small number of artifacts included in these experiments, they provide a stringent test of classificatory procedures. This was emphasised when archaeologists attempted to classify photographs of them

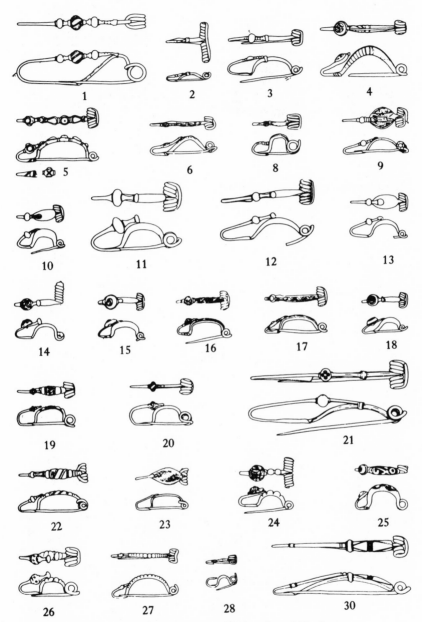

Figure 9.1. Twenty-eight bronze brooches (fibulae) from Münsingen, Switzerland, which, with those illustrated in figure 9.2, make up the test sample (see table 9.1). (Hodson *et al.* 1966.)

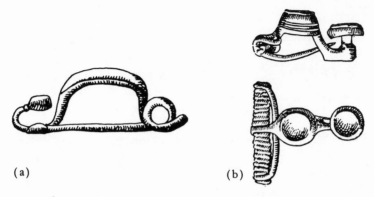

Figure 9.2. Bronze brooches (a) from the Thames near Reading, and (b) from the Hallstatt cemetery (nos. 7 and 29 respectively of the test sample, see table 9.1).

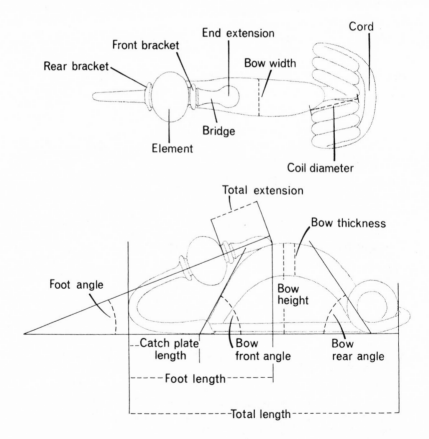

Figure 9.3. Terminology for La Tène fibula attributes.

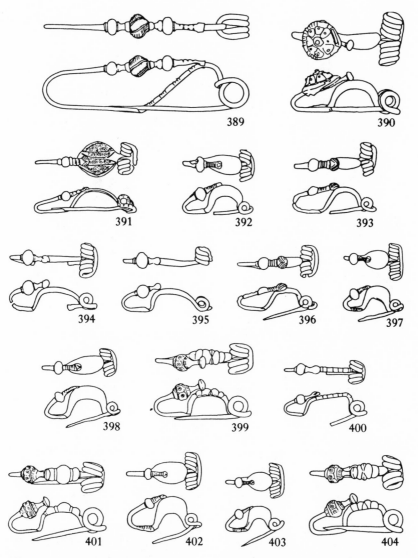

Figure 9.4. Bronze fibulae from Münsingen grave 149, all associated with the same female skeleton. Numbers correspond with the inventory of the Bernisches Historisches Museum. Nos. 389, 391, 398 and 399 are included in the test sample as nos. 1, 9, 10, 26 (see table 9.1). Some of the fibulae form obvious pairs (392 and 398, 393 and 396, 394 and 395, 397 and 403, 399 and 404), or groups (392, 397, 398, 402, 403; 399, 401, 404). (Hodson 1968, 139.)

222

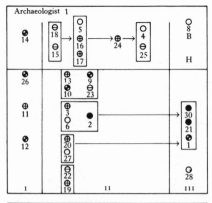

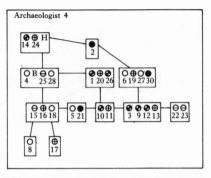

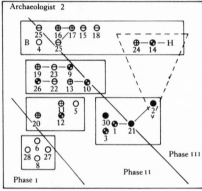

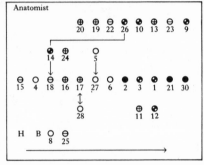

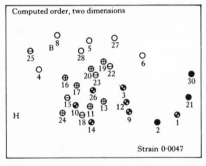

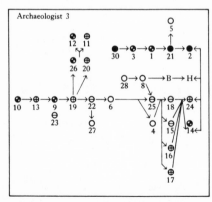

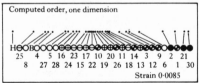

Figure 9.5. Intuitive and computed classifications of the test sample of thirty fibulae. Numbers correspond with figure 9.1 and table 9.1. Symbols from light to dark refer to five arbitrary zones in the cemetery from north to south (see figure 11.6), which in turn reflect a chronological progression, early to late. Computed classifications are given by non-metric multidimensional scaling (Hodson *et al.* 1966, 320).

by eye. Widely different groupings and ordering were suggested (Hodson, Sneath and Doran 1966; see figure 9.5).

The traditional, commonsense approach to metalwork like this sets up a hierarchy in the classification: a functional grouping splits up the material first into swords, axes, pins, fibulae and so on. Within each of these categories, a 'stylistic' classification into types is then attempted: the types are presumed to reflect changes in fashion through time, regional workshop preferences and so forth. Decoration is generally treated by a cross-classification of art-styles that may appear on different functional groups. For the period of these fibulae, Jacobsthal's 'styles' of 'Early Celtic Art' are well-known, although not entirely satisfactory (Jacobsthal 1944).

The chief practical difficulty in classifying metalwork like this has been to find a suitable level at which to define stylistic types for general description and interpretation (for example, in seriation studies of assemblages of artifacts, like those discussed in the next chapter). At Münsingen, it is possible to recognise highly specific types, where objects were clearly intended to be used as pairs or sets (see figure 9.4). However, this is too detailed a level of operation for the general description of assemblages: at such a specific level many, perhaps most items would not be grouped, but would remain classes by themselves. It is also possible to set up hypothetical series of items intended to reflect development through time, and 'typology' is understood in this sense by some archaeologists. However, this does not answer the need to *summarise*, which is essential in classification: it is really types located in a series or other configuration that are required.

The most generally accepted level for La Tène fibula types would divide them into only three groups (I, II, III) or four (A, B, C, D). For the Münsingen fibulae, the last category of both these systems is unrepresented, and so the general classification would include just two or three major types. Attempts have been made by Wiedmer (1908), Viollier (1916) and others to subdivide these major types, but the proposed classifications have differed and there is still no generally accepted set of detailed types.

The hierarchy of a functional classification splitting off all fibulae, and then the broad grouping into two or three classes, is acceptable so far as it goes, but, for detailed study, one or more further stages in the hierarchy are required. The selected sample of thirty fibulae thus represents, on a very small scale, the problem of finding one or more levels at which to define groups or types for descriptive and heuristic purposes. This does not seem to differ from the situation in other areas of study which, at first sight, may seem rather different (cf. the swords, handaxes and trace-element analyses discussed below). This means that methods found effective with this sample may be expected to have a general relevance to archaeology.

As just mentioned, the fibulae selected for this exercise are given a relative date by their context, and since it is clear from previous studies, and after specific tests, that fibula morphology is mainly reflecting changes in fashion

grave	museum no.	foot length (1)	bow height (2)	bow front angle (3)	foot angle (4)	coil diam. (5)	bow rear angle (6)	element diam. (7)	foot ext. length (8)	catchplate (9)	bow width (10)	bow thickness (11)	foot ext. width (12)	no. of coils (13)	total length
1	149	389	93	24	7	10	16	1	13	31	47	3.5	3.5	*	4	114
2	190	615	21	7	6	9	6	5	2	11	10	3.5	1.7	*	11	35
3	161	125	33	15	2	7	7	3	8	10	20	3.9	3.2	*	4	60
4	31	812	23	26	4	7	9	5	12	1	16	6.2	7.7	2.8	4	74
5	49	798	20	23	2	8	7	1	8	5	16	7.7	5.2	2.6	6	68
6	6	673	27	15	6	8	7	5	3	11	11	3.7	3.5	1.8	4	55
7	THAMES		10	16	1	10	9	1	7	0	11	6.1	4.1	0.0	4	45
8	23	643	15	18	1	10	10	1	5	0	15	3.5	3.5	0.0	4	40
9	149	391	31	13	4	9	7	4	5	11	18	17.6	1.4	3.6	6	54
10	149	398	19	17	2	7	6	2	6	10	12	9.2	6.6	3.9	6	39
11	101	491	41	23	3	8	11	3	14	15	24	7.3	5.8	8.6	6	71
12	171	149	47	17	5	9	10	4	8	14	26	5.8	4.7	6.0	6	78
13	130	545	29	15	3	8	6	3	6	10	17	11.7	3.9	6.4	6	47
14	157	085	23	13	3	8	6	2	10	7	15	5.2	2.7	5.4	12	41
15	97	478	20	15	1	7	5	1	12	4	12	4.7	4.8	3.5	6	38
16	85	436	17	16	1	7	7	1	8	3	11	5.1	3.5	2.2	6	44
17	91	464	20	15	2	7	7	3	6	10	12	5.5	3.8	3.9	6	50
18	61	821	20	13	5	8	5	2	10	5	10	4.4	4.4	5.1	6	36
19	94	474	21	18	2	9	9	1	5	6	15	8.1	2.3	1.9	4	49
20	121	348	28	17	1	10	10	2	8	6	20	2.5	2.6	2.2	4	53
21	181	212	94	15	7	10	12	5	11	31	50	4.3	4.3	*	6	128
22	68	587	22	18	1	8	7	1	5	8	17	8.8	3.0	2.4	6	59
23	61	830	20	14	1	8	6	1	3	4	14	14.3	1.4	1.7	6	44
24	130	549	22	15	3	8	7	3	13	1	17	5.0	4.6	2.5	10	47
25	80	529	12	22	1	6	9	1	9	0	11	6.8	6.4	0.0	4	45
26	149	399	27	15	1	8	10	2	9	11	19	8.2	4.0	7.6	4	53
27	48	788	15	19	2	8	7	3	3	4	12	3.7	3.5	1.9	4	56
28	44	752	10	10	2	10	6	2	2	—	9	2.0	2.3	2.2	3	26
29	HALLSTATT		9	13	3	10	4	4	9	0	8	9.6	5.0	0.0	22	28
30	193	611	68	18	7	9	9	7	3	50	18	9.3	6.5	*	4	110

Table 9.1. Details of the test sample of thirty fibulae (see figures 9.1–3). Measurements are given in millimetres, angles in intervals of 10°. Asterisks indicate that the extension to the foot is bent over and wrapped around the bow. Numbers in brackets indicate the attributes used for quantitative analyses (see table 9.2).

through time (in this case, through about four centuries), this knowledge provides a possible independent check on any morphological classifications suggested. By adding a 'known date' symbol on diagrams it is possible to see how closely any proposed clusters or series relate to this standard. This test is in some ways unrealistic. A larger sample of material is available and would normally be used: the procedures (or the guinea-pig archaeologists!) are in fact being asked to draw conclusions from an unnecessarily small, biased sample. However, for comparing different methods this is not very serious. Further, a small sample like this does not require too much computer time, and produces classifications that may be presented simply and assessed rapidly. The advantages of this small sample were soon realised after initial experiments with first 109, and then 70 fibulae (Hodson, Sneath and Doran 1966). For similar reasons, attributes were soon reduced to the smallest number that could reasonably be expected to reflect the general shape of the objects (thirteen quantified attributes; see table 9.1).

It should be stressed that these analyses were intended to test out alternative methods and *not* to provide a useful archaeological classification. This would have to be based on a much larger and less arbitrary sample, and would have to take into account more clearly defined aims (cf. Hodson 1968).

Before any analyses were attempted, measurements on the fibulae were divided into the total length (measured to the back of the coils rather than to the cord, which is often broken; see figure 9.3). This restricted the study to shape only, with size excluded as a possible basis for classification. This was to simplify comparison with traditional classifications, which are based on shape, and, generally, to exclude a possibly independent complicating factor that could be simply and legitimately excluded. In circumstances like this, when there may be doubt whether to exclude attributes, it would be possible to perform a constellation analysis and to quantify the relative effect of modification to an attribute list. However, for comparing different methods of analysing the same data, this basic set of shape attributes seems to strike a reasonable balance between simplicity and adequacy.

For the results presented here, these ratios and the number-of-coils attribute (13) were converted to logarithms (0.1 being added to all values to accommodate zero scores): see table 9.2. This transformation would be expected to counteract the skewness which generally results with ratio data (see section 5.4.5).

Principal components and Varimax components analyses of these data have already been discussed in some detail in the last chapter, and need not be repeated (see figures 9.6, 9.7 and 9.8(a)). The principal components analysis provides a two-dimensional scatter plot which is a most useful complement to other forms of analysis like cluster analysis, which will be discussed next.

Since the data are fully numeric, standard monothetic divisive algorithms cannot be considered. For a test of agglomerative clustering procedures, a matrix of Euclidean distances was first calculated. (The program initially standardised all attributes to have zero mean and unit variance, effectively giving equal weight to each attribute.) The cluster results have been published (Hodson 1970), but are reproduced here for completeness (see figures 9.9–13).

Single-linkage cluster analysis (see p. 176), and its extension in the Jardine and Sibson manner to double-linkage (see p. 177), failed to produce a

	1	2	3	4	5	6	7	8	9	10	11	12	13
1	0.285	1.579	7.000	5.000	1.966	1.000	2.214	1.314	0.924	3.487	3.487	1.411	1.411
2	0.571	1.562	6.000	4.000	1.848	5.000	2.868	1.233	1.281	2.313	3.140	1.411	2.407
3	0.652	1.411	2.000	4.000	2.133	3.000	2.054	1.808	1.131	2.741	2.939	1.411	1.411
4	1.200	1.082	4.000	2.000	2.119	5.000	1.802	3.902	1.554	2.485	2.274	3.262	1.411
5	1.253	1.118	2.000	3.000	2.230	1.000	2.104	2.617	1.470	2.189	2.580	3.262	1.808
6	0.761	1.295	6.000	3.000	2.073	5.000	2.851	1.629	1.589	2.708	2.760	3.421	1.411
7	1.482	1.040	1.000	5.000	1.668	1.000	1.932	4.606	1.389	2.015	2.407	4.606	1.411
8	1.019	0.815	1.000	5.000	1.396	1.000	2.116	4.606	1.019	2.442	2.442	4.606	1.411
9	0.577	1.411	4.000	4.000	2.048	4.000	2.293	1.552	1.095	1.118	3.616	2.681	1.808
10	0.718	0.824	2.000	2.000	1.803	2.000	1.758	1.335	1.163	1.418	1.744	2.262	1.808
11	0.604	1.160	3.000	3.000	1.863	3.000	1.615	1.591	1.118	2.285	2.514	2.122	1.808
12	0.542	1.520	5.000	4.000	2.031	4.000	2.300	1.710	1.105	2.580	2.791	2.534	1.808
13	0.542	1.172	3.000	3.000	2.071	3.000	2.122	1.543	1.026	1.416	2.501	2.028	1.808
14	0.631	1.179	3.000	3.000	1.889	2.000	1.445	1.716	1.040	2.077	2.728	2.028	2.493
15	0.693	0.971	1.000	2.000	1.947	1.000	1.160	2.202	1.185	2.104	2.084	2.407	1.808
16	0.990	1.047	1.000	2.000	1.853	1.000	1.761	2.425	1.411	2.163	2.542	3.001	1.808
17	0.956	1.235	2.000	2.000	2.008	3.000	2.068	1.629	1.452	2.219	2.588	2.573	1.808
18	0.642	1.054	5.000	3.000	1.969	2.000	1.338	1.988	1.261	2.116	2.116	1.960	1.808
19	0.892	1.037	2.000	4.000	1.744	1.000	2.272	2.072	1.215	1.816	3.063	3.262	1.411
20	0.673	1.308	1.000	5.000	1.668	2.000	1.872	2.092	0.993	3.040	3.001	3.161	1.411
21	0.438	2.147	7.000	5.000	2.352	5.000	2.442	1.418	0.971	3.388	3.388	1.411	1.808
22	1.022	1.218	1.000	3.000	2.158	1.000	2.400	2.015	1.273	1.917	2.986	3.203	1.808
23	0.833	1.176	1.000	3.000	2.041	1.000	2.625	2.407	1.176	1.157	3.450	3.262	1.808
24	0.806	1.172	3.000	3.000	1.866	3.000	1.275	3.450	1.054	2.251	2.332	2.950	2.313
25	1.348	0.765	1.000	1.000	1.629	1.000	1.641	4.606	1.430	1.905	1.964	4.606	1.411
26	0.688	1.253	1.000	3.000	1.611	2.000	1.763	1.556	1.026	1.844	2.549	1.887	1.411
27	1.345	1.115	2.000	3.000	2.149	3.000	2.868	2.526	1.562	2.721	2.779	3.558	1.411
28	0.955	0.955	2.000	5.000	1.390	2.000	2.573	4.100	1.065	2.573	2.430	2.500	1.100
29	1.115	0.815	3.000	5.000	1.917	4.000	1.147	4.606	1.281	1.099	1.740	4.606	3.096
30	0.542	1.826	7.000	4.000	2.393	7.000	3.450	0.833	1.828	2.477	2.833	1.411	1.411

Table 9.2. Data from table 9.1 prepared for analysis. Quantified estimates replace the asterisks and the missing value for fibula 28. Dimensions (attributes 1–2, 5, 7–12) are converted to shape attributes by division into total length. Together with attribute 13, these ratios are then converted to natural logarithms (0.1 being added to each raw score to accommodate any zero values).

	1	2	3	4	5	6	7	8	9	10	11	12	13
1	1.00	−0.63	−0.59	−0.23	−0.23	−0.32	−0.12	0.76	0.51	−0.23	−0.44	0.82	−0.11
2	−0.63	1.00	0.72	0.37	0.60	0.59	0.54	−0.64	−0.06	0.52	0.71	−0.66	−0.04
3	−0.59	0.72	1.00	0.29	0.51	0.72	0.39	−0.46	0.10	0.42	0.35	−0.53	0.12
4	−0.23	0.37	0.29	1.00	−0.14	0.14	0.28	0.08	−0.38	0.32	0.40	−0.04	−0.03
5	−0.23	0.60	0.51	−0.14	1.00	0.52	0.33	−0.51	0.39	0.12	0.34	−0.38	0.17
6	−0.32	0.59	0.72	0.14	0.52	1.00	0.42	−0.31	0.35	0.19	0.14	−0.35	0.16
7	−0.12	0.54	0.39	0.28	0.33	0.42	1.00	−0.34	0.36	0.27	0.61	−0.20	−0.41
8	0.76	−0.64	−0.46	0.08	−0.51	−0.31	−0.34	1.00	0.09	−0.16	−0.50	0.81	−0.01
9	0.51	−0.06	0.10	−0.38	0.39	0.35	0.36	0.09	1.00	−0.04	−0.21	0.26	−0.13
10	−0.23	0.52	0.42	0.32	0.12	0.19	0.27	−0.16	−0.04	1.00	0.30	−0.31	−0.42
11	−0.44	0.71	0.35	0.40	0.34	0.14	0.61	−0.50	−0.21	0.30	1.00	−0.37	−0.1
12	0.82	−0.66	−0.53	−0.04	−0.38	−0.35	−0.20	0.81	0.26	−0.31	−0.37	1.00	−0.00
13	−0.11	−0.04	0.12	−0.03	0.17	0.16	−0.41	−0.01	−0.13	−0.42	−0.19	−0.00	1.00

Table 9.3. Correlation coefficients computed from the data in table 9.2. Tabulated values represent correlations between the thirteen attributes.

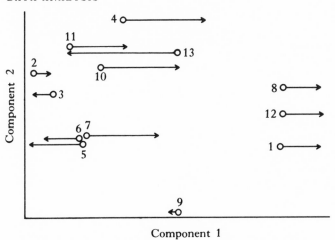

Component 2

Component 1

Figure 9.6. Principal components analysis: thirteen shape attributes for fibulae plotted against the first three principal components (see table 9.4, sections I and II).

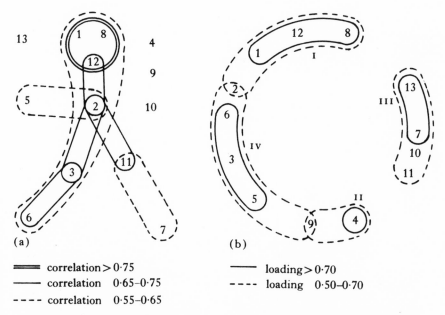

(a)

(b)

═══ correlation > 0·75
─── correlation   0·65–0·75
- - - correlation   0·55–0·65

─── loading > 0·70
- - - loading   0·50–0·70

Figure 9.7. Clusters of fibula attributes given by two alternative analyses of the correlation matrix (table 9.3): (a) cluster analysis by double-linkage, and

(b) varimax rotation to find simple structure from the loadings of attributes on principal components (see section III of table 9.4).

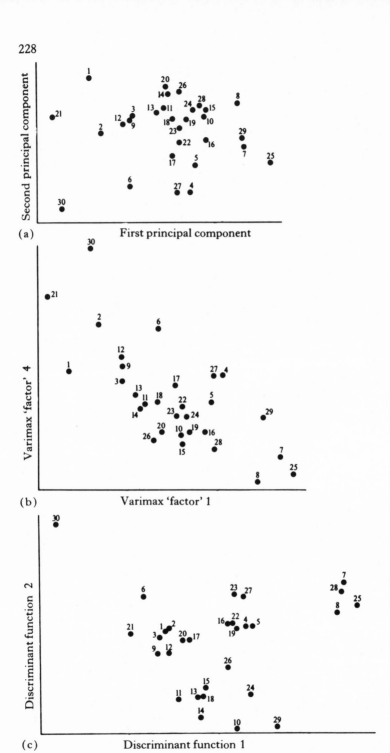

(a)

(b)

(c)

hierarchy of gradually increasing groups (see figures 9.9 and 9.10); each produced instead one main chain that progressively increased in length. However attractive theoretically, these procedures are clearly unsuited to this empirical situation.

Average-linkage analysis, on the other hand (see p. 177), produced the kind of structure that would be useful for archaeological description and inter-pretation (see figure 9.11): a definite hierarchy of progressively enlarging groups. This enables the sample to be divided into a series of types at any level that may be considered useful, down to as few as three or two clusters. (It may be recalled that any line drawn horizontally across these dendrograms will define a stage in the hierarchy, each single stem representing a cluster at that level.) Similar contrasting structures for single versus average linkage were produced from larger samples of fibulae, more descriptive attributes and a different similarity coefficient, the Simple Matching Coefficient (Hodson, Sneath and Doran 1966).

However, even if we accept that average-linkage is producing the required kind of structure, it still does not follow that the allocation of fibulae within the structure is satisfactory and meaningful: disjoint types are defined, but they may be quite artificial. The external criterion of known relative date, represented on the diagrams by a graded symbol, shows that there is, in fact, a definite relationship between archaeological significance (chronology) and the average-link types throughout the hierarchy, but this is a difficult criterion to apply too rigidly. For example, at the six-cluster level, both this and the k-means result to be discussed next (figure 9.13) seem reasonable on this criterion, but there are considerable differences in detail between them. At the very least, however, average-link would seem to produce a result worthy of consideration in itself or as a starting point for re-allocation.

The k-means analyses of these fibulae have already been mentioned in sec-tion 7.5.4. A sequence of partitions for two to nineteen clusters is shown on figure 9.13, and a graph with clustering characteristics for two to eight clusters is given in figure 9.12. This includes the range of criteria calculated for six randomised trials (dotted lines). All of these illustrated results were based on Euclidean distance and the related SSE criterion, and were obtained via the Singleton–Kautz algorithm (see section 7.5.4). The highly consistent values for criteria obtained from the randomised trials by this method are strong

---

Figure 9.8. Alternative plots of relationships between the thirty fibulae of the test sample. Each plot results from a different form of analysis summarising multivariate data: (a) principal com-ponents (see table 9.4(a) and figure 9.6); (b) varimax transformation of first four principal components (see table 9.4(b): the plot is against varimax 'factors' 1 and 4); (c) canonical variate analysis: fibulae are plotted against the first two discrimi-nant functions (see table 9.4, VI). For each diagram, the weights given in two columns of table 9.4 have been used to transform the raw scores for fibulae on the thirteen attributes. See also the plot given by non-metric multidimensional scaling (figure 9.5 lower right).

	I				II			III

RELATIVE CONTRIBUTION

	(a) Principal Components				(b) Varimax Rotated Components			
attributes	1	2	3	4	1	2	3	4
1 foot length	76	−51	25	07	90	−27	06	−
2 bow height	−94	−02	09	08	−60	31	35	
3 front bow angle	−80	−16	−11	34	−40	31	07	
4 foot angle	−32	34	53	61	01	91	18	
5 coil diameter	−61	−48	−34	−06	−33	−29	07	
6 rear bow angle	−63	−46	−21	40	−14	12	−02	
7 element diameter	−57	−44	47	−10	−07	06	72	
8 foot extension length	78	−12	31	44	88	20	−16	−
9 catchplate length	06	−95	−04	−08	47	−55	23	
10 bow width	−48	02	52	01	−18	36	56	
11 bow thickness	−69	14	37	−12	−48	31	53	
12 foot extension width	78	−29	27	28	89	−01	−08	−
13 number of coils	05	14	−73	52	−08	10	−86	

Relative importance of
components indicated by

(a) eigenvalue	5.2	2.1	1.9	1.2	80.2% of total		
(b) per cent variance	40.2	16.1	14.3	9.6	variance preserved		
(c) cumulative per cent variance	40.2	56.3	70.6	80.2●			

● for remaining components 5–13: 87.4, 91.9, 93.7, 95.5, 97.2, 98.3, 99.1, 99.6, 100

Table 9.4. Results from three metric, multivariate analyses of thirty fibulae : (a) principal components; (b) varimax rotation to find simple structure; (c) canonical variate analysis. Each analysis creates a small number of new summary attributes (axes, components, functions) from linear combinations of the old. Each column in sections II, III, V and VI represents one such new summary attribute; the tabulated values indicate

the relative contribution of original attributes to it. Using these values to transform scores on the original attributes, it is possible to compute a combined score (coordinate) for each unit on each new attribute (axis), and to draw the scatter diagrams shown on figure 9.8. The rotated components in section III are sometimes described rather loosely as 'factors' and the values in section IV as 'communalities'.

evidence of its ability to find optimal or near-optimal partitions.

Comparison between the clustering characteristics of the original data (figure 9.12 solid line) and the randomised graphs (dotted lines) implies a progressive clustering structure up to and presumably beyond eight clusters, although there is a definite hint of a shoulder to this curve at the two-cluster partition. As the date symbols show, one of these two clusters includes all of

IV	V	VI

OF ATTRIBUTES TO:

(c) Discriminant Functions for

[% original variance of each attribute preserved in 4-dimensional summaries of (a) and (b)]	two clusters	six clusters		
	1	1	2	3
91	49	55	−30	−52
90	−79	01	37	26
80	−80	29	−20	−17
88	26	−17	−02	42
73	53	−22	−12	−02
81	13	−31	−27	−07
76	−34	25	32	05
90	19	28	38	27
92	−11	−51	63	50
50	24	−17	00	−24
64	−03	−20	13	−40
85	−99	−13	−01	08
83	00	00	−14	09

Relative importance of functions for discrimination as indicated by				
(a) eigenvalue	7.85	14.6	8.5	5.2
(b) per cent of sum of eigenvalues	100	47	27	17
(c) as (b), cumulative	100	47	74	91†

† for remaining two functions 96.7, 100

the three latest fibulae (nos. 2, 21 and 30) and two fibulae related to them (nos. 1 and 3). This classification would in fact be close to the traditional division of La Tène fibulae into types I and II discussed above. Each of the five fibulae so far mentioned is of Tischler's La Tène II type, characterised by one feature: the way in which the foot is bent back and *clipped* to the bow. Of the three other fibulae grouped with these five at the two-cluster level, no. 12 was found associated with traditionally La Tène II types (like no. 21); no. 9 was associated in the same grave with another of the La Tène II types included in the analysis (no. 1), but also with the La Tène I examples nos. 10 and 26, and is in a real sense transitional; see figure 9.4. The only bad anomaly (from a chronological point of view) is no. 6, a very early fibula consistently mis-placed in numerical analyses (although not by average linkage). Typological-ly, this kind of fibula seems to have features (e.g. the long foot extension) which were tried and rejected at an early stage of development but later recalled. This is the sort of ambiguity that can often only be resolved by con-textual evidence. It emphasises how the archaeologist must be prepared to modify a mechanical result obtained from some of the available data only

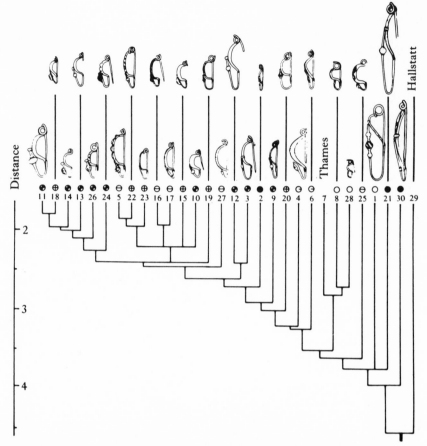

Figure 9.9. Single-linkage dendrogram for thirty fibulae. Symbols represent relative date from early (open circles) to late (filled circles) based on associations and cemetery topography (Hodson 1970, 306).

(here morphology) when other relevant evidence is available (here association). Other similar warnings will be made in discussing seriation. However, as far as this *k*-means bipartition is concerned, it is remarkable that for so small a sample, a division into two clusters was suggested that compares so closely with a long-standing, general subdivision of the material made by archaeologists. Of the hierarchy of more detailed 'types' suggested by figure 9.13, little can be said without entering into not very relevant discussions of La Tène typology. However, study of the 'best date' symbols is sufficient to show that there is a good correspondence between clusters and date at more detailed clustering levels.

A six-cluster level was chosen for some further clustering experiments. One of these was to see what modification might be suggested to these results

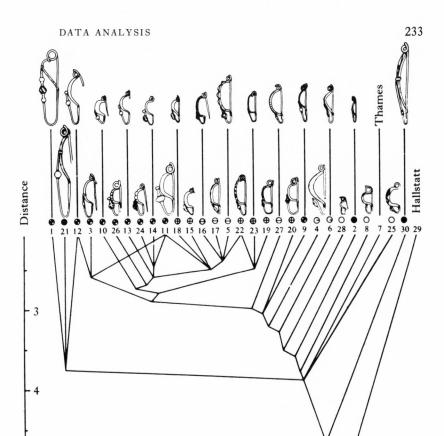

Figure 9.10. Double-linkage dendrogram
for thirty fibulae. Symbols as for figure
9.9 (Hodson 1970, 309).

if the more complex Mahalanobis distance were used as a basis for reallocating fibulae between clusters (see section 8.5). At this six-cluster level,
no reassignments were in fact suggested. At the two-cluster level already discussed, fibula no. 3 was reallocated by this procedure. Although a transitional
form, this reallocation seems for the worse rather than the better if judged on
archaeological grounds.

The computer program used to reallocate units to clusters may easily be
extended to calculate discriminate functions for a given, stable partition. As
described in section 8.5, this provides an indication of diagnostic attributes
(see table 9.4(c)), and also allows units to be plotted in discriminant space, so
that the relative separation and tightness of clusters may be assessed visually

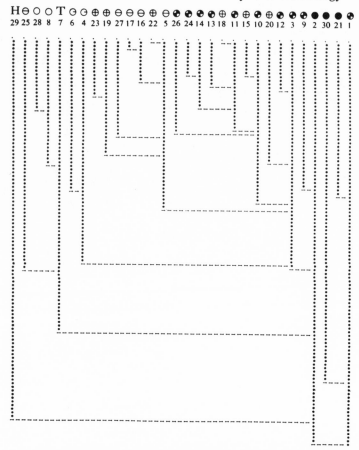

Figure 9.11. Average-linkage dendrogram for thirty fibulae provided directly by the computer line-printer. Symbols added as for figures 9.9 and 9.10 (Hodson 1970, 307).

(figures 9.14 and 9.8(c)).

For the two-cluster result, only one discriminant function is required (table 9.4(c), left). The weights which this provides show that attribute 12 (width of the foot finial) is the most important discriminator. This was just the part of the fibula singled out by Tischler in 1885 to distinguish between his major groups La Tène I and II. The values for attributes 2 and 3 in this same column show that the profile and relative height of the bow are also important for this distinction.

When the thirty fibulae are plotted relative to this discriminant function (as a histogram, figure 9.14), a clear separation between main groups is implied.

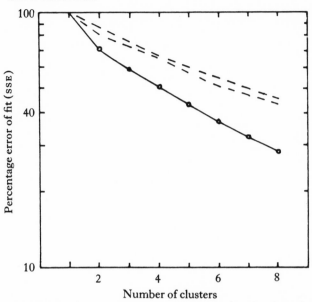

Figure 9.12. Clustering characteristics of thirty fibulae: solid line represents original data; dashed lines enclose the range of values for six analyses of randomised data (see table 9.5). (Hodson 1971, 35.)

number of clusters	2	3	4	5	6	7	8
original data	72.8	60.3	52.0	44.8	38.4	33.7	29.4
'randomised' trials							
1	88.9	76.9	67.9	62.3	55.7	50.3	45.9
2	88.7	77.4	68.7	62.1	57.0	52.0	48.1
3	85.9	76.5	68.4	61.8	55.1	50.1	46.0
4	83.9	75.5	67.7	59.4	53.0	49.3	45.1
5	84.6	75.8	68.6	61.1	54.2	50.0	46.4
6	90.0	78.2	69.5	61.0	55.3	50.1	46.0

Table 9.5. *K*-means analyses of fibula data (see figure 9.12). For each analysis after the first, columns of data (table 9.2) are shuffled independently and the *k*-means analysis repeated. Stabilised partitions for two to eight clusters are indicated by their percentage SSE (sum-squared error). Considerably less error is shown for the original than for any of the sets of randomised data (Hodson 1971).

For the six-cluster partition, five functions are required for maximum discrimination, but, as the percentage values included in table 9.4 indicate, most discrimination is given by the first two. It is instructive to note that quite different attributes are now involved in discriminating between clusters (lengths of the foot and catch plate are now most important). The plot for

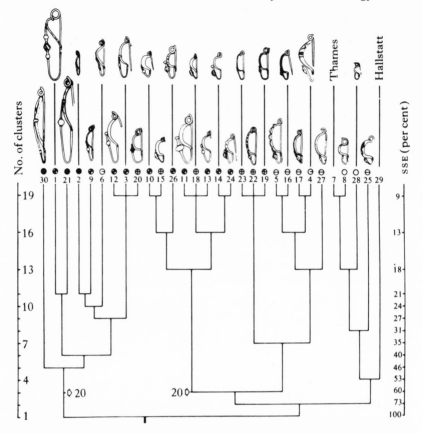

Figure 9.13. *K*-means cluster analysis of thirty fibulae. Symbols as for figure 9.9. The dendrogram is drawn from a sequence of partitions of the sample into two to nineteen clusters. At each partition an attempt is made to minimise an 'error of fit' shown at the right (see also figure 9.12). Although represented as a hierarchy, the formation of clusters is not a single continuous process, and so fibula 20 is able to migrate at the three-cluster partition (Hodson 1970, 313).

fibulae relative to the first two functions (figure 9.8(c)) shows clear separation for the extreme groups of the six, but less distinction in between.

A series of numerical classifications of a different kind (clumping, with overlapping clumps rather than clustering), were investigated for this same set of fibulae by Sparck-Jones (1970). The structures sought by their methods were mainly designed for information retrieval and, judging by these tests, do not seem to have any obvious value for archaeological taxonomy.

When the results from (a) *k*-means cluster analysis are combined with (b) a scaling analysis either metric, via principal components (see figure 9.8(a)) or non-metric (see figure 9.5, bottom right), and also (c) with a canonical variate analysis to suggest diagnostic attributes (see table 9.4(c)), a great deal of information about the interrelationships between the fibulae is obtained. In this essentially restricted experiment, each of these three kinds of analysis has produced results of direct archaeological interest.

We believe that these and other experiments have established that numerical procedures *can* produce sensible archaeological results that may be accepted as such by any archaeologist. In the next sections, the most promising of these methods are demonstrated in a more realistic context and with more comprehensively prepared data.

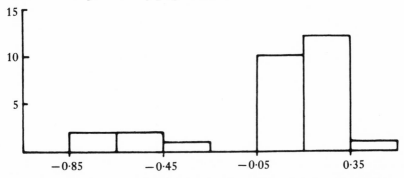

Figure 9.14. Histogram of scores on the discriminant function for thirty fibulae grouped into two clusters (see table 9.4(c)).

9.2.   HALLSTATT C SWORDS

The swords discussed in this section (see figure 9.15) provide an interesting test for numerical taxonomy. They have been studied in great detail by J. C. Cowen, and the data for analysis have been taken almost directly from his publication (Cowen 1967).

Archaeologically, the swords are of great interest: they date from the time when iron technology was first seriously introduced into temperate Europe (roughly the seventh century B C). They seem to be contextually related to this spread, as their association with the earliest native iron objects in the British Isles (at Llyn Fawr), or with iron slag in tumuli in southern France, implies. Most of the relevant swords are in fact of bronze rather than iron, but of whichever metal, they are recognised to show an unusual degree of standardisation in regions as far apart as Czechoslovakia and Ireland.

A basic taxonomic division of the swords into two types in central Europe is generally accepted, and the types are named after the sites *Gündlingen* and *Mindelheim* in Germany. However, within the Gündlingen group there are hints of distinct varieties, especially when Atlantic swords are considered as well. These are of great importance for any interpretation of the class as a whole (cf. Schauer 1972). Cowen has extended the classification taking these into account: he has separated out a *Thames type*, and has subdivided the Gündlingen swords monothetically according to the shape of the top of the hilt, the pommel piece, although clearly many other features could be considered. The most obvious contextual evidence for testing and interpreting types is geographical distribution over Europe. Cowen has already used this to support his divisions, especially for the Thames group.

The test which these swords provide for numerical taxonomy is clear: a first stage of classification should recognise the obvious contrast between Mindelheim and other varieties. A second, less obvious stage should split up these non-Mindelheim swords into 'types' that are morphologically distinctive and at the same time contextually significant.

Data were assembled on complete swords from Cowen's and other well illustrated publications, supplemented by studies of relevant examples in the British Museum. Cowen did not consider iron swords of the same shape as the

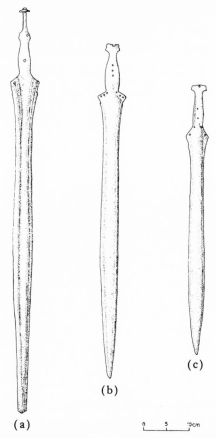

(a)   (b)   (c)

Figure 9.15. Hallstatt bronze swords: (a) from grave 126 Hallstatt (Mindelheim type); (b) from Ebberston, Yorks. (Gündlingen type); (c) from Marien-baum, Rhineland (Thames type). (Kromer 1958, Burgess 1968, von Uslar 1959.)

bronze. They tend to be badly preserved or broken, but reasonable measurements could be derived for one iron sword from Belgium (Marien 1958, figure 15). A sample of sixty-five swords resulted and these were described by nineteen attributes: mainly dimensions (see figure 9.16 and table 9.6), although counts of rivet holes were included for the top of the blade, the hilt and the pommel piece. In this section some preliminary results with standardised data will be presented.

---

1 blade length (F to L)
2 distance of widest part of blade from the top (F to J)
3 distance from blade hilt junction to maximum width at top of blade (F to G)
4 blade : maximum width (J_1)
5 blade : minimum width (I)
6 maximum width at top of blade (G)
7 blade width above tip (at K; K to L fixed as 1/20 G to L)
8 blade : maximum width of rib (J_2)
9 hilt length (C to F)
10 hilt : maximum width (E)
11 width of junction between blade and hilt (F)
12 width at top of hilt (C)
13 position of maximum width of hilt (E to F)
14 width of top pommel-piece (B)
15 height of pommel-piece (B to C)
16 height of tang or depth of cleft from top of pommel-piece (B to A)
17 number of rivet holes in top of blade
18 number of rivet holes in hilt
19 number of rivet holes in pommel-piece

Table 9.6. Attributes used to classify
Hallstatt swords (see figure 9.16).

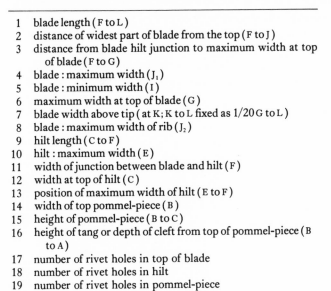

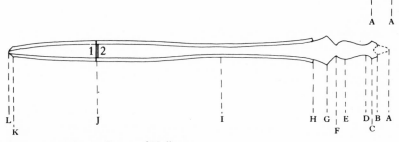

Figure 9.16. The attributes of Hallstatt
swords considered (see table 9.6).

A k-means cluster analysis has been performed, following the Singleton-Kautz algorithm (see section 7.5.4 and Hodson 1971). Partitions for two to five clusters were obtained and results for two, three and four clusters were then submitted for reallocation using Mahalanobis distance. Coordinates for the swords in discriminant space were also derived so that they could be plotted on two-dimensional scatter diagrams (e.g. figure 9.17). The advantages and disadvantages of this form of presentation have been discussed in section 8.5. Briefly, it is intended to provide as clear a visual representation as possible of the distinctness of suggested clusters.

The discriminant clustering criteria calculated suggest that it may be worth investigating more than four groups by Mahalanobis distance; a task for the future. Results of analyses carried out to date are summarised by figure 9.17, where swords are plotted in discriminant space for the four-cluster classification. Subdivisions into two and three clusters may also be discussed by reference to this diagram.

The sample was first split into two basic groups with all of the Mindelheim swords placed in the first, and the remainder in the second. They remained separated in all further subdivisions (cf. the discrete group to the right on figure 9.17). At the three-cluster level, the residue were split into two groups that correspond closely with Cowen's division between the Gündlingen type, and the Thames type with variants. However, one sword, (from Holme Pierrepoint, Notts.) illustrated with others by Cowen (1967, plate 59, 5) and classified with the Gündlingen group by him, has been grouped here with the Thames type. This is an interesting divergence, clearly caused by the contrast between monothetic and polythetic approaches: Cowen had to place the sword with the Gündlingen variety because it contained, for him, the one diagnostic attribute-state: a rectangular pommel-piece. Its overall shape (slight, short) and other detailed features such as the narrow junction between the hilt and the blade allow the polythetic computer procedure to locate this sword with the other swords that share these, perhaps more important features with it.

The four-cluster partition basically divides the Gündlingen group into two leaving the Thames group as it is (with two exceptions). The scatter diagram for four clusters in the first two dimensions of discriminant space (figure 9.17), suggests that this last division is far less marked than the previously discussed clusters. It separates Gündlingen swords into a group with very broad upper blades and broad blades in general, from a group with more slender proportions. When pointed out by this analysis this division looks morphologically convincing, although to our knowledge, it is not a division previously suggested.

These preliminary analyses do seem to say a good deal for this method of cluster analysis: it has emphasised the basic, agreed archaeological grouping into one very distinctive type (Mindelheim) and a residue. The one iron sword from Belgium (Fe on figure 9.17) is clearly located with this group. It has also supported an archaeologically reasonable division between Gündlingen and Thames types within the residue, but it is able to make this division on general grounds allowing the sword from Holme Pierrepoint to be located with the Thames series. Finally, it suggests a polythetic subdivision of the main Gündlingen series that looks plausible and that may be used and tested heuristically. From all points of view, this seems to be a most encouraging preliminary result.

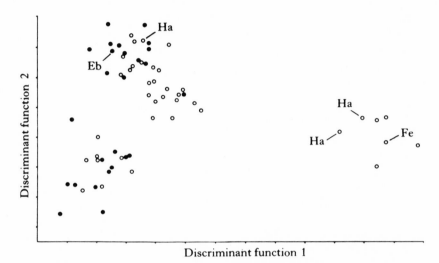

Figure 9.17. Hallstatt swords plotted against the first two discriminant functions for four clusters. Open circles represent continental swords, filled circles swords from the British Isles. Ha = Hallstatt; Eb = Ebberston, Yorks.; Fe = iron sword from Court-St-Etienne, Belgium.

9.3.   BRITISH HANDAXES
A more difficult problem is presented by the British handaxes studied by Roe (1964, 1968). He took measurements on 4 800 British handaxes from thirty-eight important sites; his purpose was to investigate *site* relationships rather than handaxe taxonomy, as was Graham's analysis of these same data (see section 8.5). However, the data which Roe collected and has made available do seem amenable to the clustering approaches discussed in chapter 7.

A report on a first set of such analyses has been given already (Hodson 1971). A random sample of 500 handaxes were taken from the overall sample using a pseudo-random number generating procedure. Twelve of these hand-axes were later rejected because of missing values, leaving a sample of 488. Five attributes were used (see figure 5.2): size as reflected by length in milli-metres (L), and shape reflected by ratios for relative width (B/L), thickness (Th/B), and pointedness overall (L_1/L) and at the tip (B_1/B_2).

The same *k*-means procedure was followed as for the swords. However, since it was far less certain that there were clusters to look for, an analysis on randomised data was carried out to provide a comparative clustering curve (dotted line on figure 9.18). This hints at clustering at the two- and three-cluster levels, and reallocation by Mahalanobis distance was carried out for

	weight	length	B/L	Th/B	B_1/B_2	L_1/L
weight	—					
length	.90	—				
B/L	−.32	.55	—			
Th/B	.15	.14	−.51	—		
B_1/B_2	.10	−.03	.16	−.08	—	
L_1/L	−.03	−.14	.20	−.10	.76	—

Table 9.7. Correlations between handaxe attributes (see figure 5.2).

partitions at these levels. Discriminant criteria and scores were also calculated (table 9.8). Figures 9.19 and 9.20 represent plots of handaxes located in this discriminant space for two- and three-cluster partitions; the former, being one-dimensional, is represented as a histogram. As might be expected, the

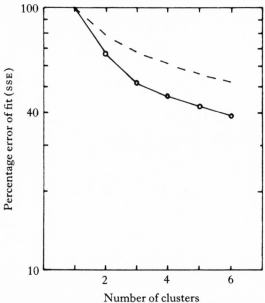

Figure 9.18. *K*-means cluster analysis: clustering characteristics for 488 hand-axes from southern Britain (D. A. Roe's data). The solid line refers to original data, the dashed line to randomised data; SSE = sum-squared error. The contrast between the two curves suggests clustering at the two- and three-cluster levels (Hodson 1971, 39).

scatter diagram shows far less evidence of clustering than for the Hallstatt swords (cf. figures 9.17 and 9.20). The histogram for two clusters suggests reasonable multivariate bimodality, but the three-cluster partition is by no means clear.

discriminant function	latent root		2 groups	3 groups	4 groups	5 groups
	1		100%	79.4%	64.6%	77.6%
1		length	2.5*	0.4	2.4	1.5
		breadth/L	−0.5	−1.4	−0.7	−1.2
		thickness/B	3.0	1.9	2.8	2.0
		pointedness 1	−1.0	−1.5	0.2	−0.4
		pointedness 2	−1.2	−2.0	0.1	−1.7
	2			20.6%	33.9%	19.8%
2		length		1.6	0.5	−1.1
		breadth/L		−1.3	1.4	1.5
		thickness/B		2.0	−0.2	−0.1
		pointedness 1		1.8	−2.0	−2.4
		pointedness 2		1.5	−2.5	−1.0
3	3				1.6%	1.4%
4	4					1.1%
determinant criterion: $LN(\,|T|/|W|\,)$			1.26	2.00	2.5	2.90

* Tabulated values represent the relative importance of the different variables for discriminating between groups. They are computed by multiplying the appropriate elements of the normalised latent vectors of $W^{-1}B$ by the square root of the corresponding diagonal element of W, where B represents the between-groups dispersion matrix, W the pooled-within-groups dispersion matrix. [See Friedman and Rubin (1967) and Cooley and Lohnes (1962, 118).]

Table 9.8. Discriminant analyses of 488 handaxes. The 'groups' are clusters defined by k-means analysis.

Since first reports of these results, Marriott (1971) has suggested further discriminant criteria for deciding whether clustering is present and at what levels. His criterion $g^2|W|/|T|$ for two and three clusters worked out at 1.13 and 1.27 respectively. These values strongly suggest that the distribution of handaxe measurements is not naturally composite (i.e. they are greater than the critical value of 1.0). However, these criteria are designed for multivariate normal distributions and indication of 'no evidence for clustering' is contrary to the randomisation test.

In view of these conflicting indications, a further random sample of 500

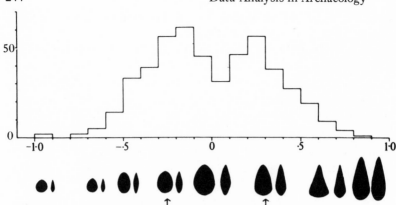

Figure 9.19. Two clusters of handaxes: frequency of 488 handaxe scores on the discriminant function plotted as a histogram. Arrows mark the position of cluster averages. Silhouettes of a range of handaxes are located below; they include the two cluster averages and the overall sample average (scoring 0). Attributes important for discriminating between the two groups are indicated by high values (positive or negative) in the first column of weights in table 9.8 (Hodson 1971, 41).

handaxes was taken. Eighteen with incomplete data were rejected, and the remaining 482 subjected to the same series of analyses as the first set. In table 9.9 the mean and standard deviation of attributes for the various clusters of the two samples are given. At the two-cluster level, the two sets of figures are remarkably similar and strengthen confidence in the belief that two clusters of handaxes are represented in the overall sample, one thicker and more pointed than the other. However, the three-cluster partitions clearly differ for the two samples: a 'thicker, pointed' group is still in evidence, but the remainder have been split in different ways for the two samples.

In spite of the doubts raised by Marriott's criterion, this replicated result at the two-cluster level, the clear hint of bimodality seen on figure 9.19 and the difference between the randomised and the real curves (figure 9.18) could be interpreted as reasonable evidence for two indistinct but discernible clusters.

It is interesting that Bordes' taxonomy for French handaxes mentioned earlier (p. 106), recognises a first basic division between thick and thin, with the critical boundary placed at the breadth/thickness ratio 2.35. This is remarkably close to the boundary suggested by the means and standard deviations of this same ratio given in table 9.9 (although here expressed in reciprocal form).

Clearly, further analyses of handaxe data, from Britain and more generally, should be carried out by these or other methods. It would also seem worthwhile attempting a more detailed attribute list for handaxes so that, potentially, a taxonomy based on more than general shape could be achieved. However future data will be prepared, it seems clear that numerical procedures will

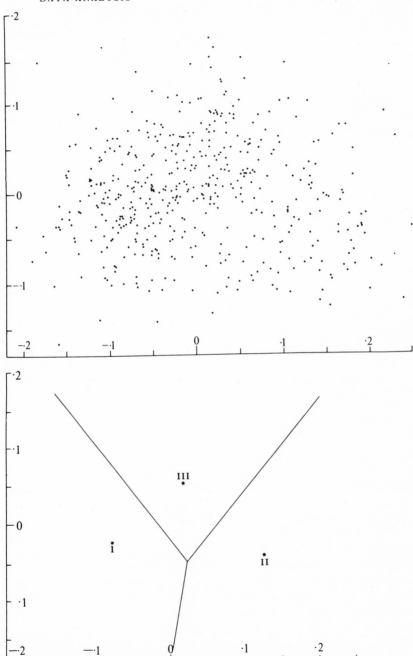

Figure 9.20. Three clusters of handaxes: (a) scatter diagram of 488 handaxes plotted against the two discriminant functions for three clusters (see table 9.8); (b) the partition suggested by *k*-means cluster analysis. Asterisks mark the location of cluster centres (averages). (Hodson 1971, 42.)

have to be both sensitive and able to deal with large numbers of units. Target populations or universes for any taxonomy will have to be carefully defined, and, if possible, some valid contextual evidence included.

						attributes		
number of clusters	cluster number	sample	number of units in cluster	L	B/L	Th/B	B_1/B_2	L_1/L
1 (total sample)	1 (total sample)	A	488	114(34)	0.65(0.11)	0.51(0.12)	0.71(0.19)	0.37(0.09)
		B	482	112(34)	0.65(0.11)	0.53(0.13)	0.73(0.20)	0.37(0.09)
2	1	A	270	095(20)	0.71(0.10)	0.44(0.07)	0.77(0.16)	0.41(0.07)
		B	230	096(24)	0.72(0.09)	0.46(0.09)	0.82(0.18)	0.42(0.07)
	2	A	218	137(33)	0.57(0.07)	0.60(0.10)	0.63(0.20)	0.33(0.08)
		B	252	127(34)	0.58(0.07)	0.60(0.12)	0.64(0.18)	0.32(0.08)
3	1	A	178	095(22)	0.75(0.09)	0.42(0.07)	0.81(0.15)	0.43(0.06)
		B	173	091(20)	0.75(0.08)	0.45(0.09)	0.77(0.14)	0.41(0.06)
	2	A	122	139(36)	0.55(0.07)	0.62(0.11)	0.57(0.18)	0.28(0.06)
		B	170	122(37)	0.60(0.07)	0.55(0.10)	0.55(0.13)	0.29(0.06)
	3	A	188	114(31)	0.61(0.07)	0.53(0.09)	0.71(0.17)	0.38(0.06)
		B	139	128(28)	0.58(0.07)	0.61(0.14)	0.89(0.19)	0.43(0.07)

Table 9.9. Two- and three-cluster partitions for two random samples (A and B) of British handaxes. Attribute means and standard deviations (in brackets) are tabulated for the various clusters. Close correspondence is seen between the two samples at the two-cluster level but less at the three-cluster level (samples drawn from D. A. Roe's data).

9.4. TRACE-ELEMENT ANALYSES: BRONZE AND FAIENCE
An area of study where efficient methods of cluster and discriminant analysis are badly needed is the classification of physical analyses carried out on archaeological objects to detect trace-elements present in their make-up. It is hoped from these analyses to isolate and locate sources of manufacture, so that industrial provinces and trade relationships may be established.

Two instances of this general problem will be discussed, both important for current work on the European Bronze Age: the classification according to their physical constituents of copper/bronze and faience artifacts.

1. *Copper/bronze artifacts* present a major problem: very many spectrographic analyses have been carried out, but relatively few trace-elements are involved. Consequently, it is possible to attribute objects to such major categories as 'pure' copper, or copper/tin bronze, but it is not necessarily possible within these categories to define consistent, local groupings based on trace-elements. This difficulty may well be insuperable for certain metal categories: almost pure copper, for example, could have been produced in many different areas and workshops, and it is probably unrealistic to suppose

that groupings based on the slightest detected presence of single trace-elements could have any workshop significance. For less pure metals, the problem is still acute, because of expected irregularities in any given ore source, possible alloying with metals from other sources, re-smelting of bronzes originally produced in diverse areas, and slight variations in smithing techniques to be expected in any one workshop: all this quite apart from the laboratory difficulties of measuring consistently small quantities of the various trace-elements investigated.

However, this does not mean that *no* useful groupings of metal profiles may be defined, and in specific regional studies, Waterbolk and Butler (1965) have shown that some groups of artifacts, that are archaeologically related by their shape and/or provenance, do have a characteristic metal content. Their approach involves first defining a hypothetical group of this kind that is likely to demonstrate similar composition. Any obvious divergences of metal content are sought by plotting general histograms for each trace element: these are hoped to reveal any major subdivisions and also outliers. Each 'refined' group is then plotted with its own set of histograms (see figure 5.10).

This essentially commonsense approach has proved extremely useful in regional studies by Waterbolk and Butler and subsequently by others (e.g. Case 1967, and Coles 1969). However, for inter-regional studies it hardly seems feasible. The increase in the number of *a priori* groupings, and the large number of unassigned outliers introduce complications that would be tedious to tackle by constant plotting, replotting and inspection of histograms. Where *a priori* groupings can be defined objectively, this approach would seem to cry out for computer treatment, not only for plotting preliminary histograms, but in calculating canonical variates for discriminating between different, hypothetical groups and for locating outliers.

However, for inter-regional studies, this whole approach is not really appropriate: it depends on the prior assignment of artifacts to groups, when what is essentially required from the whole exercise is the discovery of such groups on the basis of metal content; a cross-classification which may *then* be tested for archaeological significance on geographical and typological grounds. In other words, the situation is initially one for cluster rather than discriminant analysis.

This approach was in fact attempted from the outset by the group in Stuttgart that has carried out most of the actual spectrographic analyses (e.g. Junghans *et al.* 1960, 1968). Unfortunately, adequate techniques for detecting multivariate clusters in such large quantities of data were not, and possibly still are not available. The approach followed was (a) to look for modalities (in fact departures from normality) in the distributions of single elements, (b) to order the irregular elements into a hierarchy and (c) to set up a monothetic, divisive classification based on this ordering. Each stage in the procedure seems difficult to carry out by hand and to justify.

Because so much effort and expense has been laid out on these analyses, it

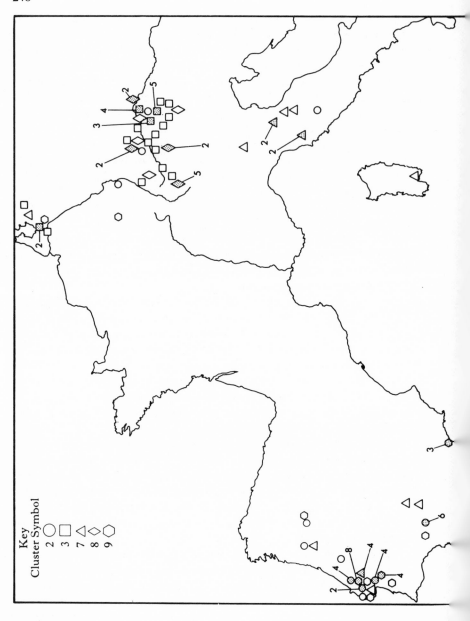

Cluster Symbol

1 □
4. △
5 ◁
6 ○

Figure 9.21. (a) and (b) Trace element analyses of copper and bronze artifacts (data from Junghans *et al.* 1960). Geographical location of clusters of artifacts with arsenic content > 1 per cent. Each symbol represents a cluster suggested by *k*-means analysis (see table 9.10). Numbers related to screened symbols indicate the number of objects from the same site assigned to a given cluster.

seems essential to extract the maximum information from them by any approach available. A suitable form of cluster analysis would seem the obvious choice, and a pilot study on 100 objects using average-linkage cluster analysis was highly encouraging (Hodson 1969). Attempts are at present under way to analyse, by other available methods, a larger sample: the entire group of 861 analyses published by Junghans *et al.* in their first major study (1960). Some preliminary results will be briefly presented.

To simplify the whole exercise, this sample has been provisionally split into three groups, assumed to approximate 'pure' copper, tin/copper bronzes, and arsenic/copper bronzes (over 1 per cent being taken as an arbitrary but probably realistic cut-off point for splitting off the latter two alloys).

Elements merely reported present as a 'trace' pose a problem in quantification. For these cluster analyses, 'traces' for elements other than bismuth were scored as 0.005 per cent; for bismuth as 0.0005 per cent. 'Not detected' was scored 0. All of the previous studies quoted have shown that logarithmic transformation of the values is required; 0.001 was added to all values before this transformation (see p. 137).

Each of the three major arbitrary groups has been analysed by *k*-means cluster analysis using the Singleton-Kautz algorithm and reallocation based on Mahalanobis distance. The significance of clusters is assessed by plotting the relevant find-spots for each cluster and judging whether the resulting geographical dispersion of a cluster is sufficiently concentrated to have workshop significance (cf. Hodson 1969).

As might be expected, little geographical significance could be attached to the clusters of relatively pure copper objects. Clusters of tin/copper bronzes also tend to produce an indistinct result. However, arsenic/copper groupings are slightly more convincing (see figures 9.21(a) and (b), and table 9.10), and localised distributions of *some* metal combinations at least are suggested (cf. the distribution for coastal Spain and Italy, cluster 4, or the distribution in the Low Countries, the Rhine Valley and Southern Germany for cluster 3).

cluster	tin	lead	arsenic	antimony	silver	nickel	bismuth	iron
1	0.0007	0.0011	1.9398	1.6859	0.6565	0.0031	0.1336	0.0032
2	0.0004	0.0011	1.6292	0.0007	0.0122	0.0092	0.0011	0.0011
3	0.0032	0.0145	1.7795	0.4383	0.0831	0.6613	0.0114	0.1016
4	0.0775	0.0027	1.6577	0.0026	0.0518	0.0025	0.0045	0.0148
5	0.0020	0.0322	2.3339	0.4914	0.1369	0.0109	0.0010	0.0056
6	0.0063	0.0557	1.4822	1.4971	0.4563	1.8645	0.0011	0.0039
7	0.0016	0.0009	2.4377	0.0014	0.0509	0.0033	0.0907	0.0043
8	0.2300	0.0622	1.3858	1.5991	0.3437	0.9065	0.0092	0.0175
9	0.0012	0.0005	4.6814	0.0015	0.0091	0.0004	0.0013	0.0020

Table 9.10. Arsenical bronzes: nine *k*-means clusters of bronzes with <1% tin and >1% arsenic. Each tabulated value shows the amount of a trace-element contained on average by objects in the cluster (data from Junghans *et al.* 1960).

At present it would seem fair to claim from this study and the earlier pilot study that it should eventually be possible to define definite combinations of trace-elements by cluster analysis. It should then be possible to distinguish clusters that represent common, natural and widely-distributed combinations of elements from those that have at least some regional significance. Within the latter, it might then be possible to distinguish highly distinctive workshop clusters from more general ore-clusters that reflect no more than well-known major ore-types.

However, far more cluster analyses using far more efficient algorithms are required for the adequate treatment of the vast sample of trace-element analyses that have already been published in Europe.

2. *Faience beads* of various shapes, dating from the second millennium BC and found in the Near East, the Mediterranean and Europe, set a similar, though more approachable problem (Newton and Renfrew 1970, Aspinall *et al.* 1972, McKerrell 1972, Harding and Warren 1973). A series of analyses of these beads were first published by Stone and Thomas (1956). Sixty-nine relevant analyses were carried out, and the quantity of eighteen trace elements recorded. This produced a highly complex body of quantitative data that could not really be exploited.

Newton and Renfrew (1970), in connection with a reinterpretation of trade patterns and general developments in Bronze Age Europe, returned to these analyses and used a computer program for 'element analysis' to extract more information about grouping from them. 'Element analysis' in this sense evidently seeks to simplify the data by eliminating attributes that are judged to contribute little to discrimination of the groups of objects concerned. It appears that where a series of attributes are found to be correlated above a certain level, one only out of the series is retained. Scatter diagrams for the units may then be plotted against pairs of remaining major variables (Newton and Renfrew 1970, figure 1). This procedure enabled Newton and Renfrew to extract far more information from the Stone and Thomas analyses than had been possible before.

Unfortunately, this kind of analysis (as would a true discriminant analysis, see p. 209) requires that a grouping of the objects is already known before the analysis can begin. This grouping is then used to evaluate the importance of the elements investigated, so that the most diagnostic may be picked out and the others ignored. Newton and Renfrew did in fact divide the beads into groups before their 'element analysis': all beads found in different areas were considered as groups, except for Egypt, where two groups were defined. This meant effectively that any trace elements that would help to distinguish alien beads traded into these areas from outside sources would be automatically played down. It would certainly be preferable in these circumstances, as for the bronze analyses, to use a method that grouped beads according to their content of trace elements alone, i.e. cluster analysis. The known find-spots of the beads could then be compared with the suggested

Data Analysis in Archaeology

clusters as contextual evidence. Therefore, it is probably worth illustrating a result obtained for the Stone and Thomas data by cluster analysis.

In view of the relatively large number of elements concerned, the uncertain number of clusters likely to be required and, at the same time, the small size of the sample (sixty-nine units), the simplest procedure seemed to be a preliminary average-linkage cluster analysis followed by reallocation by *k*-means at a suitable level of clustering as judged by the contextual evidence: i.e. to select the smallest number of clusters for the maximum amount of geographical cohesion within them. The preliminary average-link analysis is reproduced direct from the line-printer as figure 9.22. Fourteen major clusters were chosen, plus a residue ('cluster 7' on table 9.11), and the reallocation program using Mahalanobis distance was used to 'improve' these clusters. Two reallocations were made: no. 44 from cluster 6 to cluster 15, and no. 56 from cluster 15 to cluster 7. There is, as usual, no guarantee that this result is

cluster	bead	place	figure 9.22	cluster	bead	place	figure 9.22	cluster	bead	place	figure 9.22
1 ◐	25	C	1	4 ▲	24	C	11	9 ⊗	64	E	42
	59	C	5		49	E	13		65	E	41
	60	C	6	5 ▣	3	SB	7		66	E	52
2 ⬡	32	E	21		4	SB	8	10 ⊞	37	E	43
	33	E	40		5	SB	9		47	E	33
	34	E	4		7	SB	14	11 ✳	28	SIs	57
	35	E	3	6 ⬡	6	SB	37		29	SIs	58
	36	E	15		8	Sc	45		30	SIs	59
	38	E	24		9	SB	49		31	SIs	60
	39	E	16		12	Sc	51	12 ⊕	62	Sc	64
	40	E	26		13	Sc	46		68	E	66
	41	E	17		14	Sc	48		70	E	69
	42	E	28		16	Sc	32	13 ◎	55	Cz	35
	43	E	18		17	Sc	53		56	Cz	36
	44	E	2		18	Sc	47	14 ⧆	67	E	67
	45	E	19	7 ⊠	10	Sc	55		69	E	68
	46	E	25		15	Sc	39	15 ×	11	Sc	50
	48	E	12		22	M	10		19	Sc	44
	53	E	30		26	Sy	23		20	Sc	54
3 +	1	SB	22		61	Sc	65		27	Sc	63
	21	M	34		63	E	56				
	50	E	27	8 ∅	2	SB	38				
	51	E	20		57	I	62				
	52	E	29		58	F	61				
	54	E	31								

Table 9.11. Sixty-nine faience beads analysed for their trace-elements: allocation of beads (numbered after Stone and Thomas 1956) to clusters. Findspots: C = Crete, E = Egypt, S B = southern Britain, M = Malta, Sc = Scotland, Sy = Syria, I = Ireland, F = France, S Is = Scilly, Cz = Czechoslovakia.

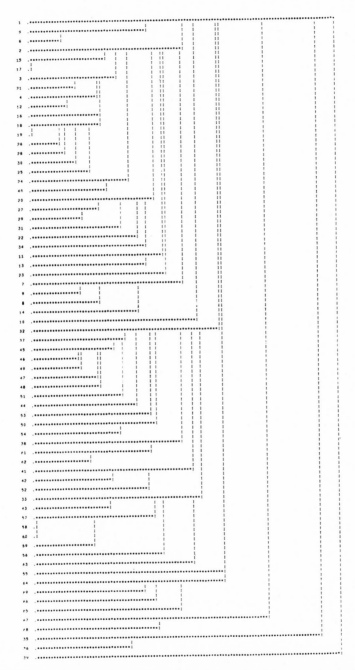

Figure 9.22. Average linkage cluster analysis of sixty-nine faience beads based on their trace-elements (see table 9.11; data from Stone and Thomas 1956).

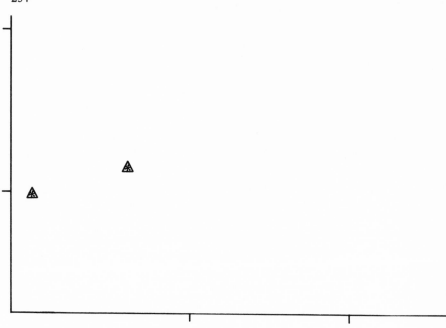

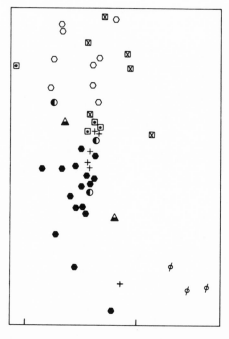

Figure 9.23. Sixty-nine faience beads plotted against discriminant functions for a *k*-means partition into fifteen groups. Symbols represent *clusters* (see table 9.11). The inset results from a further analysis for clusters of beads not well separated by the first two discriminant functions for the whole sample. Compare figure 9.24.

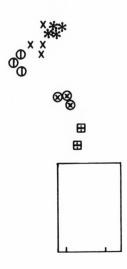

in any way optimal. A scatter diagram of beads against the first two dis-crimininant functions is given in figures 9.23 and 9.24. This shows a very clear separation of some groups (one consisting of the two central European beads), but a more jumbled residue in the centre of the diagrams. Accordingly, further discriminant functions were calculated for these groups, excluding those already separated. This result is plotted as insets.

The geographical significance of the clusters defined from trace-element evidence alone is clear from the second plot (figure 9.24) which shows the origin of beads by symbols. The need for two sets of discriminant functions is interesting: some groups are split off basically by different discriminators than others. The initial discrimination is given mainly by Li and Co on the horizontal axis, Cr and Sr on the vertical; discrimination for the 'inset' on the other hand, is given by Al, Mg, Ti on the horizontal axis, and Ti, Mn, Cu and K on the vertical axis.

Without going into details, this analysis does seem to have produced in-teresting possibilities: the two central European beads are very clearly separated from all of the others. This point was made by Newton and Renfrew and was one of the most important overall results of their study. Other detailed relationships, a group with beads found in Scotland and the Scillies, another with beads from France and Ireland, could be evidence for trade via the Atlantic seaways. A bead (no. 1) from Amesbury (Wiltshire), is placed in a cluster with beads from Egypt. There is nothing like such good discrimination

○	S. Britain
△	Scotland
□	Scilly Isles
●	Egypt
▲	Crete
■	Malta
X	Czechoslovakia
f	France
i	Ireland
S	Syria

Figure 9.24. The same plot and inset as shown on figure 9.23, but symbols now refer to *geographical location.* Comparison with figure 9.23 shows that some combinations of trace elements have a marked geographical significance.

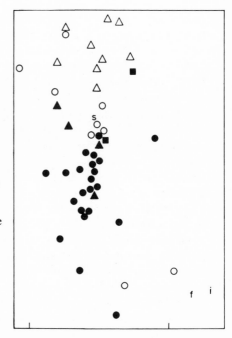

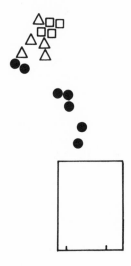

between the clusters where this bead is located, as between some other groups, but on this evidence an Egyptian source for this bead could not be excluded. On the whole, the geographical consistency within clusters is quite striking and this method seems to have produced useful archaeological information.

9.5.   PALAEOLITHIC ASSEMBLAGES: MIDDLE LEVELS OF KSAR AKIL
In earlier chapters, many of the problems concerned with the study of Palae-olithic Assemblages have been introduced and discussed separately, from the first description and classification of individual artifacts to the summary representation of whole groups of assemblages. In this section one specific case study will be followed through rapidly, from start to finish. The account is based on Azoury and Hodson (1973), where further details and references are given (see also Newcomer and Hodson 1973).

The data come from middle levels (25 to 12) of the rock shelter of Ksar Akil, near Beirut, and relate to the first Upper Palaeolithic development so far known in this important area. They form one part (about five metres) of a comprehensive depth of deposit containing earlier Mousterian and later Upper Palaeolithic industries. The absolute date for these middle levels is given approximately by one radiocarbon date from the immediately un-derlying level 26 of 41 800 ± 1 500 BC, and by another date from the rather higher level 9 of 26 890 ± 380 BC. Levels 25–12 must thus belong broadly to the ten millennia between 40 000 and 30 000 BC.

By 'levels' are understood fairly thick deposits, each distinguished from the next by a visible change in texture. The contents of such a level will necessarily represent occupation by successive human groups over lengthy periods, and the *assemblage* of material recovered must in each case be accepted as a sample, not necessarily representative, but often fairly large, of a very generalised phenomenon (see p. 107). Fortunately, from some points of view, it is just these very general, long-term distinctions that are of the greatest interest.

Perhaps a more serious defect of these particular assemblages is the virtual absence of basic ecological information to supplement the inventory of artifacts. The numerical techniques employed would allow such data (botanical, zoological, geological) to be included alongside the remains of material culture, but this was hardly possible in this study. The most that may reasonably be attempted, then, is to describe and interpret the sequence of assemblages of stone tools, which at Ksar Akil document a developing earliest Upper Palaeolithic.

This is a specific example of a host of related problems that archaeologists have tackled in various ways over the last century. The definition and interpretation of differences between Mousterian assemblages is an obvious topic of this kind that has recently received especial attention. As stated in earlier chapters, all of these studies should involve first, a clear definition of the scope of the problem and a choice of assemblages considered relevant to it; second, the adequate description of the contents of each assemblage; and third, an adequate presentation of these descriptions so that overall relationships between assemblages may be revealed and interpreted.

The basic problem discussed in this section is fairly straightforward and circumscribed: the development at one important location of a given sequence of industries. Specific comparisons are to be made only between levels from this site. As many of the levels as possible must be included, and consequently the descriptive system for the project must be adjusted to describing both relatively poor and excessively rich levels from this given site. A second rather different group of problems are concerned with general methodology, in fact in testing out alternative descriptive systems and approaches. For these enquiries the same basic descriptive system may be used in alternative guises.

The descriptive stage of this study is entirely the work of I. Azoury (1971) and represents one part of a Ph.D. project. Not all of the recorded descriptive information will be mentioned here, since it was not all compatible with a first general study of as many levels of the sequence as possible.

The scale of the descriptive problem may be appreciated from the counts given in table 9.12: over 15 000 artifacts had to be studied in detail. The material was classified for this study into a basic hierarchy with the first level differentiating (a) cores, (b) tools, (c) blanks, and (d) waste flakes. The latter category is not considered in this study. Cores were divided into seven types or clusters as originally recognised and defined by Bordes (1961). Tools were classified into a hierarchy of types: (I) major classes (e.g. end-scraper); (II) generalised types (e.g. nosed-and-shouldered end-scrapers); and (III) more detailed types (e.g. nosed end-scraper). Level III with fifty-three types corresponds closely with the level of detail at which Bordean types are defined, and indeed, many correspond with types of the Sonneville-Bordes and Perrot classification (1954–56). Level II, a short type-list with seventeen types, combines several detailed, standardised types into more general but still standardised classes. Relatively few tools had to be relegated to an 'unclassifiable' category (corresponding with Bordes' 'type' *Divers*). Cross-classifications given by such attributes as 'position of retouch' or 'edge contour' at levels I and II could not be included in this study because of the small relevant samples from the poorer assemblages.

Blanks were classified by butt type (faceted, plain or punctiform) and cross-classified by general size and shape (into bladelets, blades, flakes and Levallois points).

levels	cores	blanks	tools
25	21	32	70
24	36	52	115
23	126	650	549
22	159	2 342	1 633
21	75	487	511
20	176	1 090	912
19	132	713	578
18	46	374	266
17	550	6 182	1 541
16	76	846	349
15	17	182	51
14	4	51	14
13	29	228	130
12	135	2 227	729

Table 9.12. Counts of cores, blanks and tools from middle levels at Ksar Akil (Azoury and Hodson 1973). Level 14 was omitted from the analyses.

In the terms of chapters 5 and 7, the material has thus been described by recognising disjoint morphological clusters at different hierarchical levels, and by attributing each relevant piece to the clusters to which it belongs. Consequently, for each total assemblage it is possible to produce a direct count for each cluster defined, and the assemblages are basically described by these counts. Essentially, the whole descriptive system is based on conditional multistate qualitative attributes, and for each of the attribute states, any artifact may be scored as present, absent or inapplicable. For example, for the attribute 'tool-type', a core would be scored inapplicable in each of the fifty-three states, a nosed end-scraper 'present' for the one appropriate state, 'absent' for the remaining fifty-two states.

Of course, in practice, it would be impossibly cumbersome to list the descriptions in this form, and one shortcut would be to list for each artifact its source assemblage, and a symbolic indication of the attribute states which it possessed at the most detailed level of any relevant attribute (type) hierarchies. The computer would then build up alternative descriptive systems from this information. However, this would still require a comprehensive entry for each of the 15 000 artifacts; an unnecessarily tedious exercise, although one that we suspect has been attempted in some computerised studies reported to be under way. Since the problem is clearly defined as one of the description of assemblages, it is possible to proceed directly to assemblage description by counting for each assemblage the number of occurrences of a given attribute (type) state (for example 'nosed end-scraper' or 'faceted butt'). If more restricted stratigraphic *features* rather than general levels had been distinguished (hearth-complexes for example), it would have been possible to base the counts on these. This direct description of whole assemblages rapidly, economically and yet comprehensively is the real contribution of the Bordes' system (see p. 106). In this specific exercise, then, each of the fourteen relevant assemblages was described by an entry (representing a count of occurrences) for each of 128 attribute states—a basic data matrix with 14 rows and 128 columns—which means a relatively minor task of card-punching.

A first computer program is needed to transform these raw counts into a unified format. The obvious way is to convert each entry into percentage form. A total is required for each attribute (e.g. tool type, core type) for each level, and the count on each attribute *state* (e.g. nosed end-scraper, levallois point core) is now replaced by a percentage of the relevant total. Each entry now forms a basis for the direct comparison between assemblages, e.g. level 25 has 41 per cent chamfered pieces, level 12 has 0 per cent. A further preliminary facility is to define general classes from the more detailed where required. In this instance, the 'reduced' type-list was defined from the 'long' type list by summing the percentages of specified types. In effect, new columns of the data matrix are created in the computer to hold this information.

The complete set of totals and a labelled data matrix may now be printed out in a concise but clear format, by any standard procedure for outputting two-dimensional arrays. In practice, it proves very simple to scan this data matrix for information. Constant reference to it is necessary when interpreting any final results.

A first preliminary investigation of these data has been carried out using the technique of constellation analysis described in section 8.4 (see especially figure 8.6).

Eight general constellations were defined in an initial attempt to delineate major trends and structuring of the material. These are:

C1   short type list of 17 types
C2   short type list of 17 types, standardised data (see below)

C3 long type list of 53 types
C4 butts of blanks
C5 'types' of blanks
C6 types of cores
C7 made up of C1 + C4 + C5 + C6
C8 equivalent to C7, but data standardised (see below).

The scatter diagrams of figure 9.25 represent principal components or coordinates analyses of the levels for each constellation in turn. The numbers refer to these levels from 25 (earliest) to 12 (latest). Level 14 had to be omitted from the analyses because of its small sample (see table 9.12). These diagrams allow the interrelationships between the levels to be judged visually for each of the different categories of information defined.

Most of the diagrams result from principal coordinates analyses, where Euclidean distances are first calculated between the levels (based on the differences between corresponding percentage scores), and the levels are then referred to principal axes via these distances. This distance matrix itself may be printed out and studied; and, if desired, used as the basis for a cluster analysis. In this approach, the percentage values are used as such, and so attribute states with a wide range of percentage scores (this often means comparatively *common* types or traits) will have correspondingly more influence on the result than traits which show less variance (this often means comparatively *rare* traits).

As suggested in chapter 8, it is possible as an alternative approach, to assume that each attribute state should be given equal 'weight', whether it shows large overall variance or not. Constellations 2 and 8 represent this approach. It is achieved by standardising each column of percentages for each type so that it has unit variance. This is carried out in practice by calculating correlation coefficients between the various types defined, and then by finding principal axes from the matrix of these coefficients (see figure 8.6). The diagrams C2 and C8 on figure 9.25 result from this approach. The correlation matrices produced incidentally by this option are of great value in studying relationships between descriptors (the types and other traits). A visual summary of these relationships is also provided as part of the procedure by a plot of their weights on the first principal components. If a factor analysis of the type discussed in section 8.3 were thought desirable, these weights could be used as a basis for rotation by Varimax or any other preferred procedure.

Without entering into the detailed significance of these various diagrams, it will be seen that some suggest a more or less clearly directed sequence or seriation, corresponding with the known chronological order (especially C5, C7 and C8), while others suggest a more pronounced clustering of assemblages. In most, though not all, of the diagrams, the top two levels, 12 and 13, are placed close together and away from the remainder. This is more noticeable for the typological than for the technological constellations.

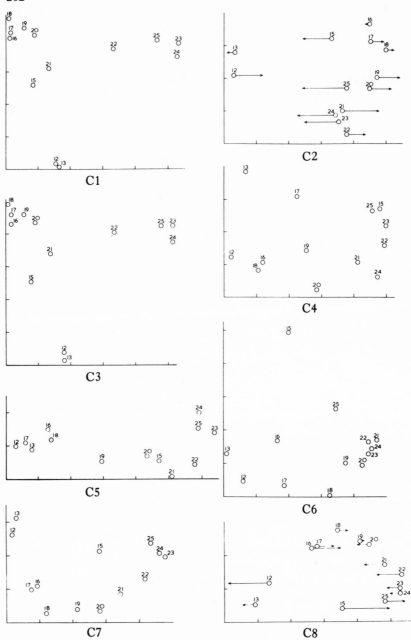

Figure 9.25. Ksar Akil (Lebanon): relationships between the earliest Upper Palaeolithic levels suggested by eight different constellations of descriptors (C1–C8). Levels are numbered from earliest (25) to latest (12). Constellations are numbered as in table 9.14 (Azoury and Hodson 1973, 300, 302).

Further summary interpretations of the significance of these diagrams will be found in Azoury and Hodson (1973).

The next stage of the analysis fits one configuration to another, and uses the residual distances between corresponding points (assemblages) as a measure of difference between the underlying constellations (see figure 8.6). For this stage, the constellations were treated in two groups, 1–6 and 1, 7 and 8. The resulting M^2 distances for 1–6 are given in table 9.13. These distances may be used as a basis for clustering or scaling, and the result of a principal coordinates scaling for constellations 1–6, starting from table 9.13, is given as figure 9.26.

	1	2	3	4	5	6
1	0.000	0.162	0.049	0.614	0.542	0.654
2	0.162	0.000	0.177	0.657	0.647	0.586
3	0.049	0.177	0.000	0.588	0.530	0.598
4	0.614	0.657	0.588	0.000	0.622	0.786
5	0.542	0.647	0.530	0.622	0.000	0.696
6	0.654	0.586	0.598	0.786	0.696	0.000

Table 9.13. Matrix of residual M^2 values between pairs of constellations after rotational fitting. The six constellations are: (1) Reduced type-list, unweighted; (2) reduced type-list, weighted; (3) long type-list; (4) blanks; (5) butts; (6) core typology (Azoury and Hodson 1973).

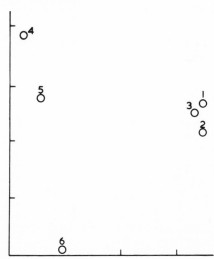

Figure 9.26. Scatter diagram representing the relationship between constellations 1–6 of figure 9.25. The configurations of levels for the various constellations are fitted against each other and the residuals computed (table 9.13).

These are treated as distances between the constellations and are referred to principal axes. The typological constellations (1–3) are closely related and contrast markedly with the technological (4–6). (Azoury and Hodson 1973, 301).

The main conclusions from this initial constellation analysis of the Ksar Akil data were that technological and typological evidence suggested a slightly different emphasis in grouping the assemblages. When both kinds of information were combined, steady overall progressive development was seen, except for a rather poor and probably mixed 'stony layer', level 15. Methodologically, it was concluded that a detailed type-list had not shown any advantages over the simpler one. Adding detail to a type-list was certainly no substitute for cross-classification suggested by technological considerations. The equal weighting of all types or categories achieved by standardisation produced a slightly, but not a markedly different result, but appeared to increased its complexity (dimensionality), so that a less satisfactory diagram of the results could be produced. The very accurate recovery of the basic sequence of levels seen, for example, on figure 9.25 C7 and C8, seems to vindicate both the descriptive system and the analytical technique used, and lends confidence to the other aspects of the analysis.

constellations		rank correlation coefficient
C1	Reduced type-list	0.56
C2	Reduced type-list, weighted	0.23
C3	Long type-list	0.57
C4	Blanks	0.71
C5	Butts	0.87
C6	Core typology	0.82
C7	Reduced type-list, blanks, butts, core typology	0.89
C8	As for C7, weighted	0.88

Table 9.14. Rank correlations between the known sequence of early Upper Palaeolithic levels at Ksar Akil and seriations given by ordering assemblages on the first principal component. Eight seriations result from the eight constellations of assemblage descriptors (Azoury and Hodson 1973).

In our opinion it would be difficult to suggest any other approaches at the present time that would be able to deal so effectively and comparatively simply with such a large body of primary palaeolithic data. The inclusion of ecological evidence, which should be available from more recent excavations, would have added little if any extra complexity to the analysis.

PART THREE
Beyond Data Analysis. Problems and Prospects

Automatic Seriation

10.1. INTRODUCTION

In part 2 of this book the emphasis was on data analysis: methods of data presentation, measures of association, automatic classification techniques, and other methods of multivariate analysis. Problems in the construction and interpretation of typologies were central to the discussion. Now we turn to other mathematical and computer techniques which may have useful application to archaeological problems. Whilst some of these have been investigated in detail, most have been much more discussed than tested in practice. The views expressed in this final part of the book, therefore, will be a good deal more speculative and controversial than those expressed earlier.

In this chapter archaeological *seriation* problems will be discussed together with the rather substantial amount of mathematical and computer work which has been directed to their solution. By an archaeological seriation problem we mean the task of arranging a set of comparable archaeological units, for example assemblages of artifacts, into a meaningful sequence solely on the basis of comparisons and contrasts between them. Notice that the objective is a sequence not a scaling: the intervals between units are not required. We must make clear at the outset our view that the mathematical work directed towards the solution of such problems has much less real archaeological value than its quantity would suggest. Our reasons can briefly be stated as follows. Where the objective of the seriation exercise is explicitly to recover chronological sequence, as has often been the case, it seems to us that the techniques so far developed so simplify the true archaeological situation that their results cannot be taken too seriously. On the other hand, if the object of the exercise is merely to find that ordering of the units which best expresses similarity relationships between them, without considering its interpretation, then we find it hard to imagine situations in which some form of scaling procedure of the kind discussed in chapter 8 would not be more appropriate. Our views will become clearer as the chapter proceeds.

10.2. THE ARCHAEOLOGICAL PROBLEM

Irving Rouse has defined seriation as follows: 'It is the procedure of working out a chronology by arranging local remains of the same cultural tradition in the order which produces the most consistent patterning of their cultural traits' (Rouse 1967, 157). Like most definitions this one is easier to understand by reference to some relatively concrete examples. Thus typical chronological seriation problems could be:

1. Given a number of assemblages of pottery sherds each including roughly the same range of types though in different proportions, determine the most likely chronological sequence in which they were deposited.

2. Given a number of burial assemblages from a single cemetery, decide the chronological sequence in which the burials were made.

3. Given a set of related artifacts, for example fibulae or swords, determine the most likely chronological sequence of their manufacture.

4. Given the remains of a number of fortifications of the same kind, determine the most likely chronological sequence of their construction.

The nub of a chronological seriation problem is that external dating evidence is either unavailable or deliberately put to one side. There are no radiocarbon dates, no stratigraphy, no inscriptions, no exactly dated parallels. The *seriation units*, be they assemblages, structures or artifacts, must be put into chronological order solely on the basis of comparison between them. A small seriation problem, by present standards, involves less than about thirty units; a very large one more than a hundred.

To make progress with such problems criteria for plausible chronological sequences must be adopted. These criteria must express reasonable beliefs about likely and unlikely trends of development for the seriation units concerned. What, for example, is a plausible process of development for a particular type of bronze sword? Such questions are usually answered either by detailed and expert assessment of directed stylistic or functional evolution, or by less sophisticated arguments which relate similarity of form and style to proximity in time—the more aspects and characteristics shared by two seriation units, the shorter the time interval between them is likely to be—or rest on simple assumptions about the dynamics of artifact types. In his definition Rouse has attempted to capture the many possible criteria by the words 'the most consistent patterning of cultural traits', perhaps not without entirely escaping the charge that his net captures boots as well as fish!

Once criteria for a plausible chronological sequence have been decided a practical problem is encountered: how to set about finding the most plausible sequence, or, indeed, any plausible sequence at all. This is not the minor problem it might at first appear. Suppose that there are ten pottery assemblages to be ordered. The number of distinct orderings turns out to be 3 628 800. Thus the practical problem is to find which of these orderings looks best on the criterion, a task which if tackled merely by inspecting one ordering after another without mechanical help would take a very great deal of time. And the number of possible orderings rises very quickly as the number of seriation units is increased. In practice the unaided archaeologist must use a combination of intelligence, insight and systematic search to obtain a plausible ordering reasonably quickly.

A fundamental difficulty in chronological seriation work is that seriation units may easily differ, not because their origins are separted in time, but for reasons such as difference in location, function or social class. Thus there is always a possibility that the sequence obtained in a seriation study may reflect not time but some other 'underlying' variable. There are two possible reactions in this situation. The first is to endeavour so to choose the seriation units at the outset of the study that any ordering obtained is bound to be chronological. Thus Rouse's definition of seriation quoted above makes explicit three conditions which must be satisfied if the results of a seriation exercise are to be taken seriously as a chronology (compare Ford 1962, 41–2):

1. The seriation units used must be drawn from a single locality; the need is to control for spatial variation.

2. The seriation units must all come from a single cultural tradition; only confusion can be expected from an attempt to seriate material drawn from two or more traditions which happen to overlap in time and space.

3. The aspects or traits of the seriation units employed in the study must be culturally, and therefore potentially chronologically, significant.

Even if these three requirements are met it does not follow that the results obtained will necessarily have chronological significance, but the chances are much improved.

The alternative response to the problem of nonchronological underlying variables is to accept that the result of a seriation study always needs interpretation; that the underlying variable or variables at work must be decided by the archaeologist. This difference of approach becomes particularly important when the objective is to quantify and automate seriation work. Where appropriate we shall distinguish between *chronological seriation* and simple *ordination*.

10.3. SERIATION BY SCALING

The reasons for quantifying and automating archaeological seriation work are apparent. Not only is there the general argument that the more that can be thrown into objective, repeatable mathematical form the better, there is the practical need to transfer to a computer the tedious business of hunting through possible orderings of seriation units looking for a good one. It is therefore not surprising that seriation began to involve mathematics and computers at a relatively early stage, around 1950. Much work has been done since then, very varied both in content and sophistication. Often archaeologists have consulted with a programming assistant and developed *ad hoc* methods without realising that their problems were only new in detail, and that a substantial body of practical experience and theoretical guidance was available to them just over the academic horizon.

Of the two attitudes to seriation mentioned in the previous section the second, ordination, accepts that the sequence derived may have no chronological significance and must always be interpreted. This immediately suggests using some of the techniques of multivariate analysis discussed in earlier chapters. The point here is that a sequence of seriation units is merely a relatively uninformative special case of a one- or two-dimensional scaling of those units (see figure 10.1). It is much easier to study a two-dimensional scatter diagram presenting the relationships between the seriation units, possibly isolating one or more 'trends' which may or may not be chronological, than it is to decide what to do with an ordering presented as a *fait accompli*. From this point of view an excellent way to solve a seriation problem, or rather to supersede it, is to calculate covariances or correlations and perform a principal components analysis or to calculate similarities and perform a principal coordinates analysis. Detailed examples of such studies are given in chapter 9. The use of these multivariate techniques only makes sense, of course, if the base assumption is the simple one that similarity between the seriation units, however measured, is correctly interpreted as proximity on the scale of the 'underlying' variables (including possibly time). It is important to remember that in such a study, as indeed is true of all of the methods to be described in this chapter, the direction of the sequence or trend is not recovered. Thus where chronology is in question there is no intrinsic means of telling which end of a sequence is early and which late.

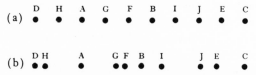

Figure 10.1. A linear scaling of a set of units (b) is visually much more informative than a simple ordering of them (a).

A technique similar to principal coordinate analysis in its aims is nonmetric multidimensional scaling, discussed in section 8.6. One of the best known and most studied techniques for the solution of seriation problems is based on multidimensional scaling. It was initially developed by D. G. Kendall, and is often known as the 'horseshoe' method from the shape of the point scatter typically generated by the scaling program (HORSHU) used.

Kendall initially considered the case where the seriation units are grave deposits from a cemetery. Specifically he attempted to throw into mathematical form a major seriation problem tackled by Petrie at the turn of the century. This problem, and Kendall's first reactions to it, are discussed below in section 10.5. The scaling procedure which Kendall finally developed is, in outline, as follows:

    1. Starting from a presence-absence matrix (a 1 in the (i, j)th loca-

tion of the matrix indicates that an artifact of type j was found in grave i; see section 5.2), compute a similarity matrix for the graves, the similarity between two graves being the number of artifact types which they have in common.

    2. Apply non-metric multidimensional scaling in two dimensions to this similarity matrix, working from several different pseudo-randomly generated starting configurations of points.

    3. Carry out a principal components analysis for each of the resulting terminal configurations projecting the points on to the principal component.

    4. Read off a sequence from each such projection.

    5. Pool these sequences to obtain the best.

When Kendall applied this procedure to data drawn from the La Tène cemetery at Münsingen Rain involving some sixty grave assemblages, he obtained results close to those obtained by a relatively conventional archaeological analysis of the same material (D. G. Kendall 1971).

    Whilst the point is not an essential one, it is worth noting that Kendall does go to some trouble to automate the process by which an actual sequence is obtained. He regards the two-dimensional scatter-diagram not as the end-point of the study, but as an extremely useful intermediate stage; useful because it enables the archaeologist to check his assumption that a single chronological dimension is sufficient to describe the similarity relationships between the seriation units. Thus Kendall is aiming at a chronological seriation (following Petrie in fact) while leaning strongly towards the ordination approach. In this he differs from the principal components work cited above, and indeed from earlier multidimensional scaling exercises (Doran and Hodson 1966; Hodson, Sneath and Doran 1966).

    Kendall's application of multidimensional scaling to seriation problems has been extended not only by Kendall himself but also by others such as Sibson (1971b), and E. M. Wilkinson in unpublished work. Developments of particular interest include the use of abundance data-matrices (for example, where the entries are percentages), the use of sophisticated mathematical techniques to straighten out the horseshoe-shaped two-dimensional point scatter and hence make it easier to interpret, and a study of which relationships between seriation units it is unreasonable on archaeological grounds to use in the analysis and how they can best be discarded. In a recent study Cowgill (1972) has taken as the units in the scaling analysis not the seriation units but the attributes or types by which they are described. Thus it is the columns rather than the rows of the data matrix which are scaled. There is a parallel here with principal components scaling from covariances rather than principal coordinates scaling from distances.

    Whilst the amount of practical experience with multidimensional scaling in actual archaeological seriation contexts is still limited, the evidence that is available is encouraging. It is important to keep in mind, however, that non-metric scaling, unlike principal coordinates analysis, involves a ponderous iterative procedure which is both fallible and time-consuming. On the other hand, it is rather more general and flexible than principal coordinates analysis.

10.4. PERMUTING SIMILARITY MATRICES

The use of multidimensional scaling to solve chronological seriation problems is a relatively recent development. Historically it has been much more common to calculate a similarity matrix between seriation units but then not to scale it but to permute it; that is, shuffle its rows and its columns (in step) until they are in the most plausible chronological order by reference to some *ad hoc* criterion. An ordering of the seriation units is thus obtained directly with no intermediate stage involving a two-dimensional configuration of points. This increase in directness is at least partly offset (many would say more than offset) by the loss of the opportunity to check basic assumptions by studying the two-dimensional configuration, and *a fortiori* of the opportunity actually to terminate the analysis with this configuration.

In complementary papers published in 1951 Brainerd and Robinson suggested a method of this direct type. Robinson, a statistician, was asked by Brainerd, an archaeologist, to provide a numerical method for seriation in the specific context of pottery assemblages. The technique developed by Robinson was based upon 'the empirically established fact that over the course of time pottery types come into and go out of general use by a given group of people', and that 'types come into and go out of use in a lenticular fashion' (Robinson 1951, 293; see figure 10.2). Robinson's technique is sometimes called, confusingly, 'matrix analysis'—a name which has no mathematical standing and

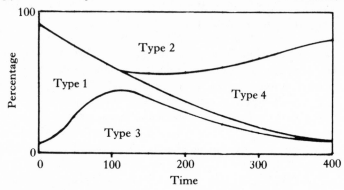

Figure 10.2. Diagram to illustrate the suggestion that types comes into and go out of use in a lenticular fashion. Four types of pottery are supposed and their differential use traced over a period of 400 years (Robinson 1951, 293, figure 89). See also figure 10.5.

is probably best avoided altogether (see section 7.4.3). It prescribed the following steps:

1. Given the percentage of each pottery type appearing in each assemblage compute a similarity measure (Index of Agreement) between

each pair of assemblages. The index suggested is the sum of the difference between the percentages for each type summed over all types (without regard to sign), subtracted from the maximum possible figure, 200 (see section 6.3).

2. Arrange the computed similarity scores into a matrix whose rows and columns correspond to the assemblages in some arbitrary order.

3. Rearrange in step the rows and columns of this matrix until the high similarity scores are, as far as possible, concentrated on or near the main diagonal (table 10.1).

lots	1	2	3	4	5	6	7	8	9	10	11	12
1	200	128	99	87	65	83	78	57	48	50	36	35
2	128	200	169	110	96	100	93	69	57	59	45	44
3	99	169	200	118	115	109	102	77	67	69	55	52
4	87	110	118	200	156	170	162	143	141	127	126	114
5	65	96	115	156	200	171	168	158	147	142	136	129
6	83	100	109	170	171	200	186	155	155	153	137	143
7	78	93	102	162	168	186	200	160	163	156	146	141
8	57	69	77	143	158	155	160	200	164	175	174	153
9	48	57	67	141	147	155	163	164	200	165	171	146
10	50	59	69	127	142	153	156	175	165	200	177	165
11	36	45	55	126	136	137	146	174	171	177	200	163
12	35	44	52	114	129	143	141	153	146	165	163	200

Table 10.1. An example of a matrix of Robinson similarity scores which has been sorted so that the larger the score, the closer it is to the main diagonal. Since any assemblage is identical with itself the values actually on the main diagonal are all 200. (Kuzara, Mead and Dixon 1966, 1451, figure 1).

The final order of the matrix rows then yields the desired chronological ordering of the assemblages without indicating, of course, which end of the sequence is early and which late. If some of the assemblages are in fact stratified deposits, then it may well be possible to use stratified sub-sequences both to direct the main sequence in time, and to check it for unacceptable anomalies.

Brainerd and Robinson applied their method of seriation to a number of small data sets derived from Mayan pottery and obtained encouraging results. Since then a wide range of variants of their method has been explored. The aspects most open to variation are: (a) the precise measure of similarity used; (b) the manner in which the matrix is sorted; (c) the exact criterion which is used to decide how good is a particular matrix sorting.

Measures of similarity have been discussed in chapter 6. The merits and demerits of the Robinson Index of Agreement, a subject of some controversy at one time, were discussed in section 6.3 and no more will be said here. Brainerd and Robinson thought entirely in terms of hand-sorting of the similarity matrix, and a number of the experiments which followed theirs did rely upon hand sorting aided at most by some simple mechanical device. However it was soon realised that a computer could easily be programmed to undertake this part of the process with a great increase in power, flexibility and precision. The first such program was published in 1963 by Ascher and Ascher, and a number of others have followed, notably those of Kuzara, Mead and Dixon (1966), Hole and Shaw (1967) and Craytor and Johnson (1968).

The most important decision the programmer must make is how to organise the search for the optimal arrangement of matrix rows and columns. Merely to look at *all* possible arrangements one by one would take inconceivably long even for the largest digital computer if the number of seriation units (i.e. rows and columns in the matrix) is more than ten or so. So all these programs use a form of iterative *heuristic search* and proceed broadly as follows. An arbitrary ordering of the rows is selected at the outset, preferably by use of pseudo-random numbers. Small modifications to the chosen sequence are then tried out, each determined by one of a large pre-selected set of sequence modifiers or *operators*. A typical operator would, for example, be that which interchanges the fifth and sixth entries in a sequence.

Every time operator application improves the ordering, the change made is retained. When a modification does not lead to an improvement it is discarded. The set of operators is scanned repeatedly until no operator improves the current ordering. The search then stops. This complete process, from the generation of an arbitrary initial ordering to the discovery of a terminal ordering which is 'locally' optimal is repeated a number of times with, of course, a different initial ordering on each occasion (see figure 10.3). The best of the terminal orderings, which may not all be different, is then the 'solution' returned by the program. There is no guarantee that this solution will really be the best possible ordering, and indeed it will normally not be. It will almost invariably, however, be relatively good.

A crucial factor is the actual set of operators employed by the program. A possible set is that of all shifts of an entry in the sequence to some other point in the sequence. A smaller and less effective set consists of all interchanges between adjacent entries. Sadly there is little mathematical theory indicating which set of operators it is best to use. The choice between the many alternatives is largely a matter of intuitive insight and experimental experience. Heuristic searches of this and similar types are frequently used in computer work. Non-metric multidimensional scaling, for example, relies upon what is essentially a form of heuristic search; a fact that has sometimes been overlooked.

The mathematical criterion used to determine the chronological validity of an ordering must in some way or other capture the intuitive idea that high values in the similarity matrix should cluster around the main diagonal. As usual there are a number of alternatives with no very easy way to choose between them. Different experimenters have different preferences. The monograph by Hole and Shaw (1967) discusses this and the preceding issues in

some detail and reports on a number of experiments. A review of this monograph by Cowgill (1968b) is also extremely useful, especially as regards practical archaeology. Another good discussion is that of Johnson (1972). It is appropriate to mention again in this context an issue discussed in section 7.4.3.
Is it reasonable to use 'matrix analysis' as a means to automatic classification
rather than merely seriation? Although there are early examples of such a
procedure, notably its use by Tugby (1958), the issue first became prominent
when Clarke (1962) used a modified form of the Brainerd–Robinson approach

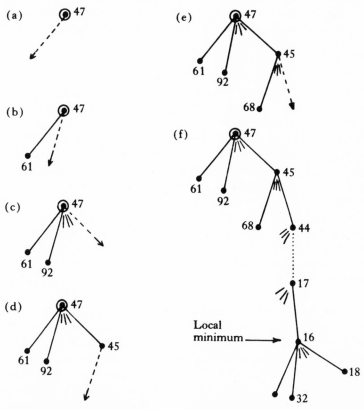

Figure 10.3. Successive diagrams to
illustrate an iterative heuristic search.
In automatic seriation work each node
corresponds to an ordering of the rows
(and possibly columns) of the matrix to
be sorted and each arc to an operator
(modification rule) which makes a small
change in an ordering. The numbers are
hypothetical scores for the orderings according to some criterion. The lower the
score the better the ordering. Diagrams

(a) to (d) show successive operators
being tried out on the initial ordering
(ringed) until an operator is found which
generates an ordering with a lower score.
In (e) operators are being applied to the
new improved ordering. In (f) the
search has reached a local
minimum—an ordering which, although
not necessarily the best possible, is not
improved by any of the available
operators.

to search (by computer) for clusters in a large collection of British bell beakers. Clarke's matrix related pairs of beaker characteristics by the number of beakers which displayed them both, a tactic which is open to severe criticism as discussed in section 7.4.3 (see also Matthews 1963, Clarke 1963). The point of importance here, however, is that Clarke sought clusters of high values in the sorted matrix and took these to indicate recurring type combinations of characteristics. More recently others have likewise worked from a seriation to a classification (e.g. Johnson 1972). Unfortunately, it is difficult to see such an approach as anything but confused and arbitrary, and therefore potentially misleading. While it may sometimes give tolerable results, there is certainly no reason to prefer it to the methods discussed in previous chapters.

10.5. PERMUTING THE DATA MATRIX

One of the stranger things about numerical seriation work is that until recent years it was almost invariably assumed that once a data matrix had been compiled, either a presence-absence matrix or an abundance matrix, the next task was to convert it into some form of similarity matrix. The seriation problem then became one of permuting (in step) the rows and columns of this similarity matrix. The strangeness lies in the fact that what is actually required is a permutation of the rows of the data matrix itself. Why not work directly on the data matrix? Why involve a similarity matrix at all? There is no real reason to think that the search for a good permutation will be any easier for a similarity matrix than for a data matrix. Perhaps there has been an element of 'follow my leader', with some of the original 'leaders' as much interested in classification as seriation and therefore prone to think in terms of similarities. On the other hand it is true that in some cases there simply is *no* data matrix preceding the similarity matrix, as when the seriation units are complex objects needing hierarchical description.

In fact, one of the earliest and most important seriation studies in archaeology, that by Petrie (1899) at the turn of the century, does not use the concept of similarity between seriation units at all. Petrie tackled the problem of arranging some 900 graves from the cemetery at Naqada on the Nile in relative chronological sequence. He did this by studying the various types and varieties of pottery found in the graves using an ingenious and intricate sequence of arguments. A particularly important principle which he used has been christened by D. G. Kendall the *Concentration Principle*. Kendall (1963, 659) states this principle as follows: 'Disturbances of the original order of graves are likely to scatter the varieties more widely, so that (other things being equal) arrangements which reduce the ranges of varieties are to be preferred to those which do not.'

In a later paper Kendall (1971, 217) put it more carefully: '*if* the typology is "chronologically significant", and when the graves have been correctly ordered (or anti-ordered), then the "sequence-date"-*ranges* for the individual types will be found to have been individually *or in some communal way* minimised' (Kendall's italics). A matrix whose rows have been so ordered that the non-zero entries in each of the columns are fully contiguous is said by Kendall to be in the *Petrie form*. At just about the time that Kendall published his first definition of the Concentration Principle, Dempsey and Baumhoff (1963) published an interesting paper in which they advocated the use of presence-absence data matrices, and in which they interpreted the basic Brainerd-Robinson lenticular hypothesis concerning the successive waxing and waning of types through time to mean for such matrices that the 'presences' should show maximum continuity; an idea very similar to the Concentration Principle.

The simplest way to make the Concentration Principle mathematically exact is to take it to mean that the rows of the presence–absence data matrix should be ordered to minimise the sum over all the columns of the range of the entries for each column. In symbols, the function to be minimised is

$$\sum_{\text{cols}} R_i$$

where R_i is the difference in value between the first and last entry in the ith column (see figure 10.4). This gives an exact criterion for a good chronological ordering of the seriation units. Further, a heuristic search for good

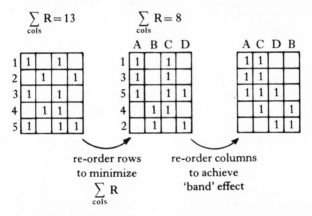

Figure 10.4. A very simple way of giving effect to the 'Concentration Principle'. The rows of the incidence matrix are reordered to minimise the sum of the spreads of entries along the columns. Subsequently the columns may be reordered as indicated to facilitate study.

orderings can be implemented just as is common in the context of similarity matrices. Experiments using this simple criterion have been reported by Doran (1971a) in which good results were obtained for the Münsingen data mentioned earlier. Doran and Powell (1972) have shown how the task of finding the optimal row ordering for this criterion can be formulated both as a branch-and-bound problem and as a linear integer programming problem.

A more sophisticated mathematical formulation of the Concentration

Principle was derived by Kendall in his 1963 paper. The word 'derivation' is appropriate because Kendall did not select the criterion on intuitive grounds but deduced it by way of a probabilistic model and maximum likelihood estimation. More will be said about this in the following chapter. The criterion itself is

$$\sum_{\text{cols}} N_i \log R_i$$

and, as before, that ordering of the rows of the matrix is sought which minimises this function. Again R_i is the range of the entries in column i, but now N_i is the number of artifacts of type i which are recorded in the matrix, assumed to be an abundance matrix of counts containing a high proportion of zeroes. This form of the Concentration Principle has been tested in practice by Kivu-Sculy (1971) on Hellenistic inscriptions but without much success; as the experimenter states, this is probably a consequence of a mismatch between the assumptions underlying the criterion and the problem to which it was applied. On the other hand E. M. Wilkinson in unpublished work has had some success on a large seriation problem using a maximum likelihood criterion similar to Kendall's.

The largest seriation problem for which a computer solution has been claimed is that tackled by Goldmann (1971, 1972). He derived a presence-absence matrix with 790 rows (assemblages) and 404 columns (types) from bronze-age material from South-Eastern, Central and Northern Europe. Working from assumptions not dissimilar to the Concentration Principle he commissioned computer programs which together generated an ordering of the assemblages in about one hour's running time on an IBM 360/75. The more important program used a form of heuristic search similar to that discussed above. The ordering obtained was consistent with evidence from stratigraphy. Unfortunately full details of this interesting study have not yet been published, and its significance is therefore difficult to evaluate.

The idea of sorting the rows of the data matrix itself can in principle be employed for full abundance matrices where, for example, pottery type frequencies are recorded. Indeed this is exactly the procedure advocated by Ford (1962) in his handbook of practical methods for archaeologists. Ford founds his procedure on the assumption that the waxing and waning of each type through time should be representable by what is sometimes called a 'battleship' curve (see figure 10.5). This is identical with the Robinson 'lenticular' assumption. In practice, direct permuting of full abundance data matrices by computer has been seriously attempted only by Regnier (1972).

Is permuting a data or similarity matrix an exercise in chronological seriation in the sense defined earlier? Or is it merely ordination? It depends very much upon one's state of mind. Certainly Robinson, Ford and Kendall were all explicitly aiming at chronology. But this does not preclude the use of their methods in more general situations and with more flexible objectives.

10.6. SOME MATHEMATICAL RELATIONSHIPS

It would be quite wrong to leave the reader with the impression that sorting the rows of a data matrix to optimise a mathematical criterion based on the Concentration Principle has no relationship to sorting the rows and columns of a similarity matrix to bring the high values close to the main diagonal. On the contrary some of the most interesting mathematical results derived with archaeological problems are the theorems that establish that there is a relationship, and do much to elucidate its precise form.

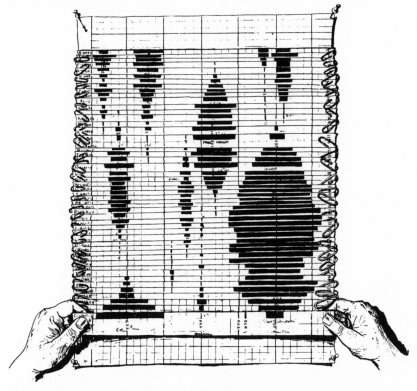

Figure 10.5. Drawing by Ford to illustrate his hand method of constructing a seriation graph. Frequencies of the types in each collection are drawn as bars along graph-paper strips. These are arranged to discover the type-frequency pattern ('battleships') as shown. (Ford 1962, figure 8.)

Essentially what has been shown (D. G. Kendall 1971, Wilkinson 1971) is that if the similarity matrix is computed from the data matrix in a specified way, then a data matrix which *can* be permuted into the exact Petrie or 'battleship' form will give rise to a similarity matrix which can be permuted into an exact 'Robinson' form, i.e. the values of the entries always decreasing away from the main diagonal. Further the permutation of the similarity matrix which gives rise to the Robinson form, is the permutation needed to throw the data matrix into the corresponding Petrie or 'battleship' form. Thus, with perfect data, solving the similarity matrix is equivalent to solving the data matrix. Unfortunately there are no results for imperfect data, which is, of course, what one always encounters in practice.

Wilkinson (1971) has extended these basic results by working with a matrix of artificially defined distances between seriation units. In the ideal case he is again able to show that sorting this matrix to have low values near the main diagonal is equivalent to sorting the other matrices as described above. However, sorting such distance matrices is equivalent to one of the more famous problems studied by mathematicians and computer scientists, the 'Travelling Salesman' problem. Unfortunately the most effective method developed for solving this problem turns out to be just the kind of heuristic search already developed independently by archaeologists for solving the seriation problem itself. Hence the relationship between the seriation problem and the Travelling Salesman problem is (so far) of theoretical interest only. Another paper relating seriation to the Travelling Salesman problem is that of Kadane (1972). However Kadane does not make use of heuristic search and works only with very small data sets.

10.7. RAPID SERIATION METHODS

Principal components analysis, multidimensional scaling and heuristic search are all impracticable without the aid of a computer for any but trivially small seriation problems. Further, if a problem is of any size (with more than thirty units say) then the computer must be a powerful one. In these circumstances it is natural to look for some seriation method which, while inevitably less reliable, requires relatively little computation; preferably so little computation that it can be carried through by hand 'in the field'. A number of such methods have been suggested.

In 1959 Meighan published a paper in which he proposed a '3-pole' method of seriation, which was then formulated algebraically by Ascher (1959). Essentially this method consists of: (a) eliminating all but three major types, or combining similar types to reduce the data to three categories; (b) computing percentage distributions as if these three types or categories constituted the entire assemblages; and then (c) plotting the resulting percentages on triangular coordinate paper (see figure 5.18) and fitting a straight line by eye through the points to approximate an ordering. This procedure rests on the usual Brainerd-Robinson assumption of lenticular change in type frequency together with the additional assumption that one can reduce the data to just three types or categories without major loss of information. When evaluated by Hole and Shaw (1967) it provided results which, when referred to archaeological truth, compared surprisingly well with those from more sophisticated procedures.

More recently rapid seriation methods of considerable interest have been suggested by Renfrew and Sterud (1969) and by Gelfand (1971). They are all refinements of the simple idea that one should select any seriation unit; find the unit most similar to it and place this beside the first, thus beginning a 'chain'; find the unused unit most similar to either end of the chain and add it to the appropriate end; and so on. The details are such that the computations can be carried through by hand for quite large seriation problems once a similarity matrix has been calculated. Unfortunately this itself will require a computer for more than a small quantity of data, so that perhaps there is little point in not automating the subsequent analysis also; a simple and rapid program will suffice. These methods have not been much tested in practice beyond their authors' original evaluation. Gelfand has proved mathematically that if an ideal Robinson ordering can be achieved, then either of his two methods will always achieve it. This is true neither of Kendall's multi-dimensional scaling approach nor, in general, of heuristic search. He also defines a criterion score which has good theoretical properties.

10.8. COMPLICATIONS

All the methods discussed in this chapter rest upon some simple assumption relating the form of the seriation units to underlying variables, especially time. Thus some methods explicitly rest upon the Petrie-Kendall Concentration Principle, others upon the Brainerd-Robinson assumption of lenticular change in type frequency, and others again on the simple idea that similarity in form implies proximity in time. As has been made clear in section 10.6, these assumptions are closely related. All of them have from time to time been claimed to be too simple or even downright self-contradictory (e.g. McNutt 1973).

Even if these basic assumptions are accepted, the most superficial study of practical problems reveals a number of difficulties which complicate the simple picture so far presented. The most important of these may be listed as follows:

1. It is rarely, if ever, the case that there is no external evidence available to help arrange seriation units in chronological sequence. Where, for example, some evidence from stratification is available is it sufficient merely to use this as a check at the end of the seriation analysis?

2. Suppose that the seriation units are assemblages of either pottery or other artifacts. Should it not influence the conclusions drawn if some assemblages are much richer than others, or if some types are much more abundant than others?

3. What if the occurrence of two artifact types is naturally positively or negatively correlated, e.g. swords and scabbards or two types of sword? Should only one of them be used? More generally, what if we intuitively regard some types as much more significant than others? Should they still just be given equal weight in the analysis?

4. What if some artifact types are more similar to one another than others; thus one type of sword is more similar to another type of sword than it is to a brooch? Again, is it good enough to treat all types as equal and independent?

5. The way in which the types used in a study were defined is of great importance. Might it not be a good idea to incorporate numerical type definition into the seriation procedure? Indeed, how often can seriation really be separated from classification?

6. Irrespective of the definition of types, might it not be useful and natural to incorporate automatic classification as a heuristic within seriation procedures as a way of simplifying large problems?

All of these issues are ill-understood, and some of them subject to considerable controversy. The best that can be done here is to comment briefly upon some of them. The question 1, of what to do with 'extra' evidence, is sometimes argued. The usual view is that this evidence is best kept either as an independent check, or for integration by the archaeologist himself when he is studying the results of the numerical seriation analysis. The contrary view, that the numerical analysis should itself take account of this evidence, meets the weighty objection that little is known about how to program computers to do this. However there has been some work done along these lines, for example by Regnier (1972), who does take into account known stratification sequences in a chronological seriation study.

Relationships between the types used in a seriation analysis (3 and 4), and the different degrees of significance which may intuitively be attached to them, generate weighting problems of the kind discussed in section 6.6. Current practice is very simple. The set of types used in the study is selected (or should be!) to avoid particularly blatant examples of correlation and so on. The analysis is then performed without worrying about these issues and the result interpreted cautiously.

Finally there is the question of incorporating automatic classification as a heuristic within seriation procedures, 6 above. The basic idea can be explained very easily. Suppose that a collection of a hundred graves is to be ordered. It might well be an effective strategy to classify the graves into a dozen or so grave types, seriate the types, and separately order the graves within each type. Assuming that the grave assemblages classify fairly naturally, it is intuitively plausible that major computational savings can be effected in this way. Classification of artifact types is similarly possible. Limited experiments along roughly these lines have been reported by Bordaz and Bordaz (1970), Hodson (1970), Landau and de la Vega (1971) and by Doran (1971a, and see section 11.7). The computer programs needed are considerably more complex than for straightforward seriation techniques and this has naturally tended to inhibit investigation of an approach which is of considerable interest.

10.9. The Value of Automatic Seriation Methods

As stated in the introduction to this chapter our view of automatic seriation methods is by and large a negative one. As we see them such methods can *either* be exercises in ordination, by which we mean arranging the units of the study in a sequence constructed to reflect as far as possible their similarity relationships, *or* be deliberately aimed at the recovery of relative chronology (or, in principle, some other specific underlying variable of interest).

As regards ordination we feel that it has less to offer than the more general scaling methods, including principal components analysis and principal coordinates analysis, discussed and exemplified in chapters 8 and 9. In our view such methods are clearly to be preferred. If the aim *is* to recover relative chronology then very different considerations arise. The formal analysis must not merely prepare data for visual inspection and interpretation by the archaeologist, but itself recover the chronological sequence. This is an essentially much more difficult task. It implies that complicating or even dominating factors such as geographical or social variation must be recognised and eliminated by the formal procedure.

Of course it has frequently been asserted or implied that a suitable choice of data can avoid complicating factors so that chronological seriation is reduced to ordination. Both Rouse (section 10.2) and Ford (section 10.5) suggest that this is so. We find such an assumption archaeologically very dubious. We believe that 'pure' chronological seriation problems are very much the exception rather than the rule (compare McNutt 1973).

Can the complexities of 'impure' chronological seriation problems be handled within the mathematics? Can mathematics distinguish, for example, between functional and chronological patterning? The answer is certainly 'no' as far as presently available techniques are concerned. Progress in such directions will require mathematical models of social phenomena which in their complexity and sophistication go well beyond the very simple general purpose models which underlie current classification and seriation studies. In the following chapter we shall discuss the prospects for the use of more sophisticated mathematical and computer simulation models in archaeological work.

It follows naturally from what has been said that where the choice of a specific sequence is unavoidable, it is best extracted from a scaling diagram generated either by non-metric multidimensional scaling, as in Kendall's work, or from principal components or coordinates analysis (see chapter 9). To go direct to a sequence by iterative search, while mathematically more elegant and more flexible in the sense that the optimisation criterion used is at choice, is archaeologically much more dangerous. It is true that really large seriation problems, where the numbers of units are measured in hundreds, have been attempted only by iterative search methods. However, ubiquitous uncertainties in the value and completeness of the results obtained and in the efficiency of the computer programs and experimental strategies employed, make it quite impossible to draw the conclusion that such methods are appropriate to the larger problems.

More generally it remains true that there has been rather little detailed evaluation of the reliability of seriation methods in practice and even less practical and theoretical comparison between them. Perhaps the most substantial study is that of Hole and Shaw (1967) cited earlier, which does not, however, take into account procedures based upon principal components or coordinates analysis or non-metric scaling. Some of the detailed experimental work presented in chapter 9 is very relevant here.

As stated in section 10.7, rapid but only approximate methods of seriation have attracted some attention and interest. In principle it is an attractive idea to carry through a rough hand analysis 'on-site' or as a preliminary to something more sophisticated. But we feel that for more than a very small number of units, say more than fifteen or twenty, the detailed calculations become sufficiently onerous and the results sufficiently uncertain that one should turn to the computer. And once this is done there is no reason to discard more sophisticated analyses. In any case, the labour of obtaining archaeological data is usually so high that it is a little perverse to put too much stress on 'cheap' methods of analysis.

Mathematical Models and Computer Simulations

11.1. MATHEMATICAL MODELS AND GENERAL MODELS

The concept of a mathematical model was introduced in section 2.10. There it was explained that such models consist of one or more mathematical equations which assert relationships between variables. The variables are extracted from some situation or system of interest, where by a 'system' is meant some complex changing whole such as a society, a dragon-fly or a river. Sometimes the equations are equivalent to geometrical relationships or patterns (see section 11.2.1). In section 2.10 an artificial example discussed in some detail served to illustrate what modelling as an activity is like, and other more realistic examples cited included the mathematical equations which model a ship rolling in heavy seas or the behaviour of a spacecraft in orbit. Models of this kind do not involve random variables and are said to be *deterministic*. Notice that specialist mathematical notations such as Venn diagrams (section 2.3), abstract graphs (section 2.3) and histograms (section 3.7), are not themselves mathematical models although they frequently contribute to modelling work.

In section 3.17 *stochastic* models were introduced. By definition such models involve random variables. Whenever a normal distribution is invoked or a regression or factor analysis used, then this is stochastic modelling but only in a rather weak sense, for the models in question are 'general-purpose' rather than designed for a particular application. Any attempt to make an existing deterministic model more realistic is always liable to involve adding stochastic elements to it. Thus a very simple model of traffic flow at a set of traffic lights could be purely deterministic, but anything at all realistic must involve random variables corresponding to the unpredictable, short-term fluctuations in traffic density.

Put at its simplest and briefest the point of using mathematical models, deterministic or stochastic, is to learn more about the situation or system modelled, by applying mathematical inference to the model equations. In particular it will be possible to make useful predictions by inferring unknown variable values from those which are known. To do this it will first be necessary to devise the model itself; that is, to find one or more equations which correctly or adequately relate the variables of interest, and then to choose or estimate parameter values. Both of these steps requires access to reliable empirical data. Then before it is accepted as sound, the model should be validated against fresh data if at all possible. An excellent general discussion of mathematical modelling, its nature, and objectives and methods, is that of M. G. Kendall (1968).

An important concept in mathematical modelling is that of a *process*. In normal usage the word denotes, roughly speaking, some continuing and relatively autonomous activity. Thus one speaks of a chemical or legal process, or more generally uses the word of the wearing of a coin, or of the excavation of a site, or of cultural evolution. Mathematicians have captured this meaning in abstract terms and have erected a *theory of stochastic processes* (section 11.4). Mathematical models frequently describe processes. The model equations relate variables, including time, abstracted from some real-world process. Computer simulations, to be discussed in section 11.5, model one process by another. A process within a computer is itself an abstracted representation of the target real-world process. Like other mathematical models, computer simulations can be either deterministic or stochastic. The mathematical concept of a process should not be confused with the more general theoretical concept of a system. This latter idea, and the embryonic body of theory associated with it, will be considered in chapter 13.

Mathematical modelling is no more than one branch of modelling as a general activity. Thus Clarke (1972) commences a lengthy discussion of the use of models in archaeology by distinguishing between 'controlling' models and 'operational' models. By the former he means the prior assumptions and attitudes with which any archaeologist approaches his data, or indeed with which anyone approaches anything! Such matters have much more to do with psychology and social science than with mathematics. Clarke uses the word 'model' in this somewhat remote sense to stress the similarity between these often unconscious preconceptions and the explicit heuristics and models used in archaeological research itself: his 'operational' models.

At the most general level models can be classified in this and a variety of other ways. Distinctions are often drawn between models which are already to be found in the real-world and those which must be constructed; between physical models and those which are abstract; between models which are scaled down replicas of that modelled and those which seek to capture only essentials; between models which involve the passage of time and those which do not. Thus possible models of a river are an aerial photograph, any stream, a scale-model constructed in a water tank, a paragraph of text describing the river, and one or more mathematical equations.

Such distinctions between classes of model tend to blur in practice. They serve more to indicate the range of models available than to identify systematic differences. Whatever the kind of model used, the aim in using it changes little. Models replace situations or systems or entities which we cannot understand or investigate or predict by those that we can understand, investigate or predict. To the extent that the model somehow captures the essentials, the exercise will be useful.

11.2. MATHEMATICAL MODELLING IN ARCHAEOLOGY

The question: 'Should models be used in archaeology?' is vacuous if the word 'model' is interpreted as widely as Clarke would have it. At that level of generality we all use models all the time. The significant and difficult question is: 'To what extent can mathematical models be useful in archaeology?' The reason why this question must be asked is that mathematical models have long been demonstrated to be extremely powerful in basic scientific work. Their use in the social sciences and the humanities is steadily increasing. It would be as unreasonable to dismiss their potential value for archaeology out of hand as it would be to accept their use uncritically. The challenge is to discover to what extent mathematical models can be useful, given that archaeology is ultimately about people rather than the physical world, and is largely unsuitable for controlled experimentation and random sampling in the mathematical sense.

When considering the foregoing question it is possible to distinguish four major contexts in which models (henceforth by 'model' we always mean 'mathematical model') might be useful in archaeological work. These are:

1. Studies of some aspect of a prehistoric society and its environment.

2. Studies of the process by which potential archaeological evidence is established in antiquity and preserved for recovery today.

3. The design and execution of archaeological excavations.

4. Studies of the archaeologist himself and how he evaluates and interprets the evidence available to him.

The categories differ substantially in the scope which they offer to the modeller and in the nature of the difficulties which they present. Thus modelling prehistoric societies is directly comparable with modelling contemporary societies, differing only, but perhaps crucially, in the even greater difficulty of obtaining reliable data. The survival of archaeological evidence can sometimes, on the other hand, be expressed very neatly and easily by a model as, for example, in the case of radiocarbon dating. Organising excavations has much in common mathematically with, for example, organising a construction site or some manufacturing process, and the problems are well-known and well-understood if not always easily solvable. Studies of archaeological inference itself must relate both to psychology and the philosophy of science. They seem to offer relatively little scope for modelling, even though the role of mathematical models in experimental psychology is well-established.

As the studies to be discussed in the next section and the remainder of this chapter will indicate, most of the attention given to modelling in archaeology has so far concentrated on the first of these four categories, that is, the modelling of different aspects of early communities or societies and their relationship to their environment. This is understandable given that such problems form the *raison d'être* of archaeology. Nevertheless a contributory factor is certainly that the interest in modelling has been generated by explicit modelling work in closely related disciplines such as anthropology and geography (e.g. Chorley and Haggett 1967). In these disciplines the human societies of interest are much more accessible than in archaeology. Problems of data reliability and interpretation loom less large. Hence it is natural that in them modelling should concentrate upon the societies themselves rather than merely the processes by which we learn about them. Archaeologists should perhaps beware of an emphasis inappropriate to their real needs.

11.2.1. *Examples of modelling in archaeology.* Many models are no more than simple formulae or equations. Sometimes they aspire to the status of law, to wide applicability; sometimes there is no suggestion that they apply to more than one specific situation. Thus Naroll (1962) has proposed an equation relating the floor area of early dwellings to the number of their inhabitants. Vértes (1968) has used a simple equation to represent the increasing rate of proliferation of technological inventiveness from Olduvai onwards. And Casteel (1972) has proposed 'two static maximum population-density models for hunter-gatherers'.

Each of Casteel's models, for example, is a mathematically very simple equation which relates maximum yearly human population density, or 'carrying capacity', to environmental variables such as the number and area of the ecosystems involved, terrestrial and aquatic food resources, and food traded. The central idea is that the human population is ultimately limited in size by the energy sources available to it. In practice the value of Casteel's models will depend upon the extent to which such a population limit indicates actual population—a weak point—and upon the accuracy with which the energy resources can be estimated in any particular case. The equation merely lays down how these estimates are to be combined once they have been obtained. The model is purely static with no attempt to allow for the reciprocal effect of the population upon its energy resources (compare the Forrester 'world model' discussed below in section 11.5.2).

Studies such as that of Casteel lean heavily upon ethnographic data and are at least as much a part of anthropology and ethnology as they are of archaeology. A similar flow of ideas from a parallel discipline, in this case geography, into archaeology is apparent in the study by Hodder and Hassal (1971) of the spatial patterning of Romano-British walled towns in Southern England (see also Hodder 1972). The authors first set out to decide whether or not the towns are located at random. They therefore carry out a 'Nearest Neighbour Analysis', the central step being to calculate the mean distance of each town from its nearest neighbour. The question is then asked: 'Is this mean distance too large or too small for it to be reasonable to treat the towns as located at random?' If the mean distance is too large then the suggestion is that the towns are regularly spaced, if too small that they cluster. The authors apply a statistical test of significance and reject the null hypothesis of random spacing. As mentioned in section 3.15, there is some logical difficulty here since it is not clear why one should ever consider the possibility of towns being randomly spaced. What matters in practice is that the mean distance is high indicating a tendency to regular spacing.

Hodder and Hassal proceed to consider various possible regular patterns for the location of the towns. These geometric models they draw from *Central Place Theory* developed by Christaller (1933) which relates the distribution of settlements and towns of different sizes to the socio-economic relationships between them. The question to be answered in as objective a manner as possible is whether or not one of the theoretical patterns 'fits' the observed distribution of towns. An affirmative answer carries with it socio-economic implications and predictions to the extent that the adopted pattern may be reliably and uniquely interpreted. In fact the authors do find a model which they feel fits the data (see figures 11.1 and 2), and they use it to make a number of

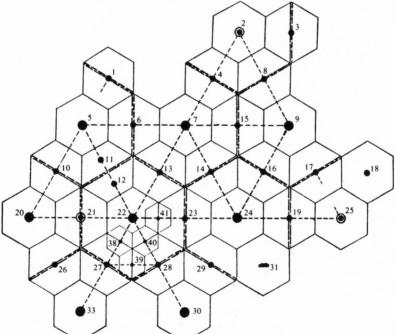

Figure 11.1. The pattern of Romano-British settlement in diagrammatic form according to the transport principle of Christaller. The numbered nodes refer to known Romano-British centres whose locations have been adjusted to fit an ideal pattern predicted on theoretical grounds—see figure 11.2 (Hodder and Hassall 1971, 399, figure 6).

predictions about the status of particular towns which they proceed to verify against independent data. The procedure they use, however, is throughout almost entirely subjective and heuristic.

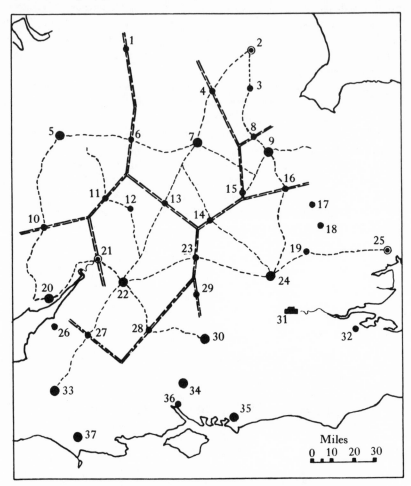

Figure 11.2. The elements of the pattern of figure 11.1 constrained to the real distribution of Romano-British walled towns (Hodder and Hassall 1971, 401, figure 7).

This is a good example of mathematical modelling in *spatial analysis*. It is especially interesting because it poses the problem of how such models should be fitted and tested objectively. This problem is touched upon below. Archaeologically the study is open to the criticism that the models deployed are manifestly too simple from the outset. They assume, for example, that Southern England is a featureless plain. They fail to take into account much information that is clearly relevant, for example the Pre-Roman tribal structure of Southern England. Although these assumptions are easily justified on practical grounds they do substantially undermine the conclusions of the analysis however carefully it is conducted. This is a situation often noted before; a piece of mathematics is no better than the assumptions upon which it is based.

A slightly different form of spatial analysis uses some objective method directly to associate with settlement centres the territories which they served or exploited. Thus Hogg (1971) has experimentally associated territories with Iron Age hill-forts in Britain south of the Thames. His basic principle is that the boundary point between the territories of two forts is closer to the smaller in accordance with the ratio of their areas (Weighted Thiessen Polygons). At the end of a particularly valuable discussion of the method and the results it yields in this context he comments: 'The way in which these forts fall into groups does suggest that this purely objective method of analysis gives results which have some real significance, but at present, it would be un- wise to claim that it provides a clue to the real territorial boundaries' (p.122). A variety of similar spatial models is deployed by Ellison and Harris (1972) in a more elaborate and perhaps rather too ambitious study of parts of southern England between 1500 BC and 1000 AD. A good general discussion of the territorial concept is that of Jarman (1972) who stresses that: 'the primary factor to be considered is the effect of increasing "cost" or difficulty of exploitation as the effort and time expended in exploitation increases'.

All the foregoing studies have used determinate models. An example of a stochastic model is that used by Orton (1973) to relate the number of rim (and base) sherds found in an assemblage of pottery to the number of vessels from which they are derived. He assumes a Poisson relationship for each vessel and uses the fact that if a number of variables each follow the Poisson distribution, then so too does their sum. This is a neat example of a stochastic model being used to aid the interpretation of archaeological evidence. Orton's work as presented in this and earlier papers repays close study (Orton 1970, 1971; and see section 5.3.3).

Much more sophisticated stochastic theory is brought to bear in a study by Ammerman and Cavalli-Sforza (1973). Here the object of study is the spread of primitive farming across Europe. The model is an equation in- volving differentials (section 2.7) as follows:

$$\frac{\delta\psi}{\delta\tau} = a\psi(1-\psi) + \beta\mathbf{\nabla}^2\psi$$

Essentially what this equation does is to relate the rate of increase of the pop- ulation density ($\delta\psi/\delta\tau$) at a given locality at any time (τ) to (a) the existing density at that time (ψ), and (b) the rate of change of density with change of locality ($\mathbf{\nabla}^2\psi$).

The equation is intended to express rigorously two basic ideas; that the population density rises to a maximum which it cannot then exceed, and that the spread of the population is the consequence of random local migration. The authors suggest that the spread of farming across Europe is the result of such population growth and displacement rather than of cultural diffusion. Thus they are attempting to model the underlying mechanism of the spread rather than merely measure it. One of the inferences that can be made from the equation is that a wave of population expansion will spread out from the central starting point with constant radial velocity. By relating this radial velocity to the estimated rate of spread of early farming across Europe (based upon available radiocarbon dates), and by taking into account available estimates of the rate of population increase at a fixed locality under primitive conditions, the authors estimate the amount of local migration needed to obtain the observed effect. This turns out to be eighteen kilometres per generation of twenty-five years. While it is easy, as with the study of Hodder and Hassal cited above, to charge the model with over simplification there is a glimpse here of the real power of mathematical models. By way of the mathematics conclusions are drawn from the assumptions that are not intuitively obvious and potentially have real archaeological significance.

As a sample of mathematical modelling in archaeology the preceding examples are representative but perhaps not too impressive. It is hard to avoid the impression that the models are still too simple and limited in scope to do much more than add an air of objective rigour to one step in a chain of inference which is still otherwise a matter of subjective, if expert, judgement. Worse, they may unduly restrict the argument as a whole. To some extent similar objections could be raised to any use of mathematics. In practice a piece of applied mathematics is always preceded and followed by subjective judgements. It is *always* possible to argue that the model used is too simple. The crucial question is whether or not the gain in objectivity and precision achieved by using a mathematical model at one point in an investigation or argument is or is not outweighed by the over-simplifications and distortions which its use requires elsewhere. There is no general answer to this question. Unfortunately we feel that for most of the work mentioned in this section the losses exceed the gains.

11.3. MODELS AND GOODNESS-OF-FIT FUNCTIONS

In the previous chapter, reference was made to a paper published by D.G. Kendall in 1963 in which he deduced a precise mathematical formulation of the Concentration Principle used to solve seriation problems. Kendall in fact made use of an interesting stochastic model. This will now be discussed together with related general issues.

Against the background of the experiments described in the preceding chapter, one would expect Kendall, presented with the Petrie problem (section 10.5), to have chosen a convincing *ad hoc* mathematical criterion for a 'good' ordering of the rows of the matrix. The next step would be to write a computer program to search for the optimal ordering in some heuristic way.

Faced with a formally identical problem of the same magnitude several years later, Goldmann, an archaeologist, did exactly that. However Kendall, as a statistician, tried to see the problem as one of estimating certain unknowns from certain observations, and therefore set out to construct a suitable statistical model and then to solve it using maximum likelihood estimation.

The essence of Kendall's model is that each type of pottery has a period of time in which it is in circulation and is, therefore, liable to appear in a grave. If a certain type of pottery is in circulation, then it appears in a grave with an abundance determined by the Poisson distribution. From this can be derived an equation for the likelihood of obtaining the given data matrix for each possible ordering of its rows:

$$\sum_i N_i \log R_i$$

where N_i is the total abundance of the pottery type in column i and R_i its spread. It is this likelihood expression which is naturally interpreted as an exact statement of the Concentration Principle.

Kendall's approach differs from those discussed in the preceding chapter in just one crucial respect; the criterion to be maximised is not invented *ad hoc*, but deduced from a precisely stated stochastic model. This might appear to be a major step forward in the solution of such problems. But, as Kendall (1971) himself has stressed, there are objections. In particular he has criticised the approach on the following grounds: (a) an inconceivably large amount of computation would be required to maximise the criterion for a matrix with 900 rows (the number of graves considered by Petrie); (b) there is no check built into the method to ensure that the graves *are* appropriately arranged in sequence; for example, there might well be a social dimension in addition to a time dimension; (c) the details of the model are extremely arbitrary; in order to carry through his mathematics Kendall made a number of exact assumptions when all that the archaeological evidence suggested was a certain kind of assumption. Kendall found these objections, especially the first, overwhelming and turned his attention to seriation methods based on multidimensional scaling as described in the last chapter.

In the time that has passed since Kendall published his study the situation has become less clear cut. The first difficulty stated above, the amount of computation needed, is both ubiquitous and, fortunately, not as overwhelming as Kendall feared. It applies in all such combinatorial studies, and, more strikingly, it applies to multidimensional scaling as much as to this approach. The lack of a check on linearity is undeniably important. It is on precisely this ground that scaling has been favoured in the preceding chapter. Nevertheless it should be recognised that such a check could probably be included in matrix permutation methods without too much difficulty. It is not essential to go all the way to multidimensional scaling.

But it is the third point which is the most interesting. As has so often been stressed in this book, conclusions drawn from a piece of mathematics are at most as sound as the assumptions made in order to apply the mathematics. Hence the criterion deduced by Kendall from his model has only as much validity as the assumptions of the model itself, and these are easily assailed. This might now suggest that mathematical modelling in such contexts is a waste of effort. One might just as well select a seriation criterion on intuitive grounds.

This raises a question of great general importance. Should the criteria used to measure how far a pattern of data corresponds to a desired pattern or model (and of which the seriation criteria of the last chapter are examples) be selected because they are intuitively plausible or because they may be derived from stochastic models? Such criteria are often called *goodness-of-fit* or *badness-of-fit functions*.

Exactly the same fundamental question arises with automatic classification. Most methods use an *ad hoc* definition of what constitutes a 'good' classification. Erecting a model tends to require arbitrary and unrealistic assumptions. However, as with seriation, there is a degree of convergence between the model approach and this *ad hoc* approach, as will now be explained.

A distinction is commonly drawn between discrimination and classification: the former concerning the allocation of a new item to the correct category, the categories being known at the outset; and the latter being the construction of a set of categories, a set of items being given at the outset. However it has recently been shown by Scott and Symons (1971) that in at least one precise mathematical context this distinction is less useful than might at first appear, and this demonstration is closely related to the issues which we have been considering.

The 'classical' discrimination problem asserts that one is given a set of multivariate normal distributions, each fully specified. Given an observation (necessarily a vector) the problem is to decide which normal distribution it was drawn from. Effectively this is a model of a certain event, the generation of the observation. The problem is solved using maximum likelihood estimation; the observation is assigned to the normal distribution which would most often have given rise to it.

This problem can be generalised and made much more difficult by supposing (a) that there is given a substantial set of observations, not just one; and (b) that while it is known how many multivariate normal populations are involved, their means, variances and covariances are unknown. To decide the allocation of each observation (and to estimate the unknown parameters) by using maximum likelihood estimation is now no easy matter. But it can be done. It turns out that in the various cases that arise, the likelihood functions which must be maximised to establish the allocation of the observations are closely related to the classification criteria used in k-means analysis (see chapter 7)—criteria selected on largely *ad hoc* grounds.

This study confirms that there is no essential contradiction between the use of *ad hoc* goodness-of-fit functions and the use of models. The issue is whether one feels more or less secure with a criterion derived from a model resting on rather arbitrary assumptions. For example, any attempt to make rigorous the model fitting process central to the Hodder and Hassall study cited earlier must either involve an *ad hoc* goodness-of-fit function or the development of the spatial models into fully specified stochastic models from which likelihood criteria can be derived.

The choice between *ad hoc* goodness-of-fit functions and actual stochastic models is in the last resort merely one aspect of the choice between data-analytic methods and classical statistics as mentioned in section 3.20. There is, of course, no sense in damning either alternative and lauding the other to the skies. Kruskal has put it very well: 'I certainly have no quarrel with stochastic models, nor do I deny their great value. However, I would argue that they present a more sophisticated situation. In many instances it is neither practical nor useful to attempt this level of sophistication. Consequently, I believe that the use of badness-of-fit functions, where no stochastic element is explicitly present in the model is a perfectly well justified procedure when greater detail and sophistication is either impractical or un-justified by the current state of knowledge' (Kruskal and Carroll 1969, 640). Contrast this view with that of Edwards (1971, 355): 'Now the only sure way to decide what form of analysis is appropriate is, in my view, to commit yourself to a specific model according to which you think the observations might have been generated. Merely to define the properties which you wish the solution to have is not good enough for critical work unless you can explain why you want those properties. I am myself guilty of having invented one such method of cluster analysis; others have invented other methods which use other criteria, but the argument over which criteria are best cannot be resolved without a model for the process of dispersion.' Whilst we have con-siderable sympathy with Edwards' view, we feel that Kruskal's is at present the more realistic in archaeological contexts.

11.4. RANDOM WALKS, CHAINS AND BRANCHING PROCESSES

Ammerman and Cavalli-Sforza, in their study discussed in section 11.2.1, argue that the spread of farming across Europe is the consequence not of the transmission of knowledge from one group to another, but of the actual move-ment of people on a small scale, of 'random local migration'. Correspondingly, the form of the model equation they use is partly determined by the assumed existence of something like a *random walk process*. In its simplest form such a process involves a particle moving on a plane in a series of steps. The length and direction of each step are chosen at random and are quite independent of those of preceding and following steps. The effect is that the particle wanders haphazardly over the plane, its path crossing and recrossing (figure 11.3).

Mathematicians have studies such processes and have worked out, for example, how far the particle is likely to be from its starting point after a given number of steps.

Random walk models have an obvious attraction in archaeological work. Intuitively they suggest small groups of nomads wandering at large; or pot sherds being knocked to and fro on a living floor until they become embedded and left to be found long afterwards. A good example of the exploratory use of simple random walk theory is the study by Hogg (1971) of late Iron Age coin distributions in Southern Britain. He tries to see whether observed departures from the coin distributions to be expected if the coins 'random walk' from the mints provide evidence of tribal boundaries. Clarke (1972) includes a useful discussion of other possible uses of random walk models.

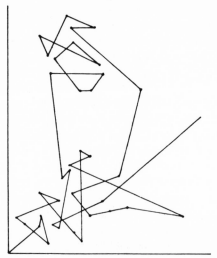

Figure 11.3. A random walk in two
dimensions (Clarke 1972, 21, figure 1.6).

Random walk models can be seen as a special case of *Markov chains*. These are the mathematical abstraction of situations where there is something, for example a cat, which can be in one of several possible alternative states (asleep, hungry, friendly, angry, dead), and which from time to time changes its state (the cat falls asleep, wakes up and is hungry, etc.). Each change of state is an independent event, but the probability of entering a state depends upon the state being left. A Markov chain is specified by a matrix of probabilities. Simplifying the cat a little we might have:

	awake	*asleep*	*dead*
awake	0.90	0.09	0.01
asleep	0.70	0.20	0.10
dead	0.00	0.00	1.00

where the entry in the ith row and jth column is the probability that when the 'chain' is in state i it will next move to state j. Notice that the sum of the entries of any row of the matrix must always be one, for the chain must be in one and only one state at any time. Notice also that the state of a chain will not change on every possible occasion. Thus once the cat is dead it stays dead.

As is true of random walk models, Markov chains are the subject of an extensive and elaborate mathematical theory. They are appealing as archaeological models in a general way, but there have been few attempts to apply them in any detail, and it is not at all clear what form such an application could take. Clarke (1968) has discussed the possible use of Markov chains as models of cultural change. Thomas (1972b), in computer simulation work to be discussed below, uses them to model the annual fluctuation in food crops.

One other type of stochastic process should be explicitly mentioned: the stochastic *branching process*. Whereas in a random walk a 'particle' moves over a plane, in a branching process the particle has no movement but splits into two or more descendants after a period of time, its descendants dividing in turn and so on possibly indefinitely. It is natural to represent such a process as a tree (see figure 2.2 (d)). Mathematical formulations of manuscript linkage problems, which have attracted considerable attention in recent years (e.g. Buneman 1971, Haigh 1971), portray the ancestral relationships of the surviving variants of some original text as a branching process. The problem is to reconstruct its exact structure, a task which is from some standpoints a generalisation of the mathematical seriation problem.

It is quite possible to combine a branching process with a random walk. Particles wander around splitting from time to time. In an informal discussion Clarke has asserted of a process of this compound type that 'this random walk model for Danubian 1 settlement expansion matches the archaeological observations in a far more satisfactory way than the east-west linear movement model customarily employed' (Clarke 1972, 22; compare the study of Ammerman and Cavalli-Sforza discussed in section 11.2.1). For a detailed application of such a model, however, it is necessary to go a little outside archaeology to population genetics. Edwards (1971) has made a long study of its application to the task of reconstructing the evolutionary tree underlying the observed distribution in human gene frequencies. He encountered major problems, not so much in justifying the appropriateness of the model as in carrying through the actual process of maximum likelihood estimation.

This brief discussion has by no means exhausted the possibilities inherent in the mathematical theory of stochastic processes. For example, the mathematical *theory of epidemics* is well developed, and has been applied to the diffusion of news and rumours. An essential idea in the theory is that of 'carriers' who for a limited time are capable of 'infecting' new individuals. The infection may or may not spread. An analogy to the diffusion of cultural traits seems obvious. A good potential source of ideas for archaeologists is a work on the use of stochastic models for social processes by Bartholomew (1967).

This includes an introduction on modelling in general and stochastic process modelling in particular.

All stochastic process models can be employed in either of two ways. They can be used in the normal manner of mathematical models: equations are set up, parameters are estimated and conclusions drawn. Or they can be actually carried out. For example, we can mark a point on a piece of paper and then start tracking its path step by step, using a table of pseudo-random numbers to choose the size and direction of the steps. Similarly pseudo-random numbers can be drawn to decide the successive states of a Markov chain. These are simulations. When a computer is programmed to do the job, we have a computer simulation.

11.5. COMPUTER SIMULATIONS

There is one awkward problem with mathematical modelling which is encountered time and again. All too often the model is so simplified a representation that it is hard to take it seriously; or it is so complex that no one knows how to solve it mathematically or, at best, only partial and unsatisfactory solutions can be obtained. This is essentially a limitation of mathematical theory. It is unfortunately true that beyond a certain level of sophistication and complexity mathematicians are no longer able to do more than admire their own equations.

Before the advent of the computer the matter had to rest there. However, with a computer it is possible to discover the implications of one or more equations not by a chain of mathematical reasoning but by designing and using an algorithm, that is by writing and running a computer program. This must specify suitable variables and iteratively change their values in accordance with the relationships in the model equations. Very often this involves following the system of variables step by step through time. Such a *computer simulation* is an effective but time-consuming way to extract information from a mathematical model, and is to be contrasted with direct mathematical inference.

Sometimes there is no mathematical model at all, just a computer simulation derived directly from the *simuland*, the system or situation of interest (figure 11.4). In such cases the simuland is often ill-understood or such that conventional mathematics can find no handhold. For example, computer simulations of group behaviour and human reasoning are usually much more useful once any attempt at a formal mathematical model is abandoned!

Any substantial archaeological problem will involve both complex processes in antiquity and the complex debris of those processes in the present. Further it may well involve our detailed knowledge of how people live and behave now, especially in primitive societies. Preferably such apparently complex archaeological problems would be solved in simple and elegant ways. Ideally there would be, for example, laws of cultural evolution similar in their importance and explanatory power to the laws of thermodynamics. Unfor-

tunately it is unlikely to be that easy. It seems unduly optimistic to assume
that such laws will be discovered if only we look a little more carefully. It can
just as well be argued that their non-appearance to date strongly suggests that
they do not exist; that social phenomena are irreducibly more complex than
physical phenomena and that our model building must accept this. This line of
argument strongly suggests that computer simulations could have an important part to play in archaeological work (Doran 1970b), and this is a view
which is gaining ground (Whallon 1972a).

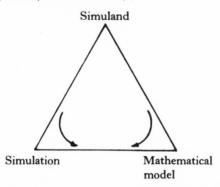

Simuland

Simulation   Mathematical
                                    model

Figure 11.4. The traditional route to a
computer simulation is from the
simuland to a mathematical model which
must be 'solved' on the machine.
However in many cases it is appropriate
to go direct from the simuland to the
simulation with any attempt to formulate a mathematical model coming
after (Brennan 1968, 7, figure 1).

11.5.1. *Monte Carlo simulations.* A rather limited kind of computer simulation occurs when the aim is not so much to investigate some complex real-
world system as to make up for some specific limitation of mathematical
theory. For example suppose that we wish to know how likely it is that in the
random walk discussed in the preceding section five successive steps will be
taken in exactly the same direction. Suppose further, that the mathematics
turns out to be too difficult for us (very unlikely in this instance!). If there is
available a reliable pseudo-random number generator an answer can be obtained by having a computer follow through a random walk step by step (this
would be *very* tedious by hand), and count how frequently five successive
steps are indeed in the same direction. Provided the simulation is kept going
long enough this will provide a good estimate of the probability required.

This is a simple example of a *Monte Carlo simulation*; the name again
betrays the origins of probability theory! In practice many such situations
arise where theory fails us and estimates must be sought by simple
simulations. An interesting and important archaeological example is provided
by D. G. Kendall's (1974) study of Thom's claim that a fixed quantum underlies many of the dimensions of megalithic sites. Here the theory is insufficient to predict how clearly the quantum should show up in a relatively

small sample, given the existence of errors and general 'noise', and Monte Carlo work is needed to provide comparative information. Similarly the model proposed by Ammerman and Cavalli-Sforza (1973) for the spread of early farming (discussed in section 11.2.1) cannot be completely solved mathematically. They have therefore programmed a simple computer simulation to investigate its properties, and remark that the simulation is potentially a closer approximation to archaeological reality than is the mathematical model itself.

11.5.2. *General computer simulation.* Full scale computer simulation, rather than limited Monte Carlo studies, is very widely used in science, business and industry. A few of the many areas where it has proved a useful tool include airport design, hospital organisation, economic development, nuclear reactor design, industrial scheduling, traffic light timing, warfare, studies of river flooding and studies of paranoid behaviour. Simulation work is supported by specially designed computer *simulation languages* such as SIMSCRIPT, GPSS, and DYNAMO. These languages facilitate the specification of the process to be studied, and the collection and interpretation of statistics on the performance of the simulation itself. The literature on simulation is extensive. Good introductory texts are those of Emshoff and Sisson (1970) and Smith (1968). A number of interesting studies have been collected together by McLeod (1968). For simulation in social science see Guetzkow, Kotler and Schultz (1972).

Any serious simulation study involves major effort at a number of stages: advanced planning; collection and organisation of suitable data; detailed specification of the simulation; writing and initial 'debugging' of the computer program; preliminary testing and validation of the program; its use in a sequence of experiments designed to achieve specific objectives; and finally the study and interpretation of the results obtained. It is easy to underestimate the magnitude of the total effort required. It is all the more important to have a clear idea of what the simulation study is intended to achieve; either a broad investigation of the behaviour of the simuland or, more likely, a determined attempt to examine the behaviour of certain variables of interest (cost? death rate? output? public approval?) and to discover to what extent they can be controlled.

An important distinction in simulation work is that between *exogenous* and *endogenous* factors. The former are variables or parameters which impinge upon the simuland from outside but are not themselves changed by it. In a simulation study exogenous factors must be set by the experimenter. In reality they may or may not be controllable and in any case their setting will require a study of the environment of the simuland. By contrast, endogenous factors are part of the mechanics of the simulation itself. They change with it and will normally include the variables of primary interest in the study. At most their initial values will be set by the experimenter.

Suppose that a simulation is constructed of traffic flow at a road junction, the aim being to discover which of various junction layouts makes for the fastest flow. Here exogenous factors include the typical pattern of traffic flow into the junction and its destination, the actual layout of the junction (controllable), and the behaviour of drivers. Endogenous factors include the number of vehicles in different parts of the junction at any time and the actual rate of flow.

In any simulation, *validation* is a matter of great importance. How can it be ensured that the model is indeed a reliable guide to reality? Where data have been collected on the simuland it will be natural to check the simulation against them. It may well be reasonable to use the simulation to generate limited predictions to be tested against the simuland. Factors that will certainly permit a simulation to be taken more seriously are internal coherence and common-sense plausibility. Once a simulation has been validated it can be put to useful work. At this point a major problem appears. During a given 'run' of a simulation on the computer, variables of interest will take on successive values. Assuming that the simulation is stochastic its behaviour will be determined partly by 'chance' on any particular occasion. Hence its behaviour on one occasion may be different from its behaviour on another. In particular the values taken by endogenous variables, including the variables of interest, will vary from one run to another. Thus any stochastic simulation must be run many times, and effectively one is sampling the behaviour of the variables of interest. This makes for much book keeping and for many complications. As mentioned above, simulation programming languages are designed to reduce these difficulties.

Simulations pose two unexpected experimental problems. First, the number of variables and parameters in the simulation is liable to be very large, giving the experimenter a task comparable with that of tuning a TV set which has several score potentially relevant knobs. Second, it may prove disconcertingly difficult to comprehend what is going on within the simulation, just as it is often difficult to comprehend a complex part of the real outside world. This is quite apart from the more mundane problem of how best to check that the behaviour of a stochastic simulation is solely determined by the factors intended and not by elusive programming errors! These problems are of more than purely technical interest. They arise from the use of a tool of sufficient complexity that its details can extend human comprehension to the limit.

Before discussing simulation work in archaeology mention might reasonably be made of what has become one of the best known computer simulation studies: the MIT simulation of mankind in its global environment, programmed and published (somewhat obscurely) in the simulation language DYNAMO (Forrester, 1971). In this model the variables which appear and are inter-related include 'population', 'capital investment', 'natural resources', 'pollution', and the 'quality of life'. Strictly, these are merely the identifiers given by the simulation designer to model variables. Whether their use is justified depends upon the extent to which the structure of the model does indeed reflect reality. The model itself is deterministic and composed of relatively simple differential equations.

Using the Forrester model it is relatively easy to predict, for example, the influence of crowding on population growth assuming that the effects of resource depletion and pollution can be contained. What is much more difficult is to decide what weight should be attached to these predictions. Since the predictions are sometimes far from encouraging this is a matter of some importance. In fact it is obvious enough that the model is no more than a very crude approximation to reality. To seek exact predictions from it would be absurd. As Forrester stresses, however, it is not the detailed predictions that matter, but the general light that the models throw upon the way in which such variables influence one another. Complex systems involving multiple feedback are not easily comprehended by human minds. We all need to learn much more about their properties and the way they react to our (often all too naive) attempts to control them. If Forrester is concerned with the future of mankind, archaeologists are concerned with its past. The mental equipment needed by each is obviously going to be much the same.

11.5.3. *Archaeological experience with computer simulation.* The idea that computer simulation techniques may be useful in archaeological work is a rather new one. Indeed, it is only in the last two to three years that the possibility has even been considered by archaeologists, and very little actual work has been completed. Before considering two interesting projects, a comment on developments in anthropology will not be out of place. An introduction to simulation for anthropologists was published as long ago as 1965 (Hays 1965). However only one piece of work has become well known since then, and this partly for an especially instructive reason. To quote at length from Allen D. Coult:

> 'One fairly complex technique employing computers and used by anthropologists is computer simulation. Some anthropologists in their haste to get into the computer business do not ask whether they should employ computers for whatever problem they have been working on but look for a problem that seems to necessitate the use of computers. One such example is Gilbert and Hammel's (1966) recent use of a simulation program employing Monte Carlo techniques for determining the number of various types of cross-cousin marriage that would occur in certain populations under varying demographic conditions.
>
> 'The results of this work were reported at a meeting of the American Anthropological Association some two or three years ago. A glance at the methodology indicated that the problem had a simple mathematical solution that could be worked out in about 10 minutes time although the programming of the simulation itself took over 500 hours. Recently the results have been published along with the

mathematical solution which Gilbert and Hammel finally realized would do the same thing. They report in retrospect that the simulation was necessary since the simulation not only gives the mean number of various types of cousin marriages but also the distribution. The distribution, however, turns out to be the binomial distribution, which it obviously would have to be since the variations from the mean were random because of the employment of Monte Carlo techniques. Gilbert and Hammel's work was essentially similar to running a program to determine the distribution of heads and tails in a number of samples of coin tossing. Probability theory is sufficient alone to tell them what the outcome would have been. The simulation was an unnecessary waste of a tremendous amount of time and money. This, of course, bears upon a very important cautionary statement; i.e. that computers if not used with reason may accomplish the opposite of what they are intended for by unnecessarily complicating fairly simple work.

'Even if the anthropologist has mastered the formal and quantitative techniques necessary for his work this does not mean that he is ready to work with computers.' (Coult 1968, 28).

No more need be said.

An archaeological simulation study is that of Wobst who has used relatively simple Monte Carlo techniques to explore the implications of a model of palaeolithic human populations. Using data from ethnographic studies and from physical anthropology a computer simulation was constructed of

'a dynamic population, which was distributed within a defined territory in which members were born, moved, married and died, all according to precisely defined probabilities and possibilities. Simulations were run of the behaviour of this model population over periods of from 100 to 500 years. In most cases, the system fluctuated randomly as it slowly settled into a relative equilibrium representing the outcome of the mutual interplay of all the parameter specifications and constraints imposed in that special case. In this way the necessary minimal equilibrium size and the minimal band size of such populations could be studied, specified, and in a sense explained. The effects of such cultural rules as band exogamy and incest were displayed . . .' (Whallon 1972a, 39).

Full details of this study have not yet been published, so that its significance, if any, for palaeolithic studies cannot yet be assessed. Nevertheless the work does indicate the possibilities which computer simulation offers.

A more ambitious project is that of Thomas (1972b, 1973). Here the initial objective was to simulate the environmental relationships influencing the life of the Great Basin Shoshoneans just before their first contact with Europeans, and thence to render explicit the origins of the archaeological record. Crucial factors are the food resources available to the

304

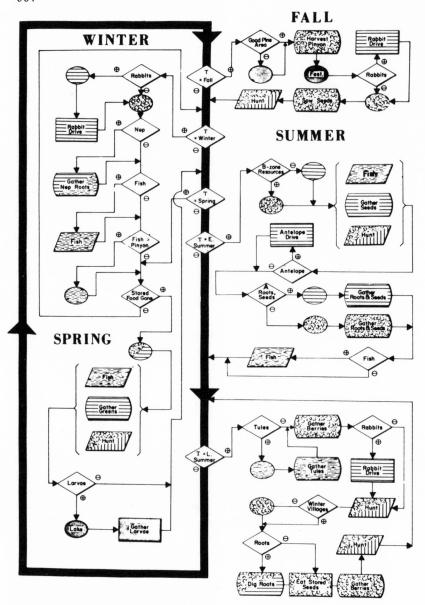

Figure 11.5. (a) Flowchart for Shoshonean economic cycle (Thomas 1972b, 679,
figure 17.3).

Shoshoneans—rabbit, fish, antelope, berries, pinon nuts—and the seasons of
the year and localities which provide them. Each procurement activity, for
example fishing, requires and discards a unique artifact combination. The
annual abundance of the different resources varies with climatic and other
factors, and so at various times of the year it must be decided which activity is
to be undertaken of those currently possible. Thus the simulation should
determine the Shoshonean activities and hence their movements and
artifactual contribution to the archaeological record (figure 11.5).

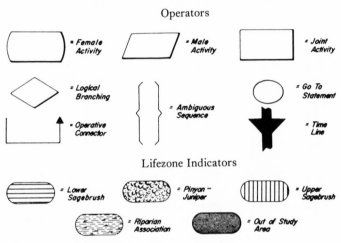

(b) Key to symbols of figure 11.5(a)
(Thomas 1972b, 680, figure 17.4).

This might seem an excellent opportunity for detailed simulation work.
Unfortunately, when it came to the point Thomas decided that only three of
the component activities were to be simulated: pinon nut gathering, Indian
ricegrass harvesting and antelope driving. Since these three activities are (to
all appearances) independent, and since the variables involved are treated
very simply (the most complex is the pinion nut harvest which is treated as a
three-state Markov chain), the 'computer simulation model', embodied as a
computer program called BASIN 1, seems hardly to have been necessary; some
straightforward mathematics would probably have sufficed. Perhaps more
ambitious simulation plans were abandoned when the amount of detailed
computer work required became apparent. Alternatively, lack of basic data may
have been important: 'Although quantitative descriptions of material culture
are becoming more available . . . , there are simply not enough data at hand to
attempt to treat BASIN 1 assemblages in quantitative fashion' (Thomas 1973,
163). Whatever the reason, this study is neither a test of nor a guide to the use
of computer simulation in archaeology. Nevertheless, taken in its entirety (for
the simulation is only one part), the study is of considerable interest and we

shall mention it again in section 13.3. A more realistic idea of the possibilities for simulation of procurement subsystems can be obtained by scanning the important text by Watt (1968). This is wholly dedicated to mathematical models and computer simulations of natural populations, with special emphasis on their control and management.

The established value of computer simulation techniques in other fields, together with the complexity of many archaeological problems, suggests that such techniques have archaeological potential. But it must be admitted that there is virtually no direct evidence in support of the suggestion. Experimental work is essential and will no doubt be forthcoming. The major limiting factor seems likely to be not the archaeologist's lack of technical knowledge, which will slowly be overcome as more introductory articles such as that of Bourrelly (1972) are written, but a lack of basic data. However, even in the absence of such data simulation work can be productive if, for example, it is used to seek insight into the dynamics of complex systems relevant to that under study, or to generate artificial data which can be used for the testing and calibration of methods of analysis (see section 11.7).

It is appropriate to end this section with the following passage taken from the book by Watt (1968, 371) cited above:

> 'Of fundamental importance in computer experimentation is the self-teaching side effect. That is, if we build a simple model of a phenomenon into the computer system by means of a program, observe the discrepancy between the behaviour of real and "model" systems, and improve the model on this basis. While we may start with inadequate and unrealistic assumptions, the pattern of the output will quickly suggest to us how assumptions must be modified to make the model more realistic. In other words, we create a feedback loop, involving the computer program, the data, and the mind of man, in which the pace of activity in the loop is largely stimulated by the computer, the fastest component. Such computer experimentation is an ideal means of suggesting how key experiments to obtain new data can clarify our understanding of a phenomenon with a minimum amount of actual experimentation.'

The relevance of this view to archaeological work is obvious. Using a computer is not merely a matter of analysing a particular body of data, it is also a process of self-education. The machine makes us see the weaknesses in our own thinking. It demands straight answers to straight questions, which is very good for all of us.

11.6. MODELS OF DECISION-MAKING AND INFERENCE

On 15 January 1595, Michael the Brave of Wallachia led a revolt against the Ottoman Empire. In a lucid and pleasantly unpretentious paper, Malita (1971) has used *decision theory* to study the decision which led to this uprising. His analysis involves: (a) listing the principal objectives of Michael the Brave's diplomacy, which included restoring Wallachia's traditional rights and stopping economic spoliation; (b) listing the possible courses of action, ranging from armed struggle to a continuance of the *status quo*; (c) listing the unpleasant consequences that could follow from action, such as internal revolt or aggravation of dependence; and then (d) quantifying both the desirability or undesirability of the various possible consequences of action, and the probability that any particular consequence will follow from any particular course of action. Given this information, which Malita derives from an examination of historical sources, it is easy to apply the formulae of simple decision theory and to obtain measures for the likely value of each alternative course of action. This indicates that an armed rising was indeed the best strategy, with an actual alliance with the Turks not far behind! The worse thing to do was nothing.

As Malita makes clear, the result of the mathematics depends heavily upon the many parameter values subjectively estimated in step (d). This is reminiscent of the situation that arises in the application of Bayes' theorem (section 3.4); it is only a small part of the total reasoning process that had been made mathematically precise. Malita comments:

'To build the mathematical model of a situation does not signify a claim to substitute a new procedure for the existing means of solution .... History will not have to be written in terms of decision comparison or game theory .... Nevertheless, modelling is of unquestionable value. This lies primarily in the increased insight it provides into the structure of events .... In particular, it develops a taste for specifying details whose necessity may have been overlooked by history as written in a qualitative language' (Malita 1971, 522).

Almost by definition prehistorians can never identify the decisions of individual rulers. So it might seem that Malita's work can have no more than a general significance for prehistoric archaeology. This is not quite the case because a society is often faced with a choice of alternative strategies in its fundamental relationship with its environment: which crops to plant, which animals to hunt, which locality to live in, which settlement structure to adopt. Each strategy will have its own potential benefits and hazards. This is not to suggest that a conscious group decision is always or even often made in such situations. More likely there will be an unsteady drift into a particular mode of activity, ultimately confirmed by success or by at least the absence of disaster.

The branch of mathematics concerned with the abstract structure of such situations is not so much decision theory as *game theory*. This has its roots in the study of the relationship between strategies and rewards in games such as chess, bridge and poker. Typically game theory soon abstracted away from its humble origins and is now a rather 'pure' branch of mathematics drawing much of its inspiration from economics. In principle it is relevant to any situation where opponents are competing against one another, including the case of special interest here in which there are just two players, one of whom is 'nature': the *game against nature* is a well known phrase. Although the use of game theory in archaeology has sometimes been proposed and its concepts aired (for example, by Clarke 1968), no substantial application of it has yet been made. The game theory concept of a *mini-max strategy*, a choice of action which minimises the maximum possible loss, is nevertheless one which is often useful in discussions of human and social behaviour.

After considering the decision making of individuals and primitive societies, it is not too great a step to consider the way in which archaeologists themselves reason and reach conclusions. Can the archaeologist be modelled? If so, what purpose would be served? To answer the second question first, a model of archaeological reasoning is a contribution to the study of archaeologist (see sections 7.3 and 10.2). This idea has been followed up in the work years. The more that can be found out about what archaeologists actually do when faced with their data, the easier it will be both to offer constructive advice to them and to design useful mathematical tools for their use. This is in no way a revolutionary idea. If the aim is to design an aircraft which is easy and safe to fly it is only sensible to make a close study of what pilots actually do when flying: and it is not enough just to ask them, an objective study is needed also!

There is a sense, of course, in which any exercise in systematic description, or automatic classification or seriation is a simulation of an archaeologist (see sections 7.3 and 10.2). This idea has been followed up in the work of Borillo (1971) who has attempted to formulate and carry through mathematically a study by Richter of a certain class of archaic Greek statues, the *kouroi*. Borillo's work involves both the creation of a suitable descriptive scheme and mathematical classification procedures. In current unpublished work he and colleagues are trying to characterise mathematically the concepts that specialists use when they consider and discuss Greek amphorae (see section 12.2).

It is difficult to accept, however, that the automatic classification and seriation procedures now in use reflect more than a small part of an archaeologist's reasoning when he is considering evidence. To make further progress more powerful modelling tools are needed. A natural candidate is Bayes' theorem which, as explained in chapter 3, does to at least some extent capture a fundamental part of reasoning: the adjustment made to an assessment of the relative plausibility of alternative hypotheses in the light of fresh evidence. Unfortunately Bayes' theorem is too abstract to be more than a general guideline in practice. Much more potentially useful are existing experiments in the computer simulation of human behaviour and reasoning (Feigenbaum 1969). These are closely associated with attempts to make machines reason intelligently whether or not in a manner similar to that of human beings. Concepts drawn from these research areas will appear in the next section.

11.7. THE SOLCEM PROJECT

Many of the topics and problems discussed in this and earlier chapters are illustrated by one particular computer project which combines elements of seriation, classification and simulation. This project was initiated not primarily to solve particular archaeological problems, but rather to explore the feasibility of having a computer undertake substantially more of a process of archaeological inference than has previously been achieved. It centres on a heuristic computer program, SOLCEM, and leans heavily upon computer science research in heuristic search and automatic hypothesis generation (Doran 1972a, 1972b, 1973).

The reader will recall that data derived from the La Tène cemetery at Münsingen-Rain have been used for a number of computer experiments, some involving automatic classification and others seriation (e.g. Hodson 1970, D.G. Kendall 1971). Enough has been learned from these experiments for it to be reasonable to attempt something more ambitious: that of having a computer accept the bulk of the evidence from the cemetery excavation, and then to draw all the conclusions that an archaeologist might reasonably draw; taking into account at least some of the relationships that exist both between the categories of evidence available and the types of conclusion which may be drawn.

More must be said about the Münsingen cemetery itself (see also section 9.1). It was excavated early this century and is of considerable importance for the study of the La Tène complex in Switzerland. It was composed of some two hundred graves (see figure 11.6), almost all inhumations and most with surviving skeletons accompanied by objects such as swords, rings, brooches and beads. The sex and age of many of the skeletons have been estimated. The location and orientation of the graves were recorded together with various other pieces of miscellaneous evidence. The standard of excavation was excellent for the time, but would not be acceptable now.

Archaeological studies (Hodson 1968, Schaaff 1966) have as yet considered the cemetery largely without reference to its regional context, focussing rather on its spatial organisation and internal chronology, on the typology and evolution of the grave objects found, and on aspects of social organisation. As already indicated, computer experiments have previously concerned either the automatic classification of a selected subset of the artifacts recovered, or the recovery of the chronological sequence of a subset of the graves by reference to the artifact types which they contain. There has been no attempt to model the total cemetery interpretation process identifying the role of classification and of chronological seriation within it.

SOLCEM is a computer program written in ALGOL-60, which tries to interpret a cemetery such as that at Münsingen as a whole. It makes use of the following categories of data, not all of which need be available on any given occasion: (a) grave locations; (b) burial age/sex; (c) objects by grave and object

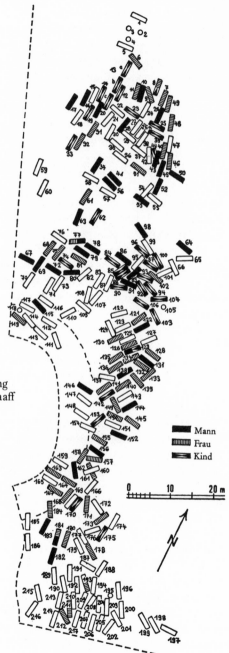

Figure 11.6. Plan of the La Tène cemetery at Münsingen-Rain showing graves as male, female or child (Schaaff 1966, 58, figure 7).

descriptions; (d) prior object classification; and (e) known chronological relationship between pairs of graves (as deduced from grave intersection).

The program draws conclusions about (a) the age/sex categories of graves (where these are not given); (b) the chronological sequence in which the graves were created; (c) whether or not the graves were clustered and/or linearly arranged and the chronological significance of such an arrangement; (d) patterns in the assignment of grave objects to graves; and (e) the different types of object which existed in antiquity and their evolution through time.

A complete hypothesis about the cemetery is, from the point of view of SOLCEM, a combination of decisions in each of these categories. Decisions in different categories are not, of course, independent of one another; this is the crux of the inference problem. An important point is that some hypotheses *assert* more than others irrespective of considerations of plausibility. Intuitively, the more evidence there is the more complex the conclusions it is reasonable to draw. This principle is embodied in SOLCEM which draws no or only simple conclusions when few data are available.

The word 'hypothesis' is used here not only because *any* conclusion drawn in such circumstances must be provisional and subject to independent support or disproof, but also because, as it will be explained, the program itself continually revises its conclusions as it takes into account more of the evidence available to it or looks again at evidence already considered. The relationship of this project to other experiments in automatic hypothesis generation has been discussed by Doran (1972a).

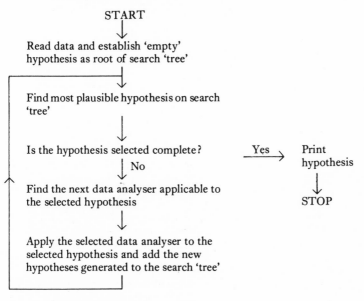

Figure 11.7. Simplified flowchart of the SOLCEM program.

The mode of action of SOLCEM is complex in detail but can very easily be understood in outline (figure 11.7). The program builds up hypotheses about the meaning of the evidence considering one category of data after another. However, it recognises that the same data can be explained in a number of alternative ways. It therefore considers in parallel perhaps a dozen or more alternative hypotheses, at any particular time working upon that which looks the most promising (see figure 11.8). This implies, of course, that SOLCEM has simple heuristics which enable it to judge when a hypotheses is plausible in the light of the data so far considered, and when it is not. The most plausi-

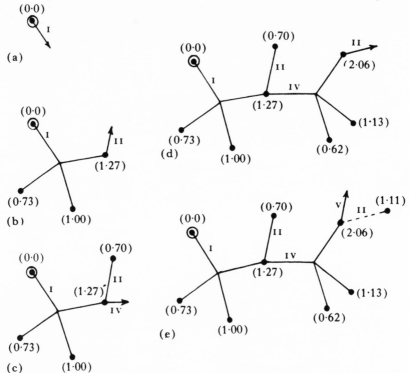

Figure 11.8. Successive diagrams showing the initial stages in the growth of a SOLCEM search tree given a typical data set. Each node of the tree corresponds to an incomplete hypothesis, the ringed node corresponding to the initial 'empty' hypothesis. The numbers give the plausibilities of the corresponding hypotheses, and the roman numerals the data analysers applied. Thus initially the grave objects are classified (data analyser I) giving three alternative classifications (a). The most plausible of these is then used as the basis of an application of data analyser II which detects associations between object classes and grave category (b). The resulting hypothesis is unattractive so the program tries the effect of data analyser IV (c), and so on. The dashed line in (e) indicates that the program has here made use of its memory of the earlier application of data analyser II (compare the much simpler search exhibited in figure 10.3).

ble complete hypothesis constructed by the program is returned to the experimenter.

More specifically, SOLCEM is made up of (a) a set of subprograms, called *data analysers*, each of which is applicable to a specific category or categories of data, and each of which returns specific categories of conclusions; together with (b) a *control section* which invokes data analysers in a coherent manner. An example of a data analyser is that which given (i) an object classification, (ii) the associations of objects with graves, and (iii) the age/sex categories of the graves, decides which classes of objects, if any, are characteristic of particular categories of graves. Other data analysers classify objects, study the spatial layout of the cemetery, and carry out seriation. There are eight in all, some of them substantial programs in their own right (see table 11.1).

I   classify objects (direct assignment to nearest selected cluster centres)

II   detect associations between object classes and age/sex categories of graves (significance test)

III   infer age/sex categories of graves by reference to significant object classes

IV   study spatial layout of cemetery (single-link cluster analysis and principal component analysis)

V   infer age/sex categories of graves by reference to spatial layout

VI   infer chronological sequence of graves by reference of distribution of object classes over graves (combinatorial analysis)

VII   compare output of VI with horizontal stratigraphy IV and vertical stratigraphy

VIII   reconstruct source types from object class definitions and other relevant data

---

Table 11.1. The eight data analysers incorporated in the SOLCEM program.

It must be made quite clear that SOLCEM is in fact very limited in its abilities. The range of hypotheses which it can consider is very narrow and unimpressive by human standards. Thus as it stands the program is certainly not a practical aid to archaeologists; it is an exploratory tool suitable for use in a variety of interesting experiments.

Eliminating programming errors from a program of the complexity of SOLCEM, and then evaluating and improving it, calls for a number of data sets (cemetery excavation records) ranging from the very simple and straightforward to the complex and demanding. Whilst it would be possible, if difficult and time-consuming, to derive such data sets entirely from archaeological sites some more convenient source is desirable. Therefore a subsidiary program, called SIMCEM, has been written to generate suitable data sets. This it does not by merely creating plausible sets of numbers, but by simulating at an abstract level the actual process by which the cemetery was formed in antiquity and by which parts of it have survived to modern times. Thus the origin and meaning of the artificial data sets are known. The most important elements of the simulation model are stochastic processes by which artifact types or traditions are initiated and evolve 'in antiquity' (random walks), by which graves are located (modified random walks), by which sets of artifacts are assigned to graves (Poisson variables), and by which evidence is lost with the passage of time (binomial distributions). Each data set generated comprises the various categories indicated above. A flow-chart of SIMCEM is given in figure 11.9.

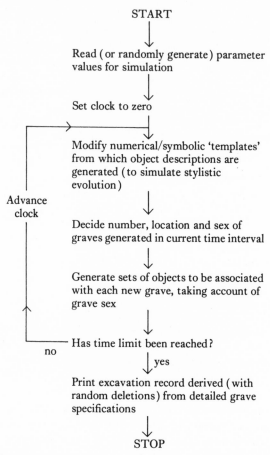

Figure 11.9. Simplified flow chart of the SIMCEM program. Within the simulation an 'object' is a set of numbers and symbols representing measurements and stylistic motifs respectively. A 'grave' consists of numbers and symbols representing spatial coordinates, sex, etc., together with a list of objects.

SIMCEM has interest, of course, beyond that of a generator of artificial data for input to SOLCEM. It is a model, albeit a crude one, of a typical archaeological process. As its parameters are varied a wide variety of 'cemeteries' can be generated which can be compared and contrasted with reality. It is not, however, feasible to fit such a model to any particular prehistoric cemetery by way of the usual simulation techniques. The data available are too few and too special. From one point of view the role of the inference program, SOLCEM, is to overcome precisely this difficulty to the extent that it can be overcome. Nevertheless the value of the SIMCEM model as a source of ideas and perspective is apparent.

Experimental work with the SOLCEM program is incomplete. Important topics to be investigated are the relationship between the soundness of the hypotheses generated and (a) the values of the parameters of the heuristic search process, (b) the complexity of artifact classification employed and (c) the extent to which secondary relationships between different categories of data are taken into account. A substantial body of data from the Münsingen cemetery has been prepared in machine readable form and is available for input to SOLCEM once development of the latter has proceeded sufficiently. The problems of preparing large data sets such as this are substantial. A number of relevant issues have been discussed in chapter 5 and more will be considered in the next chapter in the context of computer-based data banks.

11.8. SUMMING UP

This chapter has been about the various kinds of mathematical model and computer simulation which are available for the archaeologist to use in the course of his work. Since a number of actual archaeological studies have been discussed it is natural to ask how far we can now go towards answering the question posed early in the chapter: 'To what extent can mathematical models be useful in archaeology?' We shall take the question to refer only to modelling aspects of prehistoric events or societies (category 1 of section 11.2).

It seems to us that comparatively little of real archaeological value has as yet come from modelling work. It may be that this merely reflects the inexperience with such methods of almost all archaeologists, and that as more studies are completed—and certainly many more are needed before any assessment can be final—the obvious value of such work will become apparent. However, we suspect that there is a more fundamental difficulty; that the models which are mathematically tractable are too simple for most archaeological problems. The power and precision of the model itself is liable to be nullified by the restrictions inherent in its application. The implication is a commonsense one; that models need to be used with restraint and discrimination (Loynes 1971).

Computer simulations can cope with much more in the way of complications than can a mathematical model and it is reasonable to argue that their archaeological potential is much greater. But their use involves difficulties less prominent in purely mathematical work. A particular situation or process can only be simulated convincingly on a computer if there is ample and reliable data from the simuland. This is a requirement which may only rarely be met in archaeological work. Further, the sheer labour and cost of programming and testing a major computer simulation is an important limiting factor in itself. Much more practical work is needed to establish just how severe these limitations are.

It is important to remember that computer simulations can be a crucial aid to the development of general theory as well as to a specific investigation. Thus it may ultimately be more realistic to use simulations to study the population dynamics of hunting and gathering communities as a class, than to use them to study what happened to a particular community in the past. It would then be up to the archaeologist to apply the general theory as best he could in particular cases. However this is a long-term prospect rather than a development to be expected in the near future.

Computer-based Archaeological Data Banks

12.1. INFORMATION STORAGE AND RETRIEVAL BY COMPUTER

'For a number of years, a small group of archaeologists scattered around the world have been struggling toward what seems an impossible dream: the creation of a world-wide, computer-oriented data bank.' (Chenhall 1971a, 159). This statement, by one of the most active proponents of *computer-based archaeological data banks*, may be alarming. What is a data bank that it should be seen as some kind of Holy Grail, infinitely desirable but equally elusive? Can a search for such a goal be taken seriously? While it is true that the remark quoted does capture something of the motivation of archaeological data bank enthusiasts, it is also true that a great deal of serious data bank development is under way, most with limited and strictly realistic objectives. In this chapter we shall explain something of what is being done and why, and comment upon the prospects for the future.

One of the simplest things a computer can do with a piece of information—a number, a word, or some more complex data item—is to store it in memory and then to produce it on request. Since computer memories can be made very large indeed by the use of such machinery as magnetic tapes and magnetic discs, very large amounts of information can be held in them. Further, the computational powers of the machine will permit particular data items to be related to one another. Thus one is soon led to the idea that computers can be used as very large and sophisticated filing systems. Of course, this basic idea is rapidly assailed with innumerable complications and difficulties, prominent among them simply the cost of any such operation. Nevertheless it has proved workable. Indeed, information storage and retrieval by computer is now a well developed branch of applied computer science with a large and rapidly expanding reservoir of theory and practical experience. Much of the work that has been done involves library science, in particular the use of the machine to hunt down documents (described by anything from a classification number, through a set of 'key words', to a substantial abstract) relevant to some particular topic or question. More immediately relevant to archaeologists, however, are the computer data banks that have been set up and are being used in a wide range of application areas including medicine, local government, cartography, geology, pharmaceutics, company personnel records, airline reservations and police files. A great deal of experience has been obtained with such information systems.

All data banks have in common a reservoir of information, usually steadily expanding, which must be available to answer questions coming often in 'real-time', and usually from a diversity of sources with a diversity of interests. Ideally the user of such a system can gain access to the machine quickly and conveniently, can pose his question or questions without worrying about arbitrary and complex conventions, receives the kind of answer he wants in no time at all, can ask as many supplementary questions as he wishes, and so on.

In practice, of course, ideals are hard to come by. There are plenty of prominent problems with computer data banks. All too often there is too much data for the machine available, or, if there is not, the need to use large capacity storage devices means that the response time, the amount of time the user must wait for his answer, is large. This makes it all the more important to know how to organise the information efficiently in the machine. When the user finally gets an answer how does one ensure that it is the one wanted? Is there too much information, most of it irrelevant? Or is there too little? The problem of just how to tell the machine what is and what is not relevant can be both crucial and baffling. How must the user phrase his question? How close to natural language can one come? Programming a computer to 'understand' the meaning of natural language questions, rather than merely process a coded request in some routine way, is as yet barely possible even in the simplest cases. And then there are problems of security, both in the sense of privacy—only authorised users may extract information from the data bank—and of ensuring that no machine (or programmer!) malfunction can erase information that will be costly or impossible to replace.

More complications are introduced as data analysing facilities are grafted onto the data bank itself. This means that the user can not only ask questions and obtain answers, but can carry out statistical analyses on the answers he receives. The importance of such facilities in an archaeological context is discussed below.

12.2. COMPUTER DATA BANKS IN ARCHAEOLOGY

The interest of archaeologists in mathematical techniques arises partly from the vast quantities of data that they have accumulated in past years, and that they are still accumulating at an ever increasing rate. In such a situation systematic methods of analysing large amounts of information in a reliable and authoritative way are manifestly attractive. But this is not all. It is becoming more and more difficult to organise all this information so that the individual can locate and obtain access to that part of it which concerns him. Given the development of computer data banks in other fields it is natural to ask why the data cannot all be put on to a computer so that anyone can have access to it for any purpose.

One reason is that this would run counter to traditional archaeological working habits. As Gardin (1971b, 198) has put it, these 'are often those of old-fashioned scholars, working patiently to build up over the years a collection of countless pieces of information, who jealously keep all this material to themselves, like the notes and files in which it is entered, until such time as they publish it on their own account.' As he points out: 'Nothing can be more contrary to the principle of a data bank' (see figures 12.1 and 12.2). He continues: 'Professional habits and methods will both have to be radically changed before computer science can be fully exploited so as to relieve archaeologists of the endless repetitive drudgery of compilation which at present takes up most of their time'. Whilst this point of view is perhaps a somewhat extreme one it is undeniable that there is some degree of contradiction between the concept of an individual scholar and that of a pooled data bank.

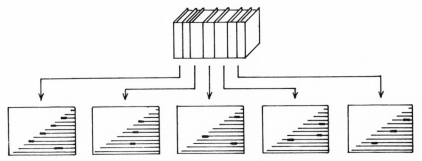

(a) In a given period, different scholars carry out independent analyses of the same data, for individual storage in separate and sometimes guarded files.

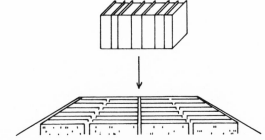

(b) The proposed alternative is that the same analyses should be carried out only once (ideally), and stored in a unique file open to public use.

Figure 12.1. Archaeological data processing in practice: a static representation of current (a) and proposed (b) usage according to Gardin (1968, 106, figure 1A).

There are, of course, plenty of other difficulties which make any idea of an 'instant' data bank for archaeologists absurd. Objections leap to mind. Who is to prepare all the data for the machine, and do we know how to do it? What conventions are to be used, and based upon what principles? Anyway, is there not far too much information around for any such wholesale operation to be feasible? Who is to pay? Who is to organise it all? And is there not a real risk that the computer will bind the archaeologist in a methodological strait-jacket, leaving him worse off than before? 'A possible danger of data banking done too soon and on too all-encompassing a scale is that it is not likely to prove particularly useful to innovative, experimental, and exploratory

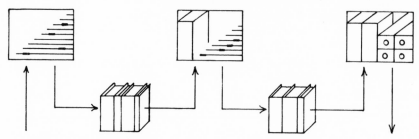

(a) Information goes through an endless cycle of analysis and synthesis, each scholar isolating data which has been assembled by others and reassembling them in a new presentation, which in turn is to be broken into pieces, etc.

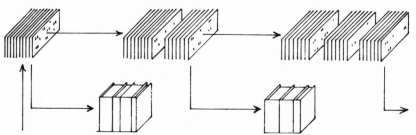

(b) The proposed alternative is that factual data should be kept in analytical form within the data bank; synthesis can then be undertaken more readily, filing being each time limited to additional data.

Figure 12.2. Archaeological data processing in practice: a dynamic representation of current (a) and proposed (b) usage according to Gardin (1968, 107, figure 1 B).

researches and may actually tend to stifle active questioning and thought ....' (Whallon 1972a, 38). To use a giant archaeological information system to propagate principles which turned out to be merely the product of short-lived fashion would be a mistake indeed!

It is clear that the idea of using computer data banks in archaeology must be analysed in a little more detail. A good starting point is the stress placed by Gardin (1972) upon the different data bank requirements of different types of archaeological activity. Thus the information storage and retrieval needs on an actual excavation site are substantially different from those associated with a regional survey covering a large geographical area, and different again from those which pertain within a museum context. And specialist files of data pose their own problems. It is therefore quite wrong to envisage one comprehensive set of conventions and standards which will meet all needs and purposes. Rather, what is required is a practical analysis which will relate the needs of each level of archaeological study to the possible forms of information system.

The range of forms which the essential data bank concept can take is easily exemplified by typical current projects:

1. It is often convenient to establish computer based data files which are suitable for a broad research project. The data files prepared from the excavation record of the Münsingen cemetery, as described in the last chapter, fall into this category. So also do data files of early amphora profiles compiled at the Centre d'Analyse Documentaire pour l'Archéologie, in Marseilles. These files are central to a project which A. Borillo (1972, 1) has described:

'un projet de traitement automatique de l'information relative à la morphologie d'un corpus d'amphores antiques de la méditerranée occidentale. Dans ce système l'information est enregistrée au moyen d'un lecteur de courbes (du type Pencil Follower D-Mac), ce qui revient à dire que le contour de l'amphore, ou celui de la section de l'anse et des lèvres par exemple, sera représenté par les coordonnées dans l'espace euclidien à deux dimensions d'un très grand nombre de points de ces contours (tous les 1/10 de mm si l'on veut). D'autre part les recherches rétrospectives sur cette information graphique s'exécutent à partir' de questions formulées dans un langage naturel—le français—à l'aide des termes mêmes dont font usage les érudits. Les conditions dans lesquelles l'expérience doit se dérouler sont celles du dialogue homme-machine en temps réel, les questions étant émises et les réponses reçues à l'aide d'une console communiquant directement (on-line) avec l'ordinateur.'

This is a particularly interesting project involving as it does questions of data capture and handling, statistical analysis, and linguistics, together with the real-time integration of these three components (M. Borillo et al. 1972). Such research-oriented data bases are becoming steadily more common.

2. Excavation or survey at a particular archaeological site generates large amounts of data, and an important question is whether and how best to transfer this information to a machine either as it is obtained, or very soon after. A major project of this type is the Teotihuacan Mapping Project where very large data files have been created from the study of a city site in the valley of Mexico. 'Records are being accumulated on all features detectable from the surface and on analyses of surface collections for each of some 5 000 separate

tracts' (Cowgill 1968a, 143). The data are organised specifically for statistical analysis. The computer programs used have either been specially written or drawn from standard statistical packages.

A project 'to test the feasibility and methodology of using a direct computer link at a remote location of an excavation or survey' (Gaines 1971, 3) was conducted in 1971 in Arizona using a remote terminal and a 300-mile telephone link.

'The area surveyed included a rincon and adjacent mesas. Twenty sites, many of multiple components, were recorded. The site chosen for excavation was a small talus-slope pueblo, consisting of approximately 20 features of well-defined rooms, a kiva, pit house and a small trash mound. This site dated from AD 925–1325.

'Daily data from both the survey and excavation, after laboratory analysis, were processed by a series of computer programs. The programs consisted of three major divisions, each containing subgroups. The first division was to verify the input data by checking for consistency of the format and syntax and providing as an output a report in a format which allowed the user to quickly scan for semantic errors which were undetectable by the program. The next major division was the file building routines which sorted and merged the data into a common "summary file". The third major division was the search and analysis programs consisting of two basic classes: a set of programs which extracted from the file specifically requested information and allowed the application of a set of standard statistical tests to the data; a series of programs which allowed logical searches of the files.'

Newell and Vroomans (1972) describe in detail a less sophisticated but very interesting example of computer recording and analysis on a Mesolithic site in the Netherlands.

3. The Arkansas Archaeological Survey has set up a computerised data bank for archaeological sites in its area, directed by Chenhall (1971a). The records held are of artifacts or features, and of sites. Conventions and procedures have been worked out in detail and the system is operational (see figure 12.3) in a limited form using programs of the Museum Computer Network (see below) and based on an IBM 360/50 machine at the University of Arkansas. Similar projects have been initiated elsewhere in the USA.

4. Museum data banks are, as one might expect, rather more developed than purely archaeological projects (Vance 1970). They often cover archaeological material and can be modified for purely archaeological work. The best known system is the Museum Computer Network based on twenty-three museums in New York, the Washington area, and the East of the USA. The program package developed at New York for the Museum Computer Network is called GRIPHOS (General Retrieval and Information Processing for Humanities Oriented Studies) and written in the computer language PL/1.

ARKANSAS ARCHEOLOGICAL SURVEY 2==   Recording Station   4==

Survey Cat. No. AAS   6==   Survey Site No. AAS   176==

Owner/Possessor (If other than Survey): Name   102==

Address   101== Cat. No.   106==

DESCRIPTION OF OBJECT: DIMENSIONS:

Object Category	32==	I	150==
Type	68==	II	152==
Style	64==	III	154==
Material(s)	48==	IV	156==
Technique	46==	V	158==
Decorative Motif(s)	42==	IV Number (If more than one)	160==
Condition	63==		136==
Provenience	178==	Photo Neg. No.	60==

Excavated or Collected By: Individual Excavator/Collector   18==

Organisation (or Survey Station)   16== Year   20==

Figure 12.3. Artifact/feature record sheet based on that used by the Arkansas Archaeological Survey. Note that the entries themselves are not coded, but that code numbers are used to designate the categories under which entries may be made. These code numbers are then used for retrieval purposes (Chenhall 1971b, 44, figure 36).

GRIPHOS is being used, in a modified form, by the Arkansas Archaeological Survey and elsewhere.

Museum projects have also been initiated in a number of European countries, including France, Germany, and Britain, but none are very far advanced (Bowles 1971). One of the more interesting is that of the Inventaire Général des Monuments et des Richesses Artistiques de la France, a department within the French Ministry of Cultural Affairs, which is compiling an inventory of all art objects and historical monuments in the country. The long-term aim is to establish a computerised data bank, but no more than pilot studies have as yet been completed (Gardin *et al.* 1972).

5. A number of projects involve the construction of computer files of specialist data. Thus the possibility of setting up a computerised inventory of radiocarbon dates is being explored by the American Journal of Science (Chenhall 1971b, 40). Similarly a computer based inventory of animal remains from archaeological sites is being developed at the British Museum (Jewell 1972). Limited initially to the generation of subject-ordered catalogues, long-term objectives are more ambitious and include direct computer response to complex specialist queries. Coverage is of all remains held in the Museum or handled there, together with full British Isles coverage of mammalian remains.

While this is no more than a representative sample of current data bank activity, it does give some idea of the diversity of possibilities that exist. Other indicators of data bank activity include conferences or symposia held at the University of Arkansas in May 1971, at Marseilles in June 1972, and at San Francisco in 1973. Following the first of these meetings a permanent international coordinating committee was set up. Recent papers which survey developments in this area are those of Chenhall (1971a, 1972) and Whallon (1972a). The earlier paper by Chenhall was reviewed by Gardin (1971a). A particularly useful overview of recent work in the USA can be obtained from Gaines (1973), where papers read at the San Francisco symposium are summarised.

12.3. DATA INPUT, OUTPUT, AND ORGANISATION WITHIN
       THE MACHINE

There are a variety of ways in which data may be collected for insertion into a data bank. In many instances where artifacts or archaeological sites are in question the procedure will involve the design of suitable data sheets, their completion and checking, card punching from the data sheets and checking, and then card reading by the machine followed by internal data screening. Clearly both the design of the data sheets and the card punching must involve standard conventions (see next section). Very often some kind of random sampling will be involved, assuming that complete data recovery is for one reason or another too difficult.

Should more sophisticated facilities be available, then it will be natural to make use of an on-line typewriter terminal, effectively leaving out the punched card stage; typing will be direct from the data sheets into the machine. Since it is now possible, even commonplace, for such terminals to be situated large distances from the parent machine using standard telephone lines, it is perfectly possible for a terminal to be located at an actual excavation site (see the Arizona experiment cited above). There are, however, likely to be hazards as well as advantages in bringing computers and excavations into such intimate contact if the limitations of the machine are not fully appreciated.

Graphical input, that is input by way of drawings rather than numbers, is more ambitious and has not been much explored by archaeologists as yet. In archaeological work Wilcock (1971), M. Borillo et al. (1972) and A. Borillo (1972) have described experiments with a D-MAC Pencil Follower, a device by which lines (straight, curved or irregular) drawn on a special drawing table are automatically converted into successive pairs of point coordinates and transmitted to the computer. The D-MAC Pencil Follower is a useful way of converting line drawings of, say, pottery profiles to a numerical coding. A functionally similar but considerably more sophisticated device is the acoustical graphics tablet used in archaeological work on an experimental basis by Irwin, Hurd and La Jeunesse (1971); see figure 12.4. Again this enables drawings to be accepted directly by the machine. Experiments have involved stone projectile points and aerial photographs.

Although these graphical input devices have only just begun to appear in archaeological experiments, they are commercially fairly easily available. A possible future development is the computer-controlled mobile TV camera capable of 'looking at' an object and of recognising, measuring and describing it. There is considerable computer science research in this direction, aimed at the automation of, for example, assembly processes in industry. While such work will have no impact on archaeology in the near future, it can potentially render fully automatic the description of artifacts and is therefore of considerable long term potential.

Retrieving information in graphical form is again possible in a number of different ways. As mentioned in chapter 3, many terminals are equipped with video-display units such that the output text is projected on a small CRT display rather than typed. If nothing else, this cuts the noise level very considerably! Digital plotters were also mentioned in the context of distribution map plotting, and other uses include computer drawings of artifact shapes from data files and plotting the results of geomagnetic surveys (see, for example, the discussion by Wilcock 1971). Line drawings continuously generated and changed by the computer can be thrown on to CRT displays and the user can modify their progress by way of a 'light-pen', a light-sensitive device with which the user can point at display features. It is also possible to program the machine to generate cine films. Once suitable archaeological data files are available, together with the experimental experience to use them, all these facilities will certainly prove useful.

Organisation of data files within the machine is a complex topic which we shall not consider here (see, for example, Welke 1972). Much depends upon both the exact demands to be put upon the data bank, and upon the particular machine hardware being used. However certain requirements always exist. It must always be possible to add new data to the bank, and to delete those judged dispensable. Provision must be made for human and machine errors: irreplaceable information must not be lost. A high degree of cross-referencing will always be desirable provided that this does not cost too much in terms of machine memory capacity used and response time. This is especially the case if the information is stored on several levels of memory, being shifted from one level to another as usage dictates.

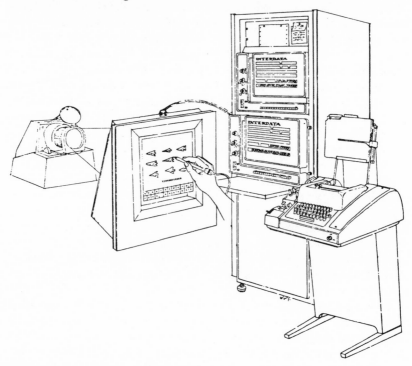

Figure 12.4. Equipment used for graphical input of archaeological data (Irwin, Hurd and La Jeunesse 1971, figure 2).

12.4. WHICH DATA, AND WHY?

Earlier in this chapter some of the more obvious problems associated with computer data banks were mentioned and it is appropriate now to look at some of them in a little more detail. They tend to arise all the more acutely the closer one comes to the large scale general-purpose data bank envisaged in the quotation which opened the chapter. Conversely much more limited projects, such as the animal remains inventory mentioned in section 12.2 should encounter rather few difficulties and be well within 'the state of the art'.

There are, as is often pointed out, two complementary impossibilities. It is quite impossible to record everything, and it is quite impossible to anticipate every need for information that may arise. In this sense, talk of a fully comprehensive general-purpose data bank is nonsense. To record the dimensions and surface features of a flint tool, any flint tool, down to the last millionth of a millimetre would itself fill any computer. Always, beyond a certain level, some detail must be dismissed as unimportant. Similarly, for how many yards or miles around an excavation should the topography be recorded? How much of the excavator's life history is relevant? Who knows, it might be important in thirty years time! Add the point that even computer memories are far from large compared with the potential amount of data coming out of a typical archaeological site, and it becomes obvious that any set of archaeological records, computer based or not, involves selecting as many as possible of those data most likely to be relevant in the future and ignoring the remainder.

That much of an archaeologist's time is spent throwing away information for purely pragmatic reasons is a point that has been stressed by Gardin (1972). It is a somewhat unexpected idea. Usually archaeologists are regarded as information collectors. Gardin has analysed the history of archaeological information (records and artifacts) from excavation, through sorting and classification to study, preservation in museums and final disintegration. At every stage the amount of information is reduced in accordance with immediate requirements but description and interpretation are strengthened. Gardin stresses the need for conscious strategies for discarding information. It should be neither haphazard nor something to be done furtively, away from the light of academic scrutiny.

All this suggests that on any excavation pragmatic and explicit decisions must be taken as to what to preserve and what not to preserve, what to record and what not to record, depending upon the declared aims of that particular excavation, the storage and other constraints applicable, and the theoretical background. This is of course just what has always happened in practice (but compare the discussion of section 13.3). At most there has sometimes been insufficient analysis of the problem and insufficient thought for what might turn out to be useful in the future.

One aspect of the problem deserves more attention. It is not simply a question of which artifacts to preserve, or which aspects of the excavation to record. Much more it is a question of how detailed the records are to be and, more generally, of just what form they are to take. As soon as the data bank concept is introduced then questions of objectivity, and of standardised coding and description, become prominent.

12.5. DESCRIPTIVE CODES

The coding and description of artifacts and assemblages of artifacts has been considered in some detail in chapter 5, in preparation for the statistical analyses discussed in following chapters. Everything said in chapter 5 carries over into the present, rather wider, context but there are one or two additional points to be made. The most important point is that the methods of chapter 5 are pragmatic and effective rather than theoretically sophisticated. To see them in perspective it is necessary to realise that problems of object description are not at all confined to archaeology and have been studied from a number of theoretical standpoints. Such studies may take account of the topological structure of the object, or of any hierarchical structure which it may possess or may even take as object descriptions algorithms by which the objects may be 'generated'. To mention these possibilities is not to suggest that they can immediately be put to use by archaeologists, far from it, but to indicate the theoretical complexities which exact and objective description of a complex artifact like a fibula could involve. The problem is not one that can convincingly be reduced to mere measurement.

It would be quite wrong, of course, to suggest that those who have worked on descriptive codes in archaeology have been unaware of the subtleties. Important general discussions such as those of Gardin (1967) and Chenhall (1967) make the difficulties clear. Gardin stresses the need for scientific standards of description in archaeology and sees the need for three classes of description rule: rules of orientation, rules of segmentation and rules of differentiation. It must be decided first how to position an object, then how to divide it into its natural parts, and finally how to differentiate the various attribute states which each part may take. While this is by itself only a general scheme it has been elaborated in detail under Gardin's supervision into a dozen or more *descriptive codes* for a variety of classes of archaeological and art objects including classes of metal tools, coins, and geometric ornamentation. More recently a number of other descriptive codes have been worked out in detail, notably for stone tools and for pottery (see chapter 5 and figure 12.5). The practical experience gained with all these codes is, however, still somewhat limited.

The central dilemma when constructing descriptive codes for archaeological material is that the more objective and 'scientific' the code, the more cumbersome and impracticable it is. A fully detailed specification of the exact spatial structure and physical make-up of an object might or might not be truly objective but it would certainly be impossibly long. Worse, it might well be objective in the wrong sense: it is certainly arguable that the code, while avoiding the biases of the coder, should take into account the significance of the object to its creator and its cultural context in antiquity. In fact, however, the issue hardly arises. 'The descriptive languages which have been proposed are *not universal*. The semiological quantification of perceptual data is unavoidably influenced by the observer's linguistic, or more generally cultural, habits . . . it is likely that other authors would have constructed other codes for the same objects' (Gardin 1967, 27; his italics). Gardin goes on to argue that no realistic artificial language can do better and that the choice is 'between culturally-bound codes, or no codes at all'.

It is this problem of the arbitrary nature of descriptive codes to which Whallon has referred in writing: 'Archaeology is not yet sufficiently scientific to establish any immutable variables, attributes or classes in our data other than perhaps some very simple ones, useful more for cataloguing than for analysis' (Whallon 1972a, 38), with the suggestion that on this ground alone

Code A: Apparent function or use

A22	Food quest		These codes will be used without sub-division to indicate the probable uses
	A222	Food gathering	made of floral and faunal remains found
	A223	Fowling	at the site; minor subdivisions will be
	A224	Hunting & trapping	used to indicate specialised equipment
	A226	Fishing	associated with these activities and not
A23	Animal husbandry		includable under Code 41.
	A231	Domesticated animals	
	A235	Poultry raising	
A24	Agriculture		
	A243	Cereal agriculture	
	A244	Vegetable production	
	A248	Textile agriculture	
A25	Food processing		This code will be used only for artifacts
	A251	Food preservation and storage	or features definitely associated with the processing of food, such as seed jars,
	A252	Food processing and preparation	mealing bins, metates, manos, etc.
A28	Leather, textiles and fabrics		This code and Code 32 will be used for
	A281	Work in skins	those items which, because of their con-
	A283	Cordage	dition, cannot be identified by use or
	A284	Knots & lashings	function for inclusion under Codes 29,
	A285	Mats & basketry	30, 41, 48, 52, 53, 77 and so on; minor
	A286	Textile fabrics	subdivisions will be used for prepared
	A287	Non-textile fabrics (barkcloth, feather-work, etc.)	materials used in these industries or for parts of objects, such as rope fiber or basket handles.
A29	Clothing		These codes will be used only for articles
	A291	Normal garb	of clothing or adornment or for toilet ar-
	A292	Special garments	ticles such as combs.
	A293	Paraphernalia	
A30	Adornment		
	A301	Ornament	
	A302	Toilet articles	

Figure 12.5. A fragment of an archaeological code. The use of numbers rather than descriptive words is optional but some degree of standardisation is essential if computer processing is to be attempted (Chenhall 1971b, 11, figure 8).

general-purpose data banks are not yet feasible. It is sometimes suggested that a strengthening of archaeological theory (consider the force of the word 'scientific' in the above quotation) will alleviate this problem. This is no doubt true to some extent, but so much depends upon human perception and cognition that it seems almost as reasonable to suggest that a better human psychology is the first requirement.

12.6. HARDWARE, ADMINISTRATION AND FINANCE

In any consideration of large computer-based archaeological data banks the question must arise whether or not present computer hardware is adequate for such a project. Naturally the answer depends upon just what kind of data bank one has in mind, but in fact it is far from obvious that the hardware available now can really cope with the enormous amounts of data that any serious large scale project must involve. A related point is whether or not such a data bank should be conceived as based on a single computer complex at a specific locality, or distributed over a network of computer installations linked by high-speed data channels. The latter concept is not at all unrealistic since a major computer network, the Advanced Research Projects Agency (ARPA) network, already exists in the United States. The flexibility and pragmatism inherent in a multiple 'hook-up' rather than one large information centre is very attractive.

If such a data bank is to be set up how is it to be financed and administered? This is a question that is only just beginning to receive serious attention. Clearly no handful of individuals can get very far without large scale support from an organisation or government. This is not inconceivable. It is worth stressing that the importance of information and information systems for scientific work is amply recognised at an international level (Gardin 1971b, 198). Some discussion of these various issues will be found in Gardin (1971b) and Chenhall (1971a).

12.7. FUTURE PROSPECTS

Few would dispute the value of relatively small archaeological data banks handling straightforward data for straightforward purposes. But do large data banks intended for the use of all and sundry have a future? Problems of data description, of hardware limitation, and of overall organisation all cast doubt on the feasibility of such projects at least in the near future. But it certainly does not follow that the concept of a general-purpose data bank should be dismissed or derided. Given the new tools and concepts being made available to archaeologists by computer science, progress is inevitable even if in unexpected directions. Science often advances by trial and error. And it should always be remembered that perfection is unnecessary; all that is required is something a little better than has gone before.

What does the future hold? According to one writer:

'The present view suggests that computerized data banks should slowly grow in size, number, and importance in archaeology in the next few years. One might venture to predict that they will find their primary and most useful application as cataloguing systems with a minimum of detailed descriptive information. As such they will be more and more extensively used by archaeologists to find the data they want for particular researches. The actual analysis of data will probably continue, on the whole, to be carried out with smaller, specialized data files containing information on certain variables and attributes measured and coded in certain ways, all specific to the problem at hand. The distinction between general-purpose and special-purpose data banks will almost certainly be maintained at least in the near future' (Whallon 1972a, 38).

This is not incompatible with our own view: that the keynote of the future will be and should be diversity rather than standardisation and the giant integrated information system. Everything suggests that technological development leads to a largely uncontrolled proliferation of possibilities far beyond anything seen by the pioneers and their critics. Consider, for example, the diversity of motor vehicles that exist. Standardisation and convention is successfully imposed only when the diversity becomes unbearable, not at the outset. More specifically, it is hard to believe that archaeologists will for long be satisfied with a situation where, as Whallon implies, data are located by way of a general data bank but analysed in a separate operation presumably requiring the researcher to return to sources. It seems almost inevitable that provision will be made for specialised data files to be 'tacked-on' to the main bank on grounds of convenience and common-sense, thereby immediately involving the latter in the storage of detailed and specialised data.

An important task for the future is to discover how best to integrate data banks with analytical programs: statistical packages and the like. Whilst Whallon may be correct to feel (see above) that the information contained by larger and more general data banks will be inappropriately coded and too diffuse for meaningful analysis there is no denying that specialised data banks are commonly created with automatic analysis in mind. Several examples were given in section 12.2, and the benefits of such integration are obvious.

It is important to remember the complementary relationship between the data actually held inside the machine, which will often consist merely of tables of numbers and symbols, and the description or measurement code itself. The latter is outside the machine, typically in a manual, and not accessible to any program. This imposes a very great limitation upon any programmed analysis. In a fairly obvious sense the analysis is acting 'blind', rather as if one were asked by a friend to arrange a group of people around a dinner table but told only their sex. It can be done, but the conversation would probably be a lot better if one knew who the guests were. Just about all computer programs used to analyse archaeological data have operated blind in this sense. The archaeologist knows what the data are all about but the program does not. *It* does know that this column of the matrix refers to bone pins and that to loom weights, nor the implications that these facts have.

This need not be so. There is reason to believe that at least part of the content of the coding manual and of the knowledge in the archaeologist's head can be given to the machine. The more this can be done, the more intelligent and effective automatic analyses can be. Much of the interest of the Marseilles amphorae project (section 12.2), with its stress on natural language communication and the mathematical description of archaeological concepts, lies precisely in its encounter with this fundamental issue. In this project archaeological research overlaps with computer science investigations into the meaning of 'meaning' from both linguistic and cognitive standpoints (Simmons 1970).

The Role of Mathematics
and the Computer in Archaeology

13.1. PAST AND PRESENT

The reader may well find it surprising that the one piece of computer work in archaeological research that is widely known both among archaeologists and non-specialists has not yet been mentioned in this book. We refer, of course, to the study by Hawkins (1973) of the astronomical significance of stone alignments at Stonehenge and elsewhere. This is quite deliberate. Hawkins' work is undeniably of great importance for our understanding of prehistoric astronomy and mathematics, but his use of the computer has no general significance for archaeological methodology. The machine is used merely to calculate significant astronomical directions in prehistoric times, and the exercise is therefore astronomical rather than archaeological. The related studies of Thom (1967, 1971) and Kendall (1973) are similarly of only special interest, though reference has been made to the latter in the context of Monte Carlo methods (see section 11.5.1). Many other special uses of mathematics in archaeological contexts could be described. Prominent among these are the techniques used in the analysis of geomagnetic survey data, and in other applications of physical methods such as thermoluminescent dating (see, for example, Tite 1972). All these instances have in common that the mathematical methods are not required by the archaeology itself but by one of the natural sciences which has come to the aid of archaeology. Thus such work is out of the main stream of the development of mathematical methods in archaeology and will receive no more than this passing reference.

The reader who has progressed steadily through the preceding chapters should have gained a reasonable idea of the mathematical techniques which have been used in archaeological work and how they have been deployed. He should also have some feel for the actual experimentation and the results it yields (see chapter 9 in particular). Multivariate analyses, automatic classification, seriation studies, and data bank work including the definition of descriptive codes, have provided most of the experiments (cf. Whallon 1972a, 41). Important surveys are those of Cowgill (1967) and Whallon (1972a), and much of the actual work has been published in conference proceedings (Gardin 1970; Hodson, Kendall and Tautu 1971; Borillo 1972). Not all the work has used a computer: far from it. But while Gardin's (1971b) remark that 'the use of statistical tools is not basically or even historically linked to the computerisation of archaeology' is undeniably true (see, for example, the sophisticated statistical work of Myers 1950), so is his immediate characterisation of the computer as an 'accelerator' in this context.

It is unreasonable to expect initial work in any research field to form a well-related whole without duplication and misconception, and any such expectation in computer archaeology has certainly been disappointed. Until very recently the picture was one of a variety of relatively isolated experiments developing from a variety of needs and theoretical orientations. These are only now beginning to yield a body of solid experience and standard practice. It is possible to identify two factors in particular which have made the initial development of computer work in archaeology particularly disorganised. The first of these is the immense academic gulf between archaeology on the one hand and mathematics on the other. This has meant that the archaeologist who has come to believe that mathematics (including therein statistics, quantification and computer work generally) may help him solve his problem or cope with his data, is obliged either to struggle himself with difficult and unfamiliar mathematical texts in the hope of finding and then understanding those minor branches of the subject related to his needs or, much more likely, to rely upon the advice of some friendly expert. Unfortunately a randomly chosen expert will recommend a method out of his own limited repertoire and is likely to do so in total ignorance of previous mathematical work in archaeology. The result can only be, and manifestly has been, a scattering of isolated *ad hoc* projects often duplicating one another and sometimes clearly ill-conceived.

The second factor which has influenced the initial use of mathematics in archaeology for the worse is that much of the impetus has come from related subjects such as geography, anthropology and social sciences generally. Frequently concepts and techniques which have been imperfectly digested by these disciplines are then picked up and used by even more enthusiastic and even less comprehending archaeologists. Examples of concepts which have been adopted in this way are those of elementary set theory, of formal linguistic and of general systems theory. Such a diffusion process is all to the good in the long-term but can easily lead to error and waste at the outset.

It might have been hoped that coherence in the content and use of mathematics in archaeology might have been imposed by coherence of the mathematics itself. This has not happened. It might have done had the techniques at issue been drawn from one central branch of mathematics. But rather they have come from a diversity of relatively peripheral branches, often themselves new and at best uncertain in application. It is a very long road to travel if one really wants to know all about multivariate analysis, and combinatorics, and computer simulation, and information retrieval by computer, and differential equations. Any two of these subjects are as far apart on the academic map as are palaeolithic and industrial archaeology. Even within applied statistics, unified traditional procedures with their emphasis upon samples drawn randomly from populations have been much less used in archaeology than the newer and theoretically uncertain data analytic methods. Thus the mathematics itself encourages discord rather than harmony.

The overall picture, then, is of much experimental work but of relatively little in the way of solid progress until recent years. Techniques of proven worth, such as k-means analysis (see section 7.5.4), are only now beginning to emerge. Nevertheless the uncertainty that attends the more sophisticated and complex techniques should not be allowed to obscure the increased frequency with which simpler methods of quantification and data presentation are being used in routine archaeological work. This is happening unobtrusively and easily as archaeologists come to realise that elementary quantitative methods are a natural and useful extension of established practice. Mathematics is not divorced from general human experience and thought, but is a natural extension of it. The passage from the informal to the formal is not an arduous one, provided that ambition is initially restrained.

A practical if relatively conservative view of the role of mathematics in archaeology is that there are certain aspects of archaeological work, and certain classes of problem, which can usefully be thrown into mathematical form and treated accordingly. Computers are often essential for the solution methods to be feasible. No radical revision of archaeological methodology need be considered. Many of the archaeologists most interested in the use of mathematical methods would contest such a view. As explained in section 1.2, the impact of mathematics upon archaeology is frequently discussed as part of the methodological debate associated with the 'new' archaeology. From a more radical standpoint formal methods in archaeology are to be seen as part of a general attempt to make the discipline more scientific, and to use 'systemic' rather than 'normative' concepts (Watson, LeBlanc and Redman 1971; Hill 1972). To the radicals, conservative usage of mathematics in archaeology is positively harmful; it merely supports a little longer an antique and misguided methodology. Although general questions of archaeological methodology are outside the scope of this book, some discussion of their more mathematical aspects is clearly relevant. Therefore we shall now look briefly at general systems theory and scientific methods as they are and as they have been interpreted by archaeologists in recent years.

13.2. ARCHAEOLOGY AND GENERAL SYSTEMS THEORY

A view prominent among those archaeologists critical of traditional methodology is the need to think in *systemic* terms (Binford 1965, Clarke 1968, Flannery 1968). The origins of this emphasis lie in a subject called *general systems theory* which has had an impact upon a wide range of disciplines in recent years. General systems theory strives to find and express in mathematical terms the common characteristics and properties of systems of all types be they physical, biological or social. However just what is meant by a *system* in general is not easy to pin down. It is probably not too misleading to say that a system is a complex of interacting elements; that systems are often studied in terms of their input, output and behaviour; and that sometimes one system is used as a model of another (for a list of twenty-four published definitions of a system see Klir 1969, 283). Any such definition is a very general one and general systems theory must be distinguished from theories of particular kinds of systems which occur in engineering science, biology, computer science, pure mathematics, management studies, information science and so on. General systems theory attempts to abstract away from all these established domains of study, capturing what they have in common.

A rather negative view of general systems theory is that of Simon (1969, 84–5) a leading computer scientist and psychologist:

'A number of proposals have been advanced in recent years for the development of "general systems theory" that, abstracting from properties peculiar to physical, biological, or social systems, would be applicable to all of them. We might well feel that, while the goal is laudable, systems of such diverse kinds could hardly be expected to have any nontrivial properties in common. Metaphor and analogy can be helpful, or they can be misleading. All depends on whether the similarities the metaphor captures are significant or superficial.

'It may not be entirely vain, however, to search for common properties among diverse kinds of complex systems. The ideas that go by the name of cybernetics constitute, if not a theory, at least a point of view that has been proving fruitful over a wide range of applications. It has been useful to look at the behavior of adaptive systems in terms of the concepts of feedback and homeostasis, and to analyze adaptiveness in terms of the theory of selective information. The ideas of feedback and information provide a frame of reference for viewing a wide range of situations, just as do the ideas of evolution, or relativism, of axiomatic method, and of operationalism.'

Simon makes two important points. Firstly, general systems theory is more an aspiration than a reality: and an aspiration that is sufficiently ambitious to attract scepticism. Secondly, the particular ideas and concepts that are current in general systems theory and in the closely related subject *cybernetics* do have general value. What Simon clearly does not believe, and what is certainly not true, is that general systems theory is something which can be applied in detail to a wide range of situations and which can produce concrete answers.

As might be expected more enthusiasm for general systems theory is shown by those actually working in the subject, and reference should be made, for example, to the publications of the founder of the subject von Bertalanffy (1950, 1968). A lucid and coherent introductory treatment is that of Klir (1969). Klir presents a number of different approaches to the specification of a system, and discusses in detail the problems that can be formulated and how the solution of such problems can be attempted. He gives many examples which relate general system concepts to real world problems. Even so he does not argue that general systems theory is sufficiently elaborated to be of significant practical value, commenting that: 'Although many results of contemporary system theories can be adopted and unified in general systems theory, the majority of problems in this field have not been solved and, thus, an intensive research is needed' (Klir 1969, 272).

Concepts important in general systems theory and central to cybernetics are those of control, self-regulation, input-output behaviour, and information (in a technical sense). The subject springs from the study of self-regulating systems such as thermostats, hormone systems, social groups, and ecological systems. The investigation naturally includes not only the effect of the regulating mechanisms, but their detailed structure (for example, the sensory/motor 'feedback' loop which enables the driver of a car to estimate and refine the effects of his actions), and the ways in which regulation breaks down (resulting in death, revolution, a road accident). A standard introduction to cybernetics is that of Ashby (1956), and Clarke (1968) has treated the subject at some length. A very brief introduction to some of the simplest ideas, together with comments on the uncertain development of cybernetics over the past decade or so, will be found in Doran (1970b).

Having said a little of the origins and nature of systems theory (we shall now drop the word 'general') it is appropriate to look at some examples of the use that archaeologists have actually made of it. Newcomb (1968) presents 'systems models' of a Courtyard House Village and of a Hill Fort. In fact these are simple block diagrams showing, in the case of the hill fort, the reciprocal relationships which in Newcomb's view hold between such factors as manpower, building materials, defence and the outside world (figure 13.1). Newcomb has performed an outline analysis of these two types of settlement, relating the various factors and components which can be detected within them. He uses systems theory terminology and is guided by its concepts. Flannery (1968) does much the same kind of thing, if at a somewhat more sophisticated level, in a study of procurement systems and regulatory mechanisms in early Mesoamerica. Neither Newcomb nor Flannery attempt to quantify, being content to analyse from a general systemic standpoint.

A much more ambitious study is that of Rathje (1973) who promises in his introduction to: 'construct synthetic systems that generate parameters of change within and between Lowland Classic Maya (800 BC–AD 900) cultural systems. The material remains patterns generated from the synthetic systems will be tested by comparison with Lowland Classic Maya burial patterns through the use of a Material Culture/Social Mobility model.' Essentially Rathje is trying to relate variability in a society's burial assemblages to its environmental variability (ecological, geographical, etc.) *via* the degree of social mobility existing within it. At the heart of Rathje's argument is the *Law of Requisite Variety* which he states as: 'Variety is required to create or destroy variety'. This is an informal statement of an exact theorem in cybernetics. Rathje uses it, informally, to predict a positive correlation between environmental variability and grave assemblage variability. These two factors are themselves assumed to be correlated positively with social mobility. Of course, this last cannot itself be measured directly. Interesting though this study is, it is difficult to take its appeal to cybernetics seriously if only because Rathje's use of the word 'variety' is itself more than a little variable. On the other hand, arguments of this general kind are potentially very powerful.

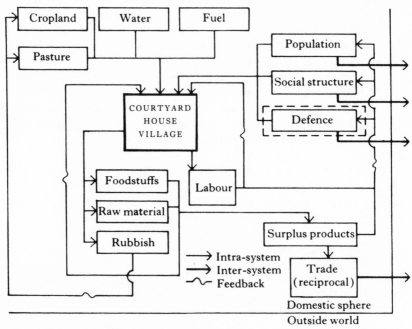

Figure 13.1. A systems model of a courtyard house village (Newcomb 1968, 10,
figure 2).

A discussion paper which indicates the impact of systems theory on archaeological methodology at the level of general debate is that of Wood and Matson (1973). They compare and contrast two models for cultural change, the homeostatic model and the complex adaptive system model, both provided by systems theory. There is, however, no solid mathematical structure and no specific application. Again, therefore, it is hard to take the discussion very seriously.

These examples of the introduction of systems theory and cybernetics into archaeological work should serve to indicate what has been attempted and with what degree of success. Unfortunately criticism seems more appropriate than enthusiasm. Thus it is surely true that the concepts deployed have been used in archaeology before if much less explicitly. It is the terminology, the emphasis, and the authority claimed or implied that is new. The source of much of that authority, the mathematics associated with systems theory and cybernetics, is either ignored completely or, worse, applied in a confused and confusing manner.

It might seem reasonable to excuse these failings in archaeologists working for the first time with difficult concepts. This would be easier to do were the faults less extreme and less confidently perpetrated: 'Terms are borrowed from ecology and general systems theory and uttered as blessings from the Bible. More critically, the terms are often flagrantly misused or misrepresented' (Plog 1973, 653). Of Clarke's *Analytical Archaeology* (Clarke 1968), which makes major use of concepts drawn from systems theory and cybernetics, Steiger (1971, 70) says that it is 'neither analytical nor rigorous' and that 'the book fails to achieve its goals because of anomalous applications of technical concepts', and supports these statements with detailed and convincing criticism. Alas, it is so much easier to make theoretical play with exciting, if a little imprecise, general concepts than to get down either to actual mathematics or to solid and detailed practical application!

Particularly relevant to this book is a tendency to relate the methods of multivariate statistics to systems theory. Thus Watson, LeBlanc and Redman (1971, 84) write: 'Various types of multivariate analysis have already been utilised [in archaeology], and further developments in this field promise to facilitate the use of a systems approach', and the context makes clear that they are referring to such techniques as factor analysis and cluster analysis. This idea is a little disconcerting because (a) the mathematics associated with systems theory has nothing to do with multivariate statistical analysis, and (b) multivariate analyses usually invoke *linear* assumptions which do not go at all well with systemic ideas. The connection, in fact, is no stronger than that archaeological systems often involve many variables.

The conclusion seems to be this. The concepts of systems theory and cybernetics do have general value in archaeology, as in many other fields, but it will be very difficult to make use of the corresponding mathematical theory. This is not merely because as yet archaeologists have no grasp on the mathematics. Much more fundamentally it is because archaeological data are insufficient for the mathematics of systems theory to be made to work (compare Steiger 1971). The essence of the archaeological problem is minimal data relative to the size of the inference problem. The mathematics used by archaeologists must be appropriate to this.

13.3. AN 'EXPLICITLY SCIENTIFIC APPROACH'

If systems theory does little to provide a framework for mathematical work in archaeology, what about scientific methodology generally? Is it not the case that in an 'explicitly scientific approach' mathematics will be assigned an exact and coherent role in archaeological research? Unfortunately this is not so. To explain why not, a brief look at the movement towards scientific methodology will be needed.

A call for a 'shift to a rigorous hypothetico-deductive method with a goal of explanation' in archaeology was made by Binford (1968) and detailed work in this spirit presented by Hill (1968). Fritz and Plog (1970) argued that 'the development and use of law-like statements by archaeologists to explain characteristics of the archaeological record has been and should continue to be one of the most important goals of archaeological research', and that 'the testing of potential laws requires a shift from an inductive procedure . . . to a deductive procedure in which the explicit formulation of potential laws and their empirical consequences precedes and directs the collection of data'. However the clearest statement of the methodological issues involved is probably that of Hill (1972). He attempts 'to demonstrate, through both argument and example, that the hypothetico-deductive approach (Braithwaite 1960, Hempel 1966) is not only more efficient, but is critical to the advancement of archaeology as a science' (Hill 1972, 63). According to Hill (p. 67):

> 'The primarily deductive researcher begins his research with an idea or hypothesis about how to interpret or explain his data; he then deduces from the hypothesis (or set of them) the kinds of evidence he would expect to find in his materials if his hypothesis is correct (or not correct). Then, by gathering and examining the relevant data, he is able to evaluate the degree to which the facts actually conform to what he expected if his proposition were correct (i.e. goodness of fit).'

This deductivist approach, with its stress on the testing of hypotheses, Hill contrasts with the traditional inductivist or empiricist approach which he follows Hempel in finding 'untenable'. He characterises (p. 66) the inductivist approach as:

> '(1) Observation and recording of all facts
> (2) Analysis and classification of these facts
> (3) Inductive derivation of generalisations from the facts
> (4) Further testing of the generalisations.'

According to Hill (p. 69): 'The important point to emphasise . . . is that in the hypothetico-deductive method we do not have to wait for a collection of mute data to somehow provide us with inferences. We may invent our own inferences, and the sources of inspiration for them are irrelevant (Binford 1967, Hill 1968).'

He stresses that: 'The idea that one can collect a body of "basic data" has merit only to the degree that a large number of our colleagues share the same problems and are testing the same hypotheses' (p. 87). Later he reaffirms that: 'If we are really seriously interested in getting answers to research questions, we must employ hypotheses to bridge the gap between our problems and the relevant data to observe' (p. 89).

How does this work out in practice? As yet there is rather little evidence to judge by. One example is the study by Hill himself (1968) of the Broken K Pueblo in Arizona, dating from about 1150–1280 AD. He studies the variability among the many rooms at the Pueblo and at an early stage formulates the proposition 'that the variability in rooms at the site has the same behavioural context as does the variability in modern pueblo rooms; the respective room types are functional equivalents' (Hill 1968, 116). He immediately continues: 'It would not, however, be profitable to terminate the analysis at this point, as is so often done; the proposition must first be tested.' He then formulates a list of sixteen 'expectations', for example that the large rooms should contain evidence that water was stored in them, and proceeds to test these propositions using, he claims, independent data. He finds that most of the expectations are satisfied and that therefore the central proposition is confirmed. Where discrepancies occur, for example the absence of large storage jars in the storage rooms, these are important in their own right. Hill uses simple χ^2 tests of statistical significance and factor analysis (not too appropriately), both to establish variability in the first instance, and then, having formulated his central proposition, to test the subsidiary propositions derived from it.

Leaving aside relatively minor doubts about the way in which Hill has used significance tests and indeed, his understanding of exactly what a significance test is, the central question to be asked of this undeniably interesting study is whether the hypothetico-deductive formulation has contributed anything at all to it. We believe not. Any competent person carefully considering the available evidence would reach the same conclusion as Hill, with the same subsidiary conclusions and speculations. Anyone would look around for fresh evidence to test each particular hypothesis. The implication that sound conclusions can only be achieved by reasoning in a rigid hypothetico-deductive manner is absurd. Arbitrary or over-simplified 'rules' of reasoning do more harm than good.

A similar reaction is evoked by a more recent attempt to construct a hypothetico-deductive argument, the important study by Thomas (1973) of Great Basis Shoshonean settlement patterns. This has already been mentioned in section 11.5.3 in the context of computer simulations. In exemplary fashion a theory is exhibited (Steward's), testable propositions are deduced from it (by means of the simulation itself and a large number of subsidiary assumptions), independent data are collected (by controlled probability sampling of the region), and a tally made of propositions confirmed and propositions rejected. But elegant though the logical structure of the argument is, it is hard to believe that it contributes anything to the archaeological value of the study that common-sense and due caution would not have done. Indeed it is arguable that the desire to complete the 'scientific' process in due style has led Thomas to simplify what he is doing to the point where, if the archaeological value of the study itself is not threatened, the justification for his use of complex mathematical tools certainly is.

Another study which aspires to be explicitly scientific is that of Borillo (1971) mentioned earlier. Borillo's study is presented both as a simulation of an archaeologist at work (see section 11.6) and as an exercise in scientific deductive archaeology. It is itself based upon a traditional study by Richter of a class of early Greek statues, the *kouroi*. Borillo sees Richter's study as directed towards the formulation of law:

> 'Richter's book aims to show that the morphological evolution of a certain type of statue (kouros) obeyed, for about a century and a half, a quite remarkable law which can be expressed in the following manner. Starting from a sculptured form of foreign origin (Egypt, Mesopotamia, etc.) characterized by the use of stable stylistic conventions, the observable evolution at the hands of the Greek sculptors presents two remarkable features: the gradual search for conformity with the anatomical natural model, and the irreversible nature of this process (presenting at no time a return to the past)' (Borillo 1971).

Later Borillo identifies the central hypothesis: 'The Greek effort was concerted, each generation building on the achievement of the preceding one, and never losing an inch of the ground gained', and sets out first to simulate formally the descriptive and classificatory aspects of Richter's study and then to reformulate the central argument in deductive terms following the hypothetico-deductive approach we have been considering.

He does this by starting with the central hypothesis and working from it to the need to compare two orderings of the *kouroi*, a morphological ordering and a temporal ordering. He then proceeds to the descriptive and automatic classification procedures needed to provide these orderings and finally discusses the definition of compatibility of the two orders. Borillo's argument as a whole is carefully structured and, of course, makes major use of formal tools.

This does not mean, however, that Borillo's paper carries complete conviction. Is it really good enough to introduce the central hypothesis out of thin air? To do so may permit a tidy argument but it has rather little to do with the realities of reasoning. And then there is a problem with the testing of this or any similar hypothesis. If we are being realistic the situation is essentially stochastic. One should be talking about the correlation between the temporal and morphological orders, not, as Borillo does, merely about their absolute compatibility. There is a general point here. The incorporation of probabilistic arguments into a hypothetico-deductive framework encounters the conceptual difficulty (it is no more than that) that there is no established theory linking formal deductive logic on the one hand and statistical inference on the other. Some archaeologists have reacted by advocating the use of formal deductive logic, which has very little practical value, while ignoring potentially much more useful probabilistic arguments.

Where there is an emphasis on hypothesis testing against independent and specially collected data it is reasonable to expect a corresponding emphasis on statistical sampling procedures, on statistical hypothesis testing and on mathematical model evaluation generally. Although this emphasis is indeed sometimes asserted by 'scientific' archaeologists, it is noticeable that in the studies just described the situation is not at all clear. Hill uses significance tests before as well as after his central proposition is formulated, and Borillo uses data analytic methods of classification as part of his testing procedure. The implication is again that the hypothetico-deductive formulation of the inference task fails to capture its essential complexity, and gives no guidance to the use of mathematical methods.

This is less surprising when one realises that it is perfectly possible to dispute the philosophical stance itself. Philosophers of science are by no means in agreement among themselves. Moberg has said of Binford's approach: 'It is exclusively that of positivism as expressed by Hempel. Is this always adequate for archaeology? The reader may be left with the erroneous impression that there exist no respectable alternatives to the science philosophy of Hempel' (Moberg 1972; see also Morgan 1973). In fact it is far from clear that an empirical and inductive approach cannot be handled systematically (Hanson 1958, 1961; Churchman and Buchanan 1969; Meltzer 1970); nor is it obvious that the development of science can realistically be separated from the social context within which it takes place (Thuillier 1971). One might even point out that the philosophy of science is not *itself* a science, and suggest that its practitioners have no more authority for their pronouncements than traditional archaeologists. They collect data, they formulate generalisations, but there is very little concrete testing of hypotheses.

The hypothetico-deductive approach to archaeological investigation does have the virtue that it encourages private and public scrutiny of archaeological procedure. It is not enough just to do, one must think about the doing. The effect must be to avoid some of the worst blunders of interpretation. But it fails to recognise that all reasoning, be it scientific, inductive, deductive or whatever is much more complex even than philosophers of science generally allow. Consequently it imposes arbitrary and damaging restrictions on procedure, and provokes time-wasting arguments by over-simple distinctions between such concepts as description and explanation, and induction and deduction. It seems that the less archaeology becomes scientific, in this sense, the better.

13.4. AN ALTERNATIVE VIEW OF SCIENTIFIC METHOD
There is more than one way to look at scientific reasoning just as there is more

than one way to approach the problem of what constitutes good archaeological method. To one accustomed to working with computer simulations of
cognitive processes (Doran 1970a, 1971b) most science philosophy suffers
from a lack of exactness and from an initial false distinction: between ordinary
reasoning and behaviour, which is ignored, and scientific reasoning and
procedure which is to be admired, analysed and explicated. In this section an
alternative view will be indicated without, however, suggesting that this is
more than the right initial perspective to adopt. There exists no fully
satisfactory theory of reasoning.

We are all possessed of a certain body of knowledge or belief. This may
loosely be regarded as a very large number of propositions such as: 'I am
sitting at my desk'; 'fire burns'; 'Winston Churchill is dead'; 'Newton's laws
of gravitation are inexact'. Some of these propositions we would normally call
beliefs, some speculations, some hypotheses, some convictions depending
upon our degree of confidence in them. Different people have different beliefs.
Where there is general agreement we tend to speak of facts or laws.

We extend our beliefs by observation (it's raining; my left foot hurts; the
newspaper placard says there's been a plane crash; the fibula is oddly shaped)
and by ill-understood processes of deduction, generalisation, concept
formation and the like (I shall get wet; perhaps my shoes are too tight; air
travel is too dangerous; invent type C/D). Where contradictions occur (there's
a draught/the window is closed), they may or may not lead to further
observation and inference intended to eliminate them (is the door open?).
Observation and inference are rarely, if ever, aimless, but directed towards the
achievement of goals which may be immediate (regain balance, pick it up,
decide if the telephone is ringing), long-term (buy a house, understand
urbanisation) or ever-present (keep warm, avoid pain). Goals are
hierarchically organised so that achieving one, with the observation, inference
and action typically required, immediately introduces another (having opened
the door, one must walk into the room; having completed the excavation, one
must write the report).

The process is, manifestly, never ending. It goes on throughout our
conscious hours and to an unknown extent in our unconscious hours as well.
With the passage of time we all develop a fixed body of knowledge and belief,
and it is on top of this that the everyday ebb and flow of observation, inference
and speculation takes place. Usually our beliefs are objectively sound, but we
all make mistakes and some of us slip into insanity.

This view of everyday reasoning is one that few would seriously dispute
and it has been explored in one form or another in a number of computer
experiments. The suggestion made here is that scientific reasoning and
scientific method is best seen as this process rendered public and communal.
Any such view at once highlights deficiencies in the more conventional science
philosophy. *Crucially the conventional dispute between alternative sequences
of methodological stages* (see last section) *merely obscures what is primarily a*

continuing cyclic process. To emphasise the deductive aspects of the cycle, at the expense of the remainder, is to court total confusion.

Thus the first requirement is for archaeologists to accept a cyclic view of knowledge acquisition as the correct one. Then it is reasonable to ask what are the prospects of putting the entire process upon a formal mathematical footing. It is natural to think first of mathematical logic, which indeed aspires to be a formal theory of reasoning. Unfortunately it still has a very long way to go. It still has rather little to say about generalisation and induction, and even purely deductive logic is very limited and very cumbersome for any practical purpose. Much the same is true of mathematical theories of probability, though some discussions (e.g. Good 1950) do place significant emphasis on belief systems and their development. However, Bayes' theorem is central to such discussions and, as has been indicated in chapter 3, some of the most fundamental statistical techniques can be interpreted as special cases of it. Thus there is some link between practical techniques and a description of knowledge acquisition and hypothesis development in terms of probability theory.

Heuristic computer experiments have more practical potential because they do try to work out exactly specified procedures in realistic contexts. Certainly it is these experiments which are doing most to elucidate the detailed structure of reasoning (Feigenbaum 1969, Simon 1969, Arbib 1972). Of particular interest are experiments which have arisen from a study of the philosophical concept of a logic of discovery, that is of a studied procedure leading to plausible hypotheses or new and important concepts. The idea of such a logic is not fashionable. Buchanan, who has examined the subject in detail, speaks of 'an overwhelming reaction against logics of discovery', and continues:

> 'Because of the confusion of the logical and psychological contexts involved in speaking of rules of discovery, and the improbability of finding rules guaranteeing the discovery of true scientific hypotheses, philosophers of science have been very anxious to avoid issues concerning the discovery of hypotheses. They prefer the oversimplified guess-and-conform model of scientific activity to charges of psychologism' (Buchanan 1966, 7).

He goes on to derive practical guide lines for logics of discovery and hypothesis generation procedures, and has put his views into practice by developing, with professional chemists, computer programs which generate hypotheses from empirical data in a particular area of organic chemistry (Buchanan and Lederberg 1972). These computer programs are widely accepted as effective and significant. If their potential can be realised then the impact upon both science and its philosophy must be substantial.

The discussion of this section obviously does not provide a clear framework for the use of mathematics in archaeology. This is simply not yet possible. But it should at least suggest to the reader that the hypothetico-deductive approach comes to archaeologists with much less authority than might at first appear.

13.5. THE ARCHAEOLOGIST AND MATHEMATICS IN THE FUTURE
As the discussions of this chapter have no doubt already made clear, we see little need for a revolution in archaeological methodology and concepts. There is, however, ample scope for archaeological procedure and reasoning to be made more systematic, more exact and more objective. This is not really a criticism of the past. It is a response to the greater variety and number of data which the archaeologist is now collecting and which generates new needs. It is a response also to the arrival on the scene of mathematical tools which generate new potentialities.

There seems little doubt that the rather heterogeneous range of applications of mathematics in archaeology will continue, no doubt with many extensions into new archaeological contexts and using, or at least trying to use, new areas of mathematics (Moberg 1971). It is sometimes suggested that archaeology requires the development of new mathematics, rather than the adoption of existing procedures. There is much to be said for this view provided it is recognised that archaeology usually shares its mathematical problems with other disciplines. Where these problems are solved by mathematicians for the first time, whether or not at the instigation of archaeologists, then the solutions are likely to be of general applicability; this follows from the abstract nature of mathematics itself.

To what extent will archaeologists need to learn mathematics? We feel that every professional archaeologist should know how to use the simpler methods of quantification, data presentation and data summary, should know something of the potentiality and limitations of the more sophisticated methods now being tested, should know enough simple statistical theory to understand, for example, the meaning of a significance test and of a confidence limit, and should have some general idea of what mathematics is. Too often in the past archaeologists seem not to have realised that simplification and assumption are ubiquitous in mathematical work and must always be recognised, and that mathematics is essentially abstract exact reasoning, not a few isolated concepts or a surfeit of numbers.

It will do no harm to stress again the generally beneficial effect of exposure to quantification and computers. The user of such tools is obliged to put his or her thoughts in order in a way which may come as something of a shock. The methodological constraints imposed are severe. The range of discussion and inference will be markedly restricted. But what is completed is much more likely to be objective and solid.

It follows from these remarks that exposure to quantitative methods must be included in standard archaeological training. This should not be too difficult to arrange once the will is there. Indeed a number of such courses already exist. Further it is natural to see the development of a new class of specialists: those who give guidance on the use of the more complex methods in archaeology and indeed, who develop and evaluate these methods. It is not too speculative to foresee the development of definite centres dedicated to such work, especially since it is the case that many of the methods at issue make heavy demands upon computing resources with the implication that these resources should be pooled.

All attempts to see into the future of archaeology are uncertain. To know what *should* happen if the agreed goals of the subject are to be achieved is not at all to know what *will* happen as social, academic, and technological forces operate. But we are confident that the use of mathematical methods and the computer in archaeological work will increase, and that far from rendering the subject lifeless, as some fear, it will add new diversity and colour to what is already one of the most varied, attractive and significant areas of human investigation. With the aid of such tools our understanding of our past can only be deepened. The benefit will be felt far outside the bounds of archaeology itself.

References

Allen, W. L. & Richardson, J. B. (1971) The reconstruction of kinship from archaeological data: the concepts, the methods and the feasibility. *Am. Antiquity*, **36**(1), 41–53.

Ammerman, A. J. (1971) A computer analysis of epipalaeolithic assemblages in Italy. *Mathematics in the Archaeological and Historical Sciences* (eds F. R. Hodson, D. G. Kendall & P. Tautu), 133–7. Edinburgh: Edinburgh University Press.

Ammerman, A. J. & Cavalli-Sforza, L. L. (1973) A population model for the diffusion of early farming in Europe. *The Explanation of Culture Change* (ed C. Renfrew), 343–57. London: Duckworth.

Ammerman, A. J. & Hodson, F. R. (1972) Constellation analysis: a study of Late Palaeolithic assemblages in Italy. *Riv. di Sci. Preist.*, **27**, 323–44.

Andrews, D. F. (1972) Plots of high-dimensional data. *Biometrics*, **28**, 125–36.

Arbib, M. A. (1972) *The Metaphorical Brain*. New York: Wiley Interscience.

Armstrong, J. S. (1967) Derivation of theory by means of factor analysis *or* Tom Swift and his electric factor analysis machine. *Am. Statist.*, **21**, 17–21.

Armstrong, J. S. & Soelberg, P. (1968) On the interpretation of factor analysis. *Psychol. Bull.*, **70**(5), 361–4.

Ashby, W. R. (1956) *An Introduction to Cybernetics*. New York: Wiley.

Ascher, M. (1959) A mathematical rationale for graphical seriation. *Am. Antiquity*, **25**, 212–14.

Ascher, R. & Ascher, M. (1963) Chronological ordering by computer. *Am. Anthrop.*, **65**, 1045–52.

Ashton, E. H., Healey, M. J. R. & Lipton, S. (1957) The descriptive use of discriminant functions in physical anthropology. *Proc. R. Soc. B*, **146**, 552–72.

Aspinall, A., Warren, S. E., Crummett, J. G. & Newton, R. G. (1972) Neutron activation analysis of faience beads. *Archaeometry*, **14**, 27–40.

Azoury, I. (1971) *A technological and typological analysis of the Transitional and Early Upper Palaeolithic levels of Ksar Akil and Abu Halka.* Unpublished Doctoral thesis, London University.

Azoury, I. & Hodson, F. R. (1973) Comparing Palaeolithic assemblages: Ksar Akil, a case study. *World Archaeol.,* **4**(3), 292–306.

Bailey, N. T. J. (1959) *Statistical Methods in Biology.* London: The English Universities Press.

Ball, G. H. (1967) *A comparison of two techniques for finding the minimum sumsquared error partition.* Stanford Research Institute Research Report.

Bartholomew, D. J. (1967) *Stochastic Models for Social Processes.* London: Wiley.

Benfer, R. A. (1967) A design for the study of archaeological characteristics. *Am. Anthrop.,* **69,** 719–30.

Bergamini, D. (1970) *Mathematics* (Life Science Library). New York: Time-Life Books.

von Bertalanffy, L. (1950) An outline of general system theory. *Brit. J. Phil. Sci.* **1,** 134–65.

von Bertalanffy, L. (1968) *General Systems Theory,* New York: Braziller.

Binford, L. R. (1963a) The Pomranky site. A Late Archaic burial station. *Anthropological Papers,* **19,** 149–92. Museum of Anthropology, University of Michigan.

Binford, L. R. (1963b) A proposed attribute list for the description and classification of projectile points. *Anthropological Papers,* **19,** 193–221. Museum of Anthropology, University of Michigan.

Binford, L. R. (1964) A consideration of archaeological research design. *Am. Antiquity,* **29,** 425–41.

Binford, L. R. (1965) Archaeological systematics and the study of culture process. *Am. Antiquity,* **31**(2), 203–10.

Binford, L. R. (1967) Smudge pits and hide smoking : the use of analogy in archaeological reasoning. *Am. Antiquity,* **32**(1), 1–12.

Binford, L. R. (1968) Archaeological perspectives. *New Perspectives in Archaeology* (eds S. R. & L. R. Binford), 5–32. Chicago: Aldine.

Binford, L. R. (1972) Contemporary model building: paradigms and the current state of Palaeolithic research. *Models in Archaeology* (ed D. L. Clarke), 109–66. London: Methuen.

Binford, L. R. & Binford, S. R. (1966) A preliminary analysis of functional variability in the Mousterian of Levallois facies. *Am. Anthrop.,* **68,** 238–295.

Binford, S. R. & Binford, L. R., eds (1968) *New Perspectives in Archaeology.* Chicago: Aldine.

Blalock, H. M. (1960) *Social Statistics.* London and New York: McGraw-Hill.

Bohmers, A. (1962) La valeur actuelle des méthodes de la typologie statistique. *Atti del VI congresso Internazionale delle Scienze Preistoriche and Protostoriche I,* 11–20. Florence: Sanzoni.

Bordaz, V. & Bordaz, J. (1970) A computer-assisted pattern recognition method of classification and seriation applied to archaeological material. *Archéologie et Calculateurs* (ed J-C. Gardin), 229–44. Paris: CNRS.

Bordes, F. (1950) Principes d'une méthode d'étude des techniques de débitage et de la typologie du Paléolithique ancien et moyen. *L'Anthropologie,* **54,** 19–34.

Bordes, F. (1953) Essai de classification des industries 'moustériennes'. *Bull. Soc. Préhist. Fr.,* **50,** 457–66.

Bordes, F. (1954) Le moustérien de l'Ermitage (fouilles L. Pradel). Comparaisons statistiques. *L'Anthropologie,* **58,** 444–9.

Bordes, F. (1961) *Typologie du Paléolithique Ancien et Moyen.* Bordeaux: Delmas.

Bordes, F. (1967) Considérations sur la Typologie et les techniques dans le Paléolithique. *Quartär,* **18,** 25–55.

Bordes, F. & Crabtree, D. E. (1969) The Corbiac blade technique and other experiments. *Tebiwa,* **12**(2), 1–21.

Bordes, F. & de Sonneville-Bordes, D. (1970) The significance of variability in Palaeolithic assemblages. *Wld Archaeol.,* **2**(1), 61–73.

Borillo, A. (1972) Problèmes de formalisation des données linguistiques dans un système intègre de traitement de l'information textuelle et graphique. *Art 68, Centre d'Analyse Documentaire pour l'Archéologie* (CADA), CNRS, Marseilles.

Borillo, M. (1971) An experiment in constructing a deductive argument through the simulation of a traditional archaeological study. *Art 57,* (CADA), CNRS, Marseilles. (Circulated at a conference on 'The Explanation of Culture Change: Models in Prehistory' held at Sheffield, December 1971.)

Borillo, M., ed (1972) *Les Méthodes Mathématiques de l'Archéologie.* Marseilles: (CADA), CNRS.

Borillo, M. & Ihm, P. (1971) Une méthode de classification d'objets archéologiques dont la description est structurée et incomplète. *Mathematics in the Archaeological and Historical Sciences* (eds F. R. Hodson, D. G. Kendall & P. Tautu), 85–95. Edinburgh: Edinburgh University Press.

Borillo, M. *et al.* (1972) Premiers éléments d'une expérience de construction d'un système intègre de traitement de l'information textuelle et graphique. *Com/53 bis* (CADA), CNRS, Marseilles. (See also article by these authors in *Inform. Stor. Retr.,* **9,** 527–60, 1973.)

Bourrelly, L. (1972) Quelques aspects de la notion moderne de simulation. *Les Méthodes Mathématiques de l'Archéologie* (ed M. Borillo), 186–199. Marseilles: (CADA), CNRS.

Bowles, E. A. (1971) Computers and European museums: a report. *Computers and the Humanities,* **5**(3), 176–7.

Brainerd, G. W. (1951) The place of chronological ordering in archaeological analysis. *Am. Antiquity*, **16,** 301–13.

Braithwaite, R. B. (1960) *Scientific Explanation*. New York: Harper.

Brennan, R. D. (1968) Simulation is wh-a-at? *Simulation* (ed J. McLeod) part II, 5–12. New York: McGraw Hill.

Brézillon, M. (1971) Les Tartarets II, habitat paléolithique de plein air à Corbeil-Essonnes. *Gallia Préhistoire*, **14,** 3–40.

Brose, D. S. (1970) *The Summer Island site: a study of prehistoric cultural ecology and social organisation in the northern Lake Michigan area.* Studies in Anthropology no.1, Case Western Reserve University.

Brown, J. A. & Freeman, L. (1964) A Univac analysis of sherd frequencies from the Carter Ranch Pueblo, Eastern Arizona. *Am. Antiquity*, **30**(2), 162–7.

Buchanan, B. G. (1966) *Logics of scientific discovery*. A I Memo 47, Computer Science Department, Stanford University.

Buchanan, B. G. & Lederberg, J. (1972) The Heuristic DENDRAL program for explaining empirical data. *Information Processing 71* (proceedings of the IFIP Congress 71; ed C. V. Freiman) vol. 1, 179–88. Amsterdam: North Holland.

Buneman, P. (1971) The recovery of trees from measures of dissimilarity. *Mathematics in the Archaeological and Historial Sciences* (eds F. R. Hodson, D. G. Kendall & P. Tautu), 387–95. Edinburgh: Edinburgh University Press.

Burgess, C. B. (1968) The later bronze age in the British Isles and north-west France. *Archaeol. J.*, **125,** 1–45.

Burleigh, R., Longworth, I. H. & Wainwright, G. J. (1972) Relative and absolute dating of four late Neolithic enclosures; an exercise in the interpretation of radiocarbon determinations. *Proc. Prehist. Soc.*, **38,** 389–407.

Cahen, D. & Martin, P (1972) Classification formelle automatique et industries lithiques. Interprétation des hachereaux de la Kamoa. *Annales, Sciences Humaines, no. 76.* Musée Royal de l'Afrique Central, Tervuren, Belgique.

Case, H. J. (1967) Were Beaker people the first metallurgists in Ireland ? *Palaeohistoria*, **12,** 141–77.

Casteel, R. W. (1972) Two static maximum population-density models for hunter-gatherers: a first approximation. *Wld Archaeol.*, **4**(1), 19–40.

Chang, K-C. (1967) *Rethinking Archaeology*. New York: Random House.

Chayes, F. & Kruskal, W. (1966) An approximate statistical test for correlations between proportions. *J. Geol.*, **74,** 692–702.

Chenhall, R. G. (1967) The description of archaeological data in computer language. *Am. Antiquity*, **32,** 161–7.

Chenhall, R. G. (1971a). The archaeological data bank, a progress report. *Computers and the Humanities*, **5**(3), 159–69.

Chenhall, R. G. (1971b) *Computers in Anthropology and Archaeology*. I B M Data Processing Application Manual G E 20–0384–0.

Chenhall, R. G. (1972) Computerised data banks for archaeologists. *Archäologie,* 3 (ed B. Heslig). Berlin.

Childe, V. G. (1956) *Piecing Together the Past. The Interpretation of Archaeological Data.* London: Routledge and Kegan Paul.

Chorley, R. J. & Haggett, P., eds (1967) *Models in Geography.* London: Methuen.

Christaller, W. (1933) *Die zentrallen Orte in Süddeutschland.* Jena: Gustav Fischer.

Churchman, C. W. & Buchanan, B. (1969) On the design of inductive systems: some philosophical problems. *Brit. J. Phil. of Sci.,* **20,** 311–25.

Clark, J. D. (1964) The Sangoan Culture of Equatoria: the implications of its stone equipment. *Miscelánea en homenaje al abate Henri Breuil* (ed E. Ripoll Perelló), Instituto de Prehistoria y Arqueologia Monografías 9, vol. 1, 309–25. Barcelona: Diputación Provincial de Barcelona.

Clarke, D. L. (1962) Matrix analysis and archaeology with particular reference to British Beaker pottery. *Proc. Prehist. Soc.,* **28,** 371–82.

Clarke, D. L. (1963) Matrix analysis and archaeology. *Nature,* **199,** 790–2.

Clarke, D. L. (1968) *Analytical Archaeology.* London: Methuen.

Clarke, D. L. (1970) *Beaker Pottery of Great Britain and Ireland.* Cambridge: Cambridge University Press.

Clarke, D. L. (1972) Models and paradigms in contemporary archaeology. *Models in Archaeology* (ed D. L. Clarke), 1–60. London: Methuen.

Clarke, R. M. & Renfrew, C. (1972) A statistical approach to the calibration of floating tree-ring chronologies using radiocarbon dates. *Archaeometry,* **14**(1), 5–19.

Clarke, R. M. & Renfrew, C. (1973) Tree-ring calibration of radiocarbon dates and the chronology of ancient Egypt. *Nature,* **243,** 266–70.

Coles, J. M. (1969) Metal analysis and the Scottish Early Bronze Age. *Proc. Prehist. Soc.,* **35,** 332–44.

Cooley, W. W. & Lohnes, P. R. (1962) *Multivariate Procedures for the Behavioural Sciences.* New York and London: Wiley.

Cormack, R. M. (1971) A review of classification. *J. R. Stat. Soc. A,* **134,** 321–53.

Costner, H. L. (1965) Criteria for measures of association. *Am. sociol. Rev.,* **30,** 341–53.

Cotton, J. W. (1967) *Elementary Statistical Theory for Behaviour Scientists.* Reading, Mass.: Addison-Wesley.

Coult, A. D. (1968) Uses and abuses of computers in anthropology. *Calcul et Formalisation dans les Sciences de l'Homme* (eds J-C. Gardin & B. Jaulin). Paris: C N R S.

Cowen, J. D. (1967) The Hallstatt sword of bronze on the continent and in Britain. *Proc. Prehist. Soc.*, **33**, 377–454.

Cowgill, G. L. (1964) The selection of samples from large sherd collections. *Am. Antiquity*, **29**(4), 467–73.

Cowgill, G. L. (1967) Computer applications in archaeology. *AFIPS Conference Proceedings 31* (1967, FJCC), 331–8.

Cowgill, G. L. (1968a) Computer analysis of archaeological data from Teotihuacan, Mexico. *New Perspectives in Archaeology* (eds S. R. Binford & L. R. Binford), 143–50. Chicago: Aldine.

Cowgill, G. L. (1968b) Review of Hole and Shaw (1967). *Am. Antiquity*, **33**(4), 517–19.

Cowgill, G. L. (1970) Some sampling and reliability problems in archaeology. *Archéologie et Calculateurs* (ed J-C. Gardin), 161–72. Paris: CNRS.

Cowgill, G. L. (1972) Models, methods and techniques for seriation. *Models in Archaeology* (ed D. L. Clarke), 381–424. London: Methuen.

Craytor, W. B. & Johnson, L. (1968) *Refinements in computerized item seriation.* Bulletin no. 10, Museum of Natural History, University of Oregon.

Cruxent, J. M. (1965) Litometría: artefactos de acabado escamoso. *Bol. Indigenista Venez.*, **10**, 193–201.

Dacey, M. F. (1973) Statistical tests of spatial association in the locations of tool types. *Am. Antiquity*, **38**(3), 320–8.

Daniels, S. (1967) Statistics, typology and cultural dynamics in the Transvaal Middle Stone Age. *S. Afr. Archaeol. Bull.*, **22**, 114–25.

Davies, R. G. (1971) *Computer Programming in Quantitative Biology.* London: Academic Press.

Deetz, J. (1965) *The dynamics of stylistic change in Arikara ceramics.* Illinois Studies in Anthropology no. 4. Urbana: University of Illinois Press.

Deetz, J. (1967) *Invitation to Archaeology.* New York: The Natural History Press.

Delaney, M. J. (1964) Variation in the long-tailed field mouse (*Apodemus sylvaticus* (L.)) in north-west Scotland, I: comparisons of individual characters. *Proc. R. Soc. B*, **161**, 191–9.

Dempsey, P. & Baumhoff, M. (1963) The statistical use of artifact distributions to establish chronological sequence. *Am. Antiquity*, **28**, 496–509.

Dollar, C. M. & Jensen, R. J. (1971) *Historian's Guide to Statistics. Quantitative Analysis and Historical Research.* New York: Holt, Rinehart and Winston.

Doran, J. E. (1970a) Planning and robots. *Machine Intelligence 5* (eds B. Meltzer & D. Michie), 519–32. Edinburgh: Edinburgh University Press.

Doran, J. E. (1970b) Systems theory, computer simulations and archaeology. *Wld Archaeol.*, **1**(3), 289–98.

References 355

Doran, J. E. (1971a) Computer analysis of data from the La Tène cemetery at Münsingen-Rain. *Mathematics in the Archaeological and Historical Sciences* (eds F. R. Hodson, D. G. Kendall & P. Tautu), 422–31. Edinburgh: Edinburgh University Press.

Doran, J. E. (1971b) Some recent models of the brain. *Machine Intelligence 6* (eds B. Meltzer & D. Michie), 207–20. Edinburgh: Edinburgh University Press.

Doran, J. E. (1972a) Automatic generation and evaluation of explanatory hypotheses. *Les Méthodes Mathématiques de l'Archéologie* (ed M. Borillo) 200–11. Marseilles: CADA (CNRS).

Doran, J. E. (1972b) Computer models as tools for archaeological hypothesis formation. *Models in Archaeology* (ed D. L. Clarke), 425–52. London: Methuen.

Doran, J. E. (1973) Explanation in archaeology: a computer experiment. *The Explanation of Culture Change* (ed C. Renfrew), 149–53. London: Duckworth.

Doran, J. E. & Hodson, F. R. (1966) A digital computer analysis of Palaeolithic flint assemblages. *Nature*, **210**, 688–9.

Doran, J. E. & Powell, S. (1972) Solving a combinatorial problem encountered in archaeology. *Some Research Applications of the Computer*, 47–52. Chilton: SRC Atlas Computer Laboratory.

Dunnell, R. C. (1972) *Systematics in Prehistory*. New York: Macmillan.

Edwards, A. W. F. (1971) Mathematical approaches to the study of human evolution. *Mathematics in the Archaeological and Historical Sciences* (eds F. R. Hodson, D. G. Kendall & P. Tautu), 347–55. Edinburgh: Edinburgh University Press.

Ellison, A. & Harriss, J. (1972) Settlement and land use in the prehistory and early history of southern England: a study based on locational models. *Models in Archaeology* (ed D. L. Clarke), 911–62. London: Methuen.

Emshoff, J. R. & Sisson, R. L. (1970) *Computer Simulation Models*. London: Macmillan.

Feigenbaum, E. A. (1969) Artificial intelligence: themes in the second decade. *Information Processing 68* (ed A. J. H. Morrell), vol. 2, 1008–22. Amsterdam: North Holland.

Ferguson, C. W. (1969) A 7104-year annual tree ring chronology for bristlecone pine, *Pinus aristata*, from the White Mountains, California. *Tree Ring Bull.* **29**, 3–29.

Fitting, J. E. (1965) A quantitative examination of Virginia fluted points. *Am. Antiquity*, **30**(4), 484–91.

Fitting, J. E. (1968) The Spring Creek site. *Anthropological Papers*, **32**, 1–78. Museum of Anthropology, University of Michigan.

Flannery, K. V. (1968) Archaeological systems theory and early Mesoamerica. *Anthropological Archaeology in the Americas* (ed B. Meggers), 67–87. Washington: Anthropological Society.

Ford, J. A. (1954) On the concept of types. The type concept revisited. *Am. Anthrop.*, **56**, 42–54.

Ford, J. A. (1962) *A quantitative method for deriving cultural chronology.* Technical manual 1, Department of Social Affairs, Pan American Union (OAS), Washington DC.

Forrester, J. W. (1971) *World Dynamics.* Cambridge, Mass.: Wright-Allen Press.

Freeman, L. G. & Brown, J. A. (1964) Statistical analysis of Carter Ranch pottery. *Fieldiana: Anthropology*, **55**, 126–54.

Freimen, C. V., ed (1972) *Information Processing 71* (proceedings of the IFIP Congress 71) two vols. Amsterdam: North-Holland.

Friedman, H. P. & Rubin, J. (1967) On some invariant criteria for grouping data. *J. Am. statist. Ass.* **62**, 1159–78.

Friedrich, M. H. (1970) Design structure and social interaction: archaeological implications of an ethnographic analysis. *Am. Antiquity*, **35**, 332–43.

Fritz, J. M. & Plog, F. T. (1970) The nature of archaeological explanation. *Am. Antiquity*, **35**(4), 405–12.

Gaines, S. W. (1971) Computer application in an archaeological field situation. *Newsl. comput. Archaeol.* VII*(1), 2–4.*

Gaines, S. W., ed (1973) *Newsl. comput. Archaeol.*, VIII(4).

Gardin, J-C. (1967) Methods for the descriptive analysis of archaeological material. *Am. Antiquity*, **32**, 13–30.

Gardin, J-C. (1968) On some reciprocal requirements of scholars and computers in the fine arts and archaeology. *Computers and their Potential Applications in Museums*, 103–24. New York: Arno Press.

Gardin, J-C., ed (1970) *Archéologie et Calculateurs.* Paris: CNRS.

Gardin, J-C. (1971a) Review of Chenhall (1971a) in *A C M Comput. Rev.*, **12**, 216.

Gardin, J-C. (1971b) Archaeology and computers: new perspectives. *Int. Social Sci. J.*, XXIII(2), 189–203.

Gardin, J-C. (1972) *The problem of sorting.* (Paper read to a conference on Computer Archaeology held at Waterloo Lutheran University, Canada, April 1972.)

Gardin, J-C. *et al.* (1972) *L'Informatique et l'Inventaire Général.* Paris: Ministère des Affaires Culturelles.

Gelfand, A. E. (1971) Rapid seriation methods with archaeological applications. *Mathematics in the Archaeological and Historical Sciences* (eds F. R. Hodson, D. G. Kendall & P. Tautu), 186–201. Edinburgh: Edinburgh University Press.

Gilbert, J. P. & Hammel, E. A. (1966) Computer simulation and analysis of problems in kinship and social structure. *Am. Anthrop.*, **68**, 71–94.

Glover, I. C. (1969) The use of factor analysis for the discovery of artefact types. *Mankind*, **7**, 36–51.

Gnanadesikan, R. & Wilk, M. B. (1969) Data analytic methods in multivariate statistical analysis. *Multivariate Analysis II* (ed P. R. Krishnaiah), 593–638. New York: Academic Press.

Goldmann, K. (1971) Some archaeological criteria for chronological seriation. *Mathematics in the Archaeological and Historical Sciences* (eds F. R. Hodson, D. G. Kendall & P. Tautu), 202–8. Edinburgh: Edinburgh University Press.

Goldmann, K. (1972) Zwei Methoden chronologischer Gruppierung. *Acta Praehistorica et Archaeologica*, **3**, 1–34.

Good, I. J. (1950) *Probability and the Weighing of Evidence*. London: Griffin.

Goodman, L. A. & Kruskal, W. H. (1954) Measures of association for cross classifications. *J. Am. statist. Ass.*, **49**, 737–64.

Gould, R. A., Koster, D. A. & Soutz, A. H. L. (1971) The lithic assemblage of the Western Desert Aborigines of Australia. *Am. Antiquity*, **36**(2), 149–69.

Gower, J. C. (1966) Some distance properties of latent root and vector methods used in multivariate analysis. *Biometrika*, **53**, 325–38.

Gower, J. C. (1967) Multivariate analysis and multidimensional geometry. *The Statistician*, **17**, 13–28.

Gower, J. C. (1970) A note on Burnaby's character-weighted similarity coefficient. *Mathematical Geology*, **2**(1), 39–45.

Gower, J. C. (1971a) Statistical methods of comparing different multivariate analysis of the same data. *Mathematics in the Archaeological and Historical Sciences* (eds F. R. Hodson, D. G. Kendall & P. Tautu), 138–49. Edinburgh: Edinburgh University Press.

Gower, J. C. (1971b) Comments (on Cormack 1971). *J. R. statist. Soc. A*, **134**, 360–5.

Gower, J. C. (1971c) A general coefficient of similarity and some of its properties. *Biometrics*, **27**, 857–74.

Gower, J. C. (1972) Measures of taxonomic distance and their analysis. *Assessment of Population Affinities in Man* (eds J. S. Weiner & J. Huizinga). Oxford: Clarendon Press.

Gower, J. C. & Ross, G. J. S. (1969) Minimum spanning trees and single linkage cluster analysis. *Appl. Statist.*, **18**, 54–64.

Graham, J. M. (1970) Discrimination of British Lower and Middle Palaeolithic handaxe groups using canonical variates. *Wld Archaeol.*, **1**(3), 321–37.

Guetzkow, H., Kotler, P. & Schultz, R. L. (1972) *Simulation in Social and Administrative Science*. Englewood Cliffs N. J.: Prentice Hall.

Haggett, P. (1965) *Locational Analysis in Human Geography*. London: Arnold.

Haigh, J. (1971) The manuscript linkage problem. *Mathematics in the Archaeological and Historical Sciences* (eds F. R. Hodson, D. G. Kendall & P. Tautu), 396–400. Edinburgh: Edinburgh University Press.

Hanson, N. R. (1958) *Patterns of Discovery*. Cambridge: University Press.

Hanson, N. R. (1961) Is there a logic of scientific discovery ? *Current Issues in the Philosophy of Science* (eds H. Feigl & G. Maxwell). New York: Holt, Rinehart and Winston.

Harding, A. & Warren, S. E. (1973) Early Bronze Age faience beads from Central Europe. *Antiquity*, **47**, 64–6.

Hawkes, J. (1968) The proper study of mankind. *Antiquity*, **42**, 255.

Hawkins, G. S. (1973) *Beyond Stonehenge*. New York: Harper and Row.

Hays, D. G. (1965) Simulation: an introduction for anthropologists. *The Use of Computers in Anthropology* (ed D. Hymes), 401–26. The Hague: Mouton.

Heizer, R. F. (1967) in *A Guide to Field Methods in Archaeology* (eds R. F. Heizer & J. A. Graham). Palo Alto: National Press.

Hempel, C. G. (1966) *Philosophy of Natural Science*. Englewood Cliffs: Prentice Hall.

Henkel, R. E. & Morrison, D. E. (1970) *The Significance Test Controversy*. London: Butterworths.

Hesse, A. (1971a) Tentative interpretation of the surface distribution of remains on the upper part of Mirgissa (Sudanese Nubia). *Mathematics in the Archaeological and Historical Sciences* (eds F. R. Hodson, D. G. Kendall & P. Tautu), 436–44. Edinburgh: Edinburgh University Press.

Hesse, A. (1971b) Comparaison par le calcul des distributions horizontales des vestiges lithiques. *Gallia Préhistoire*, **14**, 41–6.

Hesse, A. (1973) Essai sur les distributions spatiales des vestiges en préhistoire et en archéologie. *L'Homme Hier et Aujourd'hui* (ed M. Sauter), 551–63. Paris: Cujas.

Hester, T. R. & Heizer, R. F. (1973) *Bibliography of Archaeology I: experiments, lithic technology and petrography* (Module in Anthropology 29). New York: Addison-Wesley.

Higham, C. F. W. & Leach, B. F. (1971) An early centre of bovine husbandry in south east Asia. *Science*, **172**, 54–6.

Hill, J. N. (1967) The problem of sampling. *Fieldiana: Anthropology*, **57**, 145–57.

Hill, J. N. (1968) Broken K pueblo: patterns of form and function. *New Perspectives in Archaeology* (eds S. R. & L. R. Binford), 103–42. Chicago: Aldine.

Hill, J. N. (1972) The methodological debate in contemporary archaeology: a model. *Models in Archaeology* (ed D. L. Clarke), 61–107. London: Methuen.

Hill, J. N. and Evans, R. K. (1972) A model for classification and typology. *Models in Archaeology* (ed D. L. Clarke), 231–73. London: Methuen.

Hills, M. (1969) On looking at large correlation matrices. *Biometrika*, **56**, 249–53.

Hills, M. (1971) Comments (on Cormack 1971.) *J. R. statist, Soc. A*, **134**, 353–5.

Hodder, I. (1972) The interpretation of spatial patterns in archaeology: two examples. *Area*, **4**(4), 223–9.

Hodder, I. & Hassall, M. (1971) The non-random spacing of Romano-British walled towns. *Man*, **6**(3), 391–407.

Hodson, F. R. (1968) *The La Tène Cemetery at Münsingen-Rain*. Berne: Stämpfli (*Acta Bernensia V*).

Hodson, F. R. (1969) Searching for structure within multivariate archaeological data. *Wld. Archaeol.*, **1**(1), 90–105.

Hodson, F. R. (1970) Cluster analysis and archaeology: some new developments and applications. *Wld Archaeol.*, **1**(3), 299–320.

Hodson, F. R. (1971) Numerical typology and prehistoric archaeology. *Mathematics in the Archaeological and Historical Sciences* (eds F. R. Hodson, D. G. Kendall & P. Tautu), 30–45. Edinburgh: Edinburgh University Press.

Hodson, F. R., Kendall, D. G. & Tautu, P., eds (1971) *Mathematics in the Archaeological and Historical Sciences*. Edinburgh: Edinburgh University Press.

Hodson, F. R., Sneath P. H. A., & Doran, J. E. (1966) Some experiments in the numerical analysis of archaeological data. *Biometrika*, **53**, 311–24.

Hoel, P. G. (1962) *Introduction to Mathematical Statistics* (3rd edition). London: Wiley.

Hogg, A. H. A. (1971) Some applications of surface fieldwork. *The Iron Age and its Hill Forts* (eds D. Hill & M. Jesson), 105–25. Southampton: University Archaeological Society.

Hole, F. & Shaw, M. (1967) Computer analysis of chronological seriation. *Rice University Studies*, **53**(3). Houston.

Hollingdale, S. H. & Toothill, G. C. (1965) *Electronic Computers*. Penguin.

Hope, K. (1968) *Methods of Multivariate Analysis*. London: University of London Press.

Huff, D. (1970) *How to Take a Chance*. Penguin.

Huntsberger, D. V. (1962) *Elements of Statistical Inference*. London: Prentice-Hall.

Hymes, D. (1970) Linguistic models in archaeology. *Archéologie et Calculateurs* (ed J-C. Gardin), 91–117. Paris: CNRS.

Ihm, P. (1970) Distance et similitude en taxométrie. *Archéologie et Calculateurs* (ed J-C. Gardin), 309–16. Paris: CNRS.

Irwin, H. T., Hurd, D. J. & LaJeunesse, R. M. (1971) *Description and measurement in anthropology*. Report no. 48, Laboratory of Anthropology, Washington State University.

Irwin, H. T. & Wormington, H. M. (1972) Paleo-Indian tool types in the Great Plains. *Am. Antiquity*, **35**, 24–34.

Isaac, G. L. (1972) Early phases of human behaviour: models in Lower

Palaeolithic archaeology. *Models in Archaeology* (ed D. L. Clarke), 167–99. London: Methuen.

Jacobsthal, P. (1944) *Early Celtic Art*. Oxford: Clarendon Press.

Jardine, N. & Sibson, R. (1968) The construction of hierarchic and non-hierarchic classifications. *Comput. J.*, **11,** 177–84.

Jardine, N. & Sibson, R. (1971) *Mathematical Taxonomy*. London and New York: Wiley.

Jarman, M. R. (1972) A territorial model for archaeology: a behavioural and geographical approach. *Models in Archaeology* (ed D. L. Clarke), 705–33. London: Methuen.

Jewell, J. (1972) Animal remains from archaeological sites. Note in *Newsl. Comput. Archaeol.*, V I I (4), 2.

Johansen, K. F. (1919) En Boplads fra den aeldste Stenalder i Svaerdborg Mose. *Aarbøger for Nordisk Oldkyndighed og Historie 1919,* 106–235.

Johnson, L. (1968) *Item seriation as an aid for elementary scale and cluster analysis*. Bulletin no. 15, Museum of Natural History, University of Oregon.

Johnson, L. (1972) Introduction to imaginary models for archaeological scaling and clustering. *Models in Archaeology* (ed D. L. Clarke), 309–80. London: Methuen.

Junghans, S., Sangmeister, E. & Schröder, M. (1960) *Studien zu den Anfängen der Metallurgie I: Metallanalysen kupferzeitlicher und Frühbronzezeitlicher Bodenfunde aus Europa*. Berlin: Mann.

Junghans, S., Sangmeister, E. & Schröder, M. (1968) *Studien zu den Anfängen der Metallurgie II: Kupfer und Bronze in der frühen Metallzeit Europas*. Berlin: Mann.

Kadane, J. B. (1972) *Chronological ordering of archaeological deposits by the minimum path method*. Technical report no. 58, Department of Statistics, Carnegie-Mellon University, Pittsburg, Penn.

Kendall, D. G. (1963) A statistical approach to Flinders Petrie's sequence-dating. *Bull. I. S. I. 34th session, Ottawa*, 657–80.

Kendall, D. G. (1969) Some problems and methods in statistical archaeology. *Wld Archaeol.*, **1**(1), 68–76.

Kendall, D. G. (1971) Seriation from abundance matrices. *Mathematics in the Archaeological and Historical Sciences* (eds F. R..Hodson, D. G. Kendall & P. Tautu), 215–52. Edinburgh: Edinburgh University Press.

Kendall, D. G. (1974) Hunting quanta. *The Place of Astronomy in the Ancient World,* (ed F. R. Hodson), 229–64. London: Royal Society (*Phil. Trans. R. Soc. Lond. A*, **276**).

Kendall, M. G. (1968) Model building and its problems. *Mathematical Model Building in Economics and Industry*, 1–14. London: Griffin.

Kendall, M. G. (1971) Comments (on Cormack 1971). *J. R. statist. Soc. A*, **134,** 359–60.

Kendall, M. G. & Stuart, A. (1967) *The Advanced Theory of Statistics 2: Inferences and Relationship* (2nd edition). London: Griffin.

Kendall, M. G. & Stuart, A. (1968) *The Advanced Theory of Statistics 3: Design and Analysis, and Time-Series* (2nd edition). London: Griffin.

Kendall, M. G. & Stuart, A. (1969) *The Advanced Theory of Statistics 1: Distribution Theory* (3rd edition). London: Griffin.

Kerrich, J. E. & Clarke, D. L. (1967) Notes on the possible misuse and errors of cumulative percentage frequency graphs for the comparison of prehistoric artefact assemblages. *Proc. Prehist. Soc.*, **33**, 57–69.

Kivu-Sculy, I. (1971) On the Hole-Shaw method of permutation search. *Mathematics in the Archaeological and Historical Sciences* (eds F. R. Hodson, D. G. Kendall & P. Tautu), 253–4. Edinburgh: Edinburgh University Press.

Klir, G. J. (1969) *An Approach to General Systems Theory.* New York: Van Nostrand.

Koch, G. S. and Link, R. (1971) *Statistical Analysis of Geological Data*, vol. II. New York and London: Wiley.

Krieger, A. D. (1944) The typological concept. *Am. Antiquity*, **9**(3), 271–88.

Kroeber, A. L. (1940) Statistical classification. *Am. Antiquity*, **6**(1), 29–44.

Kromer, K. (1959) *Das Gräberfeld von Hallstatt.* Florence: Sansoni.

Krumbein, W. C. & Graybill, F. A. (1965) *An Introduction to Statistical Models in Geology.* New York: McGraw-Hill.

Kruskal, J. B. (1964a) Multidimensional scaling by optimising goodness of fit to a nonmetric hypothesis. *Psychometrika*, **29**, 1–27.

Kruskal, J. B. (1964b) Nonmetric multidimensional scaling: a numerical method. *Psychometrika*, **29**, 115–29.

Kruskal, J. B. (1971) Multidimensional scaling in archaeology: time is not the only dimension. *Mathematics in the Archaeological and Historical Sciences* (eds F. R. Hodson, D. G. Kendall & P. Tautu), 119–32. Edinburgh: Edinburgh University Press.

Kruskal, J. B. & Carroll, J. D. (1969) Geometrical models and badness-of-fit functions. *Multivariate Analysis II* (ed P. R. Krishnaiah), 639–71. New York: Academic Press.

Krzanowski, W. J. (1970) The algebraic basis of classical multivariate methods. *The Statistician*, **20**, 51–61.

Kuzara, R. S., Mead, G. R., & Dixon, K. A. (1966) Seriation of anthropological data: a computer program for matrix ordering. *Am. Anthrop.*, **68**(6), 1442–55.

Lambert, J. M. & Williams, W. T. (1966) Multivariate methods in plant ecology VI: Comparison of information analysis and association analysis. *J. Ecology*, **54**, 635–64.

Landau, J. & de la Vega, F. (1971) A new seriation algorithm applied to European protohistoric anthropomorphic statuary. *Mathematics in the Archaeological and Historical Sciences* (eds F. R. Hodson, D. G. Kendall & P. Tautu), 255–62. Edinburgh: Edinburgh University Press.

Laplace, G. (1968) Les niveaux aurignaciens et l'hypothèse du synthétotype. *L'homme de Cro-Magnon* (eds G. Camps & G. Olivier), 141–163. Paris: Arts et Métiers Graphiques.

Laver, F. J. M. (1965) *Introducing Computers.* London: HMSO.

Laville, H & Rigaud, J.–P. (1973) The Perigordian v industries in Périgord: typological variations, stratigraphy and relative chronology. *Wld Archaeol.,* 4(3), 330–8.

Lawley, D. N. & Maxwell, A. E. (1971) *Factor Analysis as a Statistical Method.* London: Butterworths.

Leroi-Gourhan, A. & Brézillon, M. (1966) Habitation magdalénienne no. 1 de Pincevent près Montereau (Seine-et-Marne). *Gallia Préhistoire,* 9, 263–385.

Leroi-Gourhan, A. & Brézillion, M. (1972) *Fouilles de Pincevent.* VIe supplément à Gallia Préhistoire. Paris: CNRS.

Lingoes, M. J. C. (1970) A general nonparametric model for representing objects and attributes in a joint metric space. *Archéologie et Calculateurs* (ed J-C. Gardin), 277–97. Paris: CNRS.

Litvak King, J. & Garcia Moll, R. (1972) Set theory models: an approach to taxonomic and locational relationships. *Models in Archaeology* (ed D. L. Clarke), 735–56. London: Methuen.

Lohnes, P. R. & Cooley, W. W. (1968) *Introduction to Statistical Procedures: with Computer Exercises.* New York and London: Wiley.

Longacre, W. A. (1968) Some aspects of prehistoric society in East Central Arizona. *New Perspectives in Archaeology* (eds S. R. & L. R. Binford), 89–102. Chicago: Aldine.

Lowery, P. R., Savage, R. D. A. & Wilkins, L. R. (1971) Scriber, graver, scorper, tracer: notes on experiments in bronzeworking techniques. *Proc. Prehist. Soc.,* 37(1), 167–82.

Loynes, R. M. (1971) The role of models. *Mathematics in the Archaeological and Historical Sciences* (eds F. R. Hodson, D. G. Kendall & P. Tautu), 542–6. Edinburgh: Edinburgh University Press.

McBurney, C. B. M. (1967) *The Haua Fteah (Cyrenaica) and the Stone Age of the South-East Mediterranean.* Cambridge: Cambridge University Press.

McBurney, C. B. M. (1968) The cave of Ali Tappeh and the epi-palaeolithic in N. E. Iran. *Proc. Prehist. Soc.,* 34, 385–411.

McBurney, C. B. M. (1973) Measurable long-term variations in some Old Stone Age sequences. *The Explanation of Cultural Change* (ed C. Renfrew), 305–15. London: Duckworth.

McBurney, C. B. M. & Callow, P. (1971) The Cambridge excavations at La Cotte de St Brelade, Jersey—a preliminary report. *Proc. Prehist. Soc.,* 37(2), 167–207.

McCracken, D. D. (1962) *A Guide to Algol Programming.* New York: Wiley.

McCracken, D. D. (1972) *A Guide to Fortran IV Programming* (2nd edition). New York: Wiley.

McKerrell, H. (1972) On the origins of British faience beads and some aspects of the Wessex – Mycenae relationship. *Proc. Prehist. Soc.*, **38**, 286–301.

McLeod, J., ed (1968) *Simulation.* New York: McGraw-Hill.

Macnaughton-Smith, P. (1965) *Some Statistical and Other Numerical Techniques for Classifying Individuals.* London: HMSO.

McNutt, C. H. (1973) On the methodological validity of frequency seriation. *Am. Antiquity,* **38**(1), 45–60.

McPherron, A. (1967) *The Juntunen site and the Late Woodland Prehistory of the Upper Great Lakes Area.* Anthropological Papers, Museum of Anthropology, University of Michigan.

Madsen, A. P., Müller, S., Neergaard, C., Petersen, C. G. J., Rostrup, E., Steenstrup, K. J. V., & Winge, H. (1900) *Affaldsdynger fra Stenalderen i Danmark.* Paris: Hachette; Copenhagen: Reitzel; Leipzig: Brockhaus.

Maliţa, M. (1971) A model of Michael the Brave's decision in 1595. *Mathematics in the Archaeological and Historical Sciences* (eds F. R. Hodson, D. G. Kendall & P. Tautu), 516–23. Edinburgh: Edinburgh University Press.

Marien, M-E. (1958) *Trouvailles du Champ d'Urnes et des tombelles hallstattiennes de Court-Saint-Etienne.* Brussels: Musées Royaux d'Art et d'Histoire.

Marriott, F. H. L. (1971) Practical problems in a method of cluster analysis. *Biometrics,* **27**, 501–14.

Mathiassen, T. (1939) Bundsø, en yngre Stenalders Boplads paa Als. *Aarbøger for Nordisk Oldkyndighed og Historie 1939,* 1–55.

Matthews, J. (1963) Application of matrix analysis to archaeological problems. *Nature,* **198**, 930–4.

Maxwell, A. E. (1971) Multivariate statistical methods and classification problems. *Brit. J. Psychiat.,* **119**, 121–7.

Meighan, C. W. (1959) A new method for the seriation of archaeological collections. *Am. Antiquity,* **25**, 203–11.

Meltzer, B. (1970) Generation of hypotheses and theories. *Nature,* **225**, 972.

Moberg, C. A. (1971) Archaeological context and mathematical methods. *Mathematics in the Archaeological and Historical Sciences* (eds F. R. Hodson, D. G. Kendall & P. Tautu), 551–62. Edinburgh: Edinburgh University Press.

Moberg, C. A. (1972) Review of 'An Archaeological Perspective' by L. R. Binford, 1972. *Science,* **178**, 741–2.

Morgan, C. G. (1973) Archaeology and explanation. *Wld Archaeol.,* **4**(3). 259–76.

Moroney, M. J. (1969) *Facts from Figures.* Penguin.

Mosiman, J. E. (1962) On the compound multinomial distribution, the multivariate β-distribution and correlations among proportions. *Biometrika*, **49**, 65–82.

Movius, H. L. & Brooks, A. S. (1971) The analysis of certain major classes of Upper Palaeolithic tools: Aurignacian scrapers. *Proc. Prehist. Soc.*, **37**(2), 253–73.

Movius, H. L., David, N. C., Bricker, H. M. & Clay, R. B. (1968) *The analysis of certain major classes of Upper Palaeolithic tools*. American School of Prehistoric Research Bulletin 26, Peabody Museum, Harvard.

Myers, O. H. (1950) *Some Applications of Statistics to Archaeology*. Service des antiquités de l'Egypte, Cairo: Government Press.

Naroll, R. (1962) Floor area and settlement population. *Am. Antiquity*, **27**(4), 587–9.

Newcomb, R. M. (1968) Geographical location analysis and Iron Age Settlement in West Penwith. *Cornish Archaeol.*, **7**, 5–13.

Newcomer, M. H. (1971) Some quantitative experiments in handaxe manufacture. *Wld Archaeol.*, **3**(1), 85–94.

Newcomer, M. H. & Hodson, F. R. (1973) Constellation analysis of burins from Ksar Akil. *Archaeological Theory and Practice* (ed D.E. Strong), 87–104. London and New York: Seminar Press.

Newell, R. R. & Vroomans, A. P. J. (1972) *Automatic artifact registration and systems for archaeological analysis with the Philips P1100 computer: a mesolithic test-case*. Oosterhout: Anthropological Publications.

Newton, R. G. & Renfrew, C. (1970) The origin of the British faience beads reconsidered. *Antiquity*, **44**, 199–206.

Nie, N. H., Bent, D. H. & Hull, C. H. (1970) S P S S: *Statistical Package for Social Sciences*. New York: McGraw-Hill.

Olsson, I. U., ed. (1970) *Radiocarbon Variations and Absolute Dating*. New York: Wiley Interscience.

Orton, C. R. (1970) The production of pottery from a Romano-British kiln site: a statistical investigation. *Wld Archaeol.*, **1**(3), 343–58.

Orton, C. R. (1971) On the statistical sorting and reconstruction of pottery from a Romano-British kiln site. *Mathematics in the Archaeological and Historical Sciences* (eds, F. R. Hodson, D. G. Kendall & P. Tautu), 453–9 Edinburgh: Edinburgh University Press.

Orton, C. R. (1973) The tactical use of models in archaeology – the S H E R D project. *The Explanation of Culture Change* (ed C. Renfrew), 137–9. London: Duckworth.

Ottaway, B. (1973) Dispersion diagrams: a new approach to the display of carbon-14 dates. *Archaeometry*, **13**(1). 5–12.

Ottaway, B. & Ottaway, J. H. (1972) The Suess calibration curve and archaeological dating. *Nature*, **239**, 512.

Pankhurst, R. J. (1970) A computer program for generating diagnostic keys. *Comput. J.*, **13**, 145–51.

Parks, J. M. (1966) Cluster analysis applied to multivariate geologic problems. *J. Geol.*, **74**, 703–15.

Peebles, C. S. (1972) Monothetic-divisive analysis of the Moundville burials—an initial report. *Newsl. comput. Archaeol.*, **8,**(2), 1–13.

Petrie, W. M. F. (1899) Sequences in prehistoric remains. *J. anthrop. Inst.*, **29**, 295–301.

Pielou, E. C. (1969) *An Introduction to Mathematical Ecology*. New York: Wiley.

Plog, F. (1973) Laws, systems of law, and the explanation of observed variation. *The Explanation of Culture Change* (ed C. Renfrew), 649–61. London: Duckworth.

Ragir, S. (1967) A review of techniques for archaeological sampling. *A Guide to Field Methods in Archaeology: approaches to the anthropology of the dead* (eds R. F. Heizer & J. A. Graham), 181–97. Palo Alto: National Press.

Ralph, E. K., Michael, H. N. & Han, M. C. (1973) Radiocarbon dates and reality. *Masca Newsl.*, **9**(1), 1–20.

Rao, C. R. (1971) Taxonomy in anthropology. *Mathematics in the Archaeological and Historical Sciences* (eds F. R. Hodson, D. G. Kendall & P. Tautu), 19–29. Edinburgh: Edinburgh University Press.

Rathje, W. L. (1973) Models for mobile Maya: a variety of constraints. *The Explanation of Culture Change* (ed C. Renfrew), 731–57. London: Duckworth.

Régnier, S. (1972) Sériation des niveaux de plusieurs tranches de fouille dans une zone archéologique homogène. *Les Méthodes Mathématiques de l'Archéologie* (ed M. Borillo), 157–66. Marseille: CADA(CNRS).

Renfrew, C. & Clarke, R. M. (1974) Problems of the radiocarbon calendar and its calibration. *Archaeometry,* **16**(1), 5–18.

Renfrew, C. & Sterud, G. (1969) Close-proximity analysis: a rapid method for the ordering of archaeological materials. *Am. Antiquity*, **34**(3), 265–77.

Rightmire, G. P. (1972) Multivariate analysis of an early hominid metacarpal from Swartkrans. *Science*, **176**, 159–61.

Robinson, W. S. (1951) A method for chronologically ordering archaeological deposits. *Am. Antiquity,* **16**(4), 293–301.

Robinson, W. S. & Brainerd, G. W. (1952) Robinson's coefficient of agreement—a rejoinder. *Am. Antiquity*, **18**(1), 60–1.

Roe, D. A. (1964) The British Lower and Middle Palaeolithic: some problems, methods of study and preliminary results. *Proc. Prehist, Soc.*, **30**, 245–67.

Roe, D. A. (1968) British Lower and Middle Palaeolithic handaxe groups. *Proc. Prehist. Soc.*, **34**, 1–82.

Rootenberg, S. (1964) Archaeological field sampling. *Am. Antiquity*, **30**, 181–8.

Rouse, I. (1960) The classification of artifacts in archaeology. *Am. Antiquity*, **25,** 313–23.

Rouse, I. (1967) Seriation in archaeology. *American Historical Anthropology: Essays in Honor of Leslie Spier* (eds C. L. Riley & W. W. Taylor), 153–95. Carbondale: Southern Illinois University Press.

Rouse, I. (1970) Classification for what ? (Comments on Clarke 1968). *Norwegian archaeol. Rev.*, **3,** 4–12.

Rowlett, R. M. & Pollnac, R. B. (1971) Multivariate analysis of Marnian La Tène cultural groups. *Mathematics in the Archaeological and Historical Sciences* (eds F. R. Hodson, D. G. Kendall & P. Tautu), 46–58. Edinburgh: Edinburgh University Press.

Rubinoff, M., ed (1972) *Advances in Computers 12.* New York: Academic Press (and see previous volumes in this series).

Sackett, J. R. (1966) Quantitative analysis of Upper Palaeolithic stone tools. *Am. Anthrop.*, **68**(2), 356–94.

Sawyer, W. W. (1955) *Prelude to Mathematics.* Penguin.

Schaaff, U. (1966) Zur Belegung latènezeitlicher Friedhöfe der Schweiz. *Jahrbuch des Römisch-Germanischen Zentralmuseums, Mainz*, **13,** 49–59.

Schauer, P. (1972) Zur Herkunft der bronzene Hallstatt-Schwerter. *Archäologisches Korrespondenzblatt*, **2,** 261–270.

Scott, A. J. & Symons, M. J. (1971) Clustering methods based on likelihood ratio criteria. *Biometrics*, **27,** 387–97.

Semenov, S. A. (1964) *Prehistoric Technology.* London: Cory, Adams and MacKay.

Shepard, A. O. (1956) *Ceramics for the Archaeologist.* Washington: Carnegie Institute.

Shepard, R. N. (1962) The analysis of proximities: multidimensional scaling with an unknown distance function, I and II. *Psychometrika*, **27,** 125–39, 219–46.

Shepard, R. N. & Carroll, J. D. (1966) Parametric representation of nonlinear data structures. *Multivariate Analysis I* (ed P. R. Krishnaiah), 561–92. New York: Academic Press.

Sibson, R. (1971a) Computational methods in cluster analysis. *Mathematics in the Archaeological and Historical Sciences* (eds F. R. Hodson, D. G. Kendall & P. Tautu), 59–61. Edinburgh: Edinburgh University Press.

Sibson, R. (1971b) Some thoughts on sequencing methods. *Mathematics in the Archaeological and Historical Sciences* (eds F. R. Hodson, D. G. Kendall & P. Tautu), 263–6. Edinburgh: Edinburgh University Press.

Sibson, R. (1972) Order invariant methods for data analysis. *J. R. statist. Soc. B*, **34**(3), 311–349.

Siegel, S. (1956) *Nonparametric Statistics for the Behavioral Sciences*. New York: McGraw Hill.

Sieveking, G. de G., Craddock, P. T., Hughes, M. J., Busch, P. & Ferguson, J. (1972) Prehistoric flint mines and their identification as sources for raw material. *Archaeometry*, **14**, 151–76.

Simmons, R. F. (1970) Natural language question-answering systems. *Commun. Ass. comput. Mach.*, **13**(1), 15–30.

Simon, H. A. (1969) *The Sciences of the Artificial*. Cambridge, Mass: MIT Press.

Smith, J. (1968) *Computer Simulation Models*. London: Griffin.

Sokal, R. & Sneath, P. H. A. (1963) *Principles of Numerical Taxonomy*. San Francisco and London: W. H. Freeman. Comprehensively revised and republished as *Numerical Taxonomy* (W. H. Freeman 1973).

Solheim, W. G. (1960) The use of sherd weights and counts in the handling of archaeological data. *Curr. Anthrop.*, **1**, 325–9.

Solomon, H. (1971) Numerical taxonomy. *Mathematics in the Archaeological and Historical Sciences* (eds F. R. Hodson, D. G. Kendall & P. Tautu), 62–81. Edinburgh: Edinburgh University press.

Sonneville-Bordes, D. de (1960) *Le Paléolithique supérieur en Périgord*. Bordeaux: Delmas.

Sonneville-Bordes, D. de & Perrot, J. (1953) Essai d'adaptation des méthodes statistiques au Paléolithique supérieur. Premiers résultats. *Bull. Soc. Préhist. Fr.*, **50**, 323–33.

Sonneville-Bordes, D. de & Perrot, J. (1954–56) Lexique typologique du Paléolithique supérieur. *Bull. Soc. Préhist. Fr.*, **51**, 327–35; **52**, 76–9; **53**, 408–12, 547–59.

Sørensen, T. (1948) A method of establishing groups of equal amplitude in plant sociology based on similarity of species content and its application to analyses of the vegetation on Danish commons. *Biol. Skr.* (Copenhagen), **5**(4), 1–34.

Soudský, B. (1967) *Principles of Automatic Data Treatment applied on Neolithic Pottery*. Prague: Czechoslovak Academy of Sciences.

Soudský, B. (1968) Application de méthodes de calcul dans l'étude d'un site néolithique. *Calcul et Formalisation dans les Sciences de l'Homme* (eds J-C. Gardin & B. Jaulin) Paris: CNRS.

Soudský, B. (1973) Higher level archaeological entities: models and reality. *The explanation of Culture Change* (ed C. Renfrew), 195–207. London: Duckworth.

Sparck-Jones, K. (1970) The evaluation of archaeological classifications. *Archéologie et Calculateurs* (ed J-C. Gardin), 245–74. Paris: CNRS.

Spaulding, A. C. (1953) Statistical techniques for the discovery of artifact types. *Am. Antiquity*, **18**, 305–13.

Spiegel, M. R. (1961) *Theory and Problems of Statistics*. New York: McGraw-Hill.

Steiger, W. L. (1971) Analytical Archaeology ? (review of Clarke 1968). *Mankind*, **8,** 67–70.

Stone, J. F. S. & Thomas, L. C. (1956) The use and distribution of faience in the Ancient East and Prehistoric Europe. *Proc. Prehist. Soc.*, **22,** 37–84.

Suess, H. E. (1970) Bristlecone pine calibration of the radiocarbon timescale 5400 B C to the present. *Radiocarbon Variations and Absolute Dating* (ed I. U. Olsson), 303–12. New York: Wiley Interscience.

Taylor, W. W. (1948) *A study of archaeology.* Memoir no. 69, American Anthropological Association.

Thom, A. (1967) *Megalithic Sites in Britain.* Oxford: Clarendon Press.

Thom, A. (1971) *Megalithic Lunar Observatories.* Oxford: Clarendon Press.

Thomas, D. H. (1971) On the use of cumulative curves and numerical taxonomy. *Am. Antiquity*, **36**(2), 206–9.

Thomas, D. H. (1972a) The use and abuse of numerical taxonomy in archaeology. *Archaeology and Physical Anthropology in Oceania*, **7**(1), 31–49.

Thomas, D. H. (1972b) A computer simulation model of Great Basin Shoshonean subsistence and settlement patterns. *Models in Archaeology* (ed D. L. Clarke), 671–704. London: Methuen.

Thomas, D. H. (1973) An empirical test for Steward's model of Great Basin settlement patterns. *Am. Antiquity*, **38**(2), 155–76.

Thuillier, P. (1971) Comment se constituent les théories scientifiques. *La Recherche*, 537–54.

Thurstone, L. L. (1947) *Multiple Factor Analysis. A development and expansion of the vectors of the mind.* Chicago: Chicago University Press.

Tite, M. S. (1972) *Methods of Physical Examination in Archaeology.* London and New York: Seminar Press.

Trigger, B. G. (1968) *Beyond History: the methods of prehistory.* New York: Holt, Rinehart and Winston.

Troels-Smith, J. (1937) Beile aus dem Mesolithikum Dänemarks. Ein Verteilungsversuch. *Acta Archaeol.* (Copenhagen), **8,** 278–95.

True, D. L. & Matson, R. G. (1970) Cluster analysis and multidimensional scaling of archaeological sites in Northern Chile. *Science*, **169,** 1201–3.

Trump, D. H. (1958) The Apennine Culture of Italy. *Proc. Prehist. Soc.*, **24,** 165–200.

Tugby, D. J. (1958) A typological analysis of axes and choppers from southeast Australia. *Am. Antiquity*, **24**(1), 24–33.

Uerpmann, H-P. (1973) Animal bone finds and economic archaeology: a critical study of 'osteo-archaeological' method. *Wld Archaeol.*, **4**(3), 307–22.

Uslar, R. von (1959) Jahresbericht 1954/5: Urnenfelderzeit. *Bonner Jahrbücher*, **157,** 413.

Vance, D. (1970) Museum data banks. *Information Storage and Retrieval*, **5**, 203–11.

Veldman, D. J. (1967) *Fortran Programming for the Behavioral Sciences*. New York: Holt, Rinehart and Winston.

Vértes, L. (1965) Das Jungpaläolithikum von Arka in Nord-Ungarn. *Quartär*, **15/16**, 79–132.

Vértes, L. (1968) Rates of evolution in palaeolithic technology. *Acta Archaeol. Acad. Sci. Hung.*, **20**, 3–17.

Vescelius, G. S. (1960) Archaeological sampling, a problem of statistical inference. *Essays in the Science of Culture in Honor of Leslie A. White* (eds G. E. Dole & R. L. Carneiro), 457–70. New York: Thomas Y. Crowell.

Viollier, D. (1916) *Les sépultures du second âge du fer sur le plateau Suisse*. Geneva: Georg and Co.

Waterbolk, H. T. & Butler, J. J. (1965) Comments on the use of metallurgical analysis in prehistoric studies. *Helenium*, **5**, 227–51.

Watson, P. J., Le Blanc, S. A. & Redman, C. L. (1971) *Explanation in Archaeology: an Explicitly Scientific Approach*. New York: Columbia University Press.

Watt, K. E. F. (1968) *Ecology and Resource Management: a Quantitative Approach*. New York: McGraw-Hill.

Welke, L. (1972) A review of file management systems. *Datamation*, **18**(9), 32–54.

Whallon, R. (1972a) The computer in archaeology: a critical survey. *Computers and the Humanities*, **7**(1), 29–45.

Whallon, R. (1972b) A new approach to pottery typology. *Am. Antiquity*, **37**, 13–33.

Whallon, R. (1973) Spatial analysis of occupation floors I: application of dimensional analysis of variance. *Am. Antiquity*, **38**, 266–78.

White, J. P. & Thomas, D. H. (1972) What mean these stones? Ethnotaxonomic models and archaeological interpretations in the New Guinea Highlands. *Models in Archaeology* (ed D. L. Clarke), 275–308. London: Methuen.

Wiedmer, J. (1908) Das Latène-Gräberfeld bei Münsingen (Kt Bern). *Arch. Hist. Ver. Kt. Bern*, **18**, 269–361.

Wilcock, J. D. (1971) Non-statistical applications of the computer in archaeology. *Mathematics in the Archaeological and Historical Sciences* (eds F. R. Hodson, D. G. Kendall & P. Tautu), 470–81. Edinburgh: Edinburgh University Press.

Wilcock, J. D. & Laflin, S., eds (1974) *Computer Applications in Archaeology 1974*. Computer Centre, University of Birmingham.

Wilkinson, E. M. (1971) Archaeological seriation and the travelling salesman problem. *Mathematics in the Archaeological and Historical Sciences* (eds F. R. Hodson, D. G. Kendall & P. Tautu), 276–84. Edinburgh: Edinburgh University Press.

Willey, G. R. (1961) Volume in pottery and the selection of samples. *Am. Antiquity*, **27,** 230–231.

Willey, G. R. & Phillips, P. (1958) *Method and Theory in American Archaeology.* Chicago: University of Chicago Press.

Williams, W. T. & Dale, M. B. (1962) Partition of correlation matrices for heterogeneous quantitative data. *Nature*, **196,** 602.

Wilmsen, E. N. (1968a) Lithic analysis in paleoanthropology. *Science*, **161,** 982–987.

Wilmsen, E. N. (1968b) Functional analysis of flaked stone artifacts. *Am. Antiquity*, **33,** 156–61.

Wilmsen, E. N. (1970) *Lithic analysis and cultural inference: a Paleo-Indian case.* Anthropological Papers 16, University of Arizona.

Wish, M. & Carroll, J. D. (1971) Multi-dimensional scaling with differential weighting of dimensions. *Mathematics in the Archaeological and Historical Sciences* (eds F. R. Hodson, D. G. Kendall & P. Tautu), 150–67. Edinburgh: Edinburgh University Press.

Wishart, D. (1969) *Fortran II programs for eight methods of cluster analysis* (CLUSTAN I). Computer Contributions 38, Kansas Geological Survey.

Witherspoon, Y. T. (1961) A statistical device for comparing trait lists. *Am. Antiquity*, **26,** 433–6.

Wood, J. J. & Matson, R G. (1973) Two models of sociocultural systems and their implications for the archaeological study of change. *The Explanation of Culture Change* (ed C. Renfrew), 673–83. London: Duckworth.

Young, R. K. & Veldman, D. J. (1965) *Introductory Statistics for the Behavioral Sciences.* New York: Holt, Rinehart and Winston.

Index